The Entrepreneurial Web

ft.com

Welcome to the next generation of business

There is a new world which we can look at but we cannot see. Yet within it, the forces of technology and imagination are overturning the way we work and the way we do business.

ft.com books are both gateway and guide to this world. We understand it because we are part of it. But we also understand the needs of businesses which are taking their first steps into it, and those still standing hesitantly on the threshold. Above all, we understand that, as with all business challenges, the key to success lies not with the technology itself, but with the people who must use it and manage it. People like you; the future minded.

See a world of business.
Visit us at **www.ft.com today.**

The

Entrepreneurial Web

First, *think* like an e-business

Peter Small

PEARSON EDUCATION LIMITED

Head Office:
Edinburgh Gate
Harlow CM20 2JE
Tel: +44 (0)1279 623623
Fax: +44 (0)1279 431059

London Office:
128 Long Acre,
London WC2E 9AN
Tel: +44 (0)20 7447 2000
Fax: +44 (0)20 7240 5771

First published in Great Britain in 2000

ISBN 0 273 65036 X

British Library Cataloguing in Publication Data
A CIP catalogue record for this book can be obtained from the British Library

Library of Congress Cataloging in Publication Data
Applied for.

Many of the designations used by manufacturers and sellers to distinguish their
products are claimed as trademarks. Pearson Education Limited has made every
attempt to supply trademark information about manufacturers and their products mentioned
in this book. A list of trademark designations and their owners appears on this page.

Trademark Notice
PowerPoint, Microsoft Office, Windows NT are trademarks of the Microsoft Corporation; Macintosh and HyperCard are
trademarks of Apple; OS/2 is a trademark of International Business Machines (IBM); Novell R is a trademark of Novell,
Inc.; NFS is a trademark of Sun Microsystems, Inc.; Free BSD is a trademark of the *FreeBSD* Project; SAMBA is a
trademark of the Free Software Foundation, Inc.; RealAudio is a trademark of RealNetworks, Inc.; VisiCalc is a trademark
of Visicorp, Inc.; Director, Flash and Lingo are trademarks of Macromedia; UNIX is licensed through X/Open Company Ltd
(in collaboration with Novell, Hp and SCO); and Lego is a trademark of the LEGO Corporation.

10 9 8 7 6 5 4 3 2 1

Typeset by Land & Unwin (Data Sciences) Ltd, Northamptonshire.
Printed by Biddles Ltd of Guildford and King's Lynn.

The Publishers' policy is to use paper manufactured from sustainable forests.

Acknowledgements

No book can be created by an author in isolation. This book is no exception. Indeed, the feedback from so many people during the draft stages of the writing was a major influence on the content. Below are the people (in alphabetical order) who in one way or another contributed to the evolution of this book.

Michael Allen, Geo Amundsen Carncross, Guy Anderson, Giles Askham, Bonnie Austin, Art Avery, Bruce Baikie, Perry Barile, Sheelagh Barron, Douglas and Fiona Bay, Isaac Ben, Tomer Berda, Phil and Sorel Blomfield, Vaughn Botha, Doug Brown, Cody Burleson, Dooley Le Cappellaine, Yvan Caron, Katy Cartee, Esther Garcia Castells, Delbert Chaplin, Jason Cunliffe, John Dawson, Chris Dolan, Jocce Ekström, Bruce Epstein, Pete Everett, Adrian Goddard, Ebidie Hacker, Chris Heape, Stephen Howard, Bob Hughes, Lizzie Joyce, Vahe Kassardjian, Jackie Kleinschmidt, Kate LaBore, Janet Laidler, Donald C. Lawson III, Alexander Liden, Bryan Lowes, Robert Moorhead, Anita Melling, David G. McDivitt, Ian Morrison, Nelis van Nahuijs, James Newton, Warren Ockrassa, Verne Pence, Heidi Raebeck, Joseph Rienstra, Ben Rollason, Eric L. Rosen, Matt Ross, Blane Savage, Terry R. Schussler, Birnou Sdarte, Andrew Stapleton, Warren Stolow, Peter von Troil, Dai Williams, Andy Wilson, Elias, Marcus P. Zillman.

Special thanks also to the team at Pearson Education who commissioned and edited this book for the ft.com series of books on e-commerce.

Richard Stagg
Steve Temblett
Katherin Ekstrom
Annette Abel
Alison Birtwell
Marilyn St Clair

Especially, I'd like to thank my wife, Dalida, and my two sons, Elliot and Oliver, who have had to make so many sacrifices to allow me the time to spend writing this book.

Contents

Part 2

Looking for clues   76

4   Stumbling around looking for clues   79

5   Clues from the world of investment and finance   100

6   Clues from the world of computer programming   121

Part 3

Abstractions and strategic thinking 144

7 Growing rather than planning solutions 147

8 Abstract models to think with 169

9 Difficulties in thinking with abstract models 192

Part 4
Strategies for competition and cooperation   214

Prologue

When the spreadsheet had to go

In 1979, I bought an Apple II computer and a VisiCalc spreadsheet program. I'd bought them on the advice of my accountant to enable me to create a business plan: a business plan that was to get me a $150 000 loan.

My first impression had been that this system appeared to be some kind of elaborate calculator that could make calculations and lay out all the results in neat, orderly tables. But I hadn't been working on the business plan for very long before I realized that a computer, with a spreadsheet program, had the potential to be something far more sophisticated than a calculator: it could provide a modelling environment for any kind of business idea I could come up with.

I also learned – by losing all of the $150 000 loan – that spreadsheet modelling is fallible. It can handle situations where conditions are reasonably stable and predictable, but a model can be rendered totally useless by unknowns or unexpected turns of events. Despite this serious limitation, spreadsheets can still provide an invaluable aid to business planning as long as care is taken to keep away from situations that are totally unpredictable.

For nearly 15 years, a computer and a spreadsheet program became an indispensable part of my business life; more than just tools, they became an extension to my brain. Whatever business ideas came into my mind, I could model them on the spreadsheet, try out different possibilities, test the risks, manipulate the cash flows.

In 1993, I discovered the Internet. At first, it seemed no more than a social recreation, but as I began to explore the various news groups and list serve discussion forums it became apparent that this was far more than simply a social environment: it was a rich source of valuable information and business contacts. This had no real impact on me until the advent of the World Wide Web, then it dawned upon me that this was the start of a completely new way of doing business – with virtually limitless possibilities.

There was only one snag. This new environment was totally unpredictable: full of unknowns, unknowables and unexpected changes. In short, it tendered my spreadsheet program completely and utterly useless. For a businessman, this is on a par with suddenly becoming blind. Business is about planning and thinking ahead, yet here was a business environment that precluded the use of any predictive modelling.

How then, with the obvious potential of the Internet and the World Wide Web, would it be possible to create a sensible business strategy in order to become a successful competitor in this new communication environment? It was an intriguing challenge.

A totally new world

Until I entered the digital world of electronic communications, I thought I'd learned to become a fairly shrewd and capable businessman. I'd joined the very first rush into the new technological revolution when CD-ROMs first came out. I got badly burned. The world of computers and digital communications was like nothing else I'd ever encountered before. There was too much change and too much information to deal with. I seemed to be back to square one, where I'd have to start learning how to do business all over again – from scratch.

As fast as I'd buy a piece of hardware, or a software application program, something new would come along and cause it to become out of date or redundant altogether. It wasn't simply the cost in money that was the problem, it was the time needed to get my head around the new dimensions that each new change introduced. Before very long I became totally confused because the amount I was needing to know and learn was spinning out of control. What I felt I had to do was to get off of the giddy roundabout of continuous change, step back and start from basics.

Fortunately, my educational background had been science and technology so I could get to grips with the theoretical issues. My specialities were electronic control mechanisms and systems theory; to these I'd added game theory and evolutionary biology. Mixed with a professional knowledge of marketing, finance and investment, these had seen me through many varied and exotic entrepreneurial adventures. I figured that this background was about as good as any for trying to find out what this new world of digital technology was really all about.

First I had to get at the very core of computer technology. This led to a five-year flirtation with the arcane world of computer programming. At the end of this time I began to get a glimmer of what this whole technological revolution was about and how it integrated with the everyday world of people.

In those five years, I produced two books that were a reflection of my learning process. The first explained the essence and power of computer programming: *Lingo Sorcery – the magic of lists, objects and intelligent agents*. The second book, *Magical A-Life Avatars – a new paradigm for the Internet*, expanded on the first, to explore how a programming environment in a computer memory could be used almost like an extension to the human brain – allowing humans to communicate more efficiently with each other.

By the time I'd got to grips with the fundamental concepts of computer and digital communication technology, the World Wide Web had exploded into being. For me this was especially exciting because I could combine my 20 years of entrepreneurial experience with the ten years I'd spent on the technological issues.

As I started to look around at what other people were doing, none of it was making any sense. I found a world being run by technologists, who were creating all kinds of clever and amusing tricks, but hardly any of it relating to the fundamental principles of business and commerce. It was as if the whole world of digital communication had been given over to artists and programmers to play games – impressing each other with their cleverness. This wasn't so surprising really because the people with the expertise to create this new technological environment had spent so much time acquiring the necessary knowledge and skills that they simply hadn't spent enough time in the real world of commerce to learn how to apply it efficiently.

Usually, commercial guidance for technological advance is provided by astute entrepreneurs and professional managers who have the knowledge, experience and business acumen to prevent effort being wasted on impractical solutions. Unfortunately, most hard headed business people were so completely lost in the technology that they were either ignoring it altogether or handing over the reins to technologists who were, in the main, commercially naïve.

Most perplexing of all was the gold rush mentality of investors. As I'd spent some time in the City of London writing a correspondence course in investment and finance, I had a fair understanding of the basics of investments and what I observed was not investment in any sense of the word; it was out and out speculation with values being placed upon Internet-based, start-up businesses without any regard for fundamental values. Investment valuations seemed to be anticipating the most wildly optimistic scenarios with no attempt at all to discount any of the downside risks or the emergence of competition. It is at such times, when fools rush in, that vast fortunes can be made and lost.

I read everything I could lay my hands on. I subscribed to dozens of Internet discussion forums and newsletter services. I studied multimedia techniques, Web site design technology, server side hardware and software solutions, back-end technology. At every turn, I ran into new chasms of information and 'essential to know' knowledge. I looked at thousands of Web sites, studied many emerging Internet business strategies. For two years I ran around like a headless chicken, climbing one learning curve after another, drowning in a sea of information and getting nowhere.

Then the penny dropped. It wasn't about learning and technology at all. Neither was it about planning. It was about communication and game playing. It wasn't necessary to know everything because that was impossible. It was about being able to cope with the uncertainties and the complexities better than others. This needed a radically different way of thinking from the spreadsheet mentality I'd acquired in the world of bricks and mortar.

What the book is about and who it is for

When I first started to write this book, the publisher and the readers of the draft chapters would ask me: 'What is the target audience? Who are you writing this book for?' They were always a bit disappointed when I told them that the target audience was me and I was writing the book for myself. But it was perfectly true. Writing this book gave me the opportunity to gather together all my thoughts from the experiences and knowledge I'd gained over the previous ten years of trying to understand what the digital world was all about.

What made my approach different from many others though is that the ten years I'd spent in the digital world came on top of over 20 years of experience I'd had as a pragmatic entrepreneur. Contrary to the stereotyped image, the entrepreneur is just as much a skilled practitioner as any technical expert and like any speciality profession the expertise is acquired as a result of much practical experience.

Unlike conventional specialists and technicians though, an entrepreneur has to avoid most technicalities and detail in order to be able to concentrate on more abstract issues – those involved with the higher levels of system functioning and organization. This is a woolly world where there are no logical answers to problems, no boiler plate solutions. It is a world of change and competition; where success isn't about knowing all the right answers but about making more intelligent guesses than others.

There are innumerable magazine articles and books written about digital technology, e-business and e-commerce. This published information is dwarfed by the amount of information available on the Web. It's impossible to even estimate the extent of all this knowledge let alone absorb it. What makes things even worse is that so much of the information is contradictory. Seemingly, there are few general agreements on any issues. As if that isn't bad enough, technology, techniques and recommended business strategies are changing so fast that whatever is read is almost always certain to be out of date by the time anyone gets around to understanding and applying it.

To my entrepreneurial mind, it seemed common sense that nobody could ever hope to understand what the world of digital communication is about by delving into this morass of unstable information. The only route to understanding would have to come through creating a practical working model in your mind that could be used to rise above the detail. Only in this way would it be possible to make pragmatic decisions.

Every successful entrepreneur I've ever known has worked this way. They rise above the detail – which they leave to hired helpers – in order to concentrate on the broader issues. From this high-level view of the world, they create simple, rule of thumb formulae that can be used as the basis for decision making. These loose strategies then become the engines for their success. This book is about trying to create such an engine: an abstract model that can be used to guide decision making in the seemingly incomprehensible world of digital technology.

This book is about concepts and strategies

Entrepreneurs never use books and published information as step-by-step guides to success. They are more interested in looking for abstract ideas and concepts that they can apply in novel ways. 'How to' books are of little value because if a plan or a technique has been published it means somebody else has done it before. To do the same as someone else is to play catch up, a game for technologists not entrepreneurs. Entrepreneurs leave the studying of instructional knowledge to their manager, while they concentrate on adapting and developing concepts in new and unexplored territories.

Developing ideas is seldom something that can be done in isolation. The human mind is not omniscient, there are very large gaps in anyone's knowledge and nobody can avoid having biases or limitations due to things they do not know very well or are not aware of at all. This is particularly true with anything involving the digital world of e-business and e-commerce, where the horizon is continuously expanding at breakneck speed in all directions.

Entrepreneurs can offset their lack of knowledge and counteract their biases by sharing ideas with others (it is usually the mark of a novice when they want to keep ideas to themselves). This airing of ideas can expose fallacies, reveal lack of knowledge, prompt additional information and promote fresh thinking. In the world of bricks and mortar, I'd often used cafés, restaurants, wine bars, pubs and clubs for this purpose. It is surprising how effectively informal discussions in a relaxing, social environment can help to develop and refine new ideas.

It seemed sensible then that I should use such a method to write this book. If I could gather together a suitably representative group of experts and specialists who were involved in all kinds of different aspects of the digital world, perhaps I could get them to look over my shoulder as I was writing. Better still, if I could get them all together in a café, and get them to read each chapter as I wrote it, they could then discuss the content between them and come up with all kinds of comment, criticism and suggestions. Being all together, they could bounce ideas off of each other, create a synergy that would be inspirational.

Fortunately, the technical programming books I'd written had been modestly successful. The spin-off from this had been that it had brought me into personal contact with very many people from all over the world who in various ways had become involved in different aspects of e-business and e-commerce. It occurred to me that this might be an ideal pool of knowledge to draw upon to help me with the writing of the book.

The trick would be to bring them all together to sit in a café with me, to read and discuss every chapter as I wrote it. In the physical world this would be impossible, but in the magical world of the Internet this ideal scenario was a practical reality. First I emailed about 400 of my contacts. I explained I was writing a book on e-commerce and asked if they would like to read and comment on the chapters. About 50 of them responded positively. Here is the email I sent to each of them:

Thank you for offering to read and comment on the chapters of my new book on e-commerce.

In the book, I shall be discussing various conceptual tools to help deal with the complexity of the Internet. One of these is a virtual café, where 48 of your special colleagues or contacts are present: sitting around the café at tables. The conceptualization is that you can go and sit with any of these contacts to have a discussion with them (by email), or invite a selected group of them to sit with you at a table for a group discussion (by email). In this way, the socializing aspects of a café can be simulated, even though the people in the virtual café are actually located in many different parts of the world.

Sounds silly, but in fact this idea can help create some very interesting communication strategies. Since I'm covering this in the book I thought I might use it now to see how it works. I'll be describing it in more detail in the book, so I'll explain it here just enough for you to see how it is being used for this book review process.

The café of reviewers starts with about 48 people. Most are people I've had correspondence with at various times on a variety of subjects, some I've contacted recently specifically to ask for help with this review. The 48 represent a very wide range of people – although in one way or another, each has some connection with e-commerce or digital communication technology.

They come from all over the world. Some are well-known experts in their fields; some run large companies; some are students; some are teachers. There are programmers, designers, artists, writers, hackers and entrepreneurs. Some run servers, some host Web sites. There is an extraordinary mix of different people here, most of whom I've met through the writing of my previous books or on Internet discussion forums.

I shall be randomly dividing the 48 people into six groups of seven to nine people (tables in the virtual café). So, when I send out the draft chapters, I shall be sending them separately to each group with the names and email addresses of all the people at the table in the 'To:' header.

What I should like you to do, if you have any comments, is to send them not just to me but to all the people in your group. In other words this acts like a mini list serve where everyone is responsible for serving their own posts to their own small list of people at their table. It is as if you are making comments to a table full of people in a café.

Unlike regular lists, these lists are temporary and last for two weeks only. For each new chapter there will be a random rearrangement of the tables so that the groups consist of a different mix of people each time. Not only might this random mixing of people generate some interesting discussion, it will give everyone a chance to meet a wide variety of very interesting people whom they might otherwise never have had an opportunity to meet.

Of course, I have no idea whether this will work (although I've experimented with this technique already with some quite remarkable results). It is an experiment and I'll include the results (for better or for worse) in the book. I'm very curious to see how such an arrangement might generate different kinds of discussion.

There is of course no obligation to comment. As in a real-life situation, some people just listen, others are prompted into discussion while others simply add a few apt remarks. I would appreciate, however, everyone adding at least some small comment on each chapter, so that I know they are keeping up and ready to receive the next.

Thanks again for offering to take part and I hope I can provide you with some interesting and informative reading.

The first two chapters produced a variety of responses. Unlike conventional books, I hadn't specifically stated what was going to be in the book. I had a good idea what I wanted to be in it, but I couldn't know how it was going to turn out because I was going to let the feedback from the discussions determine the exact nature of the book. This upset a lot of the readers who wanted to see a conventional table of contents and the conclusions stated right at the beginning.

I explained that I was looking at the book like a detective story: where we start with bloodstains on the carpet; find a body; discover clues; work out the motives – and then draw appropriate conclusions at the end to come up with the name of the murderer. Or, in this case, a viable way to think about e-commerce.

My bloodstains on the carpet were the difficulties many large companies are having in making any progress in the world of e-commerce. It seemed as good a starting place as any because it is a mystery. Why are many large companies having difficulties?

By the third chapter, the conclusion was drawn that the traditional structures and techniques of large corporations weren't suitable for e-commerce because it is not a stable environment. This requires a way of thinking that is quite foreign to most corporate trained managers and executives. The environment was likened to that of a complex dynamic system: a popular subject of current research, which can be described and analyzed in terms of chaos theory. This approach suggests dealing with complex environments by growing solutions rather than planning them.

I lost a few of the review readers at this point because it seemed to them to be too esoteric. They couldn't see how it was possible to build a business without a structured plan that could be closely monitored and controlled. Those that did see the logic of growing a solution began to discuss the implications and the table discussions roared into life, with some people anticipating the contents of the next chapters even before I'd finished writing them.

Up until this point, I'd been assigning the readers to tables randomly, but it became obvious that the range of different viewpoints was too wide for discussions to make any real progress without excessive disruptive discord. I began to group people at tables according to how they'd responded at previous tables. I put those who were appreciating the idea of growing solutions into groups together, separating them from those who were fixed upon the idea of having plans and managed teams. Some people weren't into the strategic aspect at all and were more concerned with technical detail; these I separated out to their own special table. I also had a table from hell: those who simply wanted to be critical and make no positive contribution to where the book was heading.

To obtain the maximum of interaction, I used a rule that if there was no response from somebody over two chapters they were deemed to have left the café. This had the result of reducing the number in the café to only those who maintained a constant interest. This also put me under pressure to try to deliver interesting chapters otherwise I'd have ended up with an empty café before I'd finished the book.

Altogether, the café produced more than 1,000 emails. A whole variety of views were put forward at each chapter. Some were critical, some helpful. The readers were adding information, introducing fresh ideas and viewpoints. I was quickly corrected when somebody disagreed with what I'd written and I was given numerable real-life examples to back up some of the theory. It was truly inspirational.

Having feedback at each chapter while I was writing the next allowed me to fill in more detail where necessary, provide extra explanation, and most importantly be able to appear to anticipate readers' thoughts. The only problem was the wide diversity of people who were reading the chapters. Some were narrow niche technologists, others were not technologically oriented at all. This has resulted in many of the explanations being repeated in several different ways in order to cater for different types of people.

The biggest problem was the explanation of the more abstract concepts. Chaos theory gave the greatest difficulty and I had to remove the original explanation and replace it with a very brief synopsis (some of the original, more obtuse theoretical stuff that was taken out can be seen on my Web site at **www.avatarnets.com**). Chapters 6 and 7 were problematic as well, when I dealt with object-oriented thinking. Several of the readers dropped out at these chapters.

Perhaps the most controversial area was explaining the idea of working without plans and letting solutions evolve. Some readers couldn't accept this at all. The problem was compounded when this approach exposed the weakness of using managed teams for the Internet side of an e-business operation. Even I was surprised at this outcome and it took an extra chapter of explanation to convince most people that this really was a rational approach.

Bringing it all together for a conclusion was the biggest challenge. Until I reached that point I didn't even know myself how everything could be tied together. Happily, it produced just the kind of result I'd been looking for when I started the book: a simple conceptual framework that could be used as a basis to confront the complexity of the Web and provide a foundation for a competitive approach to e-business and e-commerce.

Peter Small
January 2000

Introduction

Essentially, this book is about trying to understand the implications for business and commerce of the Internet and the World Wide Web. More specifically, it is about imaginative, people-to-people communication strategies that are likely to change all the rule books for competing in highly competitive markets.

Everywhere, the pundits are telling us that this seemingly innocuous new medium of the Internet holds the possibility of not only changing the way people do business but also of having a major impact on the way people live their lives. The agrarian revolution changed society from hunters and gatherers to farmers. The industrial revolution caused populations to mass into towns and cities. Now, those who should know are telling us that we are at the dawn of another revolution that is going to change society dramatically once again.

They are probably right and we are now in a transition period between the Industrial Age and the Information Age. If so, it is important that we take a serious look at this proposition and try to understand what it is really about.

Where the advances in computer technology and digital communications will eventually take us is not predictable, so we'd be wasting our time on that. More realizable and profitable will be for us to be concerned with the nature of the change itself. It is at the crest of such a wave of change that fortunes can be made, new careers forged, new businesses created, fresh and imaginative techniques and strategies formulated. We ought to be there with our eyes wide open.

To be on this wave will open up many opportunities but there will also be numerous pitfalls. Pioneering in any new territory is not for the faint-hearted; it is not for nothing that the frontiers of the digital communications revolution are known as 'the bleeding edge'. False steps can lead to disaster and oblivion, but unless risky steps are taken there is no alternative other than to play 'catch up' – not the best game in a fast-moving environment where early successes and innovations are so richly rewarded.

Those able to understand what is going on and who can respond with appropriate strategies will have the best chances to thrive and prosper. The rest are likely to find themselves falling rapidly behind. It is the purpose of this book to try to find the right mindset, the understanding and the conceptual tools necessary to be able to ride this current wave of change successfully.

Now it is easy to make all these rhetorical statements about a changing business environment, a changing world and taking advantage of the changes, but we have to look beyond the empty rhetoric. It's no good just saying there are changes ahead and we can benefit from these changes. We need to know specifically what the changes are and what we actually have to do to benefit from them.

First, let's be clear what is meant by the terms e-commerce and e-business. They will be used interchangeably and together in this book because at the time of writing there is no common agreement as to what they mean or the fields they cover. The lower case 'e' represents 'electronic'. The term 'commerce' is generally applied to the processes involved in buying and selling. The term 'business' covers a much wider area and is applied to any and all communications and processes concerned with the selling, buying, supplying and manufacture of products or services.

Whichever of these terms is used in this book, it will relate to processes that involve the use of the Internet. This is the aspect that will be our main concern: the direct or indirect effects of the Internet and its accompanying technologies of computers and digital communications. The reader is advised not to be too fastidious over the meanings and definitions of words used in this book. In a world so prone to change, words have limited permanence; their meanings can become distorted and give rise to ambiguities and misunderstandings if taken too literally. Where there is cause for ambiguity, words will be defined, but be warned, these definitions may not accord with their everyday meanings.

In the writing of this book, it has become apparent that the subject matter will involve a clash of cultures, mainly the corporate culture, the academic culture, the scientific culture, the artistic culture and the entrepreneurial culture. Each will have its own ways of approaching, using and understanding the Internet. However, there is one consideration that overrides all issues of culture: the rapid advance of computers and communications technology is throwing up so many changes that the thinking of yesterday is unlikely to be relevant today. This means that anyone who seriously wants to understand what the

Information Age is about must totally disassociate their thinking from any techniques or procedures they might have learned in the business environments of the Industrial Age.

Too often, people will want any new information they receive to fit neatly into a knowledge structure they have already formed in their own mind. This isn't always possible. A mismatch creates a situation where people talk past each other. They think they are talking about the same thing but in reality they are each talking about quite different models of reality, where words and even concepts can have totally different meanings.

Normally, this isn't too much of a problem because people from different cultures work and converse mainly in their own domain, but when all the cultures converge to discuss a subject of mutual interest – such as the new environment created by the Internet and the World Wide Web – there can be much misunderstanding and discord. The reader should be constantly on the alert to ensure that his or her cultural background doesn't get in the way of learning about and understanding the many new concepts that will be involved in adapting to the Internet.

The Information Age is new and different from the Industrial Age. Everyone must be able to step outside their personal model of the world to see the Information Age for what it really is: an 'Alice in Wonderland' world where all the conventional rules of communicating, cooperating and doing business are radically different. We are now in a new millennium and must leave the ways of the previous millennium behind us.

Mainly this book will be concerned with strategies. One of the most confusing of the issues that arise between corporate and entrepreneurial cultures is the concept of a plan or a strategy. In the corporate world, the plan is the fundamental basis of all business and commercial activity. In many instances, such plans are referred to as strategies and the two words are used interchangeably. Similarly, in the entrepreneurial world, an entrepreneur will have a plan or strategy, but an entrepreneurial plan or strategy is often conceptually quite different from a corporate plan or strategy.

Corporate plans are about applying generally acceptable rules. They are based upon knowns, knowables and statistical predictables. These are used to structure an approach to reach a goal. In contrast, entrepreneurial strategies quite often dispense with any formal or organized plan and rely on rule of thumb: a set of ad hoc rules that allow entrepreneurs to react flexibly to unpredictable situations. Such strategies are sometimes so loose and flexible that very often an entrepreneur will consider that he or she has no plan at all when setting out on a business venture – only a strategy.

Such differences in the way corporations and entrepreneurs view plans and strategies can cause much misunderstanding. For this reason this book will take the view that corporations make plans and entrepreneurs have strategies. Corporate plans, for the purpose of this book, are defined as plans that are based upon logical reasoning, past experience, training, precedence, justifiable risk and statistically based assumptions.

In contrast, the strategies of entrepreneurs will be considered to be less structured, more loose: rule of thumb strategies that might include inductive inferences, calculated risk, hypotheses and assumptions that cannot be logically justified.

With these definitions, there will undoubtedly be some corporations using entrepreneurial-type strategies and some entrepreneurs using corporate-type planning; nevertheless, it will be more useful for comparison purposes if we treat corporations and entrepreneurs as different animals who play by different rules. Seeing them in terms of black and white will save having to keep explaining the exceptions.

There is a similar conceptual mismatch of approaches to achieving goals with academics, scientists and artists. Academics will generally work from precedence and officially recognized sources of knowledge. They will build from the knowledge of others and deduce their conclusions using a top-down approach. Scientists and artists on the other hand are always looking into the unknown; they will assume that their goals are outside current knowledge and will work inductively, looking for original breakthroughs that go beyond the limits of what is known already. Their approach will be bottom-up, building creatively towards solutions. Again this is a black and white description, as many scientists and artists will work in the way described here for academics and many academics will work more in the way described for scientists and artists. Also, many more will combine a mixture of the two.

A somewhat similar conceptual confusion arises over the issues of what constitutes self-regulating systems and evolutionary design. For most corporates, the idea of a system that controls itself suggests anarchy and disorganized chaos. Products that design themselves, if they can be visualized at all, bring up visions of inefficiency and gross malformation. This contrasts sharply with the attitude of an entrepreneur, who might see self-regulation as a means of efficiency and cost saving. A self-regulating system can thus have different meanings to different people.

Entrepreneurs often rely on subjective human qualities such as trust, reliability, loyalty and duty, in place of standards and control, to effect regulation in their organizations. This might seem unsafe, even bizarre, to most corporate planners, who will want to see more tangible elements holding their organizational frameworks together. The corporate planner would see human qualities as being subjective, with very fuzzy meanings and values: far too imprecise to specify in a corporate plan.

Entrepreneurs, on the other hand, have to be more pragmatic. These human qualities are the glue that holds their organizations together. For their purposes, entrepreneurs will need to assign measurable, qualitative substance to these human attributes – a task most corporate minds might find difficult to come to terms with.

Corporates quite often misunderstand the motives of an entrepreneur. An entrepreneur will often not have the resources for careful planning, long developments or exhaustive testing that are usually available to a corporation. This leaves an entrepreneur with no alternative other than to put an unfinished, incomplete and untested product onto the market; making changes on the fly, according to customer complaints or additional demands. In the eyes of the traditional world of corporate business practice, such entrepreneurial strategies might be considered sharp practice and ethically unacceptable, but as we shall see, this seemingly unacceptable strategy of the entrepreneur is going to have to be adopted by responsible corporations if they are to succeed in the Information Age.

Already this strategy is being widely adopted. Products, in virtually prototype stages, are being distributed for free. The customers then try them out, reveal the faults and deficiencies and ask for new features. In this sense, products can be seen as designing themselves: expressing their design instructions by eliciting responses from the customer. This is the technique of evolutionary design. This is the way of the Internet.

Transition into chaos

Part 1 looks at the changes in attitudes that are necessary as the transition is made from the Industrial Age to the Information Age. It explains how the organized business environment of the Industrial Age is being replaced by a fast-changing chaotic environment where established rules, procedures and protocols are no longer valid.

It explains how the new environment of the Information Age will need business strategies more usually associated with entrepreneurs, where opportunities are anticipated and exploited in a business world full of unknowns and unpredictable chaos.

Chapter 1

Anomalies and enigmas of the Information Age

 The observation of Sherlock Holmes

It wouldn't seem that the game of poker has much relevance to the high speed, technical world of digital communications. Yet, surprisingly, it can offer many useful mental models for helping to make sense of the rapidly evolving world of e-commerce.

As a one-time professional poker player, I've always been consciously receptive to anomalies: the pattern that doesn't quite fit into the picture; the exception; the unusual; the behaviour that is out of character. In poker, such observations are an important part of the game strategy, allowing a player to make intelligent guesses about the unknowable: namely, the value of an opponent's hidden cards.

Applying this tactic of looking for anomalies to e-commerce and the Web, it immediately becomes of interest that the very large corporations, the experienced advertising and marketing companies, the weight of big money and all the factors that are effective in the traditional world of commerce are not creating the many successes in the world of e-commerce that might be expected. Indeed, many of the combinations of big money, large corporations, experienced marketing services and mass media communication experts have produced spectacular failures.

How come most of the advances in e-business and e-commerce are being initiated by the young and not the experienced business managers and executives? How is it that large corporations can invest huge sums of money to bring the best of corporate minds to bear on the problems yet be no more successful than many inexperienced start-up companies rising up out of nowhere? These are anomalies worth investigating.

The great fictional master of the anomaly was Sherlock Holmes. He looked for anomalies and would seek explanation. His was a strategy of deduction and his breakthroughs always revolved around his much-quoted observation, 'When you have eliminated the impossible, whatever remains, however improbable, must be the truth'.

In this book we are going to take just such an approach. The overwhelming evidence is that conventional corporate minds are not up to the problem of mastering the world of e-commerce. They have had sufficient time to demonstrate that their know-how can result in success. They haven't convincingly come up with the goods. So, applying Holmes' rule we must conclude the improbable: that the corporate mind formed in the twentieth century is inappropriate for dealing with the Internet in the twenty-first.

Where do we start to look for an alternative?

The temptation is to look at e-commerce ventures which are already seen to be working. However, common sense tells us that if this were the route to discovering the key to successful e-commerce trading, the optimum strategy would already have been discovered and become common knowledge by now. It is one of the most remarkable features of e-commerce that everything that anyone does is observable by millions. This is the attraction of e-commerce, but it is also a handicap.

The world of the Internet and the World Wide Web is already far too vast for human comprehension, but there are research projects putting the whole of the World Wide Web onto terrabytes of disk storage in order to study it in detail. They are setting a variety of computer programs to work on these time slices, trying to make sense of the structures that have evolved. As immense as the Web has become, it can all be contained in a physical space no bigger than the size of a single room. However, all that these researchers seem to be discovering is that they are dealing with an ever-growing system which is becoming increasingly complex. There is precious little in the way of clues to help form strategies for e-commerce. Perhaps, though, this isn't surprising because they are looking at this environment from the wrong end of the telescope.

The evidence from biological research and the history of medicine tells us that complexity isn't something that can be examined from the outside looking in. Complexity can only be understood in terms of the dynamic interactions of the components of a system: a micro rather than a macro perspective. With complex systems, understanding only comes as a result of a bottom-up approach: identifying the basic elements of a system and the rules by which they interact.

Taking a bottom-up approach, there is much that can help us to make sense of the complexity of the Internet and the World Wide Web. We have available to us all the conceptual tools that have proved so successful in unlocking many of the secrets of nature; the conceptual tools that are being used to explore the nature of matter and the universe. We have all the techniques and methods used by drug companies to explore and manipulate the complex systems of molecular biology and the many varied theories being applied to study human behaviour. There are also the software tools being used to predict the outcome of investments and stock market prices. There are sophisticated conceptual models applying game theory to various forms of negotiation and modern warfare.

All these tools and concepts come into the new and fast-growing area of complexity theory. Adapting and applying these tools and concepts to the Internet, the Web and e-commerce offers us the most likely route to finding a winning strategy.

Unfortunately, the conceptual tools we need are currently locked away in the arcane language of mathematics. Our task is to take them out of their academic settings and translate them into readily understandable and usable forms. We have to cut away all the theory and reduce these tools to simple-to-use techniques. To achieve this goal we will have to abstract the essence of the tools and apply this essence to real-world experiences.

Before going along this route, it may be worth taking a look at the corporate approach to the Internet and the Web. After all, they have the available resources both intellectually and financially to take this same approach. Why aren't they taking it?

Learning on the fly

Even though I have spent most of my life as an entrepreneur, I have had many encounters with the corporate world. I can deal with corporates in straight business negotiation, but on any other level there seems to be a problem of communication. We just seem to talk past each other. This wasn't a serious problem until, as a consequence of my books and writings, corporations started to come to me for explanation and guidance on e-commerce and e-business issues. I found I couldn't help them because there appeared to be too much of a mismatch of our concepts. Any reasoned explanations I gave were being interpreted quite differently from the way intended. At first, I found this totally perplexing. If anyone should be able to explain complex ideas to anyone I should be able to do it; this was what I had been trained for. Let me explain.

During the Second World War, the British government set up dozens of secret research establishments all over Britain. They were the places where the cream of British scientists were gathered to apply science and technology to create novel inventions which would help defeat the enemy. Many became well known, such as the Aldermaston Atomic Research Establishment, the Radar Research Establishment at Great Malvern, the code-breaking team at Bletchley Park, the biological warfare centre at Porton Down. There were many more, all exploring the myriad new possibilities opened up by the explosion of technological advances coming out of the war effort.

When the war finally came to an end, there was still a need for these research centres. It had become apparent that any future conflicts were going to be won through the application of technology. Britain couldn't afford to fall behind in this ever-increasing drive towards further technological advance.

As these research centres expanded into new and more complex areas of activity, an inherent weakness became acutely apparent – a problem of communication. Practical application of the scientific effort needed close cooperation between the theoretical scientists and the engineers who would construct the hardware. This was proving to be a weak link because the scientists and the engineers came from different worlds, they didn't speak the same technical languages and they thought with different conceptual models.

At the highest level, it was decided to build a special college in the grounds of one of the secret research establishments, to train a new breed of scientific engineers: communication specialists. They wouldn't be required to invent, design or make things but simply to provide the essential missing communication link between the theorists and the constructors.

It was as one of the first students selected for the five-year course they came up with that I found myself at the College of Electronics, situated in the middle of the top-secret Radar Research Establishment at Great Malvern, Worcester, England.

Not surprisingly, we were not taught specifically how to play this role of intermediary between scientists and engineers. Nobody had ever done it before so nobody knew what lessons needed to be taught. Instead, we were given a mixture of experiences and exposures. Half our time was spent learning theory and the rest spent working with different groups within the research establishment.

At least, this is how four of the five years were spent; the first year we were sent away from the research establishment to a giant ordnance factory where they were churning out munitions. There we joined craft apprentices and spent the time making a special set of workshop tools which involved using every type of machine used in metal working and tool making.

Returning to the research establishment after this year of exposure to the realities of industrial production, we spent the next six months in the special engineering workshops attached to the research labs, helping make components for guided weaponry. Then we spent another six months in a large drawing office, working with the draughtsmen who were planning out the work for the craftsmen to make.

It was at the beginning of the third year that I had my first real experience of the difficulties involved in turning theory into practice. We were all excited at the prospect of entering this third year because from then on the practical side of our education would take us into the scientific research labs.

Being students, working beside famous scientists on advanced secret research projects was not the greatest of interest. Our main excitement was the prospect of being able to draw all kinds of 'free' electronic components from the stores. Many of the students were keen hi-fi fans and had already constructed their own sound systems.

I wasn't one of the hi-fi buffs. I was more interested in the social side of college, so when I went along to draw a selection of 'free' components from the store I didn't know how to use them or connect them up. I randomly connected thermionic tubes, resistors and capacitors together, switched on the power and the whole thing dissolved into flames and smoke.

In itself, this incident isn't remarkable. What was significant, however, was that I'd spent the previous month of practical work, in the college lab, plotting dozens and dozens of graphs which showed the effects of varying voltages, resistances and capacitances in a circuit with a thermionic tube. As amazing as it seems in retrospect, I had made no conceptual connection between what I'd been doing in the college lab and the components I'd drawn from the stores. I simply hadn't made the necessary connection between theory and practice.

It was soon after that experience that I met Dr Utterly. He had been one of the main researchers involved in the original development of radar. He was now the head of the most important section in the research establishment: that dealing with the then-new field of electronic computing. It was to this section that I had my first assignment in the research labs.

After a few days of helping a lab technician to physically build an amplifier unit for some obscure experiment to measure fighter pilot reaction times, I was told I was to report to Dr Utterly's office.

I'd never met him before so I knocked at his door with some trepidation. When I entered, I saw a wizened old man in a white lab coat staring intently at a large sphere made out of what looked to me like fine straw. He didn't speak at first; he was too busy waving black and white cards at the sphere.

Looking closer, I noticed that the straw sphere was being gripped by a large black beetle which had been glued at its back to the bottom of a glass rod. The poor beetle wasn't aware that it was holding the straw sphere. It was under the impression that it was running across a straw landscape and away from the various shapes of black and white boards which threateningly kept appearing in its vision. The beetle was stationary and the straw sphere was revolving below, being suspended and propelled by the beetle's 'running' feet.

The eminent scientist then walked over to a blackboard on the wall and proceeded to draw a schematic of the beetle's nervous system. He explained how the black and white boards were charging up certain areas in the beetle's brain, causing it to make decisions as to the direction of its movements. At that moment, my life-long interest in biological structures was born. (I heard later that Dr Utterly was one of four scientists who had originally founded the Radar Research Establishment. All of them had been biologists.)

Briefly explaining the connection between the beetle's nervous system and the computer his department was developing, he then asked me to get to work on designing some circuitry to improve the shape of the pulses which were driving the new computer they were building. I couldn't believe he was asking me to do this. Me! who didn't even know how to connect a few components together.

Asking around among the people who were working on various other projects in the lab, I managed to get a rough idea as to what was required and the way to go about it. A trip to the library and I'd discovered how to connect things up and how to calculate the value of the components. Within a couple of weeks I'd constructed an electronic flip-flop circuit and was busy fine-tuning the characteristics of the pulse to improve its shape. It quite astounded me that I could be doing real research work after such a short period of initiation.

Three months later came my next assignment. I had to assist a physicist who was working on a machine to measure the magnetic spin resonance of atoms. It happened that he had no knowledge of electronics at all and required a special kind of amplifier which selectively filtered a broad bandwidth of very low frequencies.

With the confidence I'd gained from creating the pulse-shaping circuitry in the computer lab I went down to the library to dig out references to filtering circuits. This time I had no technicians around to give me a helping hand and I had to improvise with the circuits I'd found. Melding three frequency selective amplifying circuits into a single design seemed like it would do the trick. Immediately there were problems. It didn't work as it should; the amplification was wildly out of control.

The physicist saw I was in difficulties and tried to help out. It was a case of the blind leading the blind. Running backwards and forwards to and from the library, we tried various solutions and the number of connections and components grew and grew, giving the amplifier the appearance of a large bird's nest. It was not until we'd discovered the principle of negative feedback that we started to get anywhere.

By the end of a week of frustrating effort, it finally worked. A few tweaks of the component values and the amplifier performed perfectly, filtering the exact range of frequencies required. In that week I'd managed not only to build the circuitry but to get a strong grasp of the concepts involved in frequency filtering and feedback circuitry. So also did the physicist.

These experiences taught me a valuable lesson. Learning isn't necessarily a direct result of teaching. It can also result through practical application. The significance of this, which I was to realize much later, was that you didn't have to have an immense range of knowledge to achieve sophisticated goals; by means of a bottom-up approach you could cut straight through the complexity of surplus information to get at just whatever was necessary to achieve effective results – a very valuable conclusion when applied to the gargantuan information base available through the Internet and very useful for deciding how to go about creating an e-commerce venture.

The implications of this are best explained by observing how young children approach the use of computers. Most adults are awe-struck by the way in which young children can so easily pick up the use of complicated programs. With my own boys I was quite keen to get them started in computing early. Despite constant encouragement, threats and bribes, neither took the slightest interest in anything other than using the computer for mindless games. Then at the age of 12 the oldest boy came in from school one day and told me he wanted to use the computer to do his school homework.

Eagerly, I showed him how to start PowerPoint and immediately he started playing around with the mouse and the keyboard. When I ventured to show him how to use the program he brushed my offer aside, telling me that my explanations would only confuse him. Within an hour or two he had completed a fairly passable presentation, complete with a 3-D graphics heading. I was quite staggered and more than a little humbled that I hadn't been of any help.

I learned later that the motivation for using the computer had not been instigated by the teacher. Some of the other boys had brought in computer-generated homework submissions and my son's spidery handwriting and crude drawing were shaming him into action. It wasn't long before he was doing all of his homework on the computer, gradually progressing to various paint programs and a demand for a digital camera.

I was keen to encourage his use of the computer and made constant attempts to give him assistance but, every time, my teaching efforts were met with either indifference or an impatience to get on with what he was doing. Even when he suddenly decided he needed to use a spreadsheet program to create something or other for his French homework (yes, French homework) he would accept no offer of help at all.

Now from this description you'd think of my boy as some kind of school swot, a potential nerd. Nothing of the kind. He was a fairly average scholar and had only just discovered girls. He was using the computer more and more, simply because it enabled him to complete his homework assignments more easily and quickly.

Stepping back from this, it occurred to me that this was the modern child's natural approach to handling complexity. He hadn't read a single word from any of the computer books or manuals. He'd simply used a bottom-up approach to go directly to the solution of his particular problem: which was to complete his homework with the least possible effort. It seemed that without being encumbered by any formal instruction to set up a rigid framework, he'd simply built up his own knowledge base from scratch. There is a clue there somewhere, Doctor Watson.

This trial and error, bottom-up technique of learning accords with the way many professional computer users approach complex applications. Invariably they pay scant heed to the manual when they first encounter a new program. Their first approach is always to play around and do something constructive. It seems their learning process starts by forming a small base of knowledge and then building outwards from it. Manuals and books are used only when specific problems are encountered during use. This makes sense in an information-rich world where it is totally inefficient to take up time with information that might be redundant to actual needs.

In contrast, such an attitude is not common in most of the traditional academic world where emphasis is placed upon providing set courses which cover a broad range of information and mental constructs.

There are several possible reasons for this difference between the way professional people in the world of digital communications acquire knowledge and the way students acquire knowledge. Principally, students are given a broad range of knowledge because the teachers and most likely the students themselves have no idea what particular area of knowledge will be directly applicable to a student's post-college life. Even if this were known, it would hardly be practical to have every student studying different course material.

Once out of college, and in any occupation connected with digital communication, the range and depth of all the information applicable to any specific employment is almost certain to be far beyond any human capability to comprehend. Thus, anyone needing knowledge is forced, by the practicalities of efficient use of time, to be selectively parsimonious about what they attempt to learn. General knowledge is a luxury, which is not a practical reality for any busy careerist.

Another reason for the difference in learning between the academic and professional worlds is that the world of academia is like the world of law: it is built upon a long history of precedence. Quite rightly, the educational system is not receptive to every new idea that comes along. Looking through the history of knowledge, time and again you find instances of the great breakthroughs in thought being totally rejected at the time of their introduction. New ideas and concepts are accepted into the mainstream of education only after a suitable period of trial and rigorous examination.

In contrast, the fast-changing world of e-business and e-commerce is constantly looking for and experimenting with new concepts and strategies. The field of digital communications is moving too fast for the conventional educational system to absorb properly all the new ideas, techniques and methods that are constantly appearing.

This isn't necessarily a bad thing. Many of the new ideas and concepts arising in the environment of digital communications turn out to be very short lived. Emergent effects caused by rapidly advancing technology and the changing strategies of competitive businesses give all knowledge a degree of impermanence. Wisdom and knowledge aren't absolute or necessarily lasting in the digital communication environment. They are often temporary, subject to change and sudden reversal.

Another factor that is creating differences between the way in which students and professional workers acquire knowledge is what can be called 'the fractal effect'. Fractals are those odd mathematical functions that create lines or surfaces that look the same at whatever scale you view them. Examining a small section of a fractal shows variations seeming to look the same whether it is viewed with 10 times magnification, 100 times magnification, 1,000 times magnification or indeed any magnification whatsoever.

This fractal effect readily becomes apparent when searching for information on the Internet: the more you look into any particular detail, the more detail you will find. Searching any small area of speciality opens up a seemingly bottomless pit. The more you learn, the more you find there is to know. Pursuing a line of thought on an Internet search is seldom a satisfying experience because invariably you end up feeling less informed than when you started: the search reveals so many gaps in your knowledge.

Students are seldom aware of this fractal effect; teachers usually filter and distil information before teaching it. This often leaves post-graduate students totally at a loss when they have to build up their knowledge base without the direction of a guide or a teacher.

There is yet another problem, even more formidable than the fractal effect. The conventional world has grown used to a stable knowledge base. Education is based upon a stable society steeped in tradition and proven concepts. There are conventional rules of thought, established procedures, recognized values. These are the end results of the settling down of civilization after the industrial revolution. It is the way of the Industrial Age.

Suddenly, a new cultural, social and technological revolution is upon us. It is being called the Information Age. We find ourselves plunged into an unfamiliar world where all the rules are changed. It is an 'Alice in Wonderland' world ruled by the Queen of Hearts. It is not just that there are new rules or that some of the rules have changed. The new rules which apply in the digital world of communications and e-commerce are sometimes the exact opposite of the proven and accepted dogmas which apply in the conventional world. This is what is so unnerving: applying any Industrial Age business approach to communication and commerce in the digital world is likely to be not only ineffective but actually destructive.

This is a very serious problem for any individual or company entering the world of e-commerce. Traditional business procedures are unsuitable, traditional management techniques are totally inappropriate. Conventional marketing strategies are no longer effective. There are no suitable courses to take, no reliable books to learn from. Worst of all, the search for solutions leads mostly into the confusing and disorientating labyrinth of digital information on the Internet.

Forward planning in the Information Age

After I had finished my rather exceptional education at the research establishment, I didn't stay on to fulfil the role I had been trained for. None of the students did. As with many forward-thinking plans, some vital details had not been taken into account. The conception of the plan to train bright young students to become important links between scientists and engineers was flawless. There must have been much thought put into the course design; much money spent on buildings and teaching staff. Despite all this intellectual effort nobody had stopped to think of what the students' attitudes might be when they reached the end of their five-year training.

At the end of the course, all of us fortunate students found ourselves at the forefront of an emerging explosion of new technology. Our knowledge and training were unique. There were countless opportunities in private industry available to us; companies were vying with each other to take us on. Didn't any of the planners foresee this situation? It appeared not to be so. At the end of the five years, all of us graduating students were offered a standard graded post which would slot us into the traditional hierarchy of government employees. This fixed both status and salary and was grossly inferior to anything that was being offered by a new industry hungry for suitably educated employees.

Now it is easy to criticize such a blatant oversight in retrospect. At the time of the scheme's conception it would not have been readily apparent that such a specialized education would have been of value to employers other than the research establishment itself. Technology had suddenly taken hold. It had come at an unprecedented pace. It would have been very difficult to have anticipated and make allowances for such a seemingly unlikely outcome when the scheme was being planned.

This is the phenomenon of emergence: the unforeseen rapid change of conditions which is the dominant feature of advancing technology, particularly digital communications technology. Changes, consequences and effects occur so unexpectedly, so swiftly and so unpredictably that there is no way that allowances can be made beforehand. This results in all strategies based upon careful planning becoming redundant even before they can properly be put into effect.

How can you plan anything if you don't know what the conditions and the situation will be like when the plan reaches fruition? Time and time again, in this new world of digital technology, we are seeing companies caught out by the effects of emergence. New technological advances, new hardware, new software, competitor initiative: all conspire and interact to make a nonsense of any form of forward planning.

Yet, in the traditional Industrial Age, business strategies are always based upon forward plans and predictions.

At the commencement of writing this book, I was subscribed to an Internet discussion group focused on Web hosting. One of the subscribers asked how to go about creating a business plan. I sent in a post suggesting that a business plan would be likely to turn out totally useless in e-commerce. It was as if I'd walked into a church service at Westminster Cathedral and proclaimed 'There is no God'.

Instead of the usual polite and informative responses which are normally accorded to postings, I was immediately bombarded with derision and scorn. My post was a heresy. 'How can anyone go into business without a plan?', they wanted to know. 'How can you raise capital without providing a credible cash flow and profit and loss account?'

Knowing what I did about the chaotic variance of the Internet environment it didn't make any sense to me that any kind of forward planning could be relied upon as a credible basis for loaning money, even venture capital. Why should this not be obvious to everyone?

To check out how widespread this need for a business plan was, I made appointments to see the loan managers of several banks in my home town. I explained to each that I'd come to negotiate a loan for a business connected with e-commerce. Every loan manager started with the same question. 'Do you have a business plan?'

I then patiently explained that I was contemplating doing business in the rapidly changing world of digital communications and I didn't think it practical to draw up any business plan. 'But cash flow? You must have a cash flow?', each responded. I'd then explain why it was totally impossible to predict any kind of cash flow and finish up by adding that in any case I'd be starting off by making no charges for my services and products. Understandably, none of the managers wasted very much more time with me.

It then dawned on me that the conventional business world had no conception at all of a business structure outside of anything that couldn't be described by a formal business plan. How, then, can you plan a business without using a conventional business plan? How can you describe a business strategy without the need to predict revenues and earnings?

With a conventional business mindset, such a possibility is not conceivable. However, to anyone using the conceptual tools used for dealing with chaos, uncertainty and complexity, the solution is perfectly straightforward. The key is in taking advantage of the phenomenon of emergence: a phenomenon feared by established businesses but a boon to the entrepreneur.

Emergence belongs to chaos theory (which I'll get to later), but the game of poker exhibits this effect rather neatly and illustrates how business plans and cash flows are totally inappropriate for strategies that deal with uncertainty, competition and emergence.

Using emergence to win at poker

The most popular game in the London poker clubs of the 1960s was a variation known as 'five-card stud poker with a short deck'. This was the game preferred by most professionals because of its high skill to luck ratio. It was played with a regular deck of cards but with the twos to sixes removed. This gives a 32-card deck: ace high with the lowest card a seven.

The game starts by all players putting a small amount of money (the ante) into a central kitty (the pot). The first card is dealt face down to each player followed by a card face up. Then there is a round of betting where players can call, drop out or raise. In this round, if players don't like the first two cards they are dealt they can drop out without contributing any more to the pot. For those who stay in, another card is dealt face up and there is another round of betting. Two more rounds of face-up cards with betting sees the final betting taking place, with each player left displaying one card face down (the card in the hole) and four cards with their faces exposed.

The strategies of players vary immensely, but they can be grouped into two broad categories: the carabino strategy and the open strategy. The carabino strategy is a safe and steady style which relies upon playing from strength. At its extreme, it can mean only staying in to play a hand if the first two cards dealt are aces (one showing, the other hidden). In other words, the carabino strategy allows the players to play only if their cards cannot be beaten by any other hand on the table.

At first thoughts, the carabino strategy seems unbeatable: always playing from strength and only playing or continuing if the odds are heavily in your favour. However, the professional poker players don't play this way; they play what is called 'an open game' – a strategy that allows them to prey on the novices who adopt the more careful carabino strategy. They play with the anticipation of an emergence giving them the initiative and a winning advantage.

Let's take the case of the really cautious player who will only bet in the first round if he has been dealt two aces back to back. A professional poker player will have very quickly recognized the player's style of play and be aware of the near certainty that the careful player has aces back to back. The professional might have, say, a nine showing and a seven in the hole. He'll look around at all the other cards and if there are no sevens or nines showing he'll call the bet.

On the second round, say neither the careful player nor the professional improves – perhaps the careful player gets a king and the professional gets a queen. If no other player shows any improvement the careful player can be confident in making a large bet because he knows he has the highest cards on the table. At this stage the professional will assess the chances of each of the players improving in the next round. If another ace or king has come out he'll know that the chances of the careful player's hand improving are lessened. If there are still no nines or queens showing, the professional will know that with the short deck there is a very good chance of an improvement to his own hand. He will then call the bet, perhaps even raising the stakes even though he knows he has an inferior hand.

When the next card is dealt to each player, if the professional player improves and the careful player with the two aces doesn't, the professional will be in an advantageous position, even though he has an inferior hand. To see why, let's say the professional has drawn a nine (likely, because there are three left to come) and the careful player has drawn a jack. The careful player must assume that there is a strong possibility of the professional having more than just the two nines: probably three nines, especially if the professional had raised into the ace in the round before.

As soon as the professional has a showing advantage, he'll make an extremely high bet. This places the careful player in a dilemma. He'll know the professional might be bluffing but can he risk taking a chance? It's not only this bet he must call, he knows that there will be a further card to come and another round of betting which could force him into taking an even costlier risk. Invariably, the cautious player will fold his cards and drop out, even though he has the winning hand.

In this way a professional poker player can win more hands than the normal run of luck would allow. He will not win every time, as the careful player can get lucky, but the open play will ensure that over a series of several hands the professional will nearly always come out on a winner.

Now, if we take away from this poker game scenario the principal essence, we find that the strategy of the professional poker player is to anticipate a sudden unpredictable change. The professional poker player isn't calculating the odds of his hand against the opponent's hand, he's counting on an emergence which will provide an opportunity to engineer an advantage.

This is just the kind of strategy needed for success in e-commerce: getting into a position to take advantage of any new developments before knowing what they will be and when they are likely to occur. Such a strategy need not rely on prediction or guesswork; it can be logically calculated using special conceptual tools based upon probabilities.

Such strategies are not intuitive. To see why such a strategy cannot be envisaged by conventional business thinking, try to create a business plan for this approach. See if you can draw up a projected cash flow. Imagine the expression on a bank manager's face if you went into a bank to ask for a loan to finance a potentially winning strategy for a game of poker.

Yet this is the only kind of strategy that is appropriate for e-commerce businesses in the Information Age. Everything is changing so rapidly: the technology, the software, the hardware. All is enhanced by the speed with which information moves around the Internet. This is not a stable environment in any sense, and any strategy based upon prediction or forward planning is bound to be inferior to a strategy taking advantage of unpredictable change and emergence.

Note: Although the game of poker illustrates rather neatly the principle of using the anticipation of emergence as part of a winning strategy, the reader must not think that the game of poker itself has any relevance to e-business or e-commerce. As we shall see later, poker is a zero sum game where winners win only what losers lose. E-business is a game where everyone can be winners. It is seeking out these win-win situations that is the key to entrepreneurial success; it is also the key to successful business activity in the Information Age.

Industrial Age reactions to Information Age ideas

It is difficult to generalize on the way corporations react to the rapid advances of digital communications, so I'll recount a few personal experiences which are typical. They will illustrate some of the problems that occur when Industrial Age dogmas encounter the new concepts required in the Information Age.

A few months before starting to write this book, I'd been contacted by the owner of a multimedia production company who had read my books and was intrigued by the possibilities they presented. He explained that he was creating educational CD-ROMs for the education division of a large multinational telecoms company and thought my ideas might be of interest to them.

A meeting was arranged with the head of the education division, at which I explained my thoughts about evolving systems, group communications and leveraging knowledge. This rang several bells, as the company were currently experiencing many problems associated with adapting to digital communications technology. They seemed receptive to new inputs and asked me to start working with them straight away on a consultancy basis.

I wasn't quite sure how I'd approach their particular problems so I made it quite clear that I wouldn't be providing any positive tangible solutions, or any plans – only a strategy. This they said they understood.

The suggestion was that I work with a new group which was just being set up to bring all employees up to date with the latest advances in telecoms technology. I learned later that the pressure to improve the education had come not from within the company but from a committee of main shareholders who felt that the company was losing ground to new competitors coming into their traditional markets.

At the initial meeting with the leader of this new group, I had my first suspicions that things were not going to go well. I was shown the outline of their plan. It consisted of a bell-shaped curve that plotted the educational level of all employees in the company. The horizontal scale indicated the degree of education achieved and the vertical scale indicated the number of employees at each level of education. The bell shape, being typical of many distribution curves, showed most employees bunched around an average and falling away either side to indicate the lesser numbers who were either poorly educated or exceptionally educated.

Their plan was to move this curve to the right. That is, to increase the education of all employees an incremental amount to effectively raise the general level of employee education. They were offering a special bonus to every employee who took a set course of instruction in telecommunications that had been prepared by the company's education department. To the corporate mind of the Industrial Age this made perfect sense. To me, this plan seemed inadequate and incomplete because their stated objective was to be competitive in the Information Age.

I'd visualized this company as a kind of living organism that consisted of specialized functioning parts. It made no sense to me that you needed to provide a standard education for all the parts. For most of the employees, a standard education in telecommunications would be of very little real value. In most cases it would represent only more informational noise.

I'd had in mind a plan to encourage employees to develop their individual specializations, expanding their current areas of interest and knowledge. In this way, individual knowledge and areas of speciality could be leveraged to give the company a much wider and deeper range of expertise. My idea, I told them, was to create a pool of specialists, whose knowledge could be leveraged and shared through a suitably efficient communication network. Unfortunately, the manager couldn't seem to reconcile my ideas with the master plan.

I became even more alarmed when I was told that the company was standardizing on all its computer hardware and software. Departments that used non-standard equipment and programs were going to be heavily penalized. This I'd encountered before. If ever there was a sure sign that a company had the wrong attitude for competing in the new world of digital communications, this was it. Such a policy belongs to the sedentary world of established industrialization, the Industrial Age, not the fast-moving, rapidly changing, unpredictable environment of the Information Age.

In the Industrial Age, standardization is a deep-seated dogma. Costs are reduced with bulk buys; servicing and training costs are minimized. It all seems so logically sensible to create standards. That is, until you stop to consider that companies are now entering a period of rapid technological change. Standards are continuously being invented, revised and abandoned; new rules, new methods, new paradigms are manifesting almost on a daily basis. Standardization in this environment is not only ineffectual, it can become a serious handicap.

The motivation to standardize computer systems seems to stem from the Industrial Age tendency for companies to organize themselves into hierarchical structures of control. IT divisions are usually a separate branch of this hierarchical structure; the IT management often entrenched in ivory towers. Computing in a company is so ubiquitous, appearing in all manner of company business activities, that the influence and control of the IT department can easily become dominating and autocratic.

Even a main board of directors might not be able to exercise much control or influence over a resourceful IT management. They are the technologists at the hub of a company's nerve centre and very few people in the company have the knowledge to understand or query any of their decisions.

It goes against the grain of any corporate manager to surrender any power or control, so most IT departments try to keep all matters relating to computing tightly contained within their own domain. However, in the Information Age with its rapidly changing technology, it just isn't practical for any reasonably efficient IT department to be able to keep up with all the new and rapidly changing developments in computers and digital communications. There is just too much of it to be fully comprehended by even the largest IT department because of the fractal effect: the more you learn, the more you find there is to know.

Rather than admit any lack of knowledge or surrender any control over this technology, many IT departments will deliberately reduce the technology level of a company in order to keep it safely within the extent of their own limited knowledge. This is not a good strategy for an effective IT department to adopt if the company is to maintain competitiveness in the digital economy. The correct way to go is to allow a company to increase the range and scope of its technical competence even if it means losing control. Such an idea is anathema to Industrial Age management thinking.

The next problem I encountered was with the policy of informational exchange. I take the view that any product of a company reflects the total knowledge that the company has about that product, the corollary being that the more knowledge you can input into a company relevant to its products, the better and more competitive those products will be.

I proposed setting up a system that would encourage exchange of information with the outside world and introducing Internet communication strategies. This suggestion was greeted with horror. Mention was made of company secrets leaving the company and of staff being identified as suitable targets for head hunters. It was a no-no. The idea that people should communicate with anyone in the outside world about their work for the company was not acceptable at all.

The final straw came when I proposed introducing a communication strategy that utilized the principle of evolutionary design. I explained that I was intending to provide a piece of software that would allow employees to communicate and exchange knowledge more efficiently – specifically to take advantage of the new advances in digital technology and the Internet.

To explain the essence of evolutionary design, I likened the software to growing extensions to employees' brains. The software would evolve to adapt to individual needs and capabilities, allowing more effective individual communication strategies to be employed.

With my credibility already somewhat stretched, this did not go down too well. I think they half-expected me to start talking about brain surgery and implants. When I showed them the software I had in mind things started to go downhill fast. They began to get nervous and reacted towards me as if they were dealing with somebody who was not quite right in the head.

I'd presented them with a screen with 48 plain rectangles into which you could enter names.

'What is it?', they wanted to know.

I explained that it represented a café and into this virtual café could be entered the names of people whom the user considered to be useful contacts.

'Like an address book of business contacts?', someone asked.

I confirmed that this could be a way of looking at it, explaining that the metaphor of a café helped construct a more useful mental model. On a whiteboard I demonstrated with a little sketch how a list of names could be represented as people in a café and how you could mentally think of getting small groups of people in the café to sit together around a virtual table where you could have discussions with them. They began looking at each other with a mixture of alarm and disbelief.

They then asked me what else the software consisted of and I told them that this was all there was to it at the moment because it had to evolve as a direct response to being used. I then attempted to explain the principle of evolutionary design, where you start with virtually nothing and let the product design itself.

To illustrate what I meant I told them that any evolutionary design could start off as a green frog. No planning was needed and in time that green frog would turn into a highly complex and efficient piece of software. I might add that this explanation was not easy because the company was located in a North European country where English was not the native language. In other words, they were very far from understanding what I was talking about.

At the moment I began my explanation of the principle of the green frog, the head of the educational division joined the confused gathering. Not surprisingly, my consultancy arrangement with the company was terminated very shortly afterwards.

A conceptual divide

Now it would be easy to put this communication failure down to language difficulties, but I discovered that these ideas and concepts were difficult for almost all people from Industrial Age companies to accept: even intelligent, educated people who had a good command of the English language.

I discovered this because at the same time I'd been hosting an Internet list serve forum I'd set up for the readers of my two previous books. The stated intention of this forum was to explore the possibilities of using object-oriented design techniques for application on the Internet.

This had got off to a promising start until this subject of evolutionary design came up. It arose when discussion turned to the design of intelligent agents. A proposal was made that we began by designing a language that could be used by the intelligent agents to communicate with each other. I'd argued that this was not only unnecessary but might well inhibit the design.

'How would we start to design a system of intelligent agents if they are not able to communicate with each other?', somebody wanted to know. I explained that a language would evolve by itself by means of an evolutionary process. It was a predictable emergence of a complex system.

I was asked what I had in mind for the planning of these intelligent agents and I said that I had no plan at all as I wanted to start with a green frog and see how it evolved when we tried to use it for useful functions. At first, they thought I was joking but when they understood that I was perfectly serious about starting off a complex and ambitious programming project with nothing more than a green frog, some of them got quite cross.

At some length, I tried to explain that what we wanted to do was to create a design which would exceed our present ability even to imagine the final outcome. If such a design could go beyond our imagination, it stood to reason that we wouldn't be able to plan it from the outset. However, as with my proposal for the café, the idea of designing a software project without any preconceived plan was greeted with scepticism and total disbelief. Even worse, it was greeted with insult and derision.

Evolutionary design, I tried to explain, is an empirical, trial and error process where different ideas are experimented with. Some prove successful and some fail. The ideas that work are retained and those that don't are abandoned. Then somebody thought they had cottoned on to the idea and described it as whiteboarding (people gathering around a large sketchpad to play around with ideas). Another said this was the principle of think tanks and used by most companies prior to any major design project.

When I told them that it was not the same thing and that whiteboarding and think tank exercises were not appropriate, there was total confusion. An ambitious software design project, starting off with no planning, no previous discussion, no pooling of ideas, no initial prototype. It seemed to many that I'd taken leave of my senses.

Evolutionary design uses the same methods as nature, I explained. Nature progresses blindly. It doesn't pre-plan yet it produces unparalleled complexity to create highly efficient solutions.

At that point I lost everyone.

Chapter 2

The old ways don't work now

 **The transition into a new age**

It was a puzzle to me. I'd presented what I'd considered to be a practical strategy for dealing with complexity to two quite different groups of intelligent people and I'd failed to convince either of them. I'd explained my case as best I could and the arguments hadn't got through. Where was I going wrong? Why were these ideas so hard to accept?

It was evident that they wanted to build on knowledge they already had. They were prepared to accept new concepts but not if these conflicted with their current understandings. They were looking for clear and rational explanation in terms of what they already knew and were hostile to anything that didn't accord with their ideas of common sense.

Unfortunately, everything about dealing with the Internet, digital communications, e-business and e-commerce goes against all Industrial Age business reasoning. All education and previous experience in the conventional business world of the twentieth century don't necessarily apply in the emerging environment of high speed digital communications. Not only does this make it impossible to build upon previous knowledge, it becomes essential to have to unlearn much of this knowledge before going forward.

It then began to make sense as to why the young were making all the running on the Internet and the Web. They weren't handicapped by knowledge, experience and dogma applicable to previous times. They hadn't acquired the conflicting concepts that applied in the Industrial Age business world. They could go straight in and see the Internet for what it is: a new world that nobody knows very much about. It is just there, ready for exploration and experimentation.

Whereas Industrial Age business thinking wants to control and harness the power of digital communication to bring it in line with traditional and established practices, the young are looking at it with fresh eyes and are seeing opportunities that will take them outside of and beyond the business practices of the twentieth century. To them, all the established ways are old-fashioned and inefficient. They can see far better ways of doing business.

The question then becomes one of making a transition between the old and the new. How do you have to think about the Internet in order to escape from the established thinking and business practices of the Industrial Age? How do you get up to speed in the rapidly changing environment of the Information Age so as to avoid being left behind, fretful, baffled and confused?

It was a puzzle that Sherlock Holmes might have revelled in: the intellectual transition into a new century, a new millennium, a new age – the Age of Information.

Deduction, induction and paradox

In examining puzzles, mystery, enigma or paradox, the first instinctive reaction is to apply logic. This is the science of reasoning that looks for defensible arguments based upon sound and provable tenets. As J. S. Mill defined logic: 'Logic is not the science of belief but of proof or evidence.'

Unfortunately, when dealing with fast-changing environments like the Internet, there is very little in the way of evidence. The Internet is not only complex, it is without any sustainable precedence. There are no case histories or previous experience known today that will necessarily apply tomorrow, so pure logic does not appear to be a suitable tool to use when contemplating strategies for e-commerce.

> **In examining puzzles, mystery, enigma or paradox, the first instinctive reaction is to apply logic.**

Rhetoric and dialectic are logical processes of thought used by Hegel to merge contradictions into a higher form of truth. This is a special branch of logic which according to Aristotle was invented by Zeno of Elea and scientifically developed by Plato. This method relies on a continuous series of questions and answers to gradually bring opposing arguments together. It is the art of critical examination of the truth of an opinion through discussion.

However, as many flame wars in Internet discussion forums will testify, this well-founded traditional approach to logically resolving opposing theories is easily disrupted by paradox. As complexity in general, and e-commerce in particular, is beset with countless examples of paradox, the rhetorical and dialectical approach to understanding would appear to be inappropriate.

It is worth looking closely at this phenomenon of the paradox. It will be encountered over and over again when dealing with complexity and e-commerce strategy. For our purposes we shall define a paradox as:

> A proposition or an observance that seems at first sight to be absurd or self-contradictory, conflicting with common sense or preconceived notions of what is reasonable or possible – upon further reflection, or with new evidence or explanation, the proposition may prove to be well founded and essentially true.

In 1685, Hobbes observed: 'The Bishop speaks often of paradoxes with such scorn or detestation that a simple reader would take a paradox either for a felony or some other heinous crime – whereas perhaps the more judicious reader knows that a paradox is an opinion not yet generally received.'

Brooks, in describing the art of poetry in 1942, commented: 'Few of us are prepared to accept the statement that the language of poetry is paradox – yet there is a sense in which paradox is the language appropriate and inevitable to poetry.'

It might also be argued that paradox is the language of complex systems and, by inference, the language of e-commerce because, as we shall see, the route to understanding is littered with paradoxes of all kinds. Thus, if paradox is a hindrance to logical thought, how can we get to understand e-commerce?

Inference is a term that is often used in the context of solving problems where the rules of logic cannot be directly applied. This can be defined as the forming of a conclusion from data or premises, by either inductive or deductive methods. It implies reasoning from something known or assumed to something else that follows from it. Mill (1843) wrote: 'Cases of inference, in the proper acceptance of the term, are those in which we set out from known truths, to arrive at others quite distinct from them. In any act of perceiving, observation and influence are intimately blended.' It is interesting to note that some philosophers restrict this term to apply only to methods of induction.

Sherlock Holmes is noted for his skills of deduction, but the latter-day meaning of deduction is 'the process of inferring particular instances from general laws'. Deduction, therefore, goes from the general to the particular. Applying deduction to complexity and to e-commerce would see us having to make decisions based upon established principles and proven techniques. This is the way of the traditional business world; it makes decisions based upon procedures and concepts that have been established through experience. This is not appropriate for e-commerce, where there is precious little experience. What there is cannot be reliably applied in such a continuously evolving environment as the Internet. It would seem, then, that the methods of deduction will be of little use to us. So, should we abandon the methods of Sherlock Holmes?

W. V. Quine, writing in 1940, made the observation: 'The highly explicit way of presenting formal deductive systems which is customary nowadays dates back only to Hilbert (1922) or Post (1921).' As Conan Doyle wrote about Sherlock Holmes in the previous century, this suggests that Sherlock Holmes' method of explaining the unexplainable was not by the process of deduction as we understand it today. More likely his investigations proceeded by means of induction rather than deduction.

Induction is the reverse of deduction. It is the process of inferring a general law or principle from the observation of particular instances. It doesn't, like deduction, mean the process of looking at the general law, or big picture, and from this working out the details. It means looking at the little things that happen and then trying to discover the wider, more universal influences causing them.

Induction is the way Sherlock Holmes worked. He looked for little significant clues that suggested a pattern: a pattern of behaviour and circumstance which were part of the broad pattern of a crime. There is a story that Sir Francis Bacon gave birth to the principle of induction when he noticed the complementary similarities between the coasts of South America and Africa. They seemed to fit like pieces of a jigsaw puzzle. It cried out for a reason or a logical explanation. Three centuries later the explanation came, by way of the discovery of plate tectonics.

Confirmation of the way in which Holmes reasoned was provided by Conan Doyle's biographers. They describe how Doyle once worked with and was a life-long friend of an eminent surgeon of the time. There are several records of Doyle referring to and admiring this surgeon's powers of 'deduction' as he used small, sometimes seemingly insignificant, observations to diagnose a patient's condition. As this was before the time of the modern understanding of human biology, this surgeon must have had to use methods of induction rather than deduction.

In the research establishment where I spent much of my time as a student, it was patently obvious that there the scientists were using methods of induction rather than deduction to expand the frontiers of new and emerging technologies. They were working at the leading edge of newly emerging technologies; there was no previous work or experimental evidence on which to base conclusions or give guidance as to how to progress and move forward. The mindsets of those scientists, who used inductive methods of reasoning, were quite different from the deductive mindsets of the corporate management executives of the Industrial Age. The corporate decision makers have a wealth of procedures, techniques, statistics and previous knowledge to draw upon.

Perhaps, then, it is going to be the method of reasoning known as induction that is going to prove the most fruitful approach to understanding and being successful in the enigmatic world of e-commerce. This will not rely on the process of deduction used regularly by large companies to create new strategies out of experience and established practice. It will involve a process that looks for clues in the here and now and then searches for explanations and causes.

An example of Industrial Age attitudes

It is difficult to generalize in describing Industrial Age business attitudes to the Internet, so perhaps they can best be explained in terms of an example. Such an example came along through a chance meeting I had with an old acquaintance who had become a chief executive in a very large, old-established menswear company.

I'd enquired about the current state of the menswear market. He'd told me that clothing sales in the high streets had slumped. There was a recession and fashion goods were particularly badly affected. He then went on to tell me that they were beginning to run out of ideas as to how they could turn the situation around.

I asked if his company had started to use the Web. He told me that they'd had several meetings about possible applications but hadn't been able to decide how to use it yet. He said he didn't really think it would be applicable to their kind of business anyway. He was due to go on vacation the following week, so I bought him a copy of Kevin Kelly's book *New Rules for the New Economy* to read on the journey.

As soon as he returned from his vacation he telephoned me. Wildly excited, he rambled on about how this insight into the emerging world of digital communication had opened his eyes to all kinds of exciting possibilities. From a position of not seeing how his company could use the Internet, in the space of a single week he had begun to see countless opportunities that might benefit his company. He had seen the light.

In the month following his vacation, he was due to give a talk to a large audience of top executives in the industry to describe a strategy for marketing a new range of menswear. He was keen to include some of the ideas that had come to him while reading Kevin Kelly's book. I helped him to work out an addition to his speech so that he could propose the idea of including the Internet in the strategy, not just for marketing, but also for gathering information to influence future design.

I was quite surprised when he didn't telephone me after the presentation to tell me how it had been received. After a few days, I rang him to ask how it had gone. He told me that it hadn't gone at all well and the references to using the Internet had lost him marks on his presentation. He'd been told that the explanation he'd given had gone right over their heads. 'The trouble is', he explained, 'everyone is so caught up with efficiency, they've resorted to speaking in bullet points. Nobody has time to listen to anything conceptual.'

This rang a bell. During my ill-fated consultancy gig, I'd had an email dialogue with one of the other consultants who was also being employed by the company. He was an eminent academic from one of the country's main universities. He'd been questioning my use of a bottom-up, evolutionary design strategy. He asked: 'Would it be possible to pedagogically formulate the key points in, say, less than ten sentences?'

This was the self-same mentality. The Industrial Age corporate way, which had rubbed off onto the academic. He was asking for a bullet list summary that he could read and digest in the shortest possible time. Of course it made sense in terms of efficiency to communicate in this way, but could it be done with unfamiliar concepts?

I thought I'd have a try as the academic would probably be familiar with most of the basic concepts anyway. The bullet point summary should be sufficient to assemble the thoughts into place and just enough to explain the gist of the strategy. I then offered the following list of ten bullet point sentences:

The disadvantages of a top-down approach:

- Any pre-planned product can take into consideration only knowledge known at the time of the planning.

- Any pre-planning cannot take into account the 'emergence' effects of using the product (by definition these occur only after a product is designed and in use).

- Pre-planned designs are limited to the imagination of the planners at the time before the product is put into use.

- Changes in competitive strategies, technological changes and other innovations cannot often be anticipated in advance.

Characteristics of a true bottom-up approach:

- All design decisions are taken while the product is being used (never before).

- Design comes not from an assessment of what a user wants but as a direct response to user needs.

- Design is driven by observation and feedback (not by human intelligence).

- Observation looks for 'emergence'. That is, effects resulting from the dynamics of the product use by the users.

- Breakthroughs and competitive advantage are realized through being first to recognize and capitalize on any emergence that occurs.

- The product designs itself.

I thought I'd made a pretty good job of explaining what a bottom-up strategy did and how it was preferable to a top-down strategy. But this didn't satisfy the academic. He replied:

> I wanted a ten-liner about the very last point: 'The product designs itself.' I have no problems accepting this as an interesting concept. I just want to know *how* it can be done and whether I have missed something that can convince me that it will work well in practice.

Here then was a serious problem. The academic mind (as well as the corporate mind) has a need for absolutely everything to be summed up in neat bullet points. But not everything can be – and certainly not this final point. As you will see later in this book, a satisfactory explanation as to how a product can be set up to design itself involves several quite sophisticated concepts, many of which are not intuitive. Certainly it couldn't be summed up in ten sentences.

The dialogue with the academic came to an abrupt end when he stated that it was unsafe to apply evolutionary metaphors too literally. I explained that I wasn't using metaphors, but actual evolutionary processes that had been uncovered only in recent times. Indignantly, he insisted that evolutionary processes were not yet fully understood. What could I say? As one famous biologist once remarked: 'Evolution has been around for such a long time that everyone thinks they know all there is to know about it.'

The reality is that the principles behind the mechanisms of evolution are only just beginning to emerge and are coinciding with the emergence of the Internet. Two of the most powerful mechanisms known to man are manifesting at the same time. This is another compelling reason to have faith in the potency of the Internet.

Returning to my friend in the menswear business, his position in the company allowed him a certain degree of autonomy. I asked him why he didn't just go ahead and initiate some way to incorporate more digital communication into his area of responsibility. 'Can't be done', he explained. 'Even the directors cannot embark on any plan without specific approval and agreed funding. This would involve a procedure that, at the best, would take several months and in all probability might stretch into years.'

'On this time scale, any plan involving digital communications is almost certain to be out of date before it's approved or funded', I remarked. He shook his head. 'I know', he sighed. 'But that is the way this company works. It is the way all big companies work.'

That conversation set me thinking. If large companies were set up with this kind of internal organization, they were not going to be able to respond appropriately to the rapid changes that digital technology were ushering in. There was a structural, built-in resistance to sudden change. How widespread was it?

Further conversations with my friend revealed that this policy seemed to be an accepted dogma, fundamental to the stability of these large, old-established organizations. Big companies in the Industrial Age are owned by their shareholders, the investors. The investors need to have control over how their money is being spent. It makes sense to them to have a rigid system of detailed proposals with lengthy and rigorous examination of the details before any funding is granted. To the corporate mind of the Industrial Age, it would be totally unacceptable to allow people to take risks with money without there being a rigorous examination of the plan and a method established by which the progress could be monitored and controlled.

This is the strategy of the careful poker player, who needs to have aces back to back and be in full control before making a bet. There seems to be no way that the rigid system of corporate dogma can officially allow the funding of a strategy of open play. This would involve giving employees an open-ended assignment in the spirit of: 'Here, take this money and see if you can do something useful with it.'

I was beginning to see a possible explanation as to why many large companies formed during the Industrial Age, despite their financial muscle and their pools of intellectual resources, weren't dominating the Web. This procedural funding policy is a crippling handicap in the rapidly changing world of digital communications. In this environment, policies and planning decisions need to be made on the fly. There isn't time to hang around, waiting for intricate and detailed plans to be prepared, examined in detail and then approved. My friend just shrugged his shoulders at all this. 'If I try to change the system I'll be marked out as a trouble maker and could end up losing my job', was his pragmatic response to the situation. A company working without full financial control? It just didn't make any sense to his Industrial Age corporate mind.

Confirmation of this situation came during a conversation I had with one of the gurus of knowledge retrieval systems and groupware: David Coleman. I'm a regular reader of the monthly articles he publishes on his Web site (*www.collaborate.com*). I'd noticed that he'd begun his articles in 1996 as an enthusiastic proponent of evolutionary design strategies – systems that are grown bottom-up. Yet he'd gradually progressed to a position where he was talking almost exclusively about systems which were designed top-down: groupware solutions that are imposed as finished applications.

I asked him why he'd changed tack. He told me he hadn't lost faith in the evolutionary approach to design, it was just that the ideas it entailed didn't fit in with corporate thinking. Getting large amounts of funding for big projects required the expected results to be specified beforehand. He reiterated what I'd already deduced from the conversation with my friend: investors wanted to know what they were getting for their money before parting with it.

I pondered the significance of this. I'd seen a report that estimated the total expenditure on knowledge retrieval and groupware products for that year (1999); it was expected to top four and a half billion dollars. As far as I could see, the vast majority of this money would be going to fund top-down designs: a technique vastly inferior to the more appropriate evolutionary, bottom-up design strategies. Again, it was the aces back to back mentality. The most suitable and appropriate approach for dealing with problems involving change and complexity was being stymied by Industrial Age corporate dogma.

Looking at various other corporate attitudes to the Internet and World Wide Web, it was evident that there were many companies which were avoiding this conceptual quagmire, but they seemed to be very much in the minority.

The way of the Industrial Age

It was at this very same time that I chanced to look at the Microsoft PowerPoint application that my son was using to do his homework. This contained a number of templates to help business people make various forms of presentation (Dale Carnegie templates). What attracted my attention was that they were being provided as aids to help presenters explain and convince others of their ideas and concepts. In view of my difficulties in getting through to the telecoms company's employees, I thought they might offer me some badly needed assistance.

There were over a dozen step-by-step guides, which included how to sell your ideas, facilitate a meeting, motivate a team and recommend a strategy – templates that provided a direct entry into the corporate mind. I looked at the relevant templates which detailed the standard procedures for putting across ideas and defining strategies. They tell you to begin by defining goals, describing visions and long-term objectives. They emphasize the need to make short, clear, bullet point statements. They tell you to provide evidence and examples. They recommend producing testimonials, case histories, statistics and anything that might provide some form of concrete evidence that the idea or plan can succeed. They tell you to detail all anticipated costs and estimates of outgoings and expenditures.

The final expected outcome, they tell you, must be clearly stated and full details of anticipated benefits unambiguously defined. All assume that you are going to use a carefully worked out plan from which you can anticipate and monitor the progress all the way through to a successful conclusion.

When I tried to use these templates to help me describe an evolutionary design strategy, the results were laughable. What concrete goals could I describe, when the evolutionary process was expected to come up with something better than I could currently imagine? Technology and competition in the e-business environment is changing too fast to be able to predict progress with any reasonable degree of accuracy. How can even the most authoritative exponents of e-commerce work out all the technological changes that could take place even within the next six months?

There are too many new products and initiatives continually appearing from every corner of the planet to be able to keep up to date with developments. New techniques, software, ideas and strategies are no longer the domain of a few major players; they are coming from hundreds of thousands of different sources from every part of the world. How can any mortal mind keep track of even a small percentage of this fractal of evolving activity? Any picture of the future would be at best doubtful.

As I went through the templates, the prompts began to get even more unrealistic. How can you estimate costs without knowing where an evolutionary strategy will take you? How can you state expected benefits and outcomes when these will be determined by emergence: they will not be known until they manifest at some unknown time? As for being able to provide a step-by-step plan to allow progress to be monitored – it would be no more valid than a poker player predicting his cash flow and details of play.

Now these techniques of persuasion are going out to hundreds of thousands of people who are buying Microsoft Office. They are templates to use in presentations of various kinds. They are instructions on how to promote ideas, how to run meetings and how to sell things. These kinds of instructions are not only going to all the owners of PowerPoint, they are the tried and tested methods being taught to millions of business study students at colleges and universities all over the world. This is the standard corporate way designed for Industrial Age businesses. All potential managers are taught to think in this way: logically, with clearly planned routes to achieve optimum results and performance. How can these people be expected to perform well in the strategic world of e-business where these templates cannot be applied?

In most areas of Industrial Age corporate life, everybody is busy working in well-defined areas. Everyone can increase their efficiency by communicating with each other through bullet point memos. It works fine when most information is known or knowable. However, when it comes to tackling problems of complexity, with unknowns and unknowables, this kind of corporate mindset is found wanting. It just cannot cope with the new kind of competition which is now starting to appear in the commercial world of digital communication: the Age of Information.

These boilerplate solutions rely on having a good knowledge of the past and the present, plus a reasonable expectation of future events. They assume that most knowledge is known, obtainable or can be accurately predicted. With rapid technological advances and the near impossibility of knowing all there is to know in the Information Age – how can anyone possibly plan a strategy in advance? The templates tell you to state your vision. Vision in the environment of digital communication is about as useful as binoculars in the fog. How can you possibly know where you are going, how you are going to get there and where you are going to end up? The vision you end up with is likely to be beyond your powers of imagination in the rapidly changing world of the Information Age.

In dealing with a complex, constantly changing environment, there is not a single one of the Industrial Age template recommended points that can be satisfactorily answered. In the Information Age, goals, visions and long-term objectives can be specified in only the vaguest of terms. Bullet points are inadequate to describe the kind of strategies that will be needed. There are no credible statistics, testimonials or case histories that can be used; the successes of yesterday are not always successful today and today's successes are unlikely to be the successes of tomorrow.

In this starting phase of the Information Age there is no way to estimate costs or expenditures because the conditions applying today are unlikely to be the conditions applying tomorrow.

- Who in the beginning could have anticipated that all software products used on the Internet would start off by being free?

- Who could have envisaged the services of Internet service providers (ISPs) being offered free of charge?

- Who could have imagined a time when hundreds of people were offering free Web space, rent-free space for online shopping stores in grand, Web-based malls?

- Free shopping cart services, free CGIs and almost everything else anyone would need for e-commerce – available for free?

- How can anyone predict costs, future developments and likely outcomes in such a crazy, unpredictable world? These conditions drive the Industrial Age, corporate PowerPoint mind into apoplexy.

The way many Industrial Age corporates seem to be coping with this problem is by avoiding it. During the conversations with my friend in the menswear company, he had explained his attitude to using email. 'I don't use it', he'd told me. 'My secretary goes through the emails and puts aside anything she thinks might be important. Most of it she trashes.'

Enquiring as to why he had so little use for email, he told me that there was 'too much junk mail for it to be worth the effort of looking through'. He went on to explain that email was used mainly by employees to cover their backs. When I asked what he meant by this, he told me that when anyone in the company made any kind of initiative they'd inform just about everyone in the company they could think of. In this way, if anything went wrong and somebody reproached them, they could easily transfer the blame by saying 'But I sent you an email telling you I was going to do this. As you hadn't questioned it, I'd assumed you'd approved.' As everyone was doing this, and the overworked executives weren't reading their emails because of these irrelevant messages cluttering up their mail boxes, it was a pretty safe insurance against getting reprimands for mistakes.

This tendency for employees of all ranks to try to avoid situations where they can make mistakes is rife in large Industrial Age corporations. Perhaps this is another reason why those big companies are not leading the way on the Web.

With no adequate training to cope with the uncertainties and an inability to get to grips with the fast-expanding knowledge base, this is enough for Industrial Age employees to use all the usual corporate employee tricks to avoid getting involved with e-commerce.

In an email discussion with some of the readers of the draft of this book, Dai Williams wrote:

> Traditional corporate culture is based on operating in a largely understood, largely predictable environment. A culture of discouraging mistakes is arguably appropriate here (though only arguably, I don't happen to agree) on the premise that as long as you don't do anything stupid, like chronically mispricing your goods/services or publicly exposing your weakness, you will, by default, chunter along to an acceptable profit.
>
> Sure, you may need to be a bit more creative if you want serious growth or higher margins, but you can survive without ("No-one got fired for buying IBM"). The best way to avoid such cock-ups is to stay in your field of expertise and if you must move into new markets (geographical, product, market segment, whatever) you do so slowly and with complete clarity of direction. Novell a few years ago was an example of a company that didn't do this (buying applications business), got crucified (ended up "focusing on core business") and is used as proof that this must be true – standard, perceptual filtering, ignoring examples that don't fit the hypothesis.
>
> This premise has inevitably permeated most large corporates and results in a culture where the majority of employees have a "survival instinct" that says "Don't take risk. If you take risk, don't be seen to take risk and if you get caught taking risk it was all the next guy's fault." This turns new and radical ventures such as those involving "e-commerce" into corporate hot potatoes, where no-one wants to be seen to be too involved in case it goes wrong. Sure they would like to take the glory if it works, but, as mistakes are punished harder than successes are rewarded, the balance is to keep clear.
>
> This is illustrated by a joke I heard recently (at least, I think it's a joke). Take four chimps in a cage. Place a banana at the top of some steps in one corner. Whenever one of the chimps starts towards the banana, give an electric shock to ALL chimps. After a while, any chimp who moves towards the steps will be dragged back and beaten by the other chimps. Remove electrical shock device. Replace one of original chimps with new chimp. New chimp moves towards banana and is pulled

back and beaten by the others. Repeatedly replace other original chimps and you come to the point where four chimps can see the banana which they could easily take but they "know" they mustn't and hence won't. Isn't that corporate culture?

Yes we all know it is wrong for today's world, but you won't change it just with a flash of knowledge, it is a major culture change and one that most corporates are unwilling or, as the previous example suggests, unable to take. Hence the success of start-ups: they don't (necessarily) have the same prejudices.

Dai Williams' post sums up the situation in a nutshell. His observations further emphasize the point that not only are many Industrial Age corporations not structurally set up for tackling e-commerce, but the situation is compounded by many employees being neither trained nor sufficiently motivated to become involved.

Another problem for people who try to carry Industrial Age thinking across to the Internet is typified by another reader of the draft of the first chapter. He objected to the suggestion that a top-down approach wouldn't be appropriate for Internet products and services. He wrote:

[What about] the first moon landing. The landing was achieved (allegedly) on the back of JFK saying 'we will land on the moon before the end of the decade'. A plan had to be formulated. Scientists and engineers had to sit down and decide what they needed to build in order to achieve the goal of a moon landing. They discovered that many of the things they needed had not yet been invented! So, as well as needing to develop existing technology (rockets, for instance), other things which had not yet been created had to be developed.

Here was a top-down strategy if ever I saw one. It worked. Would Neil Armstrong and co. have got to the moon as soon if things had been allowed to evolve 'naturally'? I doubt it...

Would the space race have continued to grow instead of stagnating had it been allowed to evolve naturally?...

Here is described an application that is ideally suited for a top-down approach to design. It is a prime example of an Industrial Age project. But this has nothing to do with Information Age business. Even though in this example new technologies have to be developed, the scope of the technological initiatives would have been reasonably easy to predict. There is very little competition and most of the main factors involved in the decision making were known and predictable, even the elements of risk.

Compare this with the development of an e-business product in the Information Age. All the critical factors involved in the design would be totally unpredictable. Competition would be intense. The environment into which the product would be launched is likely to be quite different from that existing when the product was conceived and designed. To approach the design of an e-business or e-commerce product or service with the same, top-down planning approach used to design the moon landing project would be commercial suicide.

What is the alternative to the Industrial Age way of thinking?

The problem for most executives in an Industrial Age corporation is that they do need a concrete plan before taking any positive action. They abhor uncertainties or unknowns. For anyone brought up in and exposed only to this type of corporate culture, it might be difficult to see how a potential business situation can be approached without a plan. It wouldn't make sense just to do something without knowing what is going to happen next. It seems irrational to work without tangible, well-specified goals or visions.

> The problem for most executives in an Industrial Age corporation is that they do need a concrete plan before taking any positive action. They abhor uncertainties or unknowns.

A corporate planner in an Industrial Age setting usually makes business plans based upon past events of some kind. Such plans revolve around a process of extrapolating these past events into the future in order to anticipate or make predictions. This is deduction, applying the known generalities to predict instances. Practically all Industrial Age business and management courses are based upon this kind of deductive reasoning when making plans.

To find yourself suddenly in a world full of change and uncertainty, where the past isn't a guide to the future, can be truly disorientating. How can you have a business venture without a plan? This is the dilemma for the Industrial Age mindset.

The trick is to make the same distinction between a plan and a strategy that was made in the introduction. Substituting a strategy for a plan can make a move into the future begin to look decidedly more purposeful. Think of the strategy of the professional poker player in Chapter 1. The professional would have no idea what the next cards would be. No idea as to whether or not he would be encountering a winning situation. No pre-set ideas as to how the hand might progress. His strategy is just to get into the game and wait for a favourable run of the cards. Of course, he does not just wait hopefully. The wait is calculated, it is a wait of anticipation and reasonable expectation that a favourable change will occur.

The professional poker player will be constantly monitoring other cards to see if the odds of a change are improving or reducing. Any sign that he has got into a dead end (such as the aces back to back player getting another ace) and he will fold his hand immediately and wait for another opportunity to come along in another hand. Decisions are not programmed. They are made on the fly, at the turn of events.

For the Industrial Age corporate planner, the fly in the ointment is the risk factor. If the cards do not fall favourably, the game is lost. There is no way back, no insurance or cover if things go wrong. However, the poker player plays with a strategy that is not considering a single hand in isolation but a number of hands. His strategy will be based upon the net result of many games: a whole evening's play, maybe a number of evenings' play. The more games that are played, the more chance for the professional's strategy to be successful.

Unfortunately, the idea that business success is measured as an aggregate outcome of many business ventures is not something that is bred into the corporate culture of the Industrial Age. An executive's career might end abruptly at a single try if it doesn't work out successfully. However, there is more to a poker player's strategy than just winning and losing. With his strategy size is important.

The professional poker player's winning strategy also ensures that the pots (total amount bet in a hand) he wins are higher than those he loses. In other words, he will try to force up the size of the bets in the hands where he feels he has better chances of winning. In this way a few wins of high pots can more than offset a larger number of hands where he loses. In business parlance, they'd say: 'One winner pays for a lot of losers.' In investment circles they'd say: 'Cut your losses short and let the winners run.' This is a very important element in entrepreneurial strategies and will be equally important in e-business, where progress is going to be made as a result of much probing and experimentation.

One of the most intriguing aspects of the Internet is the ability to create parallel worlds. This is the trick of running many situations at the same time when in the real physical world they can only be run one at a time. We shall meet this later when we deal with communication strategies but for the moment let's apply this transformation to the poker player's strategy.

The poker player is limited to sitting in only one hand at a time; the hands (games) are played in sequence, with one hand ending before another hand starts. In business it need not be that way, businesses can be run in parallel. Several can be run at the same time. Similarly, several variations of a business can be run concurrently. In this way, the risks associated with experimenting with different businesses and business variations can be spread out so that no individual failure can have any significant effect. We shall cover this in more detail in a later chapter.

In the physical business world of the Industrial Age, such a strategy would likely be impractical for a corporate manager. It would involve a variety of different plans, much organization and probably incur high costs. In the world of the Internet, the cost of trying several different business approaches at the same time is very much less expensive. Losing businesses can be terminated quickly, at the first sign of running into a dead end. Any businesses showing promise can be left to run.

In this way, a business venture on the Internet can be constructed as a series of independent business experiments, with the net result determined by an aggregate outcome. Looked at in this way, a business strategy can be likened to that of the open play of the professional poker player: not winning every game, but winning over a series of many games.

There is of course no way to predict which business or business experiment will prove to be successful from the start; they will all appear to have an equal chance of succeeding. Only emergence, the unpredictable effect of the unknowns, will determine the winners and the losers. This means that the only skill required by the initiator is to make sure that there are at least some winners and that these winners (or winner) more than pay for the losers.

Let's look at the concepts involved here:

1 The player gets into the game to look for an emergence: a development that will throw the odds in his favour.

2 Promising situations are continued and losing situations quickly terminated.

3 The overall result is determined by an aggregate, where winning is determined by the average outcome of several plays.

If this philosophy is applied to e-commerce, it would be seen as a nonsense that a company should invest all its effort in, or allocate a large slice of capital to, any single project. With so many unknowns, with so much change and uncertainty, a more pragmatic strategy might be to invest in many small experimental ventures and wait to see which start to develop most promise.

This is not the strategy of the careful, aces back to back, poker player, or the Industrial Age corporate manager who is playing by the book. This is the strategy of the open player, the calculated risk taker, typified by the classic entrepreneur. Could it be that the strategies of the entrepreneur are superior to those of the corporate manager for competing and succeeding in the world of e-commerce? Could these be the optimum strategies to use in the Information Age?

Perhaps it is to the world of the entrepreneur that we should next start to look for clues? However, before we do, it may be wise to get a few more concepts under our belt because the world of the entrepreneur is another area that cannot be explained with a series of bullet point lists.

Dealing with a complex environment

We have considered where conventional, Industrial Age business thinking might be inadequate to cope with the Internet and how it might lead to wrong attitudes for competing in the environment of e-commerce. This begs the questions: 'What is a better way of thinking, and what other strategies might be more appropriate?' To answer these questions, the temptation is to try to get a perspective by looking at the big picture: looking to find some superior strategy that will ensure success. But this is the method of deduction used in the Industrial Age: looking at the general in order to deduce the particular.

With complexity, looking at the big picture is impossibly vague and confusing. The inability to comprehend the big picture of a complex environment makes it unlikely that a good strategy could be seen even if it were there. A strategy might be found that works for a while, but it is almost certain that change and competition will render that strategy ineffective very quickly. Successes quickly attract the herd and on the Internet the herd can move very fast.

Successes quickly attract the herd and on the Internet the herd can move very fast.

Take a moment to consider what it means when something is described as a complex environment. It doesn't just mean that there are too many things to know or remember. Complexity describes a system of interrelated parts, where each part has a direct or indirect effect on all other parts. Interacting with a complex environment is not possible without changing that environment and some of its parts through the very process of the interaction itself. Trying to get a fix on a complex environment is very difficult; snapshot pictures are no help at all. The only way to get to grips with a complex environment is to become part of it and then see what happens when you do something in it.

When Apple brought out the Macintosh computer in 1984, it heralded a new era in computer programming: the age of object-oriented systems. Besides introducing a more friendly user interface, the Macintosh included an operating system which provided a novel environment – an object-oriented environment – within which developers could create applications. It was a complex environment where complex systems could be created and controlled.

At that time, in the early 1980s, most conventional computer programs were designed specifically for a single purpose. They were highly structured, designed top-down and hierarchically organized. They were algorithmic and deter-ministic, in the sense that every command resulted in a rigidly defined sequence of events. It was almost inconceivable at that time for programs to be anything other than dedicated and well-regimented systems. This restricted them to being inflexible: neither reconfigurable nor adaptable.

Because of its friendly user interface, the Macintosh was immediately perceived as a computer for the masses; a computer where very little knowledge or training was needed to be able to use it. When the computer programmers of the day examined the way in which the operating system was designed – as a collection of independent little modules – they viewed it in much the same way as the interface: an artificially created environment that had been designed to be simple to use.

They interpreted the ready-made modules as a design strategy that would allow novice programmers to knock up quick and dirty applications. With its functions all separated out into independent modules which could be pieced together in any order, the Macintosh operating system seemed to be designed more along the lines of a Lego set than as a programming environment where professional programmers could create serious applications.

What the programmers saw, when they examined the Macintosh operating system, was many built-in functions that could be used by any application that had a need for them. These functions could be called into use merely by sending simple messages to them: nothing more complicated than a message name and perhaps a few parameters to specify how the function should perform. In this way, much of the programming a developer needed for an application was already available, in the form of modules. All that was needed to use them was a communication infrastructure – an organization – to link selected appropriate modules together.

In the beginning, many experienced programmers were completely thrown by this. It seemed to be the wrong way to go about things: starting with the objects and then adding the organizing structure afterwards. Yet, despite this apparent back to front strategy of design, it was found to work remarkably well. In fact it worked so well and was so superior to the structured, top-down conventional approach to design that Microsoft was forced to come up with a similar system.

This example is a good place to start looking for clues as to how to handle and control complexity. The Macintosh operating system is typical of a complex environment to which we can address the question: 'How did the first developers handle the problem of designing within the operating system?' This inductive approach might lead us to some useful conclusions.

An important clue comes from the way the programmers regarded the four massive technical manuals that Apple provided for application developers. A cynic once described them this way: 'To understand any part of these manuals, you would first need to have understood all the rest of what is in the manuals.' This, in many ways, sums up the attitude necessary to understand complex systems. No single part can be understood without reference to all other parts.

Quite obviously, programmers did succeed in getting to understand and control the Macintosh operating system, despite the seeming impossibility of being able to make any sense of the manuals. This is evidenced by the wealth of useful and sophisticated programs that have emerged over the years. What isn't so obvious is the way they eventually came to understand and control this complex system, when the manuals were so incomprehensible.

The trick was that they didn't even attempt to sit down with the manuals to try to understand them. They used them to provide solutions. Whenever they wanted their applications to do something they looked in the manual to see if they could find some module that would do it for them. In this way, they could create software in a modular form, much of it consisting of the pre-designed modules present in the operating system to which they then added their own custom-built modules to provide any function the existing modules couldn't provide. All modules could then be loosely coupled together within an organizing framework which simply routed messages between the modules.

In this way, the developers conquered the complexity of the Macintosh environment to create complexities of their own. Some of the independent, individual developers didn't even need a detailed plan; they could start with one module and then add other modules, one at a time, creating and extending a message routing infrastructure as they went along.

This was a radically new way to design software, adding new modules into an environment as and when they were needed. Such a strategy could allow an evolutionary design approach, where software products grow and evolve from the bottom up. This proved to be a highly effective way in which to approach design in the complex environment of the Apple Macintosh and suggests that this same strategy could be used by e-commerce traders to make effective and imaginative use of the Internet.

Such an approach to dealing with complexity is not startlingly new or revolutionary. It is the way natural systems have evolved to cope with competition and complex environments. There are numerable examples, at all levels of biological organization, which exhibit a similar bottom-up, modular approach to design; such approaches can even be found genetically programmed into the human mind.

Take the case of language. Like the Macintosh operating system, it consists of myriad small modules: words. To a non-English-speaking person, a dictionary of English words is as confusing as that set of original Macintosh computer manuals was to the developers. All words in a dictionary are described by other words, so a cynic could easily make the observation that no word can be understood without knowing all the other words.

As everyone knows, it is impossible to learn a language simply by looking at a dictionary. Language is a complex environment and cannot be understood in terms of a 'directory' (or a search engine). Each of thousands of words can be combined and configured in an almost infinite number of ways to describe almost every tangible and non-tangible entity and thought in existence. To an alien, trying to observe the way in which humans communicate with each other (looking at the big picture), it would appear to involve an awesome complexity which is seemingly impossible to unravel. Yet, a two-year-old child doesn't have a problem with this at all. It starts off by learning one or two words, then adds a few more, then puts a few of them together in combination. Within a very short time the child is talking and before the age of ten has probably mastered the complexity sufficiently well to have a reasonably intelligent conversation with an adult.

This process is similar to that of the Macintosh developers. They started out by learning what a few of the modules did, then stringing them together. Their way of progressively finding new modules to use and incorporating them into a growing design is almost identical to the way in which a small child builds up and uses a vocabulary of words. It is the process of starting with the particular and building up to the general: the process of induction.

Now if we look at this process in the abstract and apply it to any kind of complex environment, we can see how complexity can be mastered and made to grow and evolve in a controlled way. It is not necessary to understand the whole system as long as you can think in terms of small modular units that interact and send messages to each other within a communication environment. It is not necessary to design any modules if they are already in existence. The only time new modules will be needed is if the system is being developed or expanded in a totally new and novel direction.

Applying this abstraction to the Internet and the World Wide Web would see a communication network already in place and a host of versatile modules available and already connected up (the myriad software applications and components being offered for use in e-business and e-commerce solutions). As an e-commerce strategist looking to set up a system for e-commerce, the problem is no different from that of the application developers for the Macintosh. There is a complex environment in place, full of handy little modules that can be put together to create any kind of customized system required. E-commerce business people don't have to understand the whole system, or most parts of it. All they need do is to select the modules most appropriate for the application they have in mind and connect them together by messages.

Certainly, there will be small gaps in such systems where a suitable module cannot be found, but this serves to inspire design: perhaps revealing an opening for a new commercial product or service which then becomes another available module in the ever-growing sea of modules. In this way a multitude of different kinds of module becomes available for anyone to use, manipulate and organize as they see fit.

Let's now look at what these modules need to consist of. At first thoughts, the modules will comprise principally of software. It is through the software that a module will be able to receive and process messages. Through software the module will be able to carry out and perform its function. The function itself will be an operation performed by software. It is tempting, then, to think of the modules available to an e-commerce trader as being solely software.

However, upon reflection, the modules consist of much more than just software. The software is actually only a part of a wider organization which includes humans. In this wider concept of a module, the software appears as just the visible part of the module's system, much as a mound of ice protruding from the sea is the visible manifestation of an iceberg.

That human part is the design and development, the backup, the service, the marketing and all manner of different personnel that might be involved in the module's creation, function, efficiency and future performance. The actual software itself is merely a commodity. The part of the module that an e-commerce trader is really dealing with is the software module's human part.

If we begin to expand out from this system of modules, which includes humans, we can begin to get a fleeting glimpse of what the whole of the Internet is about. It is a gargantuan sea of modules interacting with each other in numerous different ways. These modules are available, usually at a price, for any e-commerce trader to use and combine for any purpose whatsoever. However, the utilization of the modules will involve direct or indirect communication between humans because the invisible supporting system for the module is a fundamental part of the module's value within a system.

The Information Age is not about technology – it is about communicating with people

One of the most intriguing paradoxes of the Internet is the way in which the progress towards more widespread order and organization is through increasing fragmentation; everything appears to be breaking up into smaller, and more specialist, niches. In the same way that information is increasing and taking many different directions, it is the fractal effect again, an inherent instability of complex systems. This phenomenon we shall deal with more specifically later; for the moment though, let's just consider the consequence of this effect. It may prove to yield several clues as to how best to make use of the Internet.

The constant expansion and increased fragmentation of Internet products and services present a crucial problem for people in the Information Age. Exploiting the potentialities of the Internet will involve not simply the use of modules, but the growing difficulties arising from their choice and selection:

- With an untold number of different possible modules to choose from, how are e-commerce business people to know which ones to use?

- How are they to know which are available or even in existence?

- Which modules are going to be the most appropriate to suit a required system?

- What are the best choices between a number of similar options?

- What are the best combinations when a number of modules have to be arranged to work together?

One of the most intriguing paradoxes of the Internet is the way in which the progress towards more widespread order and organization is through increasing fragmentation; everything appears to be breaking up into smaller, and more specialist, niches.

The practical reality of getting a viable e-commerce system into operation soon exposes this problem. It becomes apparent very quickly that no single person, or even any group of people, will know all the answers. There are too many options available, too many modules getting out of date, too many just being created. It is a nightmare situation, which would be likely to fry the brain of any resource allocation executive of the Industrial Age.

To visualize this problem, you might imagine the Macintosh manuals as consisting of millions of pages and of being put up onto a Web site with thousands of programmers constantly adding bits, altering bits and taking bits away. This would seem to make the developer's job impossible. Even with indexing and search engines, the sheer volume of information and its constant change and fluctuation would surely seem to render a modular strategy inoperable.

It would be an impossible situation if it were left only to software to handle and organize the information. However, as the fragmenting process itself bears witness, human modules start to come into play as intermediaries. Humans step in where software solutions are unable to cope. Humans can specialize in small niche areas and keep track of changes, additions and new developments. The natural evolution of the Internet encourages a network of human information sources to act as an interface between e-commerce traders and the technology and methods they will use.

It is by such considerations that Sherlock Holmes, through his technique of induction, would come to the conclusion that success in e-commerce isn't at all about knowing the technology: it is about knowing the specialists and the technologists. It is about dealing and communicating with people.

Chapter 3

In the land of the blind the one-eyed man is king

Corporates and entrepreneurs: contrasting mindsets

The first two chapters show, by way of anecdotes, how the Industrial Age mindset conflicts with the mindset required for the Information Age. This difference in the way the world of business and commerce is viewed is very similar to the difference between the way in which corporate Industrial Age managers and executives think and the way entrepreneurs think. Both types of thinking are valid in their own domains but there seems little common ground for any understanding or compromise between them. Each sees the world of business and commerce from quite different viewpoints.

This makes for an intriguing

situation because both corporate and entrepreneurial minds are being applied to e-commerce. It raises some interesting questions. Are there some areas of e-commerce particularly suited to the corporate way and others more suited to the entrepreneurial way? Corporates and entrepreneurs are certain to be in competition with each other. What happens where one way is right and the other way is wrong? Which type of thinking, on balance, is the best? Or can the two quite different modes of thought be reconciled?

Because the first two chapters were looking from the viewpoint of the Information Age, many readers who have been exposed only to the ideas of the Industrial Age might feel confused, in disagreement or even outraged by the views expressed. But isn't this to be expected? Isn't this the effect that all new paradigms have at first: when they conflict with established thinking? Different or conflicting ideas create paradoxes. Confusion reigns until the paradoxes are resolved.

We started out with an anomaly: corporations and established Industrial Age businesses aren't leading the way in e-commerce. They appear to be fumbling around in the dark, apparently no more competent than start-up companies. Despite the brainpower and the money available to them, established Industrial Age businesses seem to be playing catch up to smaller entrepreneurial enterprises.

Looking for clues, we might take into consideration that the Industrial Age corporate way is through tried and tested procedures and techniques. Conversely, an entrepreneur comes into his or her own in areas where past experience cannot be relied upon. Industrial Age corporates will apply their superior skills of planning and organization to areas where they can be most effective, while entrepreneurs will consciously seek out the areas where planning and organization are difficult or impossible to apply.

The big question is: 'What kind of areas are e-business and e-commerce?' If they are more suited to the corporate way, the entrepreneur will hold back because he or she will probably be disadvantaged. If they are more suited to the entrepreneurial way, the corporates will hold back because they will find it more efficient to wait for entrepreneurs to succeed and then buy them out.

This isn't a cynical viewpoint, it is the way corporate organizations and entrepreneurs in the Industrial Age have always complemented each other. It is often too costly for a large Industrial Age organization to experiment in new and emerging markets. It is cheaper for them in the long run to let entrepreneurs fight it out between them and then buy out the winners. The entrepreneurs for their part rarely want to take a venture on to the stage of consolidation and are happy to take a large lump sum for their efforts.

For corporate managers and executives it is about succeeding in a career, where the rewards are in the form of security, power and a regular and reasonably certain income. For the entrepreneur it is an exciting game of risk and strategy, where the winners get big prizes and the losers get nothing. An interesting situation now arises in the Information Age when corporate managers and executives may have to adopt the strategies of the entrepreneur. How will these two previously separate paradigms merge?

Coming somewhere in between the extremes of the corporates and the entrepreneurs are the specialist service areas: the contractors, the subcontractors, the consultants and the service industries that form symbiotic relationships with the corporates and the entrepreneurs. These intermediates are hybrids, each with their own individual mix of corporate and entrepreneurial traits.

There is no way to specifically categorize these hybrids because they fill all parts of the spectrum between the classical Industrial Age corporation and the classical entrepreneur. Entrepreneurs can run their businesses with the same rigidity as Industrial Age corporations. Also, corporations can have many entrepreneurial traits. Large corporations can sometimes be dominated by a chairman or board of directors who think primarily with an entrepreneurial mindset, or corporations may have special units that are given funds and the authority to employ entrepreneurial strategies.

There are no definitive distinctions that apply universally. Distinctions made here are artificial: used simply to separate out practices and attitudes applicable in the traditional Industrial Age from the more flexible, pragmatic practices and attitudes that are going to be needed in the Information Age.

 ## The Zen thing

An interesting feature about the writing of this book is that each chapter is discussed by groups of people at tables in a virtual café, as soon as it is written (this process will be covered in a later chapter). Besides providing useful feedback, this allows some relevant snippets of these discussions to be included in the text.

After Chapter 2, a discussion started at one table about how people think and plan. Mrs Brisby wrote:

I have always believed that there is a very Zen thing going on. The power of instant realization can easily be seen in large projects where the brute-force top-down look of an engineer may be less economical than that of a 16-hours-a-day coffee-driven smack-addict who can take one look at a scrolling screen of code, and find bugs with pinpoint accuracy.

Linux Torvalds pointed out in his document on 'tracking down OOPS' that there are times that he can look at a kernel OOPS (a crash page that displays register information, not far from the famous Blue Screen of Death found commonly on Wintel desktops) and tell exactly where in the source tree that is. This is a truly scary thing, for with all those thousands of lines of code, how can any one person *know* – or even be expected to know – the exact point of that crash?

He knows, because it is Zen. He has that realization of everything that is his source, and it gives him magical qualities because of it. These magical qualities are found everywhere; in every market; in every project. You can plot and plan and work it out beginning to end, but when you do, it can no longer evolve. Instead, the most successful projects seem to have been Zenned from the beginning.

I'm not saying that engineers are worthless; on the contrary. The ability to engineer a project is invaluable, and in a case of scrutiny (such as cryptography), it is a basic need of survival. Electronic Commerce is no different. We have something very infant. And it is a project so large, no one engineer (or even a team of them) should be expected to be able to see the whole thing. They Zen it; they trust their instincts.

This 'Zen thing' that Mrs Brisby talks about is something we are all familiar with. It happens when somebody makes a decision that just happens to put them in the right place at the right time. It happens when an experienced investor seems to 'know' when to buy certain stocks and when to get out of a market just before the stock prices fall. It happens when a football team manager 'knows' just the right time to bring on a player to turn a game. In all kinds of situations, people seem to be able to make canny decisions where the complexity and uncertainty involved tell you that there cannot possibly be any logical reason for their 'knowing'. Yet, the consistency with which they seem able to get it just right tells you that there must be something more than just luck involved.

A little light can be thrown onto this 'Zen thing' if we think of the professional poker player. To the frustrated novice, whose careful and cautious play finds him always ending up a loser, the professional will seem to have this 'Zen thing'. 'How can he so frequently call a high bet with an obviously losing hand and then outdraw me?', the novice might ask himself. The baffled novice can only conclude that the professional must be cheating him in some way.

Because a game of poker does not have many variables, we can easily work out the nature of the professional's 'Zen thing'. He knows the odds. He can mentally calculate the chances of receiving a card on the next deal that will turn the game in his favour. To the professional poker player this isn't a 'Zen thing', it's a statistical probability. His 'Zen-ness' comes from having a mathematical model of the game in his head.

In a further email Mrs Brisby wrote:

> In some Buddhist circles, knowing the odds is just as Zen; odds are still relatively unpredictable. Zen is to assume and trust and have faith, it's a work-out-halfway. The human mind is very good at making its own jumps and inventing its own conclusions. These kinds of things may be considered to play the odds, or whatnot.
>
> My point is that unless you calculate all the variables, and engineer every response (e.g. plot every move on a chessboard), there must be some Zen quality at work when you get what you expect.

It can be inferred that this 'Zen thing' is probably some kind of internal conceptual model that provides a rough guide as to what is going to happen next. It's not an accurate model, but it is sufficient to ensure that the decision maker is always ahead of anyone reduced to using random guesswork.

This is especially valuable when decision makers are confronted with situations too complex for logical deduction. Even though they might not be right every time, they will usually be able to make more right decisions than players who do not have this 'Zen thing'. In this chapter, we are going to look at a few mental models that might give us some of this Zen-ness: perhaps allowing us to gain a competitive edge in the world of e-business and e-commerce.

The mathematics of Zen-ness

Most internal mental models that provide this 'Zen thing' are acquired as a result of experience. In the world of e-business, where constant change and uncertainty compromise the value of experience, we have to rely, like the professional poker player, on mathematical constructs.

However, the mathematics we need for Zen-ness is not the type of mathematics that mathematicians use. We need only a rough understanding of the underlying concepts. We won't want to get into any complicated formulae or rigid proofs. For Zen-ness, we can generalize the mathematical concepts and pervert their use for our own purposes. Mathematicians might go into fits of apoplexy when they see the way we distort and misuse their concepts, but how many brilliant mathematicians become successful businessmen?

An email to an Internet discussion forum typified the hostile attitude of many mathematicians to the misuse of their precise formulations. It offered the proposition: 'The square root of minus one has the odour of garlic' as an example of a distortion of mathematical principles. This, claimed the poster, was using mathematical constructs outside their strict mathematical meaning. The poster described this as 'modal misrepresentation'. He condemned all statements of this type as being completely meaningless because they can never arrive at a point where the truth or falsity of a proposition can enter into the discussion.

The poster continued by listing a few examples of this 'modal misrepresentation': examples where he thought popularization was not accurately portraying the correct mathematical principles. His examples were 'Networks, Cellular Automata, Chaos, Fractals, Heuristics and above all, Emergence'. As these are the very concepts that we are dealing with in this book, it is worth a moment to see why he thinks it is wrong to apply these terms to situations outside their strict mathematical context.

To the poster, the items in this list came into the same category as the proposition about the square root of minus one and the smell of garlic; his reasoning told him that if you cannot arrive at a point where truth or falsity come into the picture, the proposition has no value.

What this poster had missed was that the current use of these mathematical terms is not about propositions at all: their current popularity is due to the fact that they provide practical conceptual models to give a rough understanding of some of the underlying features of complex dynamic systems. True, they cannot lead to anything mathematically exact or conclusive, but they can provide a first-order approximation of what is happening. This is a whole lot better than nothing and can give a distinct competitive advantage over a competitor who has no model at all.

Certainly, this woolly use of mathematical concepts will never arrive at any point where the truth or falsity of a proposition can enter the discussion, but it will provide that enigmatic quality of what we are calling here the 'Zen thing': a rough guide to what is going on in a seemingly confusing world. This is why there is now a flood of popular interest in networks, cellular automata, chaos, fractals, heuristics and emergence.

People are looking for this Zen-ness because it will allow them to compete successfully in the perplexing and complex environment of the Internet and e-business. Meanwhile, the more precise mathematically minded might be left behind, indignant, bewildered and probably floundering in their own attempts to understand the complexity of the Internet.

One of the readers of the original draft, Robert Moorhead from Austin, Texas, made the following comment:

> As I read, something bothered me that I couldn't put my finger on. After some reflection I came to the conclusion that the Zen analogy strikes me as fuzzy, in the sense of ill-defined. I suppose because of the unfamiliarity of the subtler aspects of Eastern thought to Western minds. I understand the point Peter is making, but I think the argument could be better served by appealing to more, I don't know..., concrete or rational, I suppose.
>
> Tor Norretranders, in his book *The User Illusion*, makes the point that human consciousness is only capable of processing a couple of tens of bits of information a second, while our senses (or unconscious) are constantly processing millions of bits per second. The difference in input is not just discarded, but in Norretranders' view, is processed at a less conscious level to appear as intuition or gut feelings. This is a VERY simplified version of the Zen concept, but it seems to me to get at Peter's (and Mrs Brisby's) point in a more direct way.

Robert Moorhead is quite right, this use of Zen to explain a non-logical approach is fuzzy, but this is the whole point of describing it as Zen – it is because the conclusions are fuzzy. But this fuzziness is a lot better than being blind.

What type of playing field is the Internet?

Judging from Industrial Age corporate attitudes and dogmas, it would seem that at some point in time, probably around the middle of the twentieth century, the conventional way of doing business became relatively stable. This stabilization allowed much of business activity to become standardized, with procedures being established and universal protocols agreed. This stabilization enabled business practice to become not only more effective and efficient, but teachable. This had many advantages, not the least of which was to allow corporations to expand and take over vast tracts of trade and commerce.

The Internet and the advances of computers and digital communication have thrown a big spanner in the works of these established Industrial Age business practices. Suddenly, there has arisen the potential for using new techniques, new strategies and on such large scales that it is almost certain to disrupt the established order of the Industrial Age. The changes are already starting to happen and more and more people are becoming aware that something new is afoot.

Despite this general awareness, very few Industrial Age managers and executives are taking seriously the evidence that these changes are escalating into chaotic turbulence. Few appreciate that the advances in computer technology and digital communication are liable to throw the whole system of trade and commerce into a radically new state. The new state is likely to involve completely new ways of doing business, requiring different attitudes, methods, procedures and protocols from those that evolved during the Industrial Age. This would make many traditional business practices redundant. Much of current training and educational material will be rendered useless; previous experience might count for little.

The industrial revolution brought people in from the countryside to work in factories and offices. Business activities became centralized at specific geographical locations. Towns and cities grew up, with populations becoming more and more concentrated at focal points. With the possibilities now available for computer-enhanced digital communication, it is no longer necessary to concentrate populations in quite the same way. This could dramatically reverse the trend for populations to concentrate at population centres, leading on to who knows what other changes in living and lifestyles.

Already, we have deskless offices and virtual businesses where employees live hundreds, even thousands of miles away from each other. There is no need to travel into work each day if the work can be done just as easily at home or in a place of exotic scenery. If the changing patterns of business allow a better lifestyle, a better way to live, isn't it likely that this is the way things will go?

Such changes do seem possible, even probable, and when talked about will get heads nodding in agreement. But of more practical concern is not 'if' these changes will take place but 'when' and 'how'. This exposes a vast conceptual divide between Industrial Age and Information Age thinking: the conceptualization as to how and when these changes might take place is totally different.

Industrial Age thinking will be familiar with order and organization and see changes taking place gradually and linearly with ample warnings and signs of impending change. Information Age thinking will be familiar with the chaotic characteristics of complex dynamic systems and will be expecting changes to take place unexpectedly, suddenly and dramatically with no warnings or signs that changes are afoot.

Zen-ness from chaos theory

Chaos theory is another paradox. The word chaos elicits thoughts of disorder and randomness, yet the theory of chaos is not simply about disorder. More importantly, chaos theory is also about the changes in states of order and stability that can arise spontaneously in complex dynamic systems. It is about the enigmatic way in which a seemingly stable system will suddenly give rise to apparent randomness and then, just as suddenly, settle down again into new and quite different steady and seemingly stable patterns of activity.

Chaotic activity can be seen in the way days of bright sunshine can suddenly give way to unsettled and changeable weather; then turn to days of constant cloud and steady rain; then, just as unpredictably, reverse the process to go back to days of sunshine once again. Chaos theory is about understanding and describing such irrational changes that can occur within a complex dynamic system. The Internet is typical of such a system and exhibits this kind of non-predictable, irrational behaviour.

For the purpose of achieving Zen-ness in the Information Age, it is sufficient to have only a simplified model of chaos in your mind: just enough to understand how chaotic disturbances can have an effect on e-business and e-commerce. It isn't necessary to learn the complicated mathematics of chaos theory. After all, it isn't necessary to know all the complicated calculations needed to make a weather forecast, to understand the weather. If you have a rough idea that high and low pressures result in changeable weather, with intermittent periods of rainy days and sunny days, you can at least have sufficient understanding to choose suitable clothes when you go out for the day. This is the 'Zen thing'. It's not exact science, it's a blurry awareness of the underlying main issues: just enough to give a competitive edge in decision making.

The Internet, and by association e-business and e-commerce, are complex dynamic systems that are affected by chaos. The theories of chaos identify the Internet and the advance of computers and digital communications as being likely triggers that could destabilize the whole of the business world. Not slowly and gradually, but in sudden unpredictable jumps.

Although chaos is a creation of mathematicians, its unpredictability can be appreciated simply by observing the effects of chaos in complex systems. One of the simplest models to demonstrate these effects is often found in novelty gift stores: the decision maker. This consists of a small metal ball suspended like a pendulum above three magnets. Swinging the pendulum over the three magnets will see the ball jerking around in a bizarre and erratic fashion before suddenly coming to rest above one of the magnets. Disturb the position of the ball with a sufficiently large push and the ball will go into another exotic dance over the magnets before coming to rest again at the same or perhaps another of the magnets.

The movements appear totally erratic and random; the ball can end up at any one of the three magnets. Yet, it ought not to happen. It is an extremely simple system where the laws and the relationships between the swinging ball and the magnets are straightforward, well known and fully determined.

It is this kind of picture that you need to have in mind in order to have this Zen-ness in e-business and e-commerce. Opinions and trends will swing widely between different current attractors and no amount of reasoning will tell you how they are going to move. A jolt in the form of a new advance in technology or an imaginative new competitive strategy can send the ball wildly jerking around with no way of knowing where it will stop. Being aware of this unpredictable nature of change can give you a distinct advantage because you can allow for it in your strategy.

Chaos, and the different states of instabilities and stabilities that can arise, is most easily observed in the world of investment. Stock market prices vary continuously but professional investors can cope with this variability because they have acquired a certain type of Zen-ness for dealing with it. As we shall see in a later chapter, professional investors use strategies very similar to the strategies employed by entrepreneurs. They get into situations with the anticipation of change and use special conceptual tools to neutralize the effects of change.

While a novice investor might be predominantly preoccupied with the details of balance sheets, the professional investor will be more concerned with the broader issues: a new government, a change of interest rates, a currency devaluation, a new technology. These are the key issues that can trigger dramatic changes of state that might move all stock market prices to new levels. No investor can predict such events or their consequences ahead of time, but being aware that such changes do occur will give them a strong competitive edge.

A strategy based upon anticipating change was illustrated in the game of poker described in Chapter 1. One player is playing the game with the anticipation that the steady state of his winning position with back to back aces will continue. The other is anticipating the probability of a new round of cards providing a dramatic change that will transfer the winning advantage. Although the game of poker itself is not a chaotic system, this captures the essence of the situation in which individuals and businesses now find themselves when doing business in the Information Age. Either they are in the unenviable position of the careful player who is blissfully unaware that there is a predator waiting for an opportunity to pounce, or they can be like the professional poker player, whose Zen-like understanding allows them to anticipate change and wait for the emergent opportunity that will throw the advantage over to them.

The most amazing and surprising consequence of chaos theory is that it undermines the value of logic. As we see from the decision-making pendulum, for no apparent logical reason, a system can become unstable and then settle down into any one of a number of several different steady states. No examination of the individual relationships between the components of the system would lead one even to suspect that such erratic and unpredictable behaviour could result. It is a strong reason for being suspicious of any logical reasoning when considering what strategies to adopt for e-business and e-commerce projects.

A real-life example of chaotic turbulence

For me, the world of computers and digital communications has involved a continuous and intensive learning process over a period of ten years.

I'd first come into the field of digital communications in 1989, when it seemed the next big thing would be CD-ROMs. I spent three years creating a CD-ROM to describe the lessons I'd learned over the 25 years I'd spent as an entrepreneur.

Those three years gave me first-hand experience of a rapidly changing technological world. I started with a top of the range personal computer: a Macintosh SE with a built-in 20 megabyte (MB) hard disk and an incredible 1 MB of RAM. At a cost of over $4,000 I bought a 600 MB external disk drive and for another $1,500 a CD-ROM reader (one of the first in the UK). I then spent a further few thousand dollars buying every possible application program I could think of that might come in useful. My intention was to produce the first-ever interactive CD-ROM book. I wanted to be a pioneer in this newly emerging industry.

I'd liked the idea of an interactive CD-ROM book because I could see how it might enable me to explain abstract ideas with animated examples. I could illustrate the effects of probability, game theory, group interaction and genetic algorithms. I could bring to life the realities of calculated decision making; introduce the concepts of compound interest, discounted risk and uncertainty; demonstrate games of strategy and competition. With all the industry experts, gurus and visionaries telling us that CD-ROMs would be the next big thing, it seemed a safe and certain way to go.

Over the three years of the CD-ROM's development, everything was changing: programs were continuously being updated, hardware constantly needed to be replaced. New techniques and programming languages had to be mastered. It was a nightmare of constant change. However, at last it was finished and I sent out review copies to every computer magazine I could think of. To my delight, I got rave reviews and immediately won a prestigious award from the *MacUser* (UK) computer magazine. I really thought I'd made it into the world of digital communications.

Sadly, it was not to be. I'd completed my black and white CD-ROM at just about the time colour computers were coming onto the market. The ease with which media could be put onto CD-ROM had attracted thousands of CD-ROM developers and artists from all parts of the planet. The anticipated huge market in CD-ROM sales had brought in hundreds of publishers who had backlogs of material that could easily be transferred onto CD-ROM. Schools and colleges were making CD-ROMs. Within a few months the whole market for CD-ROMs became saturated.

The problem wasn't so much that there were a lot of CD-ROMs on the market; the killer was that so many of them were of poor quality. The headlong rush to get into the next big thing had resulted in products coming onto the market before any proper market research or testing. Products that worked well on high-end developer machines performed poorly, if at all, on standard PCs. A 12 MB illustration looks fine on a developer's screen, but when it gets to the user and takes half a minute to load, the novelty soon wears thin.

The magazines that had begun to specialize in CD-ROM reviews and comment were swamped with samples. Some of them were so poor that it was an absolute pain for any reviewer to go through them. Most were despatched to the trash can, unseen. Retail stores, anxious to be in on the next big thing, had opened special departments to sell CD-ROMs; several big distributors had set up to service them. There were CD-ROM charts; there were CD-ROM advertisements; everything seemed to suggest that here was a whole new world of opportunity. Yet, in the space of only a few months the whole thing collapsed, destroyed by overload and an abundance of poor quality products. The promising infrastructure that had risen up in anticipation of a demand for CD-ROMs just melted away almost overnight.

 ## Phase transitions

It may not seem as if this real-life experience has much to do with theoretical considerations that can be described by mathematical equations. Yet, this CD-ROM emergence is a very typical example of the kind of unpredictable outcomes that chaos theory would predict. This short-lived rush into CD-ROMs is typical of a chaotic disturbance: a technology-induced chaotic movement in commerce, driven by the spread of information. There are many parallels to this situation on the World Wide Web today, so let us examine it more closely.

In 1989, a new technology had emerged. A small disk could now hold books to the equivalent of 42 feet (12.9m) of shelf space. Some of the world's largest encyclopaedias could easily be contained on a revolutionary new communication medium that cost less than a dollar to produce.

To creative minds, the potential for such a product was beyond the imagination. Not only could vast quantities of data be stored on these disks, it could be directly coupled with the processing power of the computer. This would allow dynamic indexing, animated displays, user interaction and many other kinds of information manipulation and sorting.

As the word spread about this new and revolutionary product, people all over the world, from a variety of backgrounds, started to think about how they might be able to use and apply this new medium in their own particular areas of interest. Corporations, entrepreneurs, marketing people, educationalists – all in their different ways saw potential uses and opportunities.

As interest grew, newspapers, magazines and other mass communication media started to take up the cause. From the research laboratories of Philips in Holland and Sony in Japan, knowledge and speculation about this new medium spread out in an ever-growing wave of optimism. It soon reached practically everybody involved in technology and communication. This was an exponential expansion of knowledge. It started slowly, emanating from just a few sources. These sources of information grew and the number of people who became aware grew even faster. At one moment in time practically nobody had heard of CD-ROMs; within the space of a year or two, everyone knew about them. A phase transition had occurred.

Phase transition is the name given to the process of a system changing from one state to another. In dynamic complex systems the change is seldom linear: it doesn't happen by means of smooth and regular incremental changes. The changes start locally, begin building slowly and then gather pace, building up to a crescendo of change which completes the process. In the CD-ROM example, at one moment in time there were no CD-ROMs; a short time later there were – with all the spectacular potential for their use and application. This is the phenomenon known as a phase transition, a typical manifestation of a system exhibiting chaos.

The gradual build-up and ever-increasing rate of change of the information spread as it goes from mouth to mouth has all the typical characteristics of an exponential function, a function that increases a value at an ever-growing rate. Mathematicians would describe this process with the aid of formulae and graphs, but it can be explained just as well by a visit to an old-fashioned music hall.

In the days before television and political correctness, a popular form of entertainment was the Music Hall: a live variety show held in a theatre. At one such show, an attractive young lady appeared on stage wearing a fur coat. In a reedy voice she rendered a few choruses of some of the popular songs of the time.

Having delivered a mediocre performance, she quickly curtsied and rapidly disappeared off stage. There was very little applause except for one single man at the back of the hall who started clapping maniacally and calling out repeatedly in a loud voice, 'Encore!', 'Encore!'

The lady duly obliged the single enthusiastic admirer and, after taking off her fur coat, returned to give an off-key rendition of another chorus. Again a quick curtsy and she retired from the stage.

The enthusiastic admirer started up his clapping and shouts for another encore. This time he was joined by a couple of others. At this, the lady returned to the stage once more but had shed the shawl which had been covering up her dress. Another mediocre performance, a quick curtsy and an exit from the stage were soon followed by a dozen men wildly clapping and calling for yet another encore.

Returning again, this time without her dress, she sang another chorus in her petticoat. When she did her little curtsy and left the stage after this chorus, she had half the men in the audience wildly clapping and calling out for her to return. After singing once more in some very skimpy underwear, her exit caused the whole audience to go into uproar: clapping and shouting for yet another chorus.

The point of this story is that it illustrates a phase transition – a transformation of the expectations of the audience as, one by one, they click on to the real meaning behind the performance. Unfortunately for the Music Hall audience there was another kind of transition, when the lady reappeared to sing her final chorus fully clothed and wearing her fur coat.

This illustrates what happened when everyone began to learn about CD-ROMs. The potential was initially realized by just a few; gradually more and more began to cotton on; it reached a peak when everybody was aware and was rushing into products and services. This has all the hallmarks of chaotic activity: the sudden introduction of a new and potent medium disturbing the steady state. The system was disturbed into chaos.

If the data retrieval rate from the CD-ROMs had been greater and if the computers of the time had been faster and more powerful, the rush towards the utilization of CD-ROMs might have resulted in many successful applications. The system might have flipped over to a new state where CD-ROMs were a massive success. This could have seen the CD-ROM becoming a ubiquitous product and providing many of the functions now being fulfilled by the Internet and the World Wide Web today.

It didn't work out that way. After a brief chaotic surge, the system quickly reverted to its initial steady state where the CD-ROM was no longer a disrupting influence. This is the typical activity of a dynamic complex system as a rapidly expanding movement threatens the stability of the current order. If you watch what is happening on the Internet and the Web today you will see countless examples of this chaotic activity as the exponential forces triggered by new advances and new initiatives take effect. How many of them will end up wearing a fur coat?

Phase transitions are common phenomena in all branches of social and physical sciences. They can be seen in catalytic chemical reactions; the spread of fear; water changing into ice; rumour spreading through a community; the condensation of intergalactic gas clouds into stars. The phenomenon can be seen to occur in a multitude of situations and environments and it is a phenomenon that we can expect to play a major role in the evolution and development of the Internet and the World Wide Web.

In the CD-ROM example, just as important to understand as the reasons for the rush towards getting in on the next big thing are the reasons for the sudden extinguishing of the enthusiasm. Seers and pundits of the type so respected in the Industrial Age had got everything totally wrong. In the Industrial Age a hierarchy of peer groups form to provide reliable opinions. Specialist and expert views are generally right. In the Information Age there are no reliable opinions; even the most authoritative views are just as likely to be wrong as those of a novice. This is what catches so many Industrial Age business people out when they enter the world of e-commerce and e-business: they believe in the experts.

It is this scepticism of widely held or authoritative views that is the hallmark of the successful Information Age businessman or businesswoman: not a cynical scepticism but a strategic scepticism that is not only distrustful of the predictions of others but also distrustful of their own opinions and intuitions. In an environment prone to chaotic disturbances, a strategy must assume that things will not go as either expected or planned.

The ubiquitous role of the exponential

Chaotic systems are driven by rapidly increasing changes of some kind or another. Mathematicians use formulae to express such changes, but they are more easily visualized by looking at graphs. Figure 3.1 is a typical exponential

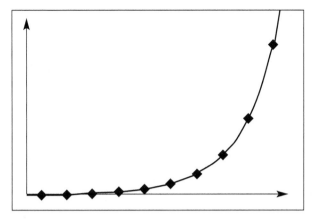

Figure 3.1 Exponential rate of change (changing at a faster and faster rate)

graph, visually showing the effect of increasing change. It could be a graph showing the rapid increase of information, computer speeds, RAM memories, hard disk sizes, transmission speeds, number of Web sites appearing, number of people starting to use the Internet. These are just some of the exponential changes that are responsible for creating the turbulence and chaos in the world of e-business and e-commerce.

The graph illustrates the way in which some events can change at a progressively increasing rate. It represents the way information gathers pace as it spreads through a community: going faster and faster as more and more people become aware and are able to tell others. It starts slowly, gathers pace, moving faster and faster towards a destination. Keep this shape in your mind. It is the mechanism that powers chaos, and, more importantly, provides the essential key to understanding how to create successful strategies in e-business and e-commerce.

In an environment of change the exponential is the single most important concept to be understood: it is the basis of most happenings and strategies in the Information Age. This contrasts strongly with the activity and plans in the traditional corporate world of the Industrial Age, where the main concerns are for stability and steady state. In the Industrial Age's corporate world of business planning and management the exponential is seldom encountered. It has very little relevance in conditions where conservatism and the status quo are at a premium. Everything is done to avoid situations that spin rapidly out of control;

strategies are used to control them and damp down the causes of rapid change.

In the Information Age, trying to resist or control change is futile. The optimum strategy is to look for and exploit runaway changes, seeing them as sources of new opportunities. There are hazards, but Information Age strategists will be aware of the dangers of riding the crests of these waves and will take suitable precautions.

Entrepreneurs are able to exploit the phenomenon of the exponential in other ways. It enables them to start enterprises from small beginnings and with limited amounts of capital and then see their businesses build at an ever-increasing rate. Small businesses can start off in niche markets and then use the power of the exponential to encroach rapidly upon corporate domains. Entrepreneurs can start businesses unobtrusively, slowly, before the corporate powers become aware.

Where an entrepreneurial business relies on its exceptional service, or some creative initiative, it can use word of mouth in place of expensive advertising: tapping into the potent power of the exponential. In the environment of the Internet, word of mouth can be immensely effective, cheap and many orders of magnitude faster than it is in the conventional world. It can easily surpass the results obtained through sophisticated marketing and advertising techniques used by large companies in the conventional world of mass media.

In the rest of this book we are going to see the ubiquitous power of the exponential appearing over and over again because it is the driving force of the Information Age. It is the force that creates chaos, and you don't have to look far to find examples of the exponential at work creating chaos and ever-increasing change:

- Consider the rapidly increasing size of computer memories, the increasing speed of computer processors, the escalating size of disk storage space.
- Cast your mind to the Internet: the increasing rate at which people are getting connected, the fast-expanding number of servers, Web sites and Web pages.
- Look at the rising speed of signal transmission, the rapidly broadening bandwidths.
- Look at the rate at which fibre cable is being laid, new satellites going up.
- Look at how businesses are increasingly taking an interest in the Internet and the Web.

The whole edifice is alive with exponentials, which are the known purveyors of chaotic activity.

If it were possible to represent the Internet as an equation, it would contain dozens of exponentials reflecting all kinds of expanding elements. This is why the environments of the Internet, e-business and e-commerce are liable to become exceptionally chaotic with the potential to produce radical new patterns of business – not only for entrepreneurs but for corporations as well. This could include government departments and involve the whole of the bureaucratic organization upon which they are founded.

The advent of the printing press, steam power, electricity, telephones, internal combustion engines, air travel and transport had major impacts on our civilization and the way we lead our lives. Yet none of these had as many concurrent exponentials coming into play at the same time and at such breathtaking speed. It is in this world of exceptional rapid changes and chaos that we have to find the most appropriate strategies for living, surviving, competing and succeeding.

Part 2

Looking for clues

Part 1 set the scene of the detective story. It presented a daunting environment: too much information, little order and no logical framework for decision making.

Part 2 is about looking for clues as to how to deal with this environment. It begins by considering new ways to think about a dynamically complex world where it is impossible to have all the answers. Like the detective in any detective story, this involves stumbling around, looking for any clue that offers a pointer towards a solution.

The main characteristics of the world of the Information Age are complexity, uncertainty, unknowns, unknowables and intense competition. Such conditions are not unique. These conditions existed in certain areas before the advent of the Internet. Two of these areas are examined here to see what strategies the professionals in these worlds are using to deal with conditions of uncertainty and complexity. Chapter 5 looks into the world of investment and finance, where uncertainty and chaotic and unpredictable events are coped with every day of the week. Chapter 6 looks at the way complexity is managed in the arcane world of computer programming.

Chapter 4

Stumbling around looking for clues

 It isn't possible to understand the Internet

Another paradox of the Information Age is that you can only begin to understand the Internet once you realize that the Internet is impossible to understand. This is true of any complex dynamic system: they are all impossible to understand in any logical, structured way. But just knowing this is knowledge itself, valuable knowledge, telling you that you cannot base any sensible strategy on trying to work out what a dynamic system is going to do next, especially if it is in a state of chaotic activity. This applies to the Internet and to any e-business or e-commerce activity involving the fast-changing world of digital communications. Just being aware of this, though, puts you at an advantage to anyone else who thinks they can base a strategy on anticipating what they think the next phase of Internet development will lead to.

Another paradox of the Information Age is that you can only begin to understand the Internet once you realize that the Internet is impossible to understand.

The value of this understanding is that it allows you to plan a strategy expecting unpredictable and unknowable changes to occur. Like the professional poker player, playing along with the player who has aces back to back, it gets you to play the kind of game that works by taking advantage of any change when it comes along. This is the classic strategy of the entrepreneur, who will anticipate change and has a strategy to be in the right place at the right time to take advantage. The first move in this strategy is always just to get in the game, without committing yourself to any major investment in time or money.

This is well exampled by Dai Williams, who describes, in another post to a table in the virtual café, how a company lost out by playing an 'aces back to back' game instead of the open play that was needed at the time:

> ... the IT organization in question historically focused on large companies and government bodies as customers. They generally respond to requests for tender (or similar documents) and then go through a (very) lengthy – in effort if not always in time – bid process, even if the net result is to qualify the opportunity out. This process inevitably means high cost of sales; hence they need large and profitable deals to come out of it in order to carry this cost of sales. This means that they cannot afford to bid for small to medium pieces of work (either for small to medium companies or less significant pieces of work for large companies).
>
> This was illustrated a couple of years ago when the company withdrew support for its Web development group. Because Web site projects were generally small in themselves, they could not be done profitably with all the sales overhead. Rather than apply different processes to this class of work, the company in question decided not to pursue this type of work. Unfortunately today most e-commerce opportunities involve, to a greater or lesser extent, a Web site element. Furthermore, many e-commerce projects are actually run as extensions to an initial Web site project and hence often awarded to the company that ran the initial (small) project. The company in question is now desperate to win 'e-commerce' projects, they still have no useful Web-based collateral (i.e. a portfolio of past

projects) and can't see that they need to have Web site development capability.

Anyway, to return to my original point, the response of these large IT companies to this problem has been logical enough though singularly unhelpful to the development of e-commerce. They have started to talk up the issues around what is fundamentally a very simple opportunity for most companies. Frequent reports highlight the need for scalability, security and total integration (all laudable aims incidentally) and conclude that anyone with a budget under $1 million for their e-com site is being naïve and simplistic.

Companies that offer to do it cheaper are painted as fly-by-night, unprofessional and probably unwashed. Unfortunately, this description appeals to many of the corporate decision makers who still don't really trust the ideas and ideals that the net represents and resent the fact that they are being harangued as too slow to react. This then becomes a self-fulfilling prophecy as the large IT companies wheel out statistics showing that large corporates ARE now spending $1 million+ on their Web sites – extra reasons for mocking a smaller budget.

This example may sound extreme but is not untypical. When Industrial Age corporate managers are used to using money and professionalism to defeat problems, they are totally at a loss when it comes to the fast-moving chaotic world of the Internet and e-business. They make big mistakes and often compound these mistakes by trying to get a result through throwing even more money and resources at the problems. They then get the kind of service that preys on this kind of mentality and it becomes, too often, a case of the blind leading the blind into an expensive fiasco.

How do you get into the game?

Dai Williams' anecdote is typical of many 'missed opportunity' situations which develop in e-business and e-commerce. They are easy to see in hindsight but they shed very little light on how to cope with any current situation in e-business and e-commerce. It may be easy to see in retrospect what a mistake it was for that large IT company not to have invested in getting their feet wet in the Web site business, but was it so obvious at the time?

There are all manner of new fields springing up. What kind of strategy will enable you to make the right choices? There are so many new directions to go that it is very difficult to be sure of what to try out and what to leave alone. In the

CD-ROM 'How God Makes God' I used a little story to depict the situation entrepreneurs find themselves in when they are trying to look for a new opportunity.

'Have you ever been out driving in the fog at night?'

'Several times.'

'Did you ever get impatient with the driver in front? Seeing his mistakes? Criticizing him for being too slow?'

'I can remember that happening to me last November when I went to pick up my husband from work.'

'What did you do about it?'

'I made such a fool of myself. It was getting late and my husband always gets furious with me if I keep him waiting, so I was getting nervous and impatient. I kept honking the horn at what I thought was a doddering old fool, a slow driver in front of me. Eventually he got fed up with my honking and pulled over to let me pass.

'As soon as I passed him, I looked out at the road ahead and the road wasn't there. All I could see was a swirling greyness. I carried on forward, trying desperately to get a glimpse of the kerb, a lamp post, anything at all that might give me some sort of direction.

'I slowed down… hit the kerb… slowed down still further. I jerked slowly up the road for about half a mile when I saw some lights appearing out of the gloom. I strained to see what they were and found myself face to face with somebody's front door.

'Somehow, I had taken my car off of the road and driven straight up the drive of somebody's private house. I have never felt so embarrassed in my life… especially when I had to ask the driver who was following me to back out. It was of course the driver I had just been honking at for being so slow.'

'Trying to make money is like that: being in a fog and having to lead the way. The road ahead looks perfectly straightforward to those following you, or those looking back and seeing only your successes… but to the entrepreneur, everything appears vague and uncertain. Nothing is obvious until after the decisions have been made. The route is taken through intelligent guesswork: calculated risks based upon uncertain clues.'

The square one position

I've read many definitions of an entrepreneur. Almost always they are written by people who haven't been entrepreneurs and are trying to describe them in such a way as to fit into conventional business paradigms. It is a little like blind men trying to describe the colour purple.

The trouble is that the activity of entrepreneurs is usually only considered after the entrepreneur has got well past square one. To truly be able to define an entrepreneur the description must include the activity at the square one position: when the entrepreneur has no funds, no ideas and quite often no contacts. Not all entrepreneurs start from this position, although many find themselves there several times. My own entry into the world of the entrepreneur started from this position. It happened when I resigned from my first and only place of employment.

The last six months at college saw us all writing out and sending CVs to every technology-oriented company we could think of. I sent out 46. In those days they were all hand-written so this was quite a considerable number.

As chance would have it, I didn't get my first job through these CVs, it came as a result of my uncle, a London taxi cab driver, chatting to one of his fares. It was an American businessman who'd just arrived in England to set up a subsidiary for his US company: The Gisholt Machine Tool Company based in Madison, Wisconsin. My uncle told him about me just finishing college, and the American gave my uncle his card and told him to send me along to see him. Within a month, I was hired at a rather generous salary and sent to the USA for six months' special training.

For the first two years, the job worked out fine. I was flying all over Europe, visiting most of the large manufacturing companies. My work was extremely varied, part customer service, part sales and part design. The team consisted of only five people: the CEO plus another director who was the son of the company's founding president, another American engineer, a secretary and myself. For me it was both exciting and interesting; that is, until they started to expand. First came the chief engineer, then the chief salesman, then the accountant. This was swiftly followed by rules and regulations, procedures and methods, costing and planning.

I decided to move on, but I had a problem. They had been paying me a salary that was at least equal to any salary I could command anywhere else – plus, I was enjoying a very generous expense account that was almost as much as my salary. A new job would entail a reduction in income.

In working out the consequences of this change in income I made a discovery that was to change the whole course of my life. I worked out how much I'd be likely to earn as a reasonably successful engineer over the course of a working life span. This is quite easy to do in career occupations as salary scales are fairly well established: sufficient at least to get a first-order approximation.

From the aggregate amount of my total anticipated earnings over a 40-year period, I started to deduct the cost of a reasonably comfortable lifestyle: buying and maintaining a house, eating, clothing, bringing up children, transportation, holidays, entertainment, insurances and pension arrangements and all the other expenditures which are more or less mandatory for a reasonably secure and comfortable life.

Before I'd reached the end of the list of things I'd noted down as being essential, I'd run out of money. Paring the costs somewhat drastically, I managed to get the expected life expenditures roughly equal to the anticipated earnings. Looking at the pared-down list and realizing that it left nothing over for any discretionary spending, I came to the startling conclusion that a career as an engineer was going to commit me to a life of bearable mediocrity.

With all of my future income committed to maintaining this modest lifestyle there seemed no possibility that anything particularly exciting was going to happen in my life. It was this revelation that prompted me to change direction and learn how to become an entrepreneur.

As ludicrous as this may seem in retrospect, it seemed a plausible proposition at the time. Surely, I thought, being an entrepreneur isn't about luck, it isn't about having the right birthright, having high connections or access to vast amounts of money? It had to be something that could be learned. It seemed eminently reasonable to me that, if it was something that could be learned, I had at least as much chance as anyone else to become an entrepreneur. After all, hadn't I been trained to be the proverbial rocket scientist? Full of confidence, I gave notice to quit my job and one bitterly cold day in February I found myself out on the street looking for a place to start becoming an entrepreneur.

Unless anyone has actually been in this position it is difficult to imagine. There is a whole world full of opportunities but no place to start. I was taken back to the time I'd played around with my first 'free' electronic components: the confusion of not being able to apply any theory or organization to the problem. It was a similar experience, a total inability to see how to make sense of the world.

To this day I don't quite know how I got started. I talked to lots of people, I went to many places. I met a man in the street who was selling personalized pencils. Through this I got into gold-blocking door bell labels. I met an old school chum and through his father who had a used car business we bought a few cars and sold them off at a profit.

Random events took me in different directions. A news bulletin announced that there was a change in the law to allow gaming clubs to be legalized. I started a gaming club. This led me to owning a discotheque. Tenant protests over noise and an ebullient local police force closed my discotheque and I started the first computer dating agency in the UK. I bought and sold some land. I ran a skiing holiday club that took weekend parties up to Scotland from London; I started a bizarre adventure holiday scheme that took people to an island in the Mediterranean. These were the winners; there were hordes of other little business adventures which were contemplated, tried out and aborted.

Most of these businesses were with partners, all as irresponsible and carefree as myself. We had a simple philosophy: that opportunities turn up of their own accord and anyone can become an expert at anything within a month. This last proposition we got from an article in *Reader's Digest*.

Becoming an expert in a month seems to be an outrageously naïve attitude to have. In fact, it made sense at the time and makes even more sense to me now in the context of the Internet. Actually, the idea didn't just come from the *Reader's Digest* article, it had come to me years before, when I was at school. All through my student life I'd been unable to learn anything in a classroom setting. After a few sentences of any lecture, my thoughts would drift away, after which I never seemed to be able to keep up. This kept me near the bottom of the class for the first year or two: until the time I was unmercifully picked on by a chemistry master.

To avoid the usual harassment I would get from this master after a poor exam result I decided at one end of term exam to cheat. I went carefully over the year's course and made a note of all the important points and wrote them down in tiny handwriting on a piece of paper that I could conceal in my sleeve. To my astonishment, when it came to the exam I found I didn't need to look at the crib sheet. I'd remembered everything. Through the process of isolating the important facts and writing them down I'd acquired an understanding that made everything easy to remember. To my surprise, and even more to the surprise of the chemistry master, I came top of that examination.

I then used this same technique throughout the rest of my school and college days. I wouldn't bother to learn anything all through the year and then make a précis of the lessons in the month before the examinations. It produced good results and many school prizes. The trick I'd discovered by accident was to isolate all the principal concepts, understand those and dispense with all the detail. This gets to become a habit and book reading then becomes a game of 'spot the concepts'.

This technique proves especially valuable when used in a 'need to know' situation – such as the kind of experience I'd had at the Radar Research Establishment where in a matter of a few weeks I'd been able to design pulse shapes and wide bandwidth amplifiers, maybe more slowly, but almost as competently as any professional electronic engineer.

Lack of knowledge seemed to be absolutely no bar to taking on any entrepreneurial venture. My excursion into the gaming world was a case in point. The club I ran was set up to play the casino game of chemin-de-fer. As I had virtually no money when the club first opened, I couldn't afford to play in the games myself and didn't actually get round to learning the rules and how to play chemin-de-fer before I was making enough money to join in. That was two or three weeks after the club had started running.

The key to understanding and appreciating the 'become an expert in a month' philosophy is to realize that a short intensive study of any subject can give you a rough guide to the principal considerations. Although you will not have anywhere near the expertise of the real experts you'll probably know more than at least 99 per cent of the rest of the population who haven't had the time or the inclination to look at the subject at all.

The value of this 'become an expert in a month' approach is not that you could do the things that the real experts can, but that you get to know enough to be able to ask the experts sensible questions when you want to do something in their areas of expertise. It enables you also to know enough about their expertise to be able to hire them to do the expert jobs for you.

There are many versions of the anecdote where parents are being shown around a school to which they are thinking of sending their child. The head master takes them into the science class and explains that these pupils will be those who go on to become scientists, surgeons, doctors and engineers. The parents are then taken to the fine arts class where the teacher explains that these pupils will go on to become musicians, bankers, lawyers, artists, writers, journalists and designers.

When they get to a third classroom, the parents ask what these pupils are studying. The teacher explains these are the children who are not clever enough for the science class and not gifted enough for fine arts and are getting just a general all-round education without too much depth. 'So what will these pupils be doing when they leave school?', the parents ask. 'They'll be employing the boys in the science and fine arts classes', the head teacher replies.

There is more than an element of truth in this trite anecdote. Specialization, by definition, confines a person to a niche. The real game is always played by the people who have the ability to organize and find employment for the niche specialists.

A reader of the draft in the virtual café wrote in response to this 'expert in a month' idea:

> If you précis something, by definition you lose some of the information the original contains. What you end up with is not an expert opinion, just an opinion... informed, perhaps... but VERY prone to error... The very thing you lose in approaching a problem this way is the subtleties that the expert is supposed to know about... This can (and often will) lead one to holding what one considers to be a strong position, based on a false reading of the details of a subject...   **Elias**

Another reader also commented:

> I don't think anyone needs to believe 'all this Internet stuff' is so readily accessible that anyone can become any kind of 'expert' in it in a short amount of time, however marginally. We already have far too many corporate droolbags out there who believe they are experts in a given endeavour because they read an article about it in *Marketing Today* or some such.   **Warren Ockrassa**

Both seem to be right, but then, if you accept their viewpoints as being valid, you are left with the realization that it is impossible to learn everything there is to know about the environment of the Internet to the standard of a real expert. This leaves only the alternative of becoming an expert in a small niche area. Yet, someone has to be able to employ and direct the specialist. The specialist, by definition, does not handle the more practical realities of getting a business up and running.

This provides another paradox: to be an expert in e-business and e-commerce you have to accept the fact that you won't be an expert in all aspects of e-business and e-commerce. This makes it imperative for e-business or e-commerce strategies to include the involvement of many different people who are niche specialists. Again, it points to the conclusion that e-business and e-commerce strategies are not about knowing the technology but knowing people.

An important distinction must be made here between two quite different uses of the 'expert in a month' technique. One use is potentially harmful, maybe even pathologically fatal to an organization. This is where the technique is used by someone to pretend they know more than they do, or even worse, allow this technique to make them think they know more than they know.

> **To be an expert in e-business and e-commerce you have to accept the fact that you won't be an expert in all aspects of e-business and e-commerce.**

Most times, a superficial knowledge is easily recognized by the real experts, but sometimes an expert might not be bothered to argue a point or may simply allow non-experts to get themselves into trouble to teach them a lesson. Even more dangerous is when a person with superficial knowledge speaks for the real experts, perhaps to a higher authority, or makes decisions without consulting them. Used as a ploy to get an order, a contract or promotion of some kind, pretending to have expert knowledge can lead to disastrous results in the Information Age.

This gives us another paradox: the really knowledgeable proponents of e-business and e-commerce readily admit their lack of knowledge. Fortunately, as we shall see later in the book, there is a strategy that will recognize, isolate and eliminate the effects of the misuse of the 'expert in a month' technique.

The proper use of this technique requires humility. It has to be recognized that the superficial knowledge gained in a month is for communication purposes only. It is not to be thought of as giving sufficient knowledge to do the job of an expert, but simply a means of finding out what you don't know. It allows strategists to be able to recognize their own deficiencies so that they can bring in the appropriate expertise.

The best managers and strategists are those who have the confidence to go around telling everyone that they don't know anything. Smart people don't pretend to know. Those who go around pretending to know everything in the Information Age will always get into trouble. Those who use a strategy that takes into consideration their *lack* of knowledge will fare much better. This is why 'expert in a month' can work, but it doesn't work if it is used to pretend to know more than you do know.

This 'become an expert in a month' concept has many forms and variations. The simplest is when you need some special information about a product or service of which you have absolutely no knowledge. At first you don't even know what questions to ask. You don't know what are the important criteria and the variables. You make a first phone call where you make a complete fool of yourself asking all kinds of dumb questions. A second phone call sees you asking more pertinent questions. After half a dozen phone calls to various people you are speaking and asking questions like an expert.

A similar experience happens at trade shows. You may start off by not even knowing what the trade show is about but by the time you've gone around all the booths and spoken to a lot of people you come out a relative expert. Or, at least, that is what you would appear to be to most people.

Speciality magazines and trade journals are other good sources to acquire a quick expertise. Reading a few issues gets you acquainted with current topics, developments and problems. More importantly, it familiarizes you with the special terminology that is used in a niche area: the conceptual phrases and buzz-words used in the communication of that world's thoughts and ideas.

Now we have the Internet, which makes the 'become an expert in a month' a highly practical concept. You can use search engines to track down some of the tangible stuff, but everything you need to know to become a relative expert you can obtain by spending a few weeks interacting with people in a special interest group (SIG) Internet discussion forum. There are thousands of these covering every possible subject you can think of.

In these groups you can very quickly pick up on the main issues, learn all the special terms and how to speak to the experts. Again, you will not become as expert as the experts but you'll glean enough knowledge to be able to communicate effectively and efficiently with them in their speciality areas of knowledge.

At another table in the virtual café, in response to a paragraph I'd written in the first draft:

> The question then becomes one of making a transition between the old and the new. How do you have to think about the Internet in order to escape from the established thinking and business practices of the Industrial Age? How do you get up to speed in the rapidly changing environment of the twenty-first century so as to avoid being left behind, fretful, baffled and confused?

Mrs Brisby responded:

> Simple. Tell them that the Internet is run by a bunch of middle management, and so long as they keep feeding money into their IT department, they'll get rich?

HAH! If only it were that simple. I'm reminded of a rather amusing anecdote where some fat-cat execs hear that NT is the new best thing.

Of course, the IT department had enjoyed running UNIX boxes in the back room for many years, and left their 'other' staff occupied with their Wintel boxes.

The goal was to link the two. The fat-cats invest some money into some outside work to bring in NT. These 'MCSE completed' folk talk local to the fat-cats (mainly because they were already rich; hence they can afford the MCSE exams) and NT boxes are brought in.

Now, the techs don't know how to run NT. Even IF the NT boxes had the easiest OS in the world, it certainly doesn't make any sense to these guys.

Why?

After all, they've been running UNIX for years!!! They know it can do anything they'd ever want to do! But now there's NT. So when NT crashes, and the tech guys figure out that NT is unstable (duh), they plead to the middle management.

Word goes around, and eventually the tech team is fired for incompetence. After all, how could NT be unstable if it's the new best thing?

Now the new tech guys come in (UNIX gurus, again), know a little about Novell and OS/2 and lie about knowing about NT (mostly what they've picked up from trade magazines). They hook up the Sun boxes with NFS mounts, turn the NT boxes into FreeBSD machines, run SAMBA and NFS loopbacked, and presto – the Wintel teams are connected.

Now what, pray tell, is the moral of this story?

Simple.

You can know anything and everything about how to hook up a UNIX network. Maintain, etc. But unless you keep building your knowledge *base* – and keep up with the 'best new thing' – you will get lost, and you will need to turn your NT boxes into FreeBSD machines.

Mrs Brisby's post illustrates several important points about this fast-changing world of information technology. Reading beyond the technicalities it contains, the post tells of a management that is hopelessly lost in the technical world of computers. A management that lives in a world of buzz-words and 'next best thing' mentality. It tells of an IT department that is managed by people who are so deeply involved with their own specialist world that they are losing connection to everything else that is happening around them. It tells of opportunists who are in the right place at the right time and apply 'expert in a month' technology to a company's problems and are rewarded by taking over the positions of the specialists who became too narrowly focused.

More significantly, it shows how a cavalier attitude towards technology can allow a powerful and expensive computer system to be rigged up to provide a minimal service that performs only to the limited requirements of a management that have no conception of its full potential.

Certainly management can't be expected to have expert knowledge, but they can become 'experts in a month' and learn sufficient to know the right experts to talk to, and how to talk expertly to them. In this way, before making decisions and taking action, they can find out what kind of options are open to them and the criteria that are relevant and important.

Probably most readers skipped through Mrs Brisby's post without bothering to make much sense of it. It contains technical words they don't understand, incomprehensible strings of letters representing arcane hardware and software solutions: the buzz-words of a technocratic elite. But these are the cynical observations of a real expert at the cutting edge of this new technology, somebody like Dai Williams, who can see the 'suits' being ripped off, bamboozled by the cowboys and the charlatans. Mrs Brisby and Dai Williams are talking sense, but how many managers would be bothered to make the effort to be able to step into their world and listen to them?

Unfortunately, many managers and executives much prefer a cosy chat over an expense account meal, or in a privileged place in a hospitality suite – where all the technicalities are swept under the table. This to them is the executive life, and they will scorn the self-effacing indignities of having to learn the ropes in an Internet special interest group forum where they will have to make fools of themselves by having to ask basic questions. If managers and their companies are going to survive into the Information Age, this attitude has to change.

Once again, the search for an optimum strategy to deal with the complex environment of the Internet, e-business and e-commerce is bringing our attention to the fact that the answers lie in our ability to communicate with people – not in the arcane details of the technology.

 ## The first inklings of a strategy

Too often, people are rushing into e-commerce on the assumption that business and commerce will work on the Internet in exactly the same way as they work in their familiar Industrial Age world. They will set up magnificent Web sites, full of technological sophistication, and then be surprised when nothing turns out as expected.

In one sense, there is some justification for assuming e-commerce should be the same as Industrial Age commerce: business is business and it should not matter what kind of environment you do it in. Fundamental values do not change; certain tenets, common-sense rules, codes of conduct and ethical considerations remain the same whatever situation you are in.

The problem is, too often, that otherwise sensible businessmen are so taken up with the technological issues involved in e-commerce that they completely forget the basic common-sense rules upon which business and commerce are founded. They seem so blinded by the complexity they find that they stumble around, becoming so involved in discovering and exploring the new that they lose sight of fundamental values.

This gives rise to yet another paradox: the ways of the Industrial Age don't work in the Information Age, but success in the Information Age must be based on the fundamental concepts of the Industrial Age.

In the last chapter, we saw how complexity was approached by the developers of applications for the Apple Macintosh computer. They ignored the complexity of the whole and concentrated upon the components. One by one, they assembled individual functions into a self-designed, interacting framework: creating a dynamic combination which lives happily within the complex environment of a Macintosh operating system.

Similarly, with young children learning a natural language, they create their own word constructs and are oblivious to the complexity of the language as a whole. They build up a personal understanding and organization, one component (word) at a time. Children, like the developers, create their own individual interface and build into the complexity; not to understand it but to interact with it. The individuality of this process is evidenced by the many different vocabularies and choices of words and phrases used by different people to communicate with one another, even when they speak the same language.

In both cases, the problem of dealing with complexity is solved by ignoring the whole and piecing together parts: integrating the combinations into a self-made complexity built from the bottom upwards. The strategy seems to be that of identifying modular units and putting them into custom-built structures: off-the-shelf components, assembled together for a purpose. Doesn't it make sense to apply this strategy to e-business and e-commerce?

Let's start by broadening the paradigm to include not just business thinking, but thinking in general. The human brain is a dynamic and complex system, so we ought to be able to apply the paradigm to our thinking processes.

Consider for a moment the proposition that human thought and thinking consist of an assembly of related concepts and rules. Although thoughts and thinking processes themselves may not be fathomable, the isolated modules of concepts and rules, of which they consist, are usually quite distinct and can be dealt with in isolation. Thoughts and thinking can then be considered as personal selections of suitable modules. These we combine in an interactive way, giving rise to the vast complexity that we know as thinking, understanding and knowledge.

This gives us a way of understanding how we use the brain as a tool without having to comprehend the whole of its complexity. We can view the brain as a collection of modules that can be put together for specific purposes. This modularity allows thinking strategies to be highly versatile and adaptive: constructs that can be consciously modified by adding or deleting different rules and concepts. It allows us to rapidly adjust our thinking on the fly, simply by recombining modules: the rules and the concepts. This is how we normally cope with a changing environment.

We don't have to know anything at all about how the brain works, we simply present it with different modules consisting of ideas and rules and the brain produces conclusions for us. If the conclusions turn out to be right, we retain the knowledge of the combination of modules that produced those conclusions. If the conclusions prove to be wrong, we can feed in some more information and reconfigure the modules to enable the brain to produce other conclusions.

Applying this modular thinking to Information Age problems, we can think in terms of reconfiguring basic rules and concepts rather than having to start from scratch. This will involve isolating some of the key fundamental components of traditional business strategies and applying them in new ways to e-business and e-commerce.

This is what we shall be doing in this second part of the book, diving into various specialist areas of the Industrial Age and picking out the building blocks so that we can use them in a different context. This can be likened to children playing with Lego. Most of the Lego my children obtained came as presents that consisted of small, pre-assembled Lego structures: a helicopter, a boat, a castle, etc. After a short while they disassembled these ready-made structures, cannibalizing them to make something new.

This is what we have to do now to adjust our thinking for e-business and e-commerce. We have to cannibalize the techniques and methods used in the Industrial Age to extract key elements that can be used to create new strategies for the Information Age.

There is no particular order to these universal fundamentals, so I'll describe them as I first came across them and then we can see how they now relate to the new age of information.

Searching for a strategy

Despite some successes and quite an interesting and varied lifestyle, my early entrepreneurial activities hadn't produced any real understanding. Everything seemed to have happened too much by chance. It was hard to see how skill had anything to do with getting a start into an entrepreneurial way of life. Apart from the simple strategy of talking to lots of people, getting into different situations and taking the opportunities when they arose, there seemed to be little that had to be learned. There was nothing that my scientific background could seize upon as a mental model to use to go about being an entrepreneur in a more efficient or purposeful way.

Searching for this ephemeral knowledge, I decided to study marketing. I wanted more than just a 'be an expert in a month' depth of knowledge so I spent several months in the library in High Holborn, London, going through the marketing books there. Libraries in London have areas of speciality and at that time the library in Holborn was the library specializing in books about marketing.

Three conceptual models from those months of study stand out in my mind. Together they form a conceptual framework that I have used successfully for many different types of communication strategies. They apply particularly well in the environment of the Internet. Keep them in mind as you read through the next few chapters.

1 Advertising only to suitable clients

Before going into that library, I'd thought advertising and marketing were about getting an advertising message across to as many people as possible. By the time the three months were up I'd realized that advertising and marketing needed to be narrowly targeted to achieve the maximum effect and efficiency.

All advertising or marketing messages have to be carefully designed to reach and to appeal only to the people who are likely to benefit from any service or product being marketed. Appealing to anyone outside this range was not only wasteful but could be deleterious.

Such a requirement needs more than just a general description of a product or service being advertised. It needs to take into account the product or service's strengths and weaknesses. Advertising the strengths is easy; more difficult is advertising the weaknesses. Weaknesses must not be covered up or glossed over. They should be advertised out in front. The weaknesses should be clearly stated because they then act as a filtering mechanism to ensure that you don't get any dissatisfied customers.

Applying that simple criterion to analyzing the strategy of Web sites would see many failing on this count. In the physical world you may be able to get away with dissatisfied customers but in the complex communicating environment of the Internet they could spell disaster.

It certainly does qualify the oft-heard statement 'Content is what it is all about'. How many Web site designs are there that sport novelty or eye candy for the sake of it? How much of the design is aimed at the actual needs of the targeted customer? How much gets in the way of a customer who goes to a site for a purpose rather than to admire the graphics or clever animations?

As Mrs Brisby says, 'Without graphics, you must be amazed by what must fill the void – and that is called content.'

2 One satisfied customer creates four more

The second really important concept that came across to me at that time was a chapter in one of the books which was headed 'Each satisfied customer creates four others'. I don't remember where that figure came from, I'm not even sure if it is accurate or not. What I do know now though – from many years of experience – is that it describes the essence of one of the most powerful and effective forms of marketing: word of mouth.

When you see the eye candy banners and the 'click through' mentality of much of Web site marketing, it makes you wonder whether these people really know what they are doing. It certainly isn't trying to capitalize on the most potent form of marketing on the Internet: the power of 'word of mouth'. If the Internet is suitable for any kind of marketing surely word of mouth (word by email) has to be the number one method.

Yet, so many marketing people seem to be quite oblivious of this and design their marketing and advertising strategies as if they were using conventional, Industrial Age mass media: broadcasting out to the masses. Not surprisingly, this error of judgement is very common with large advertising companies which are applying the skills and techniques they learned from the Industrial Age directly onto the Internet and the Web. As their clients are rapidly discovering, many traditional techniques used with mass media are hopelessly ineffective and inefficient for e-commerce.

As an important corollary to this, I've also heard the saying 'One dissatisfied customer creates eleven more'.

3   The sociogram

Remembering back to those three months, the concept that most impressed me was that of a marketing strategy used by a drug company. They had been spending quite considerable sums of money mailing out expensive literature, sales packs and samples to thousands of doctors on their mailing list and were getting very disappointing results.

Using a questionnaire to try to discover what influenced doctors in their decisions to prescribe particular drugs, the drug company discovered that by far the most influential factor was advice or recommendations from other doctors.

To investigate this clue, the drug company picked an area in the country and sent a team of investigators to call on every single doctor there. These investigators were instructed to try to find out who was speaking to whom. When these results were obtained, the marketing department took a map of the area and drew a small circle on the map to mark the geographic location of each doctor, then drew a straight line between any doctors where a communication link had been established. Such a diagram is known as a sociogram.

What they discovered, when they completed the map, was that the lines radiating out from the doctors varied immensely. Some doctors had lines connecting them with many others, some with only one or two. Looking at the overall picture it was clear that if peer-to-peer communication was a strong influence then the influence was concentrated around a relatively small number of doctors.

Changing their marketing strategy in this particular area, the drug company found that concentrating all of the marketing effort onto only these highly communicative nodes produced far better results than if the marketing effort was spread equally over all doctors.

The computer-enhanced communication environment of the Internet suggests that such a marketing strategy could be effectively and efficiently employed for all manner of products and services. Again, this is a solution involving communication between people and requires very little technological knowledge.

There is a corollary to this. When I lived in London, my family used a doctor who had a practice in the West End. Besides his practice he also spent two days a week as a consultant at the nearby Middlesex Hospital. This hospital is very close to Harley Street: the street famed throughout the world for its surgeons and specialist medical practitioners.

My family doctor, through many years spent attending patients at the Middlesex Hospital, had got to know most of the Harley Street specialists. As a consequence, whenever he found something wrong with any of his patients he could immediately recommend the best specialist for treating their condition. Although only a general practitioner, he effectively had the skills and experience of some of the world's leading specialists.

In essence, this is very similar to one of the busy nodes of the sociogram. The difference is that the doctor is using the connection to other nodes as an extension of his own abilities to provide a service to his patients. He used his network of contacts wisely. He would always refer the patient on the basis of looking after the patient's best interest – which included giving the patient best value as well as the best medical service.

Thinking about thinking

In isolation, these three conceptual models are pretty valueless. Their value can only be realized when they are mixed together with a number of other concepts to form a strategy. To be effective, the concepts must complement each other, forming a multitude of different criteria to base decisions upon.

Marvin Minsky, in his book *The Society of Mind*, writes about the quality of genius. He expresses the opinion that genius can largely be accounted for by what he describes as 'unconscious administrative skills that knit the things we know together'. This can be applied to the idea of selecting conceptual components for a suitable strategy to cope with the Internet.

He reasons that geniuses don't crop up very often because society wouldn't be efficient if everyone mixed what they know around in their heads to come up with individually different, novel solutions. Minsky says that involuntary factors are at work to curb this tendency because a cooperating group is far more efficient if everyone is working along the same lines of thought.

This natural tendency for a group to think in unison is fine when the group is coping with known and familiar environments, but as soon as it encounters an environment where the group strategy isn't working, the group is then open to new ideas. It will be more receptive to group members remixing what they know around in their heads. This is the process that is at work now as the Industrial Age changes into the Information Age. It is probably why the reader is reading this book.

Marvin Minsky describes adaptive thinking as a network of circular activities in the mind: a kind of coming together of a host of mini-minds all working independently but in unison to come up with a solution. He says it is foolishness to ask if any of the individual components of this thinking process are applicable because each in its own way contributes towards a final resolution. It makes no sense to look at any part in particular because its effect on a system's overall performance is too dependent upon the other parts. Like those original Apple Macintosh manuals, no part can be understood without knowing how all the other parts work.

This thinking process of mixing up many concepts, or mini-minds, Marvin Minsky refers to as 'multiply-connected knowledge-nets'. He suggests that the process involved is not so much dependent upon coming up with lots of novel solutions, but using ingenuity and clever tricks to weed out all the nonsense, leaving only the realistic possibilities.

Bearing this in mind, the three conceptual models above are simply mini-minds that have to be put to work. They cannot work by themselves, they'll have to be joined with many others. The trick, though, is to make an appropriate selection of other conceptual models to minimize the number of absurdities that might arise.

As we saw with the Macintosh programmers and the young children learning a language, this process cannot be arranged just by throwing hundreds of things together. It has to be built from the bottom up, starting with a few components at a time and building onto that base to expand upwards and outwards. This is the basis of bottom-up, object-oriented design that we shall be dealing with later in the book.

Here, we've made a random start with a few concepts that relate to communicating. We know this will be as good as any other place to start because the Internet is about communication. We shall now go on to add a few more concepts into this mix and see what evolves. And, please bear in mind that it is unlikely that the concepts we'll be dealing with in this book will give everyone the same conclusions. If that were to be the case, we could have started with the kind of bullet list the Industrial Age academic was calling for.

Chapter 5

Clues from the world of investment and finance

Into the world of the professional investor

Some of the most important building blocks for an entrepreneurial strategy I discovered immediately after the time I spent studying marketing. They came not from the marketing books, nor even from marketing, but from the environment they took me into – the world of finance and investment.

After studying in the library, I thought I'd try my hand at being a marketing consultant. Looking through newspaper advertisements, I began to telephone the advertisers to see if anyone needed marketing assistance. Almost straight away I got a positive response. It was from a company advertising a correspondence course to teach people the art of investment. They told me that they were looking for help because their current advertising wasn't working.

I visited the company, which was located in the heart of the City of London, just around the corner from the London Stock Exchange. They were a firm of investment advisers, managing investment portfolios for various clients. It was explained to me that making a profit on the course was not important as the main aim was that it should be a way of attracting new clients and establishing the credibility of the firm to handle client investment portfolios.

In those days, it was an original strategy. Today, it is the most common form of marketing on the Web: establishing an extensive knowledge base to generate interest and give credibility to a service or product. It is highly effective.

The head of the investment firm explained to me that although they weren't looking for a profit from the course they didn't want it to cost them any money. Their current problem was that it was costing money, because the cost of advertising the course was very much more than they were getting from the sales.

Even applying my limited, recent textbook marketing knowledge, the solution was obvious: either the advertising had to be better or the price of the product had to go up. I suggested both approaches although as far as I could judge the advertising was reasonably sound and unlikely to offer much improvement. This left a price hike as the only real possibility for making the venture viable enough to pay for itself.

As it had been a marketing ploy, the course had been designed to sell for a very low price. Unfortunately, this limited them to producing a very insubstantial product. I explained that if they were going to raise the price to cover the advertising costs they would have to improve the product – otherwise they wouldn't be giving good value. They could see the sense in this because the last thing they wanted was for the course to advertise the fact that they didn't give good value.

My ball-park assessment was that by the time they had paid for improving and supplying the course the price would have to increase fivefold. Although somewhat shocked, they agreed with my textbook solution. I then offered to set out the structure for a new course and they committed to arranging for it to be rewritten.

After the meeting, I went to Foyles, then London's largest book shop, and bought a fully comprehensive selection of books on investment. From just the chapter headings, I could get a pretty good idea as to how such a course on investment should be structured. I then divided this up into 12 lessons and proposed that it be sold as a 12-week course – sending out a new lesson each week.

This was agreed and I got busy on the advertising, which necessitated reading some of the investment books. These I found fascinating. Here was a whole world of new concepts I had never encountered before. I had been vaguely aware of interest and compound interest; I'd known how to calculate probabilities and take risks. What I hadn't been aware of was that these elements could be intricately linked to create powerful strategies to bring order to the uncertainties involved in the world of finance and investment.

I'd always considered the world of banking, insurance and investment to be areas of conservatism, safety and security. I hadn't any idea that this appearance was a mask: a façade that covered a boiling cauldron of chaotic change and uncertainty. It was simply the strategies of the investors, the brokers and the bankers that made it seem as if the worlds of banking, finance and investment were reasonably under control. These strategies were coping with chaos, uncertainty and competition: exactly the conditions prevailing in e-business and e-commerce today.

After about two months, the new lessons for the investment course started to come in. To my horror, they were really badly written. The writers included a university professor, teachers and a financial journalist, but the work was just not usable. They were providing only information and practically nothing that could in any way be described as a strategy that could help an investor to make investment decisions.

We had a meeting to try to decide what to do, at which I proposed that I should take on the writing of the course myself. They were a little taken aback by this because they knew I hardly knew the difference between a stock and a share, let alone how to invest. I then explained that for this purpose I could probably write a course better than an experienced investor. I was interested in the subject, I wanted to learn about it; writing would be a reflection of my learning process. In this way, I could write from the point of view of the student because I'd be one of them.

They saw the logic in this approach and as they were at hand to answer questions and give any assistance that might be needed I was given the go-ahead to start writing the course. This writing was monitored using four readers to work through each lesson as it was being written.

As it turned out, the course was a major success; it even got onto the London Stock Exchange's list of recommended courses. For me, personally, it provided an opportunity to spend a year in a totally different world: the world of investment and finance. More importantly, it enabled me to learn and understand the concepts that constitute the cornerstones of financial decision making. I learned how these were used as the fundamental elements in all investment strategies used by professional investors, brokers and bankers.

The key concepts I found to be: compound interest, discounting and risk spreading. These lead to the essential techniques for converting capital values into incomes (and the converse, incomes into capital values). Getting to grips with the essence of these concepts leads to the understanding of anything to do with finance and investment. As I was to realize later, these concepts also underpin all business decision making.

More importantly, from the point of view of this book, these fundamental concepts of the traditional Industrial Age also apply in the new environment of the Internet. They are the 'Lego blocks' that can provide a bed-rock foundation from which to produce imaginative strategies on the fly, to compete intelligently in the rapidly changing world of e-business and e-commerce.

The enigmatic nature of interest rates

Everyone has a basic idea of what interest is. It's the percentage of the borrowed money that has to be paid each year as a cost for the privilege of borrowing. What isn't generally realized is that interest rates are the smoothed-out average of chaotic activity. Interest rates are a kind of barometer, reflecting the current value of money and the state of the prevailing economic conditions. They are not decided by human agencies.

Many people think that interest rates are based upon some figure that is decided by a central bank or a government authority. This is a fallacy. Government agencies and banks are compelled to make official changes to interest rates by market forces. The basic determinant of interest rates is the current market value of money. This is not constant and is in a continual state of flux. Governments may change their policies to try to have an effect on the level of interest rates, but they cannot control the level simply by changing its value – at least, not without causing all kinds of unpredictable problems.

Money is a commodity and like all commodities its value will fluctuate according to supply and demand. In time of economic expansion, money is in demand and interest rates rise. In times of depression demand falls off and interest rates fall with it. In boom times money can be used profitably and so a lender will ask for and get higher interest rates. Conversely, in times of recession, when profits are scarce, interest rates are low because money cannot be used to create wealth so easily.

Money is available in the form of a large number of currencies. Each of these currencies will have a different value. Each currency value will vary against all other currencies as various different factors particular to each individual currency have an effect. These currency variations will be accompanied by varying interest rates as each currency will have its own fluctuating demand and stability.

All kinds of miscellaneous factors will affect the value of currencies: wars, weather, disasters and catastrophes, political policies, availability of resources, etc. Any number of different factors can affect the value of money and cause interest rates to change.

Just as the current price of any particular stock on the Stock Exchange reflects all the hopes and fears relating to that stock, the rate of interest reflects all the current hopes and fears relating to the value of money. The most well-known example of this is the phenomenon of inflation. Inflation is when the value of money is decreasing. If the value of money looks like going down, interest charges will go up because the cost of the borrowing will have to make allowances for the loss in value of a loan when it is repaid. This is why inflation usually produces high interest rates. The falling value of money has to be compensated for – otherwise it wouldn't be viable for a lender to provide loans.

Considering all the possibilities that can affect interest rates and the value of money, it might be expected that rates and values should vary chaotically. In fact they do, but turbulence is kept in check by the individual actions of thousands of firms and individuals who are competing with each other to take advantage of any chaotic changes that occur. The net result of their competitive strategies is to create a relatively stable financial environment in which all trade and commerce can reliably exist.

This stability is achieved through risk taking. The risk takers absorb the risks associated with change and uncertainty and make charges for doing so. These charges are transparent to everyday business and commerce because they are reflected in the various rates of interest charged.

It is through understanding how risk takers can make a profit by bringing stability to the financial markets that we will be able to work out how to profit in the unstable environment of the Internet.

 ## Discounting for risk

In trying to work out a strategy for e-business it is worth looking at the system that has evolved to deal with financial transactions because there are many parallels and similarities. Both have to deal with unpredictable environments that are too complex for logical analysis. But how do the risk takers handle risks that defy any rational form of calculation?

The solution for investors and financiers lies in a technique they call discounting. It is best described by a scene taken from the CD-ROM 'How God Makes God', where a family group are discussing the meaning of discounting. Here is their dialogue:

'Discounting is a term used in the world of finance. It is one of the most important concepts used in money and finance because discounting a price or value means allowing for risks.'

'By discounting you reduce a price or value sufficiently to allow for any risks involved.'

'It sounds complicated, can you give us an example?'

'Alright, imagine yourself to be walking along the road one day and a brand new Roll-Royce pulls up alongside you. The back window winds down and a wealthy-looking old lady pops her head out. She apologizes for stopping you in the street but explains that she and her chauffeur have inadvertently left home without any money. As it is now too late for the bank she wonders if you would lend her $20. In return, she offers to give you an IOU (I Owe You – a promissory note) for $30 that her chauffeur will redeem first thing in the morning. Assuming you had $20, would you lend it to her?'

'I would probably lend the lady the $20.'

'Now consider what you might do if it were a dirty old tramp that stops you in the street with this same proposition.'

'I think I would give him a few coins and quickly hurry away.'

'Having loaned the old lady the $20 and received her IOU, what value would that IOU have?'

'Twenty dollars? That is what it would have cost me. Or, perhaps it ought to be $30 because that is what I would get for it?'

'Now what about the tramp's IOU? Supposing you had given him the money, even if it had been out of pity, what value would you put on his IOU?'

'Zero, I shouldn't expect to get the money back.'

'Would you just throw it away then?'

'No. There's always a chance he'd pay me back.'

'Would you sell it for $5 then?'

'Yes. If I could find a buyer.'

'Now then, supposing that when you arrived home you picked up the local newspaper and the headlines blazed a story about a confidence trickster who was operating in your area using an old lady and a stolen Rolls-Royce. Also in the same paper is a story about an eccentric millionaire who is living like a tramp. What values would you now give to those IOUs?'

'The values would be reversed. The old lady's IOU would probably be worthless and the tramps would probably have full value.'

'Would you throw away the old lady's IOU?'

'No, I'd probably keep it – just in case.'

'Would you sell it to me?'

'If you gave me my $20 back I would.'

'Supposing I offered you $1?'

'I'd probably take it.'

'Would you accept $30 for the tramp's IOU?'

'I wouldn't, he might turn up the next day and give me much more.'

'Thirty-five dollars then?'

'Yes, I'd accept that.'

'You can all see now how something might have a definite nominal value, but the perceived worth can be quite different. Not only this, the perceived worth can change according to the risks associated with the real value. The perceived worth, therefore, is the nominal value discounted for various risks. Remember, also, the same apparent value might be perceived as a different worth to different people according to the information they possess.'

This dialogue provides the essence of discounting. It is the adjustment made to a value to allow for the element of risk or change. Moreover, it tends to be subjective because every person may perceive the situation differently. It is this difference in perception that brings about variations in price and provides scope for profit.

Probability theory has a mathematical approach to discounting. It assigns a value to the probability of an event occurring. This value is a number between zero and one, such that it can be used as a multiplier to modify the value. If an event is certain to happen it will have a value of one. Thus, if you were certain that the old lady in the above example would repay the loan plus the interest, the IOU would be perceived as being worth $30 multiplied by one equals $30. If there was no chance of the IOU being paid its perceived value would be $30 multiplied by zero equals zero.

Any element of doubt can be allowed for by using a value somewhere in between. If it were thought that there was a 50-50 chance of the old lady redeeming the IOU then the multiplier would be given a value of a half (0.5), in which case the value of the IOU would be a half times $30 – equals $15. An estimate that the chances of the tramp redeeming the IOU might be one chance in one hundred (1 per cent chance) would see the perceived value of the IOU reduced to $30 multiplied by one hundredth – equals 30 cents.

As you can see, where there is an element of doubt or uncertainty, it can be allowed for by reducing the value according to the element of risk. The value is reduced in direct proportion to the risk. This is the fundamental basis of all financial and investment decision making.

 ### Spreading the risk

Estimating and allowing for risk can be seen to be a perfectly logical approach to dealing with uncertainties. But it is only logical if you have some means of accurately estimating the uncertainties. What if there is so much uncertainty that you have no way of calculating the extent of the risks involved? What if there are risks that you aren't even aware exist? This is the reality of complex dynamic systems, especially those in a state of chaos.

In such environments, probabilities and the calculations for the element of risk can be no more than intelligent guesses. Values have to be assigned to probabilities on the basis of experience or common sense. But experience and common sense can also be useless in some environments, particularly in new environments that are subject to chaos. This is the environment of the Internet where rapidly changing technology and unpredictable competitive strategies afford no precise or justifiable basis for attributing discount multipliers to values or outcomes.

At first thoughts, it might seem that there is no strategy that could be effective in such an uncertain environment. Yet we do know that decisions are being made successfully in the similarly uncertain environment of investment and finance. In this environment successful strategies use a technique called 'spreading the risk'. In essence this is about making lots of decisions knowing that you cannot be certain that any particular decision is right but that the aggregate outcome is likely to be favourable.

This is similar to the strategy of the professional poker player who will know that he cannot win every hand but will be reasonably certain that he'll win over the course of many hands. However, the big difference between the professional poker player and the professional investor is that the poker player is able to calculate the chances with a fair degree of accuracy because there are only a few variables and unknowns. The professional investor on the other hand has an impossibly large number of variables, most of which are not calculable and many of which are not even known about.

The professional investor therefore has to have a more pragmatic approach to risk taking which might best be understood from another scene from the CD-ROM 'How God Makes God':

'How is your latest business venture going?'
   'It has gone bust.'
   'Broke again?'
   'Yes. Stony-broke.'
   'You remind me of the professional gambler who keeps losing, and his friend asks him why he still keeps on playing when he never wins.'
   'What was his reply?'
   'He said he couldn't give it up because it was his living.'
   'How very droll.'
   'But why don't you give up the idea of going into business for yourself and get a sensible job?'
   'Because statistically I stand a good chance of being successful in making money even though the odds would seem to be against me.'
   'That doesn't make a lot of sense.'
   'Yes it does. If there are many opportunities and if I try enough times it is highly

probable that I will succeed.'

'If at first you don't succeed try, try and try again?'

'Mock me if you wish, but the way I see it, just trying to start a business venture is more profitable than getting a job.'

'Even if you do not succeed?'

'I did not say failed attempts have value, I said the attempt itself has value.'

'What value is there in an attempt?'

'In a mathematical sense there is a very real value. It is the value of the business if it is successful, multiplied by the probability of success.'

'What is the value of your non-existent business?'

'I base most of my business attempts on building up a business which will be worth half a million dollars.'

'And what is your probability of success?'

'Each time I make an attempt I estimate that I have a 20 per cent chance of succeeding.'

'So how does that give you a value for each attempt?'

'To my mind each attempt is worth 20 per cent of half a million dollars; that is $100,000 a try.'

'But that is not a real value?'

'In a mathematical sense it is very real. Quantum mechanics and the new physics are based upon such propositions and look at their success in making sense of the world.'

'How can you earn money by keeping trying out ideas and not succeeding? You could go on failing for years and years.'

'That's highly improbable. Supposing ten people tried out ten different business ideas each with a 20 per cent probability of success; what are the odds against every single one of them failing?'

'They could all fail quite easily.'

'How easily? Come on, work it out.'

'You are the mathematical expert. You tell me.'

'Ah! This requires a conceptual twist that is not intuitive. This is the calculation that financiers and professional investors use. Try thinking about multiplying the odds of them not succeeding.'

'You mean the odds of them succeeding?'

'No. The odds of them NOT succeeding. That's the trick. If you use probability theory to work out the chances of success by using the probability of succeeding you get the wrong answer because you have to multiply probabilities. This will only allow you to work out the probability of them all succeeding. So, you have to work out the probability of them all failing and take that answer away from one.'

'That's confusing. You'd better explain in more detail.'

'If there were only one man, the chance that he would fail would be four chances in every five. If there were two men, what would be the chances that both would fail?'

'Mmmmmm... That's one of those probability things. You have to multiply the probabilities together. Four-fifths multiplied by four-fifths; let me get my calculator. I make it 0.64.'

'That's right. There is an 80 per cent chance that one would fail but only 64 per cent chance that both would fail. Now tell me the probability of ten people failing, each with an 80 per cent chance of failure.'

'Multiplying four-fifths together ten times gives me an answer of just over 0.1.'

'Yes. The chance that every one of them would fail is about one chance in ten. Now, you can turn this around to say it also means that the chance of at least one of them succeeding will be around 90 per cent certain.'

'A hundred per cent less 10 per cent. That's right, but, what does that prove?'

'Well, isn't this the same as saying that if one man tries ten times he has a 90 per cent chance of succeeding?'

'Even if at each try he only has a 20 per cent chance of success?'

'Yes. He'd be 90 per cent sure of winning through within ten tries.'

'Oh! I see it now. But you are still broke?'

'Yes, but if I make a new try every year, I'm effectively earning $100,000 a year.'

In this dialogue, notice in particular how you have to work out the probability of all failures before you can get the probability for succeeding. This is vitally important for Zen-ness because, if you need to allow for failures, you have to have an idea how many failures you are likely to be able to absorb before you can be reasonably certain of success. This is not intuitive and needs to use this little trick.

The trick was taught to me by a scientist at the research establishment at Great Malvern when I'd been a student. I'd been really disappointed at being allocated to spend three months in his department because it appeared to be the worst possible placing. Everyone else was working on missile control systems, advanced radar projects and I had to spend three boring months testing components. I had to put hundreds of components in heated damp ovens and onto shaker tables for hours on end, then test every one to see if it was still working. How more soul-destroying can life get?

Yet, these three months taught me a lesson that was to be of inestimable value in my entrepreneurial career – because I'd asked a naïve question. I'd asked what was the purpose of the testing. I'd expected the scientist to tell me that it was to help improve the design of the components. It wasn't. He replied simply, 'To find out how many radio sets a pilot has to take with him on a mission.'

I thought at first he was just joking, but he was perfectly serious. It would be disastrous for a pilot to lose contact with base because in those days all radar was ground based and the pilot needed to be warned as to where the enemy were and if they were approaching. Because components at that time were not as reliable as they are today they had to work out how long the radio lasted when the life depended upon the failure of a single component.

If they knew the probability of the worst component failing they could then work out the probability of a failure of any one of many similar components failing. This would allow them to work out the probability of a radio lasting throughout the length of a mission. In certain cases, it was necessary to take two, three or even more where conditions were particularly bad. It was in the explanation of this that the scientist taught me the trick of working with the probability of failures to get the chances of success.

In the CD-ROM 'How God Makes God' I used a nineteenth-century drawing of a mass execution to illustrate this point. It depicted 54 people being hanged on a multi-storey gallows (it was actually from a black humorous cartoon). I'd animated this to allow one of the characters at random to suddenly stop wriggling (he'd died). The game was to keep running this animation and each time to guess which one of the hanging men would die first.

The problem was then to work out how many times you'd have to run the animation and make a guess before you could be 90 per cent certain of getting a right answer. This problem cannot be solved unless you use the trick of using the probability of any of them *not* being the first to die. In the CD-ROM I could animate the formula to show how this calculation was made. In this book I'm afraid you'll have to experiment with it yourself. It is worth the effort though, because it will greatly assist in Zenning winning strategies in conditions of uncertainty, change and competition.

The dialogue of the man discussing his business strategy also makes a number of other important points. Firstly, the spreading of the risk over a number of ventures greatly increases the chances of a success even though each individual venture might be quite risky. From a banker's point of view, the financing of a single venture could be prohibitively risky. The interest return, to cover the risk of an 80 per cent chance of failure, would need to be in excess of 400 per cent for it to be viable to make a loan.

Looking at the financing of ten ventures, if one success could at least cover the cost of ten attempts then the banker would need to discount only 10 per cent of covering the cost of ten attempts. This transforms the financing of risky ventures into a reasonable proposition. Venture capital companies work on this basis. They will risk capital knowing that there might be a high failure rate but those that do succeed will cover the losses of those that fail.

Mapping this kind of thinking across to e-business and e-commerce, it is easy to see how the uncertainties and unknowns of the chaotic environment of the Internet can be allowed for. The risks can be spread across a number of decisions rather than banking on a single one. This applies not just to finance but to time and effort.

In the conventional physical world it is not usually practical to think in terms of multiple projects or multiple approaches to projects. In the world of the Internet this is not only practical, it is the only sensible way to proceed. As already discussed, it is impossible for any single person or even a group of people to have complete knowledge of all the developments that are constantly occurring in the digital communication environment. This means that any company or entrepreneur who invests in a single approach is going to run a greater risk of making a wrong move than those who invest in several.

The final statement in the dialogue between the two men – 'I'm effectively earning $100,000 a year' – would seem to be a nonsense. However, in a theoretical sense that statement is quite correct. The man is effectively earning $100,000 a year. It is not possible to see this as being a truism by thinking solely of this one individual; however, if 1,000 individuals were using this strategy their average earnings would be $100,000 a year.

It is this statistical approach to thinking that will be important in the chaotic environments of e-business and e-commerce, as we shall see when we cover game theory in the next chapter.

Examples of spreading the risk

Let's look at a few businesses where unknowns and uncertainties prevail and see what strategies they employ. The simplest example I could find was my local newsagent. He has a thriving business, part of which is based upon delivering newspapers door to door in the locality. This work is carried out by school children, local teenagers.

Having a teenage son myself and knowing how fickle and unreliable they can be, especially when it involves getting up each day at the crack of dawn, I was intrigued as to how the newsagent always seemed to arrange reliable deliveries. It turned out that the unreliability of his workers was a factor taken into account. He always had an extra boy available and arranged the rounds so that each round could be completed in a fairly short time.

This seemingly inefficient arrangement allowed him to compensate for the known unreliability of his staff. If one boy didn't turn up he had a replacement. If several didn't turn up, the rounds were short enough for him to be able to ask some of the boys to do extra rounds. In this way he could ensure that he could maintain a constantly reliable and efficient service, even though he was employing an inherently unreliable staff.

The arrangement allowed the newsagent to dilute the risk, spreading it over a number of boys. If he'd planned to use each boy in an optimally efficient way – employing just a sufficient number to cover the rounds and giving all of them an amount of work to completely fill their time – any lateness or absenteeism would have seen a breakdown in the reliability of his service. With many unreliable boys involved, this would likely have seen the service impaired almost every day.

If you now substitute boys with hardware, software and elements of a business plan, it will be seen how an e-business or e-commerce strategy will almost certainly break down unless there is sufficient redundancy and duplication built in. A fixed plan with predetermined elements can be likened to a chain: it is only as strong as its weakest link.

Time and time again, examples of e-commerce solutions can be seen on the Web that are totally dependent upon an assembly of predetermined elements built as if every element was an optimal and reliable selection. There is seldom any backup, no duplication of elements, no alternatives to switch into. They are constructed like a chain: vulnerable to any weak link.

There is so much uncertainty and so many unknowns involved in e-business and e-commerce that any planned e-business or e-commerce solution will be vulnerable to failures in the same way as a group of unreliable paper boys. This situation requires a complete change in attitude by those responsible for the design of e-business and e-commerce solutions. It calls for the downgrading of expertise and elitism and the promotion of realism and humility.

Failures and mistakes must be an accepted by-product of a successful strategy. A strategy that does not produce failures and mistakes must be suspect, perhaps designed to underperform. Strategies must assume that every decision could be wrong and backups, alternatives and redundancies built in. It may seem inefficient, but as my local newsagent has discovered, this is the only way to provide a reliable service that will survive and be able to keep ahead of its competition.

Another business that has similar unknowns and uncertainties is the book publishing business, particularly the technical book publishing field. Although acquisition editors try to keep up with technological events as much as possible it is impossible for them to be fully knowledgeable in any particular area. Authors make proposals, acquisition editors make intelligent guesses, sales and editorial teams have selection meetings, but nobody can really know how a book is going to turn out before it is written.

This is particularly true of books to do with computer technology, digital communications, the Internet, e-business and e-commerce. Technological changes happen fast, but the production time cycle for a book starting from its commission to its eventual printing and distribution can take several months. This is a long time in such fast-changing fields.

The publishers' strategy is to gather all the information they can, trying to spot market trends and the directions of technological advances. With whatever clues they can muster they will then make woolly judgements and commission a range of books, knowing that many of them will be failures. They will try to ensure, though, that their selections are such that there is a strong possibility of there being winners among them – enough to show a profit on the whole range.

The publishing industry is well established. It has evolved strategies to cope with unknowns and uncertainties. It is dealing with similarly technologically influenced products as e-business and e-commerce. Shouldn't we be looking here for some clues as to how best to approach e-commerce? It can be observed how the book industry follows trends. It can be seen how, following a trend, one often sees a subject swamped with the publication of many similar competitive titles all coming out at the same time. It can be noticed how rapid changes in technology can so quickly cause books to become out of date – sometimes even before they get onto the bookshelves.

Some books are right on the ball, up to date and complete with all the latest advances. Some are incomplete, missing whole swathes of new developments. How are the publishers to know before the book goes on sale? Even with good technological reviewers, inadequacies are often missed. Yet the industry copes and remains profitable by using a strategy of risk spreading.

E-business and e-commerce have many parallels with the technical book publishing business. The decisions and choices in e-business and e-commerce are similarly affected by changing events, new technological developments and competitor initiatives. Like a publisher's book selection, isn't any hardware, software, technological choice, solution or strategy just an intelligent guess that is made from a position of incomplete knowledge?

The strategy of the publishers is to go for a broad selection of titles. They will not publish a single book on a particular topic, they'll publish several. They keep their initial costs down so that they can produce a variety of possibilities. They stop printing the losers and let the winners run. Shouldn't e-business and e-commerce ventures be approached in the same spirit?

The resolution of some paradoxes

A paradox, as we have already defined, is: 'A proposition or an observance which seems at first sight to be absurd or self-contradictory, conflicting with common sense or preconceived notions of what is reasonable or possible... upon further reflection, or with new evidence or explanation, the proposition may prove to be well founded and essentially true.'

Let's look at a couple of the paradoxes from Chapter 1 and see if we are now in a position to resolve them. First was the paradox of the proposition that 'planning is not appropriate to current e-business or e-commerce'. This was the single most contentious issue when this chapter went out to reviewers. It does seem implausible, even though a distinction is made between a plan and a strategy.

However, plans are not very reliable guides in the world of the Internet. They are subject to all kinds of unreliability problems. We have seen how other businesses cope in this kind of situation. They do so by breaking up the solution into units and then concentrate on the overall effectiveness of the units without relying on any single one. This is also the strategy of the investment manager, who will have insufficient knowledge of any particular stock but will spread the risk over many selections.

On the assumption that the risk-spreading strategies of the investment manager are applicable to the design of e-business and e-commerce solutions, consider the way in which the business of investment is carried out. Think of the relationship between the investment manager and the client. Would you think it appropriate for the investment manager to offer the client a detailed plan – in the kind of format described by the PowerPoint templates? Would it be considered a reasonable request for a client to ask for such a plan?

How can investment managers provide an accurate cash flow projection that is backed up by example and precedence? Could they be expected to detail how they would be switching investment money in and out of different investments over a period of time? Common sense tells you that they wouldn't be able to provide such an undertaking. All investment managers can do is to ask the client to take them on trust and rely on their ability to spread the risks in such a way as to ensure that the capital remains reasonably safe and will earn an acceptable return.

Secondly, it may have seemed preposterous that a corporate plan could be financed without a fully accountable plan that can be monitored for progress all along the way. Yet, this arrangement is the norm when millions of investors place their life savings with investment corporations. The inescapable fact is that when clients allow an investment agent to invest for them they are giving the agent carte blanche to deal for them in an unpredictable, turbulent market. The long-established and traditional procedure is for the clients effectively to say to the investment manager, 'Here is my money. Do the best you can for me.'

Looking at this situation with a conventional corporate attitude, it would seem criminally insane to fund an activity on this basis. It wouldn't be allowed. Can you imagine telling corporate fund managers that you can't explain exactly what you are going to do with the funding you are requesting, they'll just have to trust you? I know what they'd say. They said it to me after I'd explained about the green frog.

Yet, in the world of investment this is the only way investments can be funded. There are obviously too many unknowns and unknowables for the investment manager to be able to make predictions. In fact, an investment manager has no better way of knowing how stock prices move than the client. At least, a good investment manager will not. Every known factor that could influence a share price is already discounted in the price. How, then, can any investment manager know where best to invest? Any particular 'view' an investment manager might take would simply be a gamble and any responsible investment manager does not gamble with client accounts.

This is probably the most remarkable discovery I made during my year in the City. The best investment managers, brokers and bankers were not experts: they were strategists. The relationship between investment managers and their clients is one of trust. This is not based upon the skills of the investment managers to pick winners. It is based upon the ability of the investment managers to act responsibly and apply a viable strategy with the clients' money, providing them with an acceptable return with the minimum of risk – a strategy that is based primarily on the concept of spreading risk.

The strategy of an IT department

Consider the idea of a corporate information technology department standardizing all the computer equipment and programs within a company. Seems sensible at first, until you start to realize that IT people are fallible. No IT person or group of IT specialists can possess total knowledge. It isn't just a question of ability or training, it is the amount of time needed to know all there is to know and to keep abreast of all the new developments and initiatives that affect IT decisions. Knowing even a fraction of this, with any degree of depth, is not a practical reality for even the most gifted scholar.

This means that in standardizing they are 'taking a view': they are gambling. Investing in an IT department that commits a company to a single technological solution is similar to using an investment company that invests in only one type of stock. A single IT solution commits a company to only one interpretation of the rapidly changing events in the digital communication environment. There is no spread of risk to offset any bias or lack of knowledge within the IT department.

Additional to this, in entering the fast-moving environment of digital communications, there is a crucial need for a company to be versatile and flexible. This necessitates that a company can select from a variety of tools and techniques. It must be able to bring many different points of view to bear on solutions and problems. It must be able to choose from a range of options. The traditional Industrial Age's preference for standardization and efficiency is at odds with these requirements.

In this age of information, computers should not be considered as items to be standardized. They shouldn't even be treated in the plural. Computers should be thought of as part of an individual: each treated as a unique extension of a particular employee's ability to fulfil a function. In the Information Age it is not appropriate to think of computers as part of some robotic process. They must be considered as individual enhancements – to people.

Committing everyone in a company to using the same computers with the same programs is the equivalent to decreeing that every person in the company must have identical experience and educational qualifications. Organizations owe their power and strength to the variety of skills and knowledge that can be brought to bear on their business activities. It isn't sensible to curtail this variety. It doesn't allow the company to adjust to the unusual, adapt to changing conditions, seize new opportunities. By standardizing, a company will lose out to other companies which are more likely to have the right people, the right knowledge and the right tools.

Why, then, do so many companies gamble their investment in IT departments which are 'taking a view'? Surely the most sensible strategy in the environment of information technology with so many unknowns and unknowables is to spread the risk. This must entail the employment of a variety of hardware and software solutions. Maybe this does involve more cost, maybe it does mean some loss of control for the IT department, but it is far better than being tied into an inflexible solution that may not be optimally suitable for all parts of the company.

Corporations head-hunt for highly qualified people to run their IT departments. They want them to be experienced and expert in a wide and extensive range of appropriate computer technologies. Is this realistic? Even if there were such people, it is questionable whether this would be the best kind of person to head up an IT department. As good as they might be, it is unlikely that they would know everything. As specialists and experts they would be very likely to take a view on technological issues. They may not want to risk options where they have incomplete knowledge or control. This would limit the technology of the company to the knowledge of the head of the IT department.

Many well-paid technologists are defensive of their knowledge base and feel it a weakness to be seen to be unaware of any new technological developments. They'll often declare a specific preference when they have very little experience of the alternatives. On the other hand, pragmatic technologists will realize and accept the limitations of their knowledge and allow ample opportunity for unfamiliar technology to coexist with their own.

In a fast-moving technological field where it is impossible to know everything, wouldn't it be better to deal with technologists in the same way as the newsagent deals with his paper boys? Allow for fallibility? Assume that they do not know everything and provide cover, duplication and backup?

With the strong possibility that a real expert would take a narrow position, there is a case to be made for a non-expert to run an IT department. If the heads of IT departments knew that their knowledge was insufficient, they'd have to rely on others. They'd have to assume that they didn't know enough to judge whether or not a technologist was competent or expert enough to get a particular job done. They'd then be forced to cover themselves and use a strategy that included backup and duplication. They'd have to employ a variety of solutions because they wouldn't be able to decide which is the best.

With the conventional mindset of the old Industrial Age, this would seem a grossly inefficient and woolly way to work, but it is similar to the strategy of the newsagent who is creating a reliable business out of unreliable paper boys. It is the strategy of investment managers who know that their knowledge is limited and satisfy their clients by spreading the risk. By dividing up the risks into as many different compartments as possible, a non-expert can cover all possibilities and at the same time expose the company to a wealth of different knowledge and option possibilities. This is the way of the Information Age.

The same thinking must be applied to creating Web sites. Who really knows what is the best strategy, the best design, the best software and hardware? A large investment in a single plan is again equivalent to handing your capital over to an investment manager who is going to 'take a view'. There is no justification at all for limiting an e-business or e-commerce project to a single solution.

Why go for a single Web server, when a similar result can be obtained with many? Even an 'expert in a month' philosophy will tell you that there are so many different ways to run a Web site that you'd be crazy to be stuck with a single option. There are innumerable hardware configurations, innumerable software applications that can be employed. Why be stuck with a single choice when it is virtually impossible for anyone to decide on the best possible combination of options to use?

What is needed is flexibility. A system may be more suitably configured if it uses the combined resources of a number of different hosts. A server hardware configuration may be suitable for one part of an operation, a quite different server may be configured more appropriately for another. It is likely to be far more efficient to use several specialist servers rather than to compromise with only one.

An e-commerce project is likely to need a variety of different specialist software packages. Would it be reasonable to expect the optimum of each package to be present at a single location or emanate from a single source? Is it reasonable to expect one person or even one team to make all the right choices? Surely a strategy should avoid the possibility that a project should be shackled to a single rigid solution, or dominated by a single line of thought?

How about Web site design? Here is an area that is totally subjective and is fraught with technological bias. With the large number of possible ways to design and run a Web site it would be totally irresponsible to trust this to a single creative source. There are a large number of Web authoring tools that require highly specialist practitioners. It stands to reason that no one person can know enough about all of the capabilities and limitations of all the different approaches to be able to categorically come up with an optimum solution.

Again, we are coming to the conclusion that it is not about technology, it is about people. It is about combining people's abilities. It is about being aware of their abilities and strengths but taking account of and safeguarding against their limitations. The successful player in the world of e-business and e-commerce will have to play the game like the newsagent – dealing primarily with people rather than the technology.

Chapter 6

Clues from the world of computer programming

 Object-oriented thinking

It is quite clear that any e-business or e-commerce solution is going to need the cooperation and collaboration of a large variety of different kinds of people. They can be grouped into four main categories: financiers, initiators, organizers and technical experts. Although their roles may be completely different they will need to be able to communicate with each other and be aware of each other's strategies.

The strategies of these groups will of necessity have to be quite different. However, they will also have to be complementary. It is important therefore that everyone involved has some common understanding as to the way in which e-business and e-commerce projects develop and evolve. This is what we shall attempt to do in these next few chapters. We'll take a pragmatic look at the kind of problems that are likely to be encountered at the higher levels of structure and organization and try to work out how these may be solved. We can get on to the particular strategies for each of the four categories later.

The anecdote about the school children who are less clever and less talented than their peers but eventually go on to employ them has a ring of truth. The idea of the 'expert in a month' being better able to organize businesses than the real experts is also generally true. The reason for this is simply a matter of available time: how it is used.

To become an expert in any field it is essential to narrow down interests in order to concentrate on the area of expertise. Any time spent learning and working in a speciality area will reduce the time available for thinking and working in others. Choosing not to become expert in technicalities frees up time to be spent either on leisure activities or on a different level of organizational activity.

A computer programmer might spend 60 hours a week puzzling over the intricacies of complex software projects. A graphic designer may spend 60 hours a week creating clever visual interfaces. Not all this time, though, is spent entirely on coding or design; far more is spent on maintaining a level of competence. This involves reading about new developments, learning new techniques, communicating with peers and, most of all, just spinning around all the ideas in their minds. This leaves precious little time for exploring broader issues.

Business initiators and organizers may commit just as much intellectual effort as the technological experts, but confine their research, communications and thinking time to organizational issues. In its own way, this requires a particular kind of expertise. It may not have any tangible or definable form or subject matter, but nevertheless it requires the same dedication.

In the Industrial Age industries, initiators and organizers can acquire a generally clear picture of the broader aspects of business and its organization. There are ample textbooks to study, a host of examples and case histories to learn from. There are many experienced guides and advisers. It is quite different in the world of the Information Age. The initiators and the organizers are faced with a bewildering range of options and there is no wealth of previous knowledge and experience to draw upon.

Assuming that initiators and organizers are not omniscient or do not have superhuman brains, the complexity of choice in the design of e-business or e-commerce systems can overwhelm the ability to think logically and clearly. There are so many different ways in which systems and presentations can be initiated and organized that no single person can even hope to know enough to make a perfect combination of right decisions. This is a problem to be solved.

Initiators or organizers coming from an Industrial Age industry might be so bewildered by the extent and complexity of Information Age technology that they give up on it entirely. More likely though, they will put their e-commerce strategy into the hands of somebody who seems to understand what it is all about: usually a technical specialist.

Stepping back from this situation to see it in perspective, it isn't a very smart thing to do. In the industrial world, would it make any sense to hand over control of the business strategy to a specialist engineer or a research worker? Would it be sensible to leave all the business strategy to an advertising agency or a marketing organization? Yet, this is what seems to be happening over and over again when people with Industrial Age thinking try to get on a fast track into e-business and e-commerce.

How many initiators and organizers are happily giving people without any kind of real business experience carte blanche to design e-business or e-commerce schemes for them, trusting their commercial judgements simply on the basis that they seem to understand some of the technicalities? Many corporations put their e-commerce solutions into the hands of advertising or marketing organizations. These often have no more idea than the corporations themselves and simply pass the problem on to subcontractors: firms of technologists whose business experience is nearly always limited to creating multimedia or building pretty-looking Web sites.

Only too often, the main business strategists of companies lose control of their strategies because they get lost in a profusion of technical detail. In the environment of the Internet all expert technologists, by definition, are narrowly focused. They have to be because each area of speciality requires so much knowledge, learning and thinking time.

The plain fact is that nobody can know all there is to know about a highly complex evolving system that contains so many areas of speciality. Anyone who claims to be able to design a perfect solution for an e-business or e-commerce project is a charlatan. Yet, how many companies have put their trust in charlatans, people who claim they are going to provide them with optimum solutions? How many companies are going to be stuck with inflexible systems that have fundamental flaws? Who is going to be able to try to fix the flaws? The charlatans?

Any pragmatic assessment of the world of the Internet will see that a single, planned and logical approach to the design of e-business and e-commerce solutions must be flawed. It is the realization and acceptance of this that must be incorporated into a design strategy.

Here is an email I received from a correspondent, Ebidie Hacker, who had recently been hired by a large advertising company which had come to realize that their reliance on technical experts was getting them nowhere:

> I run around, learning, playing with all kinds of new toys, spending their money, experimenting, making mistakes, and they pay for it, and pay me to do it, and the more audacious I get, the more they want to pay me.
>
> Think about it – why would one of the biggest advertising companies in the world want to hire me to give them an efficiency procedure? I am a high school dropout, an ex-rock musician. Great credentials.
>
> The oddest part of all is that I do a good job. But I sure as heck scare the hell out of my bosses – because they do not understand how I work. The way I work also looks like chaos until the end, when it all miraculously comes together – but that is the plan. I lay a broad foundation and take risks at the same time.

This email speaks volumes. It tells of an Industrial Age company at a total loss as to how to cope with e-commerce. They bring in a person who in normal circumstances they wouldn't give the time of day to, yet this person has a down-to-earth, pragmatic approach that is achieving results.

Where then does this leave the initiators and the organizers? How are they going to be able to apply their expert knowledge of business strategies when they are out of their depth in this age of information overload? In the world of computer programming they have found an answer to this seemingly intractable problem. They call it object-oriented design (OOD). It comes in two quite different flavours: top-down and bottom-up.

Top-down, object-oriented design

First we'll take a look at this from an abstract point of view, then we'll get on to the examples. Top-down, object-oriented design was originally conceived as an answer to the ever-growing complexity of computer programs. With the demands of the military, aerospace, and the many other large industries that were exploiting the use of computer technology, computer software systems were becoming impossible to visualize. As computer programs began to run into hundreds of thousands, even millions of lines of code, modifications became ghastly nightmares and even the smallest of faults or mistakes could become major, expensive problems to solve.

With so much interaction between various sections of the programs it was impossible to track down sequences of events. An innocuous alteration to one small part of a program could have serious repercussions in others. This made modifications and corrections to a large system impossibly difficult. This problem was exacerbated when programs became so large that the programming had to be divided up between several design teams. Then, an alteration by one team could present an insoluble problem for another team when the different sections of the full system were brought together.

A rationalization of the programming procedures saw it as being necessary to separate large programs into parts that could function and be tested quite separately from each other. Out of this was born the programming technique known as OOPS (object-oriented programming systems). This technique allowed the development of highly complex programming environments that could be regulated and controlled.

The essence of top-down, object-oriented design is basically very simple. The idea is that you take a planned system and break it up (decompose it) into separate parts (objects). These objects are connected to each other only by means of communication links. This requirement for communication links necessitates that, for any component of a system to qualify as an object, it must have the means and ability to receive and transmit information.

The key to the success of this technique is the principle of encapsulation; this is where each object must be private to itself so that its internal working need not have to be known or understood by any other part. It is this element that is so foreign to the thinking of the Industrial Age where a preoccupation with standards and control precludes this possibility.

Considering e-commerce and e-business solutions in terms of systems of objects, each object might be seen as a black box that provides functions or services to other black boxes. The functions and services of the black boxes are provided as a response to messages received, the messages being accompanied by any relevant information (parameters) needed to carry out the function. Re-emphasizing, because this is of paramount importance, each black box object is restricted only to communicating with other black boxes. It cannot make alterations or interfere with the internal workings of any other black box.

Taking this principle outside of the technical context of computer programming would see black boxes as being ordinary everyday things like people, companies, departments, contractors, subcontractors, Web sites, computer programs, manufacturing processes, advertising agents, servers, shopping carts, electronic shopping malls, credit transfer software, programmers, graphic designers, etc. Any of these things can be considered as black boxes that can communicate with each other but not alter or interfere with each other's activities. Any e-business or e-commerce solution can be decomposed into a communication infrastructure and these kinds of black boxes.

Confusingly, things that are called objects in the everyday world, such as a Web page, a piece of artwork, an animation, a field of text, etc., are not considered to be objects in an object-oriented environment because they cannot communicate. In an object-oriented environment they are called components. Such components can only become objects if they are combined with an object that can communicate. Thus, an artwork isn't an object but an artwork combined with its artist is an object.

The concept of object-oriented design can be very difficult to grasp without seeing several different kinds of examples, so we'll start by decomposing the business of the newsagent into black boxes. The newsagent's customers need not be aware of the complexity of the newsagent's strategy to provide them with newspapers. To them, the newsagent would simply be a black box that they could instruct to deliver newspapers to them each day. They don't know or care how this newsagent black box arranges this service: they just want it done. In his turn, the newsagent would see his customers as black boxes, each of which could fit into a component that was a newspaper round. He'd think of all of his delivery boys and girls as black boxes and he'd assign these to specific newspaper rounds in order to turn each round into a black box.

Having made these assignments into black boxes, the newsagent can forget details. He can arrange his delivery service at a higher level of organization where the names of the customers are not relevant. He doesn't have to know whether or not the delivery boys and girls have new tyres on their bikes or whether or not they've had breakfast before they come out. It's not important whether they are boys or girls. Paper delivery boys and girls can all be considered to be black boxes that each have a statistical ability to carry out a part of a procedure that allows the newsagent to provide a reliable newspaper delivery service to his customers.

As simple as it seems from this example, it is not easy to decompose systems into appropriately sized black boxes. It is not easy to see how they can be linked only by means of communication. For this reason we'll now go through several other examples so that many different ways of applying this thinking can be appreciated. It is vital to do this because object-oriented thinking is going to be as important to communication age strategies as hierarchical structuring was to the Industrial Age.

Let's start with a technological example to illustrate the principle of encapsulation: that all-important and necessary characteristic for all objects in an object-oriented environment. Imagine an e-commerce solution that involves a database. The database will contain some formatted or catalogued collection of items. It will also incorporate software that will be able to communicate with other software. It will include software that adds to, subtracts from, or modifies the records in the database. It is thus completely self-sufficient: it is an object.

Object-oriented design specifies that no other objects will be allowed to make changes to this database. If changes need to be made they cannot be made directly by any other part of the system. Changes have to be specified and sent to the database object as the parameters of a message so that the database's own software can make the necessary alterations to the records.

In this way, a software object, acting as a database, will be like a factory stock room complete with a stock room manager. The stock room manager will not let anyone go into the stock room to take components away or add components to the shelves. A responsible stock room manager will make sure that all deliveries go through him and he is the only one able to put things on the shelves. He'll also make sure that if anybody wants something from his stock room they have to ask him to get it for them. In this way the stock room manager is in complete control and will be able to ensure that his stock room is kept orderly, and he will always be in a position to know what is in stock and where it can be located.

Similarly, another software object might be responsible for the information that goes onto a computer screen. This is the object's function. It keeps a record of what goes on screen and no other objects are allowed to alter or change the display at all. If another software object performs a function that requires a human observer to be made aware of something, the object must send the necessary information to the object that is responsible for the screen display and not make its own alterations to the screen.

In many respects, an object-oriented system acts like an old-style unionized factory where each type of worker is restricted to their own union's range of responsibilities and not allowed to encroach upon the responsibilities of others, i.e., only electricians would be allowed to do electrical jobs even if it is something as simple as changing a fuse. In the industrial world of high efficiency, such a restriction might seem ridiculously petty, but in the world of objects it is crucially important.

Object-oriented techniques in the world of computer programmers

Most readers will not be computer programmers, but if they are to be involved at all in e-business or e-commerce they will have to have some kind of superficial knowledge of the ways in which programmers work otherwise it will be difficult to see how programming fits into the overall scheme of things. That would be a severe handicap. For this reason we'll now take some examples from this speciality area so that the non-technical reader can see how it can be understood without the need for any serious technicalities.

In the world of computer programming, as the advantages of object-oriented thinking began to be more fully appreciated, the parts into which a system could be divided started to get smaller and smaller. Groups of people could become smaller, more focused. Even individuals could work on sections alone.

This allowed single programmers to work independently, creating their own little software modules that could be designed without having to know what other programmers were doing. All they had to do was to make sure that their modules responded adequately to the messages being sent to them. In this way, individual programmers didn't have to know or care what the whole system did or indeed what any other parts of the system were doing. All the programmer needed to know was what was happening in his or her own private module when it received a message.

Such a modular system allows each programmer to specialize in a particular area of programming. The programmer responsible for creating the database module, for example, could concentrate all his or her knowledge and expertise solely in the area of database technology. A specialist database programmer wouldn't have to worry about or need to know about monitors or display techniques or any other specialist areas; other specialists could specialize in these and make a far better job of it.

In this way a vastly complicated program can be designed where all kinds of speciality skills and knowledge are required without any programmers having to improvise and design in areas where they are insufficiently knowledgeable. Thus each separate part of the total design can be covered by an appropriate and professional expertise.

Breaking up a large software system into discrete and isolated modules (objects) has the added advantage that any faults, bugs or mistakes can be confined to a specific module. They are easier to locate and rectify. In most cases, only the code of one single module will need to be examined to find a particular problem.

As each programmer realized the advantage of working in modules they began to divide their own modules into modules. On a smaller scale, they could have the same advantages of being able to easily locate bugs and make adjustments and alterations. They also discovered that certain modular parts of their designs could be reused in other modules they had to design. Gradually a whole new approach to designing software began to evolve.

 ## At the system level

There are two, even more significant, consequences that have come out of this new way to design software. Firstly, as the OOP system is designed within a messaging framework, the messages can be intercepted and redirected to new modules. This allows faulty, redundant or outdated modules to be bypassed, isolating them from the main system. The intercepted messages can then be redirected to a replacement module that is fault free or to an updated version of the original.

This is somewhat similar to the way in which complex equipment like television sets is designed. The design of a TV set splits the electronic circuitry up into plug-in modules. This means that when a fault occurs, the person responsible for repairing it doesn't have to spend time checking all the circuitry for the fault, but simply locates the fault to a particular module and then replaces the module. As it usually costs more to track down the fault in a particular module than to buy a new module, modules are treated as disposables and simply thrown away when they develop a fault.

This attitude of treating system modules as disposables can also be applied to software objects in object-oriented systems. Moreover, there is not even a need to remove the old modules: messages can simply be diverted around them. In this way the modules can still be ready to be reconnected if the replacement module isn't working properly. Also, a simple switching arrangement can allow switching between the old and the new modules. This leads to switching between different kinds of modules to allow the system to react differently to different situations. Simply by including message switching objects, which respond to messages, systems can become intelligently flexible, adapting to environmental stimuli simply by re-routing messages to appropriate alternative modules.

This modular system of communicating objects also provides a simple way to change, modify or improve the system itself; new modules can easily be inserted into a finished system. This is typified by the plug-ins that are used with Web browsers. Here, new software modules tap into the browser's internal messaging system and give the browser new or extended capabilities.

What this seemingly innocuous change in design strategy has accomplished is to allow complex rigid and inflexible systems to become highly flexible. Systems can be built that can easily and inexpensively be changed or adapted to cope with any new situation, specification or environmental vagary.

Out of the hands of the technical specialists

The second important consequence of object-oriented programming was that it took the main system design out of the hands of the technical specialists. Designs could be managed at a higher level of organization: a level not cluttered up with technical detail. Systems engineers could concentrate on the larger issues of system design with no need to be technically proficient in the finer aspects of computer programming. As long as they had enough knowledge to be able to communicate sensibly with speciality programmers, they could treat projects simply as systems of communicating black boxes.

Unfortunately, the birth and evolution of object-oriented design occurred mainly in large, traditional Industrial Age corporations, where hierarchical management structures were still in vogue. It was anathema to treat the programming and the modules as black boxes in a literal sense. Managers wanted to look inside, have a say in what went on in the black boxes. Corporate dogma required procedures and standards. Managers looked into the boxes and wanted to see how they were coded. They wanted neat and formalized layouts, with approved coding conventions. The black boxes had to conform to regulated, top-down structured design specifications.

In this way the full value of object-oriented design was lost; the technique was compromised. The regimentation and standardization broke the most important principle of object-oriented design that all modules have to be encapsulated: insulated against any outside interference.

The usual reason given for standardization and design regulations is that somebody else at a future date may need to be able to look at the programming to see how it works. Somebody else may have to change or alter the code after the programmer has left the job. It all seems so perfectly reasonable to the thinking of an Industrial Age. But in terms of object-oriented thinking, it is sacrilege. Nobody other than the original designer should ever be called in to repair or change a module in an object-oriented environment once it has been created. If it isn't working it ought to be discarded: not changed or interfered with. This is a very hard principle for the mind of the Industrial Age to accept.

So, instead of object-oriented techniques freeing up programmers to do whatever they wanted to do in their black boxes, they were hampered with rules and regulations. The elegant simplicity of object-oriented programming strategies was corrupted and turned into a complex and inhibiting procedure.

 ## What is an object?

Industrial Age thinking sees objects as things to be fully understood and controlled. Information Age thinking doesn't know or care how objects work. Objects are just sent messages and they are expected to respond appropriately. If objects don't respond properly, they are eliminated, or messages are diverted to bypass them.

Industrial Age thinking separates an object from the object's creator. Information Age thinking sees the creator as part of the object. This is the key to understanding the difference between the various approaches to object-oriented design.

Most people who have difficulties in coming to grips with the concept of object-oriented thinking are usually stumbling over the definition of an object. An object is hard to conceptualize because it can describe literally anything. This is one of those complexity problems that can completely blank out the mind. With an infinite range of objects, it is not possible to think of any single example that would be representative of all.

The trick, though, is to concentrate on the definition and not on any particular example. The definition of an object is elegantly simple: it is anything that has a boundary, a function and can receive and transmit messages. The function can be anything you want it to be. The ability to receive and transmit messages is understandable. The only enigmatic quality of an object is its boundary. This can be thoroughly confusing until you appreciate that objects can combine with each other to form virtual objects.

The boundary of an object is described by the functions and features you want to give an object. For example, a piece of software that stores data can be called an object: i.e., a database object. Such a database object is designed to communicate with the operating system of a computer. However, a computer that has database software can also be called a database object. It is a virtual object because it is made up of two other objects: the database software and the operating system.

This virtual database that includes a computer and a computer operating system could then communicate with a human: a human object. The human need have no knowledge at all as to how the database communicated with the operating system; the human would just see a computer with which they could communicate to obtain information.

Someone asking the computer operator to get data for them from a database wouldn't care how the computer operator communicated with the computer. In fact, to them, the operator represents the database: the computer operator would simply be a single object that could be seen as a database object.

In a company providing a service to supply information, clients will see the company as a virtual object. They simply communicate with somebody in, say, the information department, make a request and the necessary information is returned without them having to know what objects are involved inside the company to get the information to them.

The internal messaging goes to and from the internal objects: the software, the operating system, the computer operator, the person who communicates with the client. All this is transparent to the clients. They will not know or care what the name of the computer operator is. They will not care if it's a happily married woman or a drug addict. They don't know or care what kind of computer is used or the type of database software. The clients are solely concerned with how efficiently they can get their request for information fulfilled by the one single virtual object: the company.

This is what is so enigmatic yet so powerful about object-oriented systems: boundaries are flexible and can exist in different forms with different combinations of objects. Even more enigmatic and powerful is the way objects in a virtual object can be arranged to form new virtual objects without changing the original virtual object.

This is not as confusing as it sounds. For example, any company can be considered to be a virtual object made up of people objects. The company can thus be considered to be a virtual object made up of other virtual objects: the departments. Now imagine this company to have a bowling team. This bowling team can also be considered to be an object that is made up of people objects taken from different department objects of the company object. In this way virtual objects can exist in many different forms composed from the same set of objects.

It is this ability to metamorphose objects into different conceptual configurations of virtual objects that gives object orientation its power and versatility. This, as we shall see, makes object-oriented design ideal for devising solutions for e-business and e-commerce. The structures and constructs can be built as systems of interacting modules that are reconfigurable and replaceable. Each of these objects and virtual objects can then be dealt with in the same way that the newsagent deals with his paper delivery boys and girls. They can be arranged to be dispensable and replaceable.

Object-oriented thinking allows you to analyze and construct systems at several different levels of organization. It allows you to break up an e-business or e-commerce solution into hierarchical patterns of virtual objects, each of which can be further decomposed into more basic objects.

In this way the design of a Web site, for example, needn't be considered as a single project. It can be considered as consisting of myriad independent objects that fit into a communicating framework. This would allow the decomposing of a site into a group of interacting and communicating servers that are run by different groups that are physically separated, even separated by oceans and national boundaries. The trick is to think of the servers as virtual server objects that each consist of the hardware, the programs and the expertise that can be tapped into.

An object-oriented software product

Before moving on from the technical area of computer programming, let's use it a little more to see what effect it has on the programmers themselves and the system designers who have to organize the work of the programmers. Bear in mind, though, that what is being applied here to programmers can be mapped across to any area of technical expertise.

A computer software system can be visualized as little modules of computer code, each designed by a different programmer. Expanding the boundary of each of the software objects, you can visualize each object as a virtual object consisting of the code and the programmer: together forming a complete virtual object separate from the rest of the world but connected to it by communication links.

Treating a programmer as part of the object that he or she designs would allow the system designer to be able effectively to speak to the objects (via the human part of the object), telling the object what function it had to do when it received messages from other objects. Any non-functioning of an object, or alterations to its performance, could be discussed on a human-to-human level. This then describes a system that consists of objects with two levels of communication, one at the programmed response level, the other at a human-to-human level.

With such a system, a system designer doesn't have to be concerned with any technical low-level detail at all. The designer can treat each object like a black box that needs to perform one or more functions within an interacting system. If there is a problem the system designer doesn't have to worry about the cause of the problem, he or she just informs the human part of the object to fix the problem so as to respond appropriately to messages from other objects. It either works or it doesn't work. If it doesn't then the complete object should be eliminated from the system in some way, if necessary along with the programmer.

The advantage of taking the principle of object-oriented design literally, applying it to the programmers as well as to the modules that they design, is that the programmers need not be part of any regulatory regime. The programmers needn't conform. The programmers can be free to concentrate on speciality areas of programming where their services can be made available to many different system designers.

This also frees up the system designers, who will not have to worry about setting and checking details. They would be able to select programmers only on the basis of the kind of modules they needed and how well they did their job. They wouldn't have to worry about the styles, knowledge or competence of the programmers that created them. This attitude is not a product of the Industrial Age, it is particular to the very different Information Age: the age of communication.

For the programmers' part, they can work more efficiently, supplying a better product because they can concentrate all their efforts into speciality niches instead of having to be a jack of all trades and master of none. They won't have to spend time superficially learning some new field as they change around to different aspects of the product's design. Probably they might spend much time experimenting with new techniques or even in new areas of expertise, but in the professional application of their skill and knowledge they can confine themselves to the areas where they are truly expert. In this way they can build solid reputations for themselves based upon effective and efficient professionalism that ensures a job well done and gives good value.

Of course, the Industrial Age way will work to some extent, but this will not be appropriate in the fast-changing, competitive world of the Internet. A designer for an e-business or e-commerce solution who has to work with a set team of improvisers with a limited knowledge base is going to be handicapped when competing against a designer who can call on the services of a large assortment of specialists that can be assembled and configured on the fly. Notice again there is this same emphasis on communication with people rather than on the technology.

Viability of breaking up a project into small objects

In the traditional world of the Industrial Age, it was not practical to think in terms of breaking projects up into small modules. With the limitations of Industrial Age communications, it wasn't possible to call on a wide variety of specialists and hire their services for perhaps only a few days or weeks at a time.

For the technical specialists themselves it wasn't viable to work for many different organizations for short periods because such a way of working would see them needing more clients than they could realistically hope to find. Not only that, most work in an Industrial Age environment usually necessitates a physical presence, restricting a client base to within a fairly local area.

In the environment of the Internet all this has changed dramatically. Most e-business and e-commerce projects do not require the physical presence of the programmers and media creators. Almost all communications can be handled via the Web. Code modules can be transferred as email attachments. Web pages, graphic designs and animations can be demonstrated, discussed and modified by using a Web site as a virtual screen that can be reproduced simultaneously in different studios separated by hundreds, even thousands of miles.

Neither system designers nor specialists will be restricted to dealing locally. Systems designers can have the whole planet to source for technical expertise. Technical experts, for their part, can comb the planet for clients, using discussion groups and personal email contacts to spread the word of the availability of their expertise rapidly and inexpensively.

A suitable strategy for system designers would be to make sure they had scores, maybe hundreds of specialist designers to call upon to meld together into a system of small virtual objects. In their turn, programmers and media designers could endeavour to build up a large number of clients who would occasionally have need of their particular specialities.

All it takes for this to work is for system designers, programmers and media creators to have a suitable communication strategy to get enough contacts to satisfy their needs. Building contact lists is not something that can be done by flicking through Yellow Pages. It takes time. It requires a strategy: credibility has to be established and a word of mouth operation put into effect. Once again it is emphasized that the key to success in the world of e-business and e-commerce is effective communication with people rather than mastering the technology itself.

The Christmas tree light problem

The top-down, object-oriented approach is dependent upon having a planned structure in place. The system has to be visualized structurally in order to be able to decompose it into appropriate objects or modules. This requires that the basic framework, messages and modular functions have to be planned beforehand.

Using the strategy of spreading risk, any problem areas ought to be covered and allowed for. However, the top-down, structured approach has a few inherent problems that it is difficult for even a risk-spreading strategy to deal with. It has to do with the effect different parts of a system have upon each other and the performance of the system overall.

We have discussed above how a system can be decomposed into different modules. For the system – and by that is meant the e-business or e-commerce project – as a whole to perform effectively and efficiently all the modules must be working properly. If any one fails, like the link in a chain breaking, the whole system fails.

Seems straightforward enough: to fix it, you just have to mend or replace the link. However, it may not be that simple. Think of a set of Christmas tree lights connected up in series such that if one bulb fails all the lights go out. To solve the problem you'd have to get a new bulb and gradually go along the string of lights replacing each bulb in turn with the new bulb until you reach the faulty bulb. When the faulty light is replaced, all the lights come on again and you breathe a sigh of relief.

Now imagine what would happen if more than one bulb were faulty. Supposing the new bulb itself was faulty? Perhaps the new bulb and several of the original bulbs are faulty? Suddenly, you'd find yourself with a very difficult problem on your hands. How would you attempt to solve it? There are just too many variables involved; the Christmas tree lights would have to be trashed.

This is the fundamental problem of any structured pre-planned design in a fast-changing competitive environment. If the system doesn't perform properly it may be too difficult to spot where the fault or faults are located.

The perplexity of this problem is delightfully analyzed by a discussion at one of the tables in the virtual café where the reviewers were reading the chapter on risk spreading. The discussion centred mainly around three reviewers.

Chris Heape wrote:

I've taught design students for a number of years now and I try to get them to understand or be aware of the necessity for a design process, when tackling a design project. Apart from introducing them to an awareness of a structure over time, it has been very important to enable them to utilize their world of associations to come up with a richer form or visual world of expression.

This inevitably leads to the description of 'Killing Your Darlings'. That it just isn't sufficient to proceed with a design project if you've got only ONE idea. What will happen if that idea fails?

I've always encouraged them to come up with at least five *different ideas* that they develop parallel to each other in the design process, and along the way to drop the weak ideas and to use what they can to get a final result.

My point is that I've always used as my teaching motivation the notion that the students should touch on as broad a base of their world of association as possible. What occurs to me now, after reading this last chapter, is that what I've been asking them to do is 'to hedge their bets'. To allow the students to *plan for partial failure*. That they give themselves enough areas of potential that they can allow some of these to fail in order to come up with a successful design.

The book is about e-commerce and as chapter after chapter comes in I'm gaining a far greater understanding of the *potential* of this area and at the same time getting a confirmation that my way of thinking can be used within this area. You're making me aware that this isn't an exacting science that I have to learn. No! I can use my own human potential and intuitive understanding to get hold of this new world of possibility and commerce. I can't help feeling that this is where your book will succeed. You're touching other people's intuition and understanding that might be contrary to the up-to-now or Industrial Age's way of doing things, but which now has the potential of being put to use in a fruitful way.

Ben Rollason wrote:

I agree with the concept of stripping away elements, so as not to cloud issues, but sometimes I feel in this sheer compelling simplicity, some of the subtleties of situations are lost. Some of the more fuzzy concepts are overlooked. Swings and roundabouts!

In the last chapter, I found the concepts of success and failure rather black and white. Of course, this is necessary in order to illustrate a mathematical point. But personally, if I were to fail or succeed all the time, I would feel like a great success. The hardest thing of all is to succeed partially... mediocre success. Failure can be a success too, as the entrepreneur in the probability example is pointing out, but you have to fail well enough. The worst that could happen to him to foil his plan, perhaps, would be if one of his enterprises half took off... stick or twist?

Chris Heape wrote:

I do feel the operative word here is compensating. Or trying to compensate for the unknown. I used the term 'hedging their bets' when considering an area of risk that isn't involving such large strategies that, for example, investment companies use on a daily basis. But I feel that the point is still the same. That one starts out on a project or venture with several different fronts, in order to achieve a success, because one recognizes the fact that some of these fronts or paths are going to lead to a dead end. That one actively contributes to one's success by planning for partial failure.

Ben, you wrote 'partial success'. I really feel that there is a fundamental difference. By planning for partial failure, one accepts that, along the way, one can cut away the deadwood or weak parts of a fledgling venture, and this will leave you with a few healthy shoots that can then grow and emerge as a fully fledged business.

By planning for partial success, I feel that it is implicit that one will never succeed fully. Some of Peter's phrases spring to mind: Emergent solutions. A humility of spirit. This I have always felt is at the heart of the matter. That one should have a respect and a humility for the chances and opportunities that present themselves, having set a process going. That one then, with respect for one's original idea or venture, somehow allows oneself to be led/guided along the way whilst at the same time using the new information to forge some kind of successful result. That one pays attention to the solution that is emerging, and not kill it off or put it into a box by some very structured, preordained or wished-for result.

Could one say – planning for a surprise result? Sounds a bit of a paradox, I know. This might sound a bit woolly, but I think it reflects my intuitive sense towards this issue. But that Zen thing springs to mind again. Maybe one has to bring these things up to the surface, examine them, maybe learn them, but then *forget* it all, to finally be able to use what was once a heavy concept, in a light and capricious way.

Ben Rollason wrote:

> The idea of spreading risk has been well argued and is no doubt a good strategy. A gamble that isn't a gamble. Although once it's brought down to the level of hedging your bets, it doesn't seem quite so appealing. One of the issues I seem to remember having been raised at the beginning of the book was how larger corporations can emulate the success of start-up companies, such as Yahoo! Now I don't know a great deal about the history of Yahoo!, but I would guess that they didn't achieve their success by hedging their bets.
>
> What I am trying to say is that there are many sites that will have been started up as a labour of love and end up capturing the imaginations of the public at large in the way that it captured the imagination of its inventors in the first place. Tenacity, vision and single mindedness can suffice where bet hedging may fail (by resulting in a partial success).
>
> As I understood it, at the beginning of the book, the corporates were not totally failing to break into e-commerce, but were simply not flying in the same way that the start-ups were. Perhaps, paradoxically, it is being prepared to fail totally for something you believe in that distinguishes the small start-up success stories from the corporates, for whom simple, quantifiable, financial success is an end in itself. Undoubtedly many, many start-ups did fall flat on their faces. A total failure! Brilliant… next attempt.
>
> The risk-spreading argument also assumes unlimited resources, human and financial. This isn't the case always. I also perceive the risk-spreading strategy as slightly heavy and certain, whereas the start-up mentality is light, capricious and flippant. Perhaps corporations just can't emulate this.

Perry Barile wrote:

> Half-baked success is hard to deal with. Terminate or continue? I think before measuring how successful a success is, you have to predetermine exactly what will constitute success. At what point will this venture be a success? Knowing these things can be difficult. I think experience would play the biggest part.

Ben Rollason wrote:

> My comments on bet hedging were not really a direct response to your posting. I have nothing against the idea of spreading risk at all and I agree the two terms are pretty much the same. It's probably the more prosaic emphasis on the term

'hedging your bets' that prompted my meanderings. Like many things, a small shift in perceptual emphasis leads you along a quite different (and not wrong or worthless) tack. I had forgotten that you had mentioned partial failure, so my comments on partial success were unrelated, but in retrospect, parallel, I think.

Don't get me wrong; I wouldn't advocate planning for partial success. I was trying to say that to me a partial success is more a failure than an all-out, proper, face-down-in-the-mud failure, and hence, something to be avoided. But meanwhile that partial success is an easy situation to slip into and a hard one to get out of. Whether to try to capitalize on the partial success or to fail properly and start again, I suppose is the core dilemma.

I often found that the moment of ditching a partial success, the moment of destruction, turned out to be the most seminal and creative moment. I recall learning to model portrait heads at college and an elderly teacher by the name of Monty who was famed for keeping an eye on students progressing down the wrong track modelling a feature, a nose for instance, in great detail, having got the fundamentals of proportion and volume quite wrong. He would wait a bit and then take great delight in removing the nose in its entirety... Eventually, some of the students would start to pre-empt Monty by pulling the features off their own efforts if things were progressing in an unfavourable direction. A good teacher!

As Perry commented, success is a very hard thing to quantify and to do so, you will probably have to set some measure. I think that success goals would be likely to shift though. In this sense that one's perception of one's own success or failure is likely to move and evolve with whatever unfolding venture one is trying to quantify. I must point out as well that I am not talking specifically about an entrepreneurial experience, never having set up a business. I am talking really about a personal and creative process, but I think there are probably strong resemblances. If I was to set up some kind of business, it would be this experience that I would expect to draw on most strongly.

In rereading your [Chris Heape's] original response to the last chapter, I came across 'This inevitably leads to the description of "Killing Your Darlings"'. If I understand your meaning correctly, I have always found 'killing your darlings' a laudable aim. The ability to destroy the things that you have invested most time and love in. It's hard, but the best cure for the onset of creative inertia.

Again though, I have always found this hardest when confronted by a partial success. Accident and failure have to be embraced in order to succeed. You're right, embracing partial success is not an option. I think perhaps there are moments when one has to spread risk and times when one has to rush in where angels fear to tread. The glue perhaps is the Zen thing. The intuition that tells you when and how to act, when to stick with something and when to 'kill your darlings' and shake yourself right up. At the end of the day, you can own the world's biggest rule book, but without the intuition, it is useless.

Chris Heape wrote:

Whilst making the supper I jotted down these thoughts: this is it!/bouncing back and forth/in and out of intuition/what turns up/chance and logic. Progressing with some kind of rational conclusion is now a little difficult. There is an interplay here. How does one know when to 'kill off a darling'? How does one know when a partial success has to be decapitated? When does one use something from a good idea/venture and then throw the rest out with the bath water?

I feel that this has to do with a back and forth between logical rational thinking and maybe more inspired intuitive/creative thinking. On second thoughts logical and analytical thinking is of course just as creative! One engages both these areas (intuitive thinking and logical thinking) in a creatively strategic plan? Maybe some kind of: creatively-planned-allowing-oneself-to-try-out-mistakes in order to strengthen-one's-initial-goal plan. I find it difficult to very quickly apply deeply rational arguments for these thoughts. That I feel is Peter's job!!!

I feel OK with an intuitive understanding of this way of relating to a development process. I think the most important thing about this way of constructively using risk and intuition is that one has beforehand allowed/planned for several approaches. One has defined beforehand some kind of goal. This allows one's subconscious or world of association to link in/latch on. Allows a series of gates to be opened. One has accepted that within this almost intangible, defined space/railway track, one will accept whatever turns up, relative to the goal that one has *temporarily* set. One has accepted that there will be a series of choices, from a range of alternatives that one has set in motion, that one will have to make in order to weed out the weak parts.

Ben, getting to your point of: 'Whether to try to capitalize on the partial success or to fail properly and start again, I suppose is the core dilemma...' You're not starting again. This is the whole point. You're building, expanding on a sense of movement that you've set in motion. This I think, unless I'm completely off the mark, is what the aspect of *engaging the will to apply risk in a creative and growth e-commerce venture* is all about. One learns so much by what has gone wrong, especially if this has been planned for! This is fundamentally how any creative process develops.

This discussion elegantly illustrates all the problems that occur with top-down structural solutions, even when object-oriented thinking is super-imposed over them. Like the Christmas tree lights, the faults are not easy to isolate. The final arrangement, the solution, may only partially work. It may perform, but only moderately well. It may be filled with modules that are 'special darlings' that are emotionally difficult to remove. A brilliant feature like Monty's nose might be blinding the designer to a fundamental fatal flaw in the main structure.

This is the inherent problem with top-down design strategies. They can work fine if you are working in stable areas of business and commerce where there are few unknowns and relatively little uncertainty. They work fine in areas where there are set protocols, standards, rules and regimentation. These are the conditions of the Industrial Age.

In the age of information, where everything is changing and uncertain, the top-down approach is found to be severely wanting. Here, solutions require the other flavour of object-oriented design: the bottom-up approach. This will be the subject of the next chapter.

Part 3

Abstractions and strategic thinking

The human brain doesn't appear to come as a standard package that works the same way for everyone. Some people have a flair for mathematics, others cannot get to grips with it at all. Some find foreign languages easy to learn, others find them impossible. Some people find talking and discussion easy, others become tongue tied or can't get the words out before the conversation has moved on. Some can write down their thoughts clearly, others have difficulty composing even a simple letter. Some people are naturally good at art or music, others can't draw to save their life or have absolutely no ear for music. Some people have a sense of direction, while others can turn just two corners and become hopelessly disorientated.

Probably humans have evolved this way because it then becomes essential for them to cooperate with each other. Partnerships and groups are formed on the basis of benefiting from each other's special abilities and compensating for any deficiencies. Cooperative groupings are always favoured by the evolutionary process, so it is not surprising that this oddity of everyone having different types of brain has evolved as a survival characteristic of our species.

Bearing in mind these differences in the way brains can handle information, this next part of the book might be particularly difficult for some people to appreciate because it deals with abstract concepts. Apparently, according to many empirical studies (I can't vouch for any of them), less than 50 per cent of people have the natural ability to make abstractions to allow lessons learned in one environment to be transferred to another. I don't believe that this ability is so rare, it's more likely that such methods of thinking are not adequately covered by conventional education (perhaps because teachers are typical of the population as a whole and more than 50 per cent aren't aware of this phenomenon, so are unable to teach it to others). Whatever the truth is about people being able to use abstract models of thought, it does seem as if the ability to use abstractions is not universal.

Generally speaking, the people who can think in abstractions tend to be strategists. Those who can't tend to be tacticians. Tacticians and strategists work well together because tacticians concentrate on developing specialist skills and abilities that are essential for any strategist's plans to succeed. This part then is written with the strategist in mind, who will need to be able to use abstractions and mental modelling to be able to make decisions in the uncertain and complex environment of the Information Age. Tacticians will also benefit from this section because their ability to get appropriate commercial benefit from their particular area of expertise or speciality will also need to use a suitably efficient strategy.

Chapter 7

Growing rather than planning solutions

Bottom-up, object-oriented design

The idea of object-oriented design, splitting a project up into communicating modules, is reasonably easy to understand if it is used with an overall, formulated plan. However, as we saw in the last chapter, with the extreme conditions of uncertainty and competition in the Information Age, using a formulated plan will produce severe 'Christmas tree light' problems.

The only way round this is not to use a plan at all, but to use a bottom-up strategy where a design is grown upwards without any planned way for it to grow. This involves starting with a single module and then creating new modules, one at a time, to add onto the growing structure.

Each new module is designed, tested and completed in a working environment before going on to start the next. In terms of Christmas tree lights, this is equivalent to constructing a string of lights one light at a time. At each addition, a check is made to ensure that they are all working properly together. Only when this partially built string is seen to be working properly is another light added.

The full set of modules is not decided beforehand. There is no overall plan. However, designing without a plan is not a concept that is readily accepted by the psyche of the Industrial Age: it is the antithesis of all corporate thinking. This was apparent in my dealings with the large telecoms company and their academic advisers from the university. The idea of working without a plan seemed to them to be completely crazy.

It does seem crazy, until you realize that a plan, however sensible, cannot take into account any unknowns that crop up, such as emergent effects that appear only when a structure is in use. No plan can plan for these, so you have to have a strategy that allows for these unknowns to appear singly, leaving you room to deal with them before too many get together to make the problem of sorting them out too complex.

Not everyone, though, is confused and disorientated by bottom-up strategies where you create a design without a plan. Truly creative people grab hold of the concept immediately because to them it is just plain common sense. An artist, working in oils, may start out with just a hazy idea of what he or she wants to paint and let the painting evolve into a work of art as inspirations take hold during the painting process. Often, the results are as much of a surprise and delight to the artist as they are to the viewing audiences.

A writer might start with a single character: placing the character into a situation, then, by giving the character random personality traits, visualize how the character might react. The interaction will prompt other randomized characters to be introduced and their interactions trigger ideas for a story line. The writer might well begin with only a starting place for a plot and then let the story develop by itself. Many writers have expressed the mystical nature of this process, explaining that the characters seem to acquire a life of their own and in some mysterious way the story tells itself.

All this is anathema to the corporate minds of the Industrial Age. They cannot imagine a world where you just set the workers free to go off and do their own thing. But there again, it would seem ridiculous to anyone: until they click onto the bottom-up paradigm.

Chris Heape, commenting on the above in the virtual café, put his finger on the problem when he wrote:

> If one just takes the artist for a moment, at his canvas. To a certain degree you're right, Peter, but you also have a very romantic idea of what it is to stand and paint that wretched canvas. It looks at you every morning, in its virgin canvas colour, grinning at you until you make a move. Things move along, and mark after mark, brush stroke after brush stroke is applied and one is reasonably satisfied that one is 'attempting to reach that goal that one set in the beginning'.
>
> But as the whole canvas gets more complicated with each new brush stroke, one is in an *intuitive dance* with the canvas and oneself, balancing each new stroke with THE WHOLE CANVAS of MARKS. Each stroke affects the rest of the picture. No stroke is something in itself. This is a scenario I have obviously been involved in many times and I know is what many other artists have battled with. It is the balancing of many entities into a very subjective harmonic whole.

The way Chris sees the painting of a picture, it does seem to be a frustrating and perplexing process, but this is the very way many people view the creation of an e-business or e-commerce solution. There are too many alternatives to choose from. The possibilities are endless, hardware and software are evolving even as you try to work out the solution. Every new item added increases the complexity. There seems to be no way to approach the problem of design logically.

Yet, the way out of this dilemma is simple, once you click upon the right paradigm. It needs a trick way of thinking that allows you to approach the problem from a different perspective. In this case, the trick is to see the artist as three people: 1) a creator of initiatives, 2) an expert craft worker, 3) a decision maker. It is only when these three different roles are separated out that the problem seems soluble.

Seeing the painting of a picture as a team effort where creative initiators and craftsmen are trying to satisfy a decision maker can break the problem up into three neat categories that can be dealt with separately. The enigmatic problem then comes down to determining what is the basis of the decision maker's decisions.

Once you get into this area you then have to start asking questions about the purpose of the artwork. Is it to please the decision maker, or is it to please the people who will see the finished work: the viewers? If it is being designed to please the viewers this immediately puts a restraint on the decision maker's vision. The vision then becomes the decision maker's interpretation of what the viewers would like to see as a vision.

This shifts the role of visionary over to the viewers and the role of the decision maker then becomes one of interpreting their requirements. The decision maker's role thus changes from a visionary to a communication specialist who communicates the requirements of the viewers to the craftsmen and initiators.

This begs the question: 'Who is now the designer? Is it the initiators and craft workers? Is it the decision maker? Or is it the viewers?' It is how this question is answered that lies at the heart of e-business and e-commerce solution design.

The uncertainty of prediction

The conceptual difficulty in understanding bottom-up design strategies is identical to the conceptual hurdle that has to be crossed in understanding evolution. It is a matter of trying to look across time slices.

The human mind appears to be able to predict the future by extrapolating past and present events. We can do in our minds with the fourth dimension, what artists can do on paper or canvas with the third when they make 3-D drawings. We model the future to simulate future possibilities, events and consequences. What we cannot do, though, is accurately visualize the future when there are too many uncertainties involved.

During the many Internet discussions I've had on the subject of bottom-up design, I've found that most people who have problems with the concept equate bottom-up design with brainstorming or whiteboarding because these techniques are often used prior to devising a fully structured Industrial Age plan.

In brainstorming, everyone is invited to contribute ideas, however unrelated they may seem. In whiteboarding, a group gathers around a large sheet of paper upon which anyone can sketch out their ideas or add to the ideas of others.

Chris Heape describes how he sees them being used:

The principal reason for having brainstorming sessions or whiteboarding sessions is not to my mind just a question of 'to predict outcomes or events'. No way. These are techniques to allow people (myself, my students, and my working colleagues) to access their world of association and to allow them to bring their 'TACIT KNOWLEDGE' up to the surface, enabling them to communicate what it is difficult to put into words and understand the problem in hand. This technique is a brilliant tool to get round the cliché thinking that bedevils the innovative mind. It allows one to *paint* one's thoughts, word by word, onto the canvas of the whiteboard, in order to find some kind of sense, pattern or meaning which allows for the next step or decision, without having to refer to some given plan, but to some initiated goal or attracted towards some goal.

The key here is in understanding that these techniques can only be used to provide initiatives for 'the next step' in the Information Age, because it isn't valid to look any further. Bottom-up design involves a continuous series of short 'next steps' with evaluations and brainstorming at every step. Industrial Age planning uses brainstorming only at the conception of a plan.

When the future involves too many unknowns for reliable prediction, predictions have no value. You have to work only with reality and this means waiting for the future actually to arrive before taking action. This is the biggest paradox of all: that you can exercise reasonable control over a future design by waiting for the future to arrive before taking any action. Understanding this is not immediately intuitive. It is an elusive concept that is beset with paradoxes.

It will need practical examples to enable the concept to click into place. When it does, the understanding arrives, not gradually, but as a sudden transition. Just like learning to ride a bicycle, when you first try to ride you think it is absolutely impossible and then suddenly you find yourself cycling along and wondering why you ever saw it as being difficult.

In much the same way as it is difficult to learn to ride a bicycle from a list of instructions, so it is impossible to try to learn about bottom-up design from an explanation. For this reason, we'll spend the rest of this chapter going through various kinds of anecdotes and examples to bring out the essence of this enigmatic strategy.

The business that designed itself

The secret of utilizing the power of bottom-up design is to think of the product or business as being attracted towards some goal – and you get to set that goal. As an example, I'll explain a bottom-up process that happened to me almost by accident. It saw me owning a string of head shops in all the trendy tourist areas of London's West End. (What are head shops? It was a term used in the 1970s to describe places that sold bizarre and unusual gifts. This was at the time of the flower people, love, peace and psychedelia.)

My speciality at that time was old clothes: clothes from the 1920s and 1930s that were very fashionable with the trendy hippies. I had a successful old clothes boutique in London's Carnaby Street and a chance came up for me to rent a large area in a shopping mall that had opened next to my shop. I split the area up into small trading units and let them out.

When this mini-market opened, I had two empty units. One was extremely small, about 20 square feet (1.86 m²), and the other was around 200 square feet (18.58 m²) but was stuck in the corner with a very small entrance. Not wanting to open with two empty units I decided to run them myself. The small unit was suitable only for small tourist gifts so I went round to a local wholesaler, gave him a few hundred pounds and said to him, 'I haven't the faintest idea what to buy. I've got to set up a small sales kiosk in Carnaby Street, give me what you think will sell.' I added, 'If they sell well I'll be back for more.'

The other unit I decided to make into a really nice antique shop. Most of the buying of the stock for the old clothes shop was in and around antique markets and I'd developed quite an interest and some expertise. I spent a few thousand pounds stocking the unit, making careful selections to build an exquisite range of interesting antiques.

The market opened under the name of 'The Flea Market'. As this was in Carnaby Street, a top tourist attraction, it was immediately successful. Every unit was taking lots of money, except for my beautiful antique shop. Everybody marvelled at it, took photos and said how brilliant it looked. But nobody was buying any antiques.

The weeks went by and although I bought more and more antiques, the shop still wasn't taking any money. On the other hand, my little gift shop was doing really well. I was down to the wholesaler every day to replace the sold stock.

One day, a scruffy-looking Asian trader came into the antiques unit. He showed me some cheap-looking replica swords that had been made in India. They had brass handles and bright red velvet scabbards. He offered to sell them to me and I explained as patiently as I could that this was an antique shop and these cheap imitations just wouldn't fit in. He was persistent and insisted that he left them in the shop for me just to see the reaction. To humour him I let him leave them and as soon as he'd gone I put them into a dark corner where they wouldn't stand out.

At the end of the day I went to the antique shop and to my delight found we'd actually taken some money. 'What did you sell?', I asked the sales girl. 'Those funny swords', she told me.

When the Asian returned, I bought some more swords from him and he showed me some hideous-looking carved wooden boxes. Seeing the look on my face, he told me to try them. 'You'll be surprised', he said. Sure enough, I was surprised, they sold well. When he came back he had some funny-shaped knives and some African drums. I put those in with the antiques and they sold. He brought in brass horns, leather whips, ornamental daggers. Then he brought in incense. In no time at all it was looking like a weird Indian bazaar.

Then the incense attracted a wholesaler of pipes and chillums for smoking funny tobacco. He said they were selling like crazy in the tourist shops. He was right, they did. Other wholesalers came along and supplied me with other items that were selling well in trendy shops catering for the flower people. Soon this unit was taking more money than any other unit in the market. And I hadn't taken any intelligent part in the success at all. The unit had grown on its own.

One day, a guy showed up at the unit and said this was the most original shop he'd seen in London and asked me if I'd like a prime site in a market he was opening in Piccadilly Circus. I jumped at the chance. That was one of the busiest tourist sites in the world. It couldn't help but be successful.

Soon, I was going every day to wholesalers getting stock. I still couldn't judge for myself what would sell or not sell. So, apart from stock that had to be replaced, I left the stock selection to them. It was working well, why change the system?

Then, other people approached me to open units in their markets. I soon had units in all the main tourist centres: Leicester Square, Oxford Street, Kings Road, Kensington High Street. In no time at all I had a mega-business taking thousands of pounds a week. Yet, it seemed to me I hadn't really done anything to create it. It had just grown: from the bottom up.

Although at this time I'd never heard of object-oriented design strategies I was forced into treating all these units like objects. It was impossible to organize the stock properly. There was so much and of such a variety that any kind of stock control or inventory check was impossible. To make it worse, all the units were run by unsavoury characters. They were mostly foreigners who had come to England on the pretence of studying.

If this choice of staff seems strange, you have to take into consideration that these were central tourist locations and were open till late at night. Sensible and respectable people would not work in such an environment and I had to hire anyone I could get and these were the people who were not suitable to take regular jobs. They were the flotsam and jetsam that hung out in busy tourist areas.

As it was obvious that these characters were not particularly loyal and certainly not scrupulously honest, I had to accept a large amount of pilfering. I couldn't check the stock, there was a lot of shoplifting, so any kind of control was out of the question.

Taking a pragmatic view, I decided to leave well alone. I told them I trusted them and didn't even pretend to check up on the stock. I left them to cheat me as much as they liked. This probably sounds ridiculous, but although my staff were pretty unsavoury they were all intelligent and streetwise. They knew I couldn't check up on them but they also knew that they wouldn't last very long in their lucrative jobs if their units were making a loss. So, they had to exercise some discretion as to how much they stole and had to work really hard at selling to cover up their pilfering. Any who overstepped the mark were removed immediately.

The system worked really well. The way I looked at it was that I had units that were producing a profit. I didn't have to get involved in how they worked because I had keen, conscientious staff who were working to cover up the extra money they were taking from the business. I employed somebody to get the stock from the wholesalers and deliver it to the units and my sole job was to go round each day to collect the money. All I had to do was to make sure that the money I was paying out was less than I was getting in.

Now it may seem that this has nothing at all to do with e-business and e-commerce, but in fact it is a better model to work from than any you'll find in any business college textbook. It illustrates what can be seen happening on the Web all the time: starting with a fine-looking solution that is inappropriate for the environment; the initial reluctance to have any changes made to 'a darling' even though it is patently obvious it isn't working. It shows how just by being in an environment can allow an efficient solution to be grown without any need for creative input from the designer. It shows how humility pays off.

If system designers, or solution providers, can subdue their opinions and biases they can let other, more expert people provide the initiatives. In this way a project is not led from the front with a super-mind making all the decisions;

the project leader can take a back seat and let the project find its own way.

This example also shows, like the newsagent example, how a group of seemingly inappropriate people can be brought together to run a successful business. Sure, the business seemed to be running inefficiently, but it was working. Maybe I was being ripped off, but the bottom line was that the people who were ripping me off were working hard and efficiently and with a lot of motivation. But there again, were they really ripping me off? Weren't they deserving of a fair share of the profits? Were they not in fact doing all the work and giving me a share for setting up the business for them? It's all a question of getting an appropriate mindset that you can feel comfortable with.

Without knowing it, I'd employed a bottom-up evolutionary design strategy to create a business and used an object-oriented structure to maintain it. The business grew of its own accord, ran itself. My part in it was simply collecting the money.

The follow-up to this business is even more telling. I sold it to a company who decided to run it along more conventional business lines. They introduced inventory controls and checks. They got rid of all the streetwise sales people who were weeding money out of the till. They employed a buying manager and advertised for respectable sales people, selecting them from CVs and interviews. Within six months the business had collapsed.

Taking a pragmatic look at the environment of e-business and e-commerce, there are many parallels. Most of the really good programmers and media creators I know look just as dishevelled and unsavoury as the people I employed to run those units in London. They have CVs that would put off most conventional employers. Yet, given the freedom to work how they like, when and wherever they want, they can really come up with the goods: probably a whole lot better than any graduate with a string of qualifications who is shackled and supervised within a cubicle of a large organization.

Starting in the kitchen

An example of a bottom-up strategy that occurs by accident rather than design does not have the same credibility as one that is carried out by deliberate intent. We shall see a real-life, intentional, bottom-up strategy in the next chapter, but before going there, we had best take an intermediate step and create an artificial scenario that highlights the main features contained in a bottom-up strategy. We'll do this by taking a look at a hypothetical Industrial Age structure that is normally designed top-down, and perversely approach the design using a bottom-up strategy.

The building of a private house provides a good example of a top-down, Industrial Age design process. Before plans are made or the building work started, the design of an individual house is given much thought. The client discusses with the architect his or her preferences and special requirements. Together, the architect and the client go through many design possibilities. This might involve making numerous sketches, looking at photographs and drawings of other houses.

After lengthy discussions and considerations, the architect will draw up detailed plans. These may be modified several times by the client before final approval. Once the plans are finalized, the architect will order all the necessary building materials and arrange for suitable contractors to carry out the construction. This is the classic procedure of a top-down, structured design strategy.

In sharp contrast to this, a bottom-up design strategy wouldn't start with any plans at all. It would assume that the client would be the only one who could judge how best to build the house. The client would be given all the initiatives and made to push the building through at every stage. The architect would take a back seat, providing expert services only when they were needed by the client. As unlikely as this situation may seem, it is the optimum strategy for designing e-business and e-commerce solutions. It is about letting the customers or the clients design the products for themselves and the experts being on hand to help them get what they want.

In the real world of house building, such a way of working wouldn't be efficient or practical. The last thing a firm of architects would want is for clients to be around at the building stage, telling them what to do and changing things around all the time. So, to use a house-building metaphor to explain bottom-up design, it is necessary to step outside of reality for a while and just imagine a world where practical considerations do not matter. Such a way of thinking is constantly necessary for making the conceptual jump from Industrial Age to Information Age thinking.

The hypothetical bottom-up, house-building process may start with the potential house owner selecting a building plot and appointing a firm of architects. Onto this plot the architect would build a front door and construct a temporary structure to be used as a bedroom so that the client can move onto the site straight away. The equivalent, for a Web site construction as part of an e-commerce solution, would be to put up a temporary home page.

Next, the client might decide on a size and a position on the plot for a kitchen. This may be a logical starting point as eating is going to be essential whatever kind of house is being built. The client would then instruct the architect to arrange for the kitchen to be built while she – we'll assume it's a female client – organized for the various kitchen equipment and other kitchen items to be brought in.

The key point here with this strategy is that at this stage the kitchen is physically built without having any definite ideas about how the rest of the house might be designed or constructed. The client moves in and starts to use the kitchen.

Individual items in the kitchen wouldn't be left to the architect. The client would want to hand-pick those herself from different speciality suppliers. All the various electrical equipment she'd use in the kitchen would also be chosen without reference to the architect: just plug-in modules obtained from the most appropriate sources.

In this isolated kitchen, the client starts her cooking and as different needs and ideas arise she adds to the kitchen: decorations; micro-wave oven; sinks; refrigerators; and various other types of kitchen equipment and utilities. She might add tables and chairs and other furniture, install lighting, plumbing and electricity (yes, these will come after the physical construction in this way of doing things). If the kitchen starts to feel cramped, no problem: just move the walls back to make the kitchen larger. Ceiling too low? Increase the height of the walls. Cooker doesn't match the refrigerator and the washing machine? Change it. Need an extra sink? Move everything else along and put another sink in. The client doesn't compromise the way she works in order to adapt to a pre-planned kitchen: she makes the kitchen adapt to suit her.

Before moving on to other rooms in the house, the client would want to make sure everything in the kitchen works satisfactorily. She'd make sure there were enough plugs and sockets; sort out all the plumbing, etc. In this way the client could complete this segment of the house so that she'd be free to think about the rest.

This strategy is equivalent to isolating a few of the Christmas tree lights to get a small group working before moving on to check out the others. A whole string of Christmas tree lights with several faulty bulbs would be impossible to get right, but starting at one end with a few, getting those working first before adding another small group of lights to test, makes the problem solvable. It is also the equivalent of the viewers designing the painting. The architect may be quite an expert at house design, but that isn't relevant because the house has to be built for the client's convenience and comfort, not as a theoretical product created in the mind of the architect.

We might consider at this juncture the question of who is the designer of this hypothetical house. Is it the client or the architect? Who are the craft workers? Who are the instigators? Who is the decision maker?

The roles are not clear cut. The client seems to make most of the decisions, but there will have to be other decisions made that the client hasn't the technical expertise to make. It seems that the client is making all the initiatives but where do the ideas come from? Most likely many of them will come from the architect. Who does the actual building work? It won't be either the client or the architect, it will be given out to various contractors and subcontractors who will be under the direction of the architect.

It can be seen that the design and building work are being carried out simultaneously, all within an environment of constant interaction and communication. In the world of real bricks and mortar this would be chaotic, but the equivalent situation in the environment of the Internet can be coordinated quite easily and efficiently within a suitable communication framework and strategy.

This is the way bottom-up design works. It may seem inefficient in the world of bricks and mortar, but it is the only way to go with e-business or e-commerce projects where a plan may contain too many different ways for the system as a whole to go wrong or underperform.

Having got the kitchen sorted out to her satisfaction, the client could then start to think about the kind of dining room she would like to be serving into. Now in this imaginary world of house building, there is no overall plan so she can look at the design of the dining room quite separately from the kitchen. There is no reason then why she shouldn't have a different architect for this part of the house. Maybe she chose the first firm of architects because kitchen design was their speciality. Why not choose another architect for the dining room: one that specializes in dining rooms?

With no overall plan, it will be the client herself who'll be the judge of how well all the rooms work together, so it isn't necessary to have everything under the control of a single architect. Spreading the designs of different rooms over a number of architects also makes her less vulnerable to any single specialist. She'll not know how good an architect is until after the house is finished, so, like the newsagent and the investment manager, she will be far safer spreading the risk over several architects.

Using another specialist architect then, the client would have a dining room built onto the kitchen, fitted out with suitable décor and furnishings. She'd then invite people around for dinner. She'd see how it went with her kitchen and, if necessary, make improvements or adjustments to one or other of the rooms. She'd discuss with her guests how well they liked the décor, the furniture and the way the kitchen works. This may lead to further changes or improvements that she could pass on to the appropriate architect.

She could even get the architects into a joint conversation with her. They'd not be in competition because they'd know each was a specialist in a different area. Maybe she'd invite them both round together to have dinner with her, her family and guests. Who knows what fresh ideas they might bounce around together?

After being satisfied that the kitchen and dining room were working out, the client could then think about the lounge. She might want to use it for entertaining her guests after a meal and also for relaxing in the evening to watch television with her family. She'd then engage a new architect whose speciality was lounge design. When the lounge was finished to her personal satisfaction she'd invite her dinner guests into the lounge after the meal. She'd see how this worked out, taking her guests' comments into consideration to make any necessary changes or alterations. More comfortable chairs? A larger room? A fireplace? More heating? No problem, just inform the lounge architect to make the changes according to the needs as they are revealed.

She'd then spend some time in the lounge with her family. She'd see how this worked out, listening to their suggestions and arranging for the suggested alterations. She'd invite in more guests. If the changes made by the family didn't work so well with a room full of guests, no problem, she'd just build another lounge that was more suited for social entertaining. If two groups cannot be satisfied in the same room, why compromise? Build two, then both groups can be optimally catered for.

The bedroom? Perhaps the lady and her husband couldn't agree on design and décor. That's okay, they'd each have a separate architect and build two. They could then try out each of their separate designs and pick the one they both agreed was the best. The children's playroom? So many possible alternatives and the lady has no idea which is best. The solution? Get half a dozen architects each to build different playrooms and let the children decide by seeing which playroom they spent the most time in.

All different kinds of needs would come into her mind as she created her house. It would grow in an unpredictable way. If it started to feel awkward or messy, she could just scrap parts of the construction and remake them; if necessary, she could scrap a whole room and bring in another architect to make another. In this way, the design would evolve into her perfect house. It would evolve out of her having ideas; using many different specialists; satisfying needs and necessities; trying things out to see if they worked as expected and seeing if they worked well together. Unlike a house designed in the conventional way, she does not have to adapt to a finalized plan.

Let the imagination stretch a little further. Imagine that instead of doors she could install the kind of transporters used in the Star Trek science fiction television programme that can send people instantly through space to a new location. Why would she then need to have all the rooms in the house on the same plot? Why not have the kitchen looking out onto a white sandy beach with palm trees? The bedroom situated on a mountainside with panoramic views? Why not have a reception room situated near a main road with ample parking that would make it easy for guests to visit? With travel only a transporter click away, the rooms in the house could be spread all over the planet.

All these things are possible in an imaginary world of house building, but they are also possible in the communication environment of the Internet. Expensive? Inefficient procedure? Well, it's not expensive if it leads to a flexible e-commerce system that sees you a leader in the field. And it could turn out to be a far less expensive solution than a top-down structured plan that leaves you trailing the field with the business performing poorly on the Internet.

Now, let's once again consider those design roles. Who now is the decision maker? Is it the client, or the client's guests and family members? Is the role shared with one architect or with many? How many people are involved as instigators? How many different types of craft workers are involved? This surely would be a nightmare situation in the real bricks and mortar world, but all connected through a suitable communication network they could interact to gradually shape the ideal structure.

As bizarre as this building scenario seems, it is exactly the way many e-business and e-commerce solutions will have to be constructed in the Information Age. Experts and specialists cannot make full and complete plans for whole systems without quite considerable risk. Fast-changing technology and increasingly sophisticated business and marketing strategies will make conventional Industrial Age-type planning too prone to error and mis-judgement. Above all, the clients, customers and users will take a major part in the design process.

A serious communication problem

The difference in approach between Industrial Age and Information Age strategies creates a serious communication problem when Industrial Age thinkers have to use Information Age technology. The most serious problem is the acceptance of a degree of ignorance.

In the worlds of Industrial Age business and commerce, it is possible for specialists and bright executives to have a reasonably complete knowledge of all the technicalities their professional roles entail. They can justifiably claim to be experts. This is not the case in the world of the Information Age. All specialists, executive managers and experts have incomplete knowledge. This unavoidable state of affairs is very hard for Industrial Age planners to come to grips with.

Having written two technical books on multimedia programming strategies, I am considered to be somewhat of an expert, even among some of the experts. The truth is that I feel completely fraudulent in this role. My narrow area of technological knowledge has thrust me deep into the world of the experts and, far from allowing me to feel knowledgeable, it makes me feel woefully inadequate. My expertise in one area has exposed me to all the other expert areas that I know little or nothing about.

This came home to me after a meeting of Web-building specialists that I attended at the offices of a major player in the IT world. A few of us finished off the day with a few beers and a chat at a local English pub. Immediately the conversation became quite technical as the specialists began to talk about some of the practical issues involved in creating Web sites. I could only barely follow the conversation, particularly as they kept using the initials of the various software techniques and programs they were dealing with.

I expressed my awe at the amount of expertise that they all had. To my surprise, everyone else had the same feeling: they were all in awe of each other. The ensuing conversation revealed that everyone was aware that they were existing in a make-believe world where everyone had to pretend to know much more than they really believed they did. Once this came out, some amazing stories started to be told. Sales people agreeing designs with a client and instructions going out to designers, only to find all kinds of problems occurring after the product was delivered. Inferior products being delivered based upon the fact that the client wouldn't know they were inferior.

They told stories of high-flying companies that had gone from start-up to employing a hundred or more designers and programmers in just a few months, their managers living in a constant state of nervous tension because they were swamped by all the technological problems. They talked of the difficulties in getting competent staff and the ridiculous amount of knowledge being asked for by some companies in the CVs of applicants.

The head of a technical division of a large e-commerce solution provider told of his interviewing techniques. 'You know they can't have all the knowledge they claim to have in their CVs', he said. 'I place them in three categories. The first is when they come in and tell you they find it easy to write in all the computer languages and can use all the technical authoring tools with ease. Every technical issue you ask them about they will tell you they find it easy. The second type is where every special area of technicality you ask them about they tell you it is too complex for them to handle. I go for the third type, who come in and readily admit they are not very proficient in the technical areas you ask them about but have read about them somewhere and seem to want to expand their knowledge in those areas.' This developer told us he didn't take any notice of what people told him they could do because everyone lied; he was more interested in their approaches and attitudes, looking for those who appeared to be keen and interested in exploring new avenues.

All gave similar stories of a world where everyone was in a constant state of incomplete knowledge; where people learned on the job, the management driving by the seat of their pants to fulfil impossible client expectations. Most surprising of all, nobody seemed convinced that any of the projects they had worked on was in any way a commercial success for their clients. They all agreed that the vast majority of e-commerce success stories seemed to be coming from the entrepreneurial start-ups that had built into a situation. Rarely did they come from the kind of clients who pre-planned e-commerce solutions and then contracted out the plans for the technologists to build according to the instructions.

This was confirmed by my friend Ebidie Hacker, who was called in by a leading advertising agency in New York to sort out a Web site for a Fortune 500 company. He wrote, telling me:

> ... this guy throws me into a site, OK it's a tiny, eight-page site and it is all templates, pre-designed. But there was nothing there! There was a vague, inconsistent idea and a couple of pieces of badly written copy on paper. That was the site. To help me they assigned one part-time, oversensitive, unprofessional copywriter who not only tried to do things his own way but at one point actually changed and deleted my edits!
>
> I had one part-time coder who had a full-time day job. I hired him because my boss said I needed a part-time coder! It turns out I didn't need a coder because the coding doesn't happen for another month, what I needed was a layout graphics person. So the coder tells me he can do it, no problem, but it turns out that he really can't!
>
> So I am trying to convince the client that everything is under control and cool, when in fact it is a nightmare! But somehow I am making my deadlines and deliverables and getting good work out of these people. I also hired one more person in the very beginning on one day's notice to bail me out because no one had told me when I got on board that there was a deliverable in two days!
>
> My boss had told me that her production manager would be doing the production so I wasn't very worried, but guess what? She was on some emergency priority project and I was left in the cold. My part-time coder, turned art director, said he would hire a part-time graphic designer to help him out, and that he had someone, so I relaxed. Guess what? He never hired her! Last minute I hire someone, on one day's notice, to bail me out again. I get the guy and it is all set up. Well I tell my boss and she forbids me to work with him because she happens to know him and hates him!
>
> The coder quits – right before a deliverable to the client! I would have been completely screwed and thrown off the project. I use every bit of charm and psychological insight I can muster and convince him to see me through that deliverable and then leave. He is completely stressed out.
>
> Anyway, I could go on... but you get the idea. I never once complained or

blamed anyone at all. I said everything was going fine and I just pulled it all together by sheer will power and by working insane hours.

Ebidie's email describes the way many highly respected companies are handling Information Age projects for clients. There is now a huge industry grown up on the back of the hysterical demand to get into e-commerce, mostly feeding on ignorance. Businesses are targeted and offered routes into the Information Age. High pressure salesmen will get a company interested in the possible advantages of Web sites.

They seldom talk about a strategy for the core business, they'll talk about a Web site as if they were going to build a broadcasting station for the targeted company. They'll provide examples of stunning graphics, clever animations, interactive shopping and ordering systems.

Once they have the client hooked, they can hit them with all the technicalities:

- Ftp facilities for clients to download animated demonstrations, information brochures, demos and software
- Software for streaming audio and video support
- Utilization and supply of special server plug-ins
- Intelligent database management systems
- Software that generates Web pages dynamically
- Sophisticated customer service
- Programs for handling a growing and rapidly changing product catalogue
- Software for customer tracking
- Software that will identify repeat customers
- A system for remembering a specific customer's buying patterns
- A method of targeting particular customers with appropriate advertising and special offers
- Facilities for running manufacturer audio and videos
- Secure ordering software
- A search engine
- An encryption scheme

- Programs for presenting and processing forms
- Custom-designed CGI scripts.

The list can be endless. Sounds impressive, doesn't it, yet all this information can be obtained from the Web. I got it from some excellent white papers written by Bruce Baikie, Strategic Alliance Manager, IP Network Services, SunTelco, Sun Microsystems, Inc. These papers explain in simple language all you need to know for an overview of server technology, Web hosting and Internet service provision. The papers were written to assist software and hardware buying decisions for Web hosting and Internet service providers, but they also provide an excellent sales pitch for the less than scrupulous e-commerce solution providers.

When the client sees the impressive list of technology that needs to be brought to bear in building a commercial Web site, they will be in awe. They will be convinced that having a Web site will take them into the big time. The more money they are charged, the more sure they will be that this expenditure will take them into a new big league that only the big hitters can survive in. After all, who but the big players could afford to harness all the technical expertise necessary for building a Web site? They'll willingly shell out obscene amounts of money to get into this game.

The problem is, in shelling out all the money, the Industrial Age accountants will want to see a solid plan to justify the expenditure. So, they are given a plan: a string of Christmas tree lights. It looks pretty, but they are seldom warned that there may be quite a few faulty bulbs when it is delivered. More often than not, they end up buying an expensive can of worms for their money. Instead of a cash cow they get a money sink, an expensive folly that is continuously eating up funds and producing very little in the way of actual business results.

Those items listed above are only some of the more obvious divisions. Less obvious are the subtleties involved with the types of server facilities that might need to be taken care of. Decisions have to be made about:

- the amount of server disk space required;
- system backup facilities;
- record storage and analysis;
- bandwidth;
- special server scripts and dedicated programs.

It may seem logical to pre-plan these factors but there are too many areas to get wrong, or worse: slightly wrong. Like the lady with her bottom-up house building, these decisions are best made one at a time, while a system is up and running.

Compounding all these problems will be the reality that people visiting a Web site will be using a huge variety of computers to access the site. They will be using different browsers, different versions of browsers and different computer operating systems. To attempt to provide for all these inherent difficulties and at the same time run a credible marketing strategy puts the most complex of Christmas tree light problems into the shade. If the system underperforms, who will be able to put the finger on what is going wrong? Where do you look when everyone is putting the blame for underperformance onto others?

The uncertainties involved in e-business and e-commerce make it absolutely essential to have the hosting facilities as flexible as possible. With the rapidity of technological change it would be folly to be locked into one set of hardware or a single hosting solution. The server hosting can be divided up between a number of server hosts. Even though it may involve different hosting companies separated by continents, the separations will only be a link click away and totally transparent to clients or customers. Like the lady building her house with transporters, why put all the rooms on the same plot?

Trusting the design of a complete system to a single contractor runs the risk of being stuck with them for at least a very long time. Who'd want to look into the complexity if the system underperforms? A company could be dead in the water before they have either the courage or the finance to replace an inferior consultant or contractor.

To be totally realistic, nobody should expect anyone to be able to plan a complete e-commerce solution. It needs a risk-spreading strategy. E-commerce projects have to be put together one module at a time. The modules have to be duplicated and given to competing specialists so that the best of a choice can be used. Like the newsagent's paper delivery boys and girls, all experts and contractors should be easily replaceable and expendable.

This needn't apply only to large installations. In an e-commerce talk group, a student, Katy Cartee, described how her Internet service provider had tried to bump up the charges because her site had become so busy and was using too much bandwidth. She'd explained how she'd overcome the problem by taking advantage of the free Web space being offered by some promotional companies.

She'd used her main site simply as a portal, a front door that contained links to all her free sites. These contained the bulk of her site content, spreading the bandwidth over a number of different free servers. Like the lady building the imaginary house, Katy was no expert. Here's an email from her when she was reading the draft chapters of this book in the virtual café:

Well, I'm reading this from an entirely different perspective than most of you I'm sure. I'm a college student and have had no experience of the workings of businesses. But I have been around the net (or the 'digital world') for almost three years now and many of the points made are very real. Things are changing at an incredible rate of speed!

I started out on the Web chatting and surfing my way around it – back when the net was still quite young. From there I became interested in making my own Web page. It started out very simply as a fan site (of 80s' cartoons) and continued to grow for two more years until it was a huge archive of pictures, sounds and information.

I was getting so much traffic that I was forced to disassemble it and spread it around several servers! I looked at other 80s' cartoon sites on the net, and wondered why they were not encountering the same problems as me – and the fact is, they weren't moving fast enough. I started out with simple wav files of theme songs for people to download. But as soon as I became aware of RealAudio technology, I researched it and put it into use on my site.

It seems that most people see a technology like RealAudio and think, 'That's too complicated or expensive… I'd never be able to do that myself' and don't even try! And so they stay in the 'dark ages' of the www. In the world of e-commerce, you have to take chances… and you have to realize that you don't know all there is to know. You have to be willing to seek out new technologies and implement them.

I like the idea of starting out with a green frog and seeing what it turns into. That's essentially what I did with my site – I started from the bottom. When I began, there was NO way I could have known what it would be like two years from then. If someone had come to me and said 'In two years you're going to be utilizing a scanner, digital camera, and RealAudio technology', I would have responded: 'What are those?'

There's no way you can 'plan' for those kinds of changes. Like you said, you start out with something simple, then change it as your desires and needs change. I guess the only thing to watch when using this strategy is to be careful of letting it get out of hand – or too 'messy'. That's another problem I ran into. Since I started small and kept building on top of that, by the end it was so extensive that you could easily get lost in it. But part of that was just that I didn't have the time to sit down and think about its organization too carefully – with a business, I'm sure you'd take the time.

Katy's approach is the way all the pathfinders are leading the way on the Internet. They are not planning. They are just getting onto the Web and building upwards and outwards. They are learning about new things by looking at other Web sites, other e-business and e-commerce solutions. If something looks interesting and they don't know how it is done they ask on an Internet discussion group. Almost certainly they will be able to get answers, or referrals to Web sites where answers can be obtained. And, if required, be given contact names and email addresses of relevant experts and specialists.

At first sight the technical complexity of an e-commerce project may seem overwhelming. But is it? Consider the scenario of the client building her house using a bottom-up design strategy. She doesn't have to have any technical expertise: all that is handled by experts. She doesn't even have to make the decisions and choices. These are made for her by the observations she makes and by listening to friends and family. All she has to be pretty good at is communicating with people. But there again, so do all the other people involved in the project.

Chapter 8

Abstract models to think with

 Directing a bottom-up design process

As the astute reader might have realized, this book has been written using a bottom-up design technique. It wasn't planned: it evolved. As each chapter was written, it was passed on to several groups of review readers to read and comment upon during the time I was writing the following chapter.

In the ensuing discussions, it quite often happened that one or other of the readers would seem to anticipate the content of the next chapter. This chapter is a case in point. When I had just completed writing this chapter and before sending it out, one of the readers, Yvan Caron, a senior systems analyst from Canada, sent in the following post to his group of reviewers. I was quite surprised because in some ways it provided a short, sharp summary of what I had just been writing. Here is Yvan's post:

One of the things that I have noticed in reading Peter's new book is that he did not address specifically the never-ending project syndrome.

In reading this book the corporate mind will fear that without very specific plans, IT overhauls can easily zoom out of control. When *snip* Insurance Inc wanted to replace a system that collected data from third-party administrators, it was expected that the project would take three months to finish. A year later, the project was still far from complete, and the company undertook a major reassessment. The conclusion: it would take another three months.

If you think this is unusual, think again. The never-ending IT project has become a staple of corporate America. 90% of projects exceed their deadlines. Not surprisingly, at least half of all IT projects go over budget, and almost as many are eventually abandoned altogether.

Why does this happen?

There is no single reason why IT projects so often run out of control, but one explanatory phrase has taken on some notoriety in this regard: 'scope creep'. This is an insidious disease that takes hold when the scope of a project slowly and almost imperceptibly increases in size. There's no deliberate pattern here. The designers simply ask to be given, say, a particular set of tools or technology licences; after getting them, they ask to add on features. Sometimes, without anyone noticing it, expectations change, goals change, technologies change, and the project keeps stretching to accommodate all these changes.

The corporate mind says poorly defined objectives can also be a serious obstacle to the successful completion of a project. Without a concise and comprehensible set of objectives, the project keeps going and going. There tends to be a lack of structure about what the up-front goals of the project are. There are unclear expectations on all sides.

There are some corporate minds, however, that are willing to do whatever it takes to avoid a never-ending project, including what is called a 'ready–aim–fire' approach. First, on any given project, you ascertain user needs and wants and define a set of very specific objectives. Then, you devise a quick solution, usually deliverable within three or four days, sometimes even a day. Users then provide immediate feedback, and IT does an almost instant redesign. The project goes back and forth between IT and users, until the users are happy. This is what could be called 'fast-paced solution building'. In today's technology environment, even the most innovative design will become obsolete in the near future. If the solution becomes obsolete or is inadequate in some other way, it can quickly and efficiently be brought up to snuff.

What particularly appealed to me about this post was that the last paragraph had neatly summed up a strategy that I'd taken this whole chapter to explain. What Yvan calls 'ready–aim–fire' and 'fast-paced solution' approaches describe in a nutshell the bottom-up approach to designing e-commerce businesses. So, if you have any difficulties in understanding this chapter, when green frogs and throwing marbles into a field are mentioned, just refer back to this last paragraph of Yvan's post.

The most perplexing problem for top-down thinkers to grasp about the bottom-up approach is the seeming lack of direction. Many don't see how a process that is allowed to evolve freely can home in on exactly the right solution without random wanderings. This is another of those paradoxes where the resolution is not easily seen until you click upon the right idea.

> **The counter-intuitive reality is that the bottom-up – the 'ready–aim–fire', or fast-paced solution – actually achieves its goal more directly than any carefully planned and controlled approach.**

The counter-intuitive reality is that the bottom-up – the 'ready–aim–fire', or fast-paced solution – actually achieves its goal more directly than any carefully planned and controlled approach. It is the top-down, procedural approach that is vulnerable to directionless wanderings, or 'scope stretch' as Yvan calls it. In this chapter we shall see why.

In the book *Magical A-Life Avatars* I likened the process of bottom-up design to a strategy for finding a small hole in the middle of a large field. The key is to have an observer, or a means of feeding back results to modify a process. To find a hole in a field, imagine that you use ten marbles. From any place in the field you drop the ten marbles. An observer tells you which of the marbles is closest to the hole. You then pick up all the other marbles and drop them over the marble that has been identified as the nearest.

The observer then indicates which of the newly dropped marbles is now the nearest to the hole, and you pick up all the other marbles and drop them over this new marble that has been identified as being the nearest. Repeating this process over and over again must eventually lead to reaching the hole in the field as the route is continually guided by following the marble that falls closest to the hole at each throw.

At first thoughts, this doesn't make any sense because it implies that you already know where the hole is: the answer to the problem. But that is the whole point: you do know the answer to an e-commerce solution – the answer is that you want to be profitable. You want to move towards profitability. If there are competitors, you want to move to the position where you are more profitable than the others.

This might be less ambiguous if we change the metaphor: using the marbles to find the northern part of the field. If somebody can tell you which of the ten marbles is most northerly you can gradually move the marbles increasingly towards the northern perimeter at each successive drop. This can be more easily associated with moving to a state of profitability.

Now map this across to the scenario of my head shop business in the last chapter. Instead of marbles, think of sales items. The observer, me, identifies those items that point towards the solution I want: profitability for the business. As I keep following in the direction of the items that are proving to be profitable, I am effectively following the marbles that are dropping nearest to that goal.

The paradigm shift is to realize that the designer of the system is not the person dropping the marbles but the observer. The observer does nothing except for noting the results and providing the necessary feedback. In the case of finding the hole in the field, this feedback goes to the person who drops the marbles. Thus the designer, or decision maker, is the one who says which is the nearest marble and the one who drops them is the expert or specialist.

That is the twist. The expert or specialist isn't leading the design. Experts and specialists are providing random suggestions and initiatives. The designer is testing these against some main system criterion and selecting those that seem to be leading to the goal. Now map this across to the picture creation model in the last chapter the observer is the decision maker; the marble-dropper is the initiator; the marbles are the work of the craft workers.

This can also be related to the 'fast-paced solution' described by Yvan Caron. It's analogous to the process he described when he wrote: 'Then, you devise a quick solution. Usually deliverable within three or four days, sometimes even a day. Users then provide immediate feedback, and IT does an almost instant redesign. The project goes back and forth between IT and users, until the users are happy.'

Now you can extend this model to have one observer (the system designer) with ten people who are dropping the marbles (the experts or specialists). The observer can give them all feedback – telling them which of their marbles is nearest – and allow them all to converge on the hole. The marble-dropper who gets there first will be the most expert, or the expert that was nearest to the hole (the solution) from the start.

This begins to make sense if you think of all the marble-droppers as being somewhat eccentric. Imagine one to have bad eyesight, another to be a bit deaf, another to have a twitch, another not to trust the observer's judgement, another to do the opposite to what the observer indicates. The observer (the designer) won't know these things and will just be aware that there are ten marble-droppers (experts) working on the problem and, unless the designer is very unlucky with the choice of experts, can be reasonably confident that one of them will eventually locate the hole in the field (or the northern perimeter fence).

Notice that the observer (the designer in this system) does not have to be involved in the marble-dropping activity at all. All the observer does is to make an observation after the action and then communicate. The order of events is: 1) Action; 2) Observe; 3) Communicate.

Relating this back to my head shop business, it can be seen that the business was able to design itself because of the role I was able to play as the observer: the non-participating designer. This, as I explained, happened accidentally, so it may be clearer if I describe another personal experience where I used this technique deliberately as a calculated strategy for design.

Strategy in the world of high fashion

It wouldn't seem that business strategies in the world of high fashion had much relevance to the strategies needed for businesses in the Information Age. Yet there are some startling parallels. Known as the 'rag trade', the industry involving high fashion and designer clothes is as tough and competitive as anything likely to be encountered in e-business and e-commerce. Like the world of digital communications it is an environment of continuous and unpredictable change. Fashions come and go. Trends develop and then quickly disappear. It is the perfect environment for the entrepreneur using bottom-up strategies for design and communication. Understanding the way in which this industry works provides many valuable clues for designers of e-business and e-commerce solutions.

The rag trade can be split into four separate sections: designers, manufacturers, wholesalers and retailers. To see how various entrepreneurial and corporate strategies coexist and complement each other within these categories it is essential to realize that the fashion industry isn't about clothes and designs at all: it is about information. It is about people's need to establish themselves in a social pecking order and associate with a particular social group. Fashionable clothes are communication devices; they make a statement about the wearers, identifying them with a group and their position within a group.

Changing fashions exhibit all the characteristics of a complex dynamic system. Change is erratic and unpredictable. Stable fashions or trends emerge; these will suddenly change and destabilize. For a while there is a mixture of different fashions and then this suddenly settles down into a new emergent style. This has all the hallmarks of chaos. It is unpredictable; it has erratic periods of stability and instability and the phenomenon of emergence.

To understand the fundamental mechanism driving this chaotic environment we'll look at another of the dialogues from the CD-ROM 'How God Makes God'. It is a conversation between a man and a woman. It is in the 1970s and the man is trying to explain to the woman how he chooses the fashions to buy for his boutique.

'Do you remember a few years back there was a craze to wear a gold or silver razor blade on a chain about the neck?'

'Yes, I do. My friend Annie had a pair of solid gold earrings in the shape of tiny razor blades. They were all the rage then.'

'The razor blade, as you may or may not know, is associated with cocaine because a razor blade is used to chop up cocaine crystals into a fine powder and spread it into thin lines to make it easier to sniff into the nose.'

'What sort of people are you talking about?'

'In the early 70s, the use of cocaine was confined mainly to pop stars. Within the groups that hung around with the pop stars it became fashionable to wear a razor blade around the neck because it identified the wearer, by association, with the exclusive pop group sets.'

'You mean it was a signal that only those in the know could identify with?'

'That's right, and as pop stars associated with fashion leaders the razor blade decoration was adopted by some of them, causing the razor blade to become associated with the top fashion sets. The razor blade decoration was then copied by people who copied the fashion leaders. These in turn were copied by others who were one step further removed from the top fashion set. Gradually the fashion spread out to the whole population, as people in groups followed their own group's trend setter, triggering the copying actions of other groups further and further away from where it all started. By the time the craze reached the high street shops it had completely lost its association with cocaine and most of the wearers would have been horrified if they had been aware of its significance.'

'How does this relate to you buying dresses for your boutique?'

'It is a good model to explain how fashions and trends spread. Ideas starting from an influential group spread through the population because people want to identify themselves with others. Group leaders take ideas from the groups above them in a perceived hierarchy and the groups follow their leaders' initiatives.'

'I get it. Trends and fashions spread through the population in the same way that ripples spread out over a pond when a stone is thrown into the middle. So how can you benefit from knowing this?'

'If I observe people at the centre of fashion and watch how their ideas trickle down to the groups my customers belong to, I can anticipate their needs. I can arrange to buy my stock just before they need it.'

'But I thought your boutique was successful because you had an eye for what looks good?'

'No, I watch people. I look for groups. I try to distinguish between the leaders and the followers. To be a successful fashion buyer, you have to look beyond your own immediate surroundings to see how it's being influenced by the rest of society. The world isn't a haphazard conglomeration of people meeting and interacting with each other at random; there is order and organization out there if only you can see it.'

The idea behind this simple model allowed me to break into the fashion business. Not only to break into it, but to create one of the trendiest fashion companies in London at a time when London was leading the world of fashion in the early 1980s. All that was needed was an appropriate communication strategy.

It all began from a small boutique I had in Newburgh Street in London, a little street that runs parallel to Carnaby Street. I called the shop 'Street Theatre' and started off by buying dresses from some of the designers who were trading in Kensington Market.

At that time, Kensington Market, the former hippie market in Kensington High Street, was populated by many graduates from the various London fashion colleges. Failing to get employment in the fashion industry, they had set up their own little workrooms and retailed their products from stalls they rented. As retailing was so precarious, most of them also wholesaled their products to boutique owners like myself.

As the business expanded I could no longer get enough stock from Kensington Market and had to set up a small workroom myself. I had a friend who'd worked for many years as a dressmaker and pattern cutter and I employed her to run the workroom. She bought a few sewing machines and other technical equipment for making dresses. But we were then faced with the problem of what to make.

I'd used the same strategy for buying from the designers in Kensington Market as I'd used with my head shop wholesalers. I simply told the designers to provide me with the designs that were selling, i.e., the designs they found to be selling best in their own retail units. Thus, when it came to deciding what designs to make in my own workroom I didn't have a clue. Unfortunately, neither did the lady I had employed to run the workroom. Although technically skilled, she had no more idea than I had as to what fashion designs to create.

I'd noticed that of the clothes I'd bought from Kensington Market, the items that sold best were those I'd bought from young trendy designers who were always out clubbing. As the Carnaby Street area was very near to the centre of the London rag trade (the streets just to the north of Oxford Street), it was frequented by many trendy young designers. Most of these were either fashion design students or graduate designers looking for work.

There are probably as many young people aspiring to be fashion designers as there are aspiring to be pop stars. Fashion design colleges all over the world turn out hundreds of thousands of fashion designers every year. Quite a considerable number of these are exceptionally talented and creative, but unfortunately only a very small percentage ever make it into the commercial world of fashion where their designs are actually worn by people.

Talking to some of them, I found they would be only too delighted to have an opportunity to create designs for my workroom. So, choosing on the basis of how trendy they were and which clubs they went to, rather than how skilled they might be at making dresses, I employed them on a freelance basis to create designs.

Most of the garments they produced were not very practical, but the designs reflected the designers' interpretations of what they were seeing in the trendy London clubs. Combining the essence of these designs with the professional skill of the lady who ran the workroom, many of these designs could be turned into very saleable and highly fashionable products.

What I'd produced, out of necessity, turned out to be an extremely effective design strategy. The young and inexperienced designers were producing design information about the latest trends and fashions in London's trendiest clubs. They weren't describing them or drawing them; they were producing samples that reflected the trends and at the same time added some originality. It was the perfect information for the experienced dressmaker to work with.

Not surprisingly, the shop began to acquire a reputation. The fashion press were visiting the shop and the Street Theatre designs started to appear regularly in the fashion pages of prominent fashion magazines and even in the fashion pages of national newspapers.

It wasn't long before this attracted the attention of other boutiques who began to buy dresses from us. It also attracted the large multiples who offered us concessions (sales space in their stores where they took a percentage of the takings). The demand soon outstripped the capabilities of our small workroom and we had to use the services of a manufacturing company to make up our designs. Within a few months we'd grown into a fair-sized business.

The way I was seeing it at that time was as a business made up of flexible modular units. We had many retail units, a wholesale unit, a workroom unit, a manufacturing unit and a nebulous creative unit. It was this creative unit that most interested me because I saw it as the engine that was driving all the other parts. If this creative unit ran out of steam all the rest of the units would grind to a halt.

I then increased the number of designers who were producing the samples and asked them to produce at least one a week and bring them along to the workroom on Friday afternoons. I also arranged for many of the sales staff to be in attendance so that we could hold a private fashion show, with staff and designers wearing the week's creations and strutting across the large fabric cutting table in the workroom. Sales staff and designers would then comment and vote on the selections. In this way, the system had a constant flow of design input and a selection procedure.

It soon became apparent that the feedback from the staff was an important factor in this process and I started to employ people who were totally unsuitable as employees in the normal sense but who were invaluable in this interactive design selection process. They were club people: wannabe models and wannabe pop stars. In fact some of them did make it. There were two who went on to become successful designers in their own right, and another who became a highly paid international model.

The most bizarre of all the staff I employed at that time was a pop-mad, gay guy who lived in a squat and always arrived late for work exquisitely made up and dressed like a woman. However, he was a great influence on not only the designs but the whole atmosphere of the company. He didn't do much actual work except for some imaginative window displays and spent most of his time on the telephone getting a pop band together. He called his band 'Culture Club' and went on to become world-famous pop star, Boy George.

As with the head shop business, I had virtually no participation in any of the actual functioning of the company. Apart from some hassling, I tried as much as possible to keep my opinions completely out of the picture. I simply set the system up and let it self-organize and as a result Street Theatre became one of the most famous fashion companies of that time.

In retrospect, what I had done was to ignore the technicalities of manufacture, ignore the creativity of the designers and set up an information flow that came from the trendy London clubs, directly into the garment manufacturing unit.

It's about communication strategies

It may be difficult to map this exotic scenario across to e-business and e-commerce. The trick is to use an abstraction: extracting out the essence of the system, shorn of all the detail. The bottom line here is that an unconventional business approach had organized people into a communicating framework.

It is quite obvious that the real work was being carried out by the professionals: the lady running the workroom and the expert technicians in the manufacturing unit, but it is not so obvious that these professionals were working on designs that had evolved from the erratic and inexpert opinions of a small group of totally unreliable people, most of whom wouldn't have any chance at all of being selected for a position in a respectable company.

The significance of this can only be truly appreciated if seen in the context of the whole of the rag trade. There are thousands of designers, wholesalers and manufacturers vying with each other for the attention of the public and the fashion press. Some of the companies are large, employing hundreds of people that include dozens of top-class designers with CVs as long as your arm. Yet a motley crowd of amateurs had come from nowhere and got out in front.

It might be pertinent here to ask who was the designer or the decision maker. Who created the successful designs that took this company to the front in a highly competitive field full of experts? It certainly wasn't me. It wasn't any of the staff. It was the system: designing itself.

The success was not brought about by expert knowledge and skills (although they were an essential part of the evolving organization); success came through the creation of a suitably focused communication network. Isn't this what the Internet is about? Isn't it a perfect environment for creating imaginative communication strategies? Again we are back to the same common denominator. It isn't about the technology: it is about communicating with people.

Starting with a green frog

Almost guaranteed to send any Industrial Age corporate planner into a frenzy is to tell them that a system design starts off with a green frog. It's like one of those enigmatic Zen stories where the novice goes up to the Master and asks for a solution to a problem and the master says, 'It is there' and points into empty space.

The point is that the green frog is a starting place that has no predispositions. It is devoid of any subjective points of view. It contains no assumptions or opinions; no guesses; no calculations; no precedence. It is just there and it is obviously not going to do whatever it is that a system is supposed to do.

The mindset then is to tell the green frog to do the thing you want your system to do. For example, you can tell it to become an efficient electronic communication system. Of course, it sounds ridiculous, but it is no more ridiculous than asking someone with a handful of marbles to find a small hole in a field.

Immediately, you know a frog can't do this, so you make an intelligent guess and replace the frog with a computer. The computer is useless without a link to the Internet. So another intelligent guess gets you connected to the Internet. Already, with just two guesses you have transformed the green frog into a computer with an Internet connection. You've started a bottom-up design process. You've moved towards the hole with a couple of throws of the marbles.

This is where we need to have a little bit of Zen-ness. We need a mental model that will allow us to understand how we might guide this process towards producing an efficient electronic information system without wandering about all over the place producing nonsensical results.

In the book *Magical A-Life Avatars*, I usurped an abstract mathematical model known as Hilbert space and showed how it could be used as a model to help design intelligent software systems with simulated human emotions. I used it to explain how software can be trained to adapt to an environment and learn in human-like ways to compete in a complex game situation. We can use this same model here to think about design communication strategies and e-commerce solutions.

At first thoughts, Hilbert space appears to be one of those abstract devices that you'd need to be a mathematical genius to understand. It is a space with an infinite number of dimensions. However, a dimension is only a general name for a characteristic or a quality. If you can imagine the green frog in such a space it would have a dimension of 'colour'. Its position in this space would coincide with where the dimension of 'colour' was green. Push the frog along this dimension in Hilbert space and it will change colour. The dimension would include all possible colours so the frog can be in Hilbert space and be any colour just by moving it along the 'colour' dimension.

The valuable feature of Hilbert space is that you can move an object along a dimension without changing or disturbing any other dimension. In this case, all aspects of the frog remain unchanged except the colour. This is the equivalent of being able to concentrate on a single light in a string of Christmas tree lights, the other dimensions being all the other lights in the string.

Similarly there will be a dimension of 'legs'. Push the frog along this dimension in Hilbert space and it can have one leg, two legs, three legs; in fact it can have any number of legs just by pushing it along the 'legs' dimension. Now, the clever part of Hilbert space is that you can move an object along dimensions simultaneously. You can move the frog along the 'colour' dimension and the 'legs' dimension at the same time so you can get red frogs with 12 legs, blue frogs with one leg, etc. You can get all possible combinations of legs and colours on the frog just by appropriately moving it around in Hilbert space.

Again, no other dimensions are affected: only the colour and the number of legs. This is the equivalent of isolating two of the lights in a string of Christmas tree lights. In this way it is possible to take any group of dimensions and deal with them as an isolated group, where playing around with the values of this group has no effect on other dimensions.

This can easily be demonstrated by picking up a green frog and moving it around a room. Everything about the frog remains the same except the three dimensions that describe its physical position in conventional 3-D space. The values of these dimensions are being varied quite independently of any of the green frog's other dimensions.

With an infinite number of dimensions you can do some very weird things to that frog. Push it to colour grey, zero legs, square shape and you have a grey box. By adding several other dimensions you can push it to a place where it becomes a computer. Somewhere in the computer dimension, another dimension can connect it to the Internet.

With this idea in mind, any possible object that you can think of can have its position defined in Hilbert space simply by making a list of characteristics and qualities. Changing the items in the list will be like pushing the object into a different position in Hilbert space and, conversely, pushing the object around in Hilbert space will effectively be changing the items in the list.

This may seem a peculiar thing to do until you realize that we are talking about controlling the evolution of an object. As an object can be described by a list of its characteristics, the evolutionary process effectively changes the list. It is difficult to think of controlling a list but not so difficult to imagine controlling the position of an object in a space (even if it is a multidimensional space). This is why we need this model: to get a convenient picture in our minds to be able to manipulate a list of characteristics. Then we can manipulate that list of characteristics to be exactly right for doing a specified job, effectively and efficiently.

A strategy that can ignore the unknowns

It is at this point that a top-down, logical mindset gets stymied. It is logical that you can represent a system by a descriptive list of its qualities and characteristics. It is logical that you can use that list to represent the system as a point in multidimensional space. But the fallacy appears to be that with a complex system, most of the list is likely to be missing and the Hilbert space location will be short of many of its dimensions. The top-down mindset will then ask, 'If these dimensions are unknown or unknowable, how can you possibly accurately fix a system's position in Hilbert space?'.

This seeming impasse reveals why the concept of Hilbert space is so powerful in a complex environment. With Hilbert space you don't need to have a full list. Dimensions can be separated out and dealt with in isolation, so the list can be incomplete and yet still have a position in Hilbert space. You can deal with any unknowns simply by ignoring their existence.

Just like the observer with the marble-throwers, there is no need to know all there is to know about the marbles or the marble-throwers to get to a point in space. All you need to know is which is the nearest marble to the hole. The observer, that is, the designer or decision maker, doesn't have to know anything other than where the marbles fall when they are thrown. By the same token, a designer of a complex system doesn't have to know what the system consists of. All that needs to be known is whether or not by altering one or more of a system's parameters or components the system becomes more or less efficient.

In *Magical A-Life Avatars* I showed how this model could be used to design complex software systems, where the dimensions were in the form of a list of software modules (objects). Together, all these modules of computer code combined and interacted with each other to form a single complex system. The list of these software modules could then be thought of as describing where in Hilbert space the complex object was positioned, with each module representing a dimension. Changing the way any module functioned, or adding or removing modules, caused the whole system of interacting modules to react differently in any particular situation.

Having a list of the modules isn't enough. They are simply the dimensions that can provide variable responses. What is also needed is a value for each dimension. Just as the colour dimension of the green frog needs to be set to the green position along the colour dimension, so each of the modules has to be set to the appropriate place along the dimension line that covers its range of possibilities.

The system described in *Magical A-life Avatars* could make decisions and take actions according to artificial emotions. (Note: These artificial emotions were not esoteric metaphysical states; they were simply values given to variables acting as weighting factors to enforce decision rules.) There was an emotion associated with each module in the system.

These emotions could be arranged to be positive or negative, strong or weak, each emotion controlling a particular action. The problem was that the object had to learn how to play a competitive game and it started out without having any settings for the emotions that guided its decision making and actions. How could it acquire values for those emotions if there wasn't a designer with the knowledge to set them?

In other words, each module is flexible enough to perform a number of different variations of its function and you have to specify exactly the right emotion value for each and every module to get the system to respond appropriately. This would seem to be impossibly difficult and even more complex than any Christmas tree light problem.

If we think of the system as being described in Hilbert space, we can forget about the details of how the code modules are constructed and just concentrate on the emotions that influence the way the system reacts. This allows us to use Hilbert space where the dimensions are not the modules themselves but simply the emotions. It will be Hilbert space where every dimension is an emotion, and wherever the system is in this Hilbert space will specify the values of all the emotions.

In this way, we can think of the system as having different sets of emotional response in different places in Hilbert space. If we keep testing different places to see how each place causes the system to react we can know when one place is better than another. In other words, which set of emotions is better than another set.

If this seems somewhat confusing, just think of Hilbert space as having just three dimensions, where the dimensions are fear, hunger and interest. Then think of this Hilbert space as being an object with these emotions and this object sees an exotic-looking fruit growing on a strange tree. At one point in that space the value of the fear emotion might be very great and the emotions of hunger and interest small. At this point in its Hilbert space the object will move away from the fruit.

At another point in this Hilbert space the fear emotion might be very low and the hunger and interest might be very high. With the object's emotions set at this point in Hilbert space it will rush eagerly towards the exotic fruit.

By varying the values of the emotions of fear, hunger and interest effectively moving around in Hilbert space, the object will elicit a whole range of different reactions upon seeing the exotic fruit. A suitable mix of emotions would see the object approaching the fruit cautiously. Another mix would see it reluctantly moving away. By moving a point around in this object's Hilbert emotional space its actions and attitudes towards the fruit can be made infinitely variable.

If you wanted to find a place where this object would stand still, you could play around with the values of the emotions until you came to a point where the object was torn equally between its fear of the fruit and its interest and hunger. At this point in Hilbert space the values for the emotions would be cancelling each other out and cause the object to stand still, not being able to decide one way or another whether to go forward or backwards.

Finding this place could fairly easily be arranged by altering the different emotions one way or another to gradually slow up its movement until it stopped – a sort of trial and error guided by observing what the object does after you make adjustments to the values of its emotional dimensions.

Isn't this similar to the hole in the field problem? There we had to find a position in space. Didn't we solve that by throwing marbles? That is what we can do in Hilbert space. We can do the equivalent of throwing marbles, by randomly choosing sets of emotions. The set nearest to the response we are looking for is the equivalent of being the marble nearest to the hole.

This is where a paradigm shift is needed. How do you determine the right values to make the system perform optimally? The trick is to start by giving all the emotions a random value. This will send the software object into a random place in Hilbert space. At this random position you can try out the object to see how well it performs the required function – with the emotions that are specific to that location. This is like throwing a single marble into a field.

Using the emotional Hilbert space and the exotic fruit example you would simply give random values to fear, hunger and interest to see what it did. This is the equivalent of initializing the system to get a first fix on what effect the values have.

Now if you repeat this ten times with different random values for the emotions, this would be the equivalent of throwing ten marbles into a field where they land in ten different positions. By seeing how the system performs each time you change the value of the emotions, you can find out which set of emotions performs best. So, ten trials with randomly different emotional value settings will allow you to choose the set of random emotional values that works best. It is not the optimum values, but, like the first throw of the marbles, it allows you to take a positive directional step towards the goal.

By changing one or more emotional values and testing again each time, you can see if the changes cause the system to perform better or worse. Retaining good changes and cancelling bad changes, you can steadily steer the system towards a position in Hilbert space where it is performing optimally. At this place, the emotional values will be set at their best values. No calculations, you just follow a route marked out by trial and error testing that will lead you directly to the solution.

This can be easily visualized by creating a control system for an object where forward and backward movements are controlled by three variables. You wouldn't have to know anything about the system itself; you could get the object to take up a stationary position simply by steadily adjusting the values of the variables to different values to make it slow up and eventually stop altogether. Who cares whether it's an electro-mechanical system, a software system or a biological system? You don't have to know: all you need to care about is that you can get the system to a state where it will do what you want it to do.

This example is describing a system of objects made up of computer code, but the magic of Hilbert's multidimensional space is that it can be used to model practically anything. Hilbert himself said it could be used to model tables, chairs, beer mugs and beer mats. More importantly, from the point of view of e-commerce, it can model Web sites, e-business and e-commerce solutions and, most valuable of all, communication strategies.

As this is so important, bear with this abstract explanation for a moment while we flesh it out a little, then, in the subsequent chapters, we can develop some really powerful paradigms for use in Internet strategies.

The abstraction of this model

As mentioned earlier, the idea of using abstract models to represent real-world systems is that you can cut out all irrelevant detail. The simpler you can make the model the less chance there is to get side-tracked and go off at a tangent. Such models can then be used to acquire the Zen-ness that allows you to be more competitive.

Without these models of the marbles and Hilbert space it might be very difficult to see how a bottom-up strategy can achieve efficiency. This leaves you no alternative but to use a top-down approach. But now imagine a top-down approach competing against a bottom-up approach. Think of how each has to react if the other gets an advantage. The top-down strategy would have to expensively examine and redesign the system; the bottom-up strategy would simply alter a few dimensions to change the system's position in Hilbert space so that the results were better than those of the competitors.

The way we are working here with the concept of Hilbert space modelling an object is simply manipulating a list of dimensions; this can be a numbered list. Instead of using the descriptions of the dimensions, you can just use the line numbers on the list to represent the dimensions and another number to represent the value of the dimension, i.e., line 1 of the green frog's dimensions might be 'colour', with the number 5 representing 'green'. In this way the colour dimension in Hilbert space would be '1:5'.

In the case of the emotional Hilbert space and the exotic fruit, the emotions can be given numbers and the extent of each emotion given a value on a scale of 1 to 10. Thus the emotional reaction of the object represented by its Hilbert space could be (1:3, 2:9, 3:7) where its state could be described as: 1 (fear) = value 3; 2 (hunger) = value 9; 3 (interest) = value 7.

By using such numerical codings, an object descibed by its Hilbert space could be represented as arrays of numbers. By changing the numbers, you can effectively push something around in Hilbert space to make it morph into all kinds of manifestations to function flexibly in a variety of different ways and test how effective it is at anything you want it to do.

This is the essence of genetic algorithms where you use numbers to effectively push something around in Hilbert space with a computer program. After every push, you can check to see if it is functioning efficiently and if not you can change a number to push the software somewhere else where its performance may be better. Genetic algorithms go one stage further, though; they mix and match different combinations in a way that moves the solution more quickly towards the desired result.

Once you can get this picture into your mind – of pushing an object that is described by its dimensions around in space by changing the values of its dimensions – you have a powerful model to deal with complex environments. This is because you don't have to know what every dimension is or what values or parameters are associated with the object. All you need be aware of is that by picking a dimension and changing its value you can make the object in Hilbert space move somewhere else where it performs differently.

If we go back to the marble model, it's as if all the marble-throwers are objects in Hilbert space and their marbles are the dimensions. If a throw of the marbles results in getting nearer to the hole you know that object is making an improvement. If the throw doesn't result in getting nearer to the hole you know that the throw didn't work. You don't have to know anything about the marble player or the way the marble-thrower throws, all you have to know is whether or not a throw gets the marble-thrower nearer to the target.

One of the special features about object-oriented thinking is that you can combine objects to make them form virtual objects. So, if we put all the marble-players into a group we can get them all to throw their marbles together. Then, when they all throw their marbles, the nearest marble will point the way to the target: effectively choosing the best out of many haphazard, random, different positions. This will get the whole group progressing faster towards the target than any single marble-thrower.

This is exactly what was happening with the Street Theatre designers. Their designs were all over the place. But we were taking the nearest (closest to what was judged as best by the group) as the direction to go. These selections were then made the dimensions of another object in Hilbert space, the retail shop, to see which sold best there. Those that sold best indicated the direction for the shop to go in the same way as the nearest marble points the way to the target.

Again, in a general way, it is the same as Yvan Caron was describing as a 'ready–aim–fire' approach and 'fast-paced solution building'.

 ## Strategies in Hilbert space

You can always be sure that you have a winning system if it is used in biological systems. After all, nature has had three or four billion years' start on us. This system of objects randomly spreading around is the way our genes have sorted themselves out. These are the dimensions of our human form and as this arrangement has moved around in Hilbert space they have been progressively selected as our organisms move closer and closer towards some perfect optimization for survival and reproduction.

We don't need to go into the intricacies of molecular biology to appreciate how nature performs its optimization tricks; all we need be aware of is that it has managed to optimize these genes and our human form without the need for any forward planning. It manages to do this blindly, just by selecting for best results.

Instead of an observer, nature simply uses a rule to decide which of its marbles is nearest to the hole. That rules is: 'Those organisms that manage to reproduce are counted as being nearest to the hole.' In this way, organisms and the genes that describe them move progressively towards a state optimal for reproduction.

This then is the key to controlling the direction of a bottom-up design process: trial and error and selecting those that perform the best according to any given rule or rules. In the case of organic evolution, the fundamental rule is simply to survive, but this rule can easily be qualified to control the direction of the evolutionary process. This is readily apparent when we observe the human qualifications imposed on this rule when we breed domestic pets or farm animals, and generate agricultural products.

Humans impose conditional rules on the reproduction to steer evolutionary progress along lines convenient for human purposes. This is why we have cute and friendly dogs that evolved from fierce wolves; it's why we have cows with huge malformed udders; it's why we have fields of uniformly sized corn with gigantic seeds. Humans have just added an extra rule to the selection processes that changes the positions of animals or plants in Hilbert space.

All this would be of only academic interest if it weren't for the extensive flexibility of Hilbert space to be able to work with abstract dimensions. For example, a strategy can be thought of as a set of rules: rules we can define and put into a list. These can be regarded as the dimensions of a strategy.

If a strategy is placed into Hilbert space we can think of the rules changing as the strategy is moved around. Or, conversely, by changing the rules we can change the position of the strategy in Hilbert space and because the rules are changing, the strategy works more or less efficiently according to where it is in Hilbert space.

As is done with domesticated pets, farm animals and agricultural products, we can move the strategy around in Hilbert space by means of an evolutionary process that selects appropriate rules according to the qualifications placed upon the conditions of reproduction. This is elegantly demonstrated in the CD-ROM 'How God Makes God' by giving software objects behaviours that are activated by simulated emotions.

The objects are placed into an artificial competitive environment where only particular behaviours will be successful. By arranging for these objects to breed and selecting the objects that are most successful in the competition, the simulated emotions gradually evolve to cause the objects to act in the best way to achieve success in the competitive environment.

This in itself is remarkable, but even more remarkable is the fact that acting in groups the individual objects evolve emotions that cause them to behave in ways less than optimal for the individual but more appropriate for the success of a group. In other words, altruistic behaviour emerges out of the blind evolution of objects competing with each other in a competitive environment. Emotions evolve that maintain the efficiency of a group, rather than individual competitive performance.

Hilbert spaces within Hilbert spaces

In this chapter we have seen how any kind of system, either tangible or intangible, can be represented in Hilbert space. We have seen how selected dimensions can be chosen to represent a system.

The simplest Hilbert space was two-dimensional, where the value of the dimensions gave the position of marbles. By observing the nearest marble to the target hole we could guide a marble-thrower to the target. We saw how clothing designs were put into Hilbert space and through selection by sales we saw how a fashion design company could be steered towards success. We saw how software could be placed into Hilbert space and advanced to where it could make suitable emotional responses. We understood how groups could progress through the evolution of the individual group member's emotions. In every one of these examples, there is no element of planning – it is just inspiration, intelligent guessing or random chance followed by a testing then a selection procedure; this steers any kind of construct in a straight line towards any specified solution.

In previous chapters, we saw how an e-commerce project can be set up as a number of modules. As the bottom-up house-building strategy demonstrated, each module (room) can be evolved independently of the others. Putting this scenario into the context of Hilbert space would see each room having its own Hilbert space and then the whole building or any combination of rooms being in Hilbert space. Hilbert space can then contain other Hilbert spaces. This is the flexibility that gives this model its power to create imaginative solutions within the complexity of a dynamic system.

In this way, all parts of the system plus the system itself can be grown from nothing more than a green frog.

Where this is taking us

Green frogs, marbles and Hilbert space? It may seem that we are heading for an insanely complicated way to create e-commerce and e-business solutions. But remember we are not trying to arrive at some logical procedure. We are looking for Zen-ness: that enigmatic understanding that will give us an inexplicable ability to create counter-intuitive strategies.

By now you will have some sort of fuzzy idea about how objects can be placed into Hilbert space and be manipulated for optimum performance. With this fuzzy picture in mind it is time to reveal the most powerful of the Hilbert space magic: it can be used to deal with people.

With all the systems we have considered, each modular part of any system has always been found to be associated with people. People, then, are dimensions of all modules and all systems. Using the ability of Hilbert space to select particular dimensions to define the space, we can set up Hilbert space where the dimensions are people.

This is more than just an idiosyncratic conclusion. This is of major significance. It means we can create an optimally performing system where our only dealing is with people and there is no need to reference any underlying technology.

If the dimensions of a Hilbert space object are people, you might then ask what does this object represent: how would you describe such an object? The answer is: the object is a solution. For every different combination of dimensions (people) you'll get a different solution to a problem. Moving around in such a space will produce an infinite variety of different solutions and the game is to find the place in this space (the right combination of people) that will provide the best solution to a particular problem.

The trick, though, is to find an efficient way of moving around in this Hilbert solution space. To do this we shall need to use communication, but this is what the Information Age is all about. And, by means of the Internet, we'll be able to use communication strategies that were not possible in the Industrial Age.

However, it cannot be just any kind of communication strategy; we shall need some help from the sophisticated teachings of game theory. This is where we shall go next.

Chapter 9

Difficulties in thinking with abstract models

The difficulties caused by the green frog

Having had many different experiences of explaining the concept of the green frog and Hilbert solution space – in one-to-one discussions, in corporate meetings, in technical workshops and in college lectures – I knew I'd get a range of different reactions when I sent out Chapter 8 to the reviewers in the virtual café. I wasn't disappointed.

Many immediately recognized Hilbert space as a hugely versatile mental modelling environment that could be used as an approach to thinking about all kinds of problems. Simply by choosing different kinds of dimensions to work in, any kind of bottom-up design process can be visualized. Mostly, artists and people working in creative fields found the concept easy to understand. This was exemplified by Blane Savage, a multimedia designer from the UK, who wrote to a café group explaining why he'd deliberately rub out a successful individual feature of his work in order to go beyond his imagination:

> For me this process is more to do with letting go of some small piece of beauty (which when looked back upon is flawed beauty) to risk capturing a greater whole – it is also about pushing your work to destruction (past the instinctive stopping point of a piece) to expand the envelope of your understanding.
>
> How can you develop your self and your art unless you grow beyond your present boundaries? Creation of art is not about methodical stages – it is about starting with nothing and developing in a very 'design up' way. My experience, and that of other designers I have spoken to, is that creativity is a difficult process – it does not come easily. Failure is constantly there and success is almost painfully achieved with a leap of inspiration – a single successful feature is a short-term resting place to hide in before moving on. If you safely stay and develop around that point you will never achieve what you are trying to find. …
>
> … do programmers ever find that the code that is most eloquent and that they are most proud of is actually stopping the program running once it is complete?

Others couldn't seem to connect it to any real-life experience. Another multimedia designer, from France, provided this pragmatic assessment of the green frog and Hilbert solution space paradigms:

> A green frog with 12 legs, a blue one with one leg, or a grey one which becomes a grey box… I give up, Hilbert got me….
>
> Chapter 8 made me sleep… maybe, (or for sure) I'm the kind of person that Elias described as: 'the poor client trying to work out what the hell you are talking about…'
>
> Finding out the best strategy for optimizing the use of the Internet for e-commerce and e-business is discussed since Chapter 1 with different concepts and samples for illustration. I agree that within a concept must arise an idea, but if this concept drives [one] to intellectual masturbation, it becomes quickly boring and somewhat unproductive. We have to focus on a strategy that is real and feasible for it to be productive.

Fair comment. It does seem to be a completely unnecessary and complicated way to approach e-commerce solutions because it isn't dealing with any reality.

But the reality of e-business and e-commerce is too complex to deal with. There are just too many variables to be taken into consideration to be able to think clearly. We need a technique, a mental tool, that allows us to see through the confusion created by the detail. The point of the green frog and Hilbert space is to be able to have a way of getting at the essence of problems without getting bogged down or side-tracked by any irrelevancies.

To be able to think of starting at a random point like the green frog and moving from that point around in space to find a better position enables us to cut out all the side issues, prejudices and emotive issues that keep cropping up to cloud real-life issues. It also allows general strategic policies to be discussed without having to use specific examples that cover only a limited range of applications.

This is particularly important when it comes to dealing with people because human interaction is so beset with emotive overtones that rational strategic thinking is severely handicapped. This is particularly true of Internet communication because human emotions have evolved to deal with real-world communication and they conflict quite strongly with communication tactics and strategies appropriate for the environment of the Internet.

Yvan Caron, the Canadian systems analyst, had another kind of problem which he explained in an email to a table discussion in the virtual café:

> Maybe it's me, trying to distort this idea, but I don't quite understand it. The observer knows where the hole is, that I can understand, but what about an observer in the complex world of the Internet; how does he know where the profitability is? From an economic point of view, how many experiments can we afford to exploit?
>
> How are you going to convince an entrepreneur or a corporate entity to start from the metaphor of a green frog? Is not that the reason why, when someone wants to have a Web site, he gives 'carte blanche' to an expert to design it? This is what we do when we want to invest our money. We go out in search of an expert to manage it.
>
> I don't see how I could afford to change my choice when I started with a so-called expert. There would be penalties to pay if I decided to change to another expert. This economic problem is also present in the WWW. So my question is, how are we going to cope with this if we choose to keep the same designer?
>
> Also, to complicate the problem a bit more, what strategy would we use if the

small hole in the middle of the large field started to change its position in the process of trying to locate it? To me, this new dynamic property reflects more the situation that we may find in the WWW. Everything is moving, the only discernible pattern is that there is no permanent pattern. This is where I get lost when I try to understand the science of random fluctuation that we find in complex systems.

Yvan sees three problems here. Firstly, the connection between the model and the real world. He is mixing up the goal with the solution. The observer, the person using Hilbert solution space to find a solution, has to have in mind what problem is to be solved. It is not necessary to know the final answer in advance to act as an observer to guide this process. The marble-throwing example was a simplified view, where the answer was a physical location. For this, the observer would have to know where the hole is. But most times the answer will not be specific: it will be relative.

Top-down, structured thinking involves knowing where you want to go before you start out on a journey. Bottom-up thinking is where you have no way of knowing where you are going to end up. This doesn't seem to make sense until you realize that in the world of e-commerce the goal posts are constantly moving. In the case of the marble-throwers, it's as if the hole is constantly on the move.

Even worse than the hole constantly being on the move, the hole may suddenly make a jump to a different part of the field. There may be many different holes and you have to decide which is the best hole. Just imagine trying to create a route map (the equivalent of a structured top-down plan) to reach a hole in a field when there are lots of holes in the field all jumping around like crazy. This is the kind of problem that has to be solved for e-business and e-commerce solutions and is why it is necessary to use an abstract modelling tool like Hilbert solution space to devise a suitable strategy.

Yvan's second problem is with the association with the experts that are needed to help find an e-business or e-commerce solution. He accepts that no one knows everything there is to know about e-commerce solutions, so there is a need to commit to advisers and experts of various kinds. Having committed to any expert, Yvan sees it as creating a relationship that has some degree of permanence. Yvan is suggesting that this imposes either a moral obligation or a financial penalty if that commitment is cancelled. To answer this second problem, we need to solve Yvan's third problem.

This is, as explained above, that he recognizes that the best solution for any particular e-business or e-commerce venture is continuously changing with the fluctuations of technology and competitive strategies. A solution at one point in time may be totally inappropriate at a later date. In other words, the place (or hole) in Hilbert space that describes the best solution is constantly on the move. The goal posts are moving.

This can be a serious problem if your strategy is to stick with the same group of expert advisers and specialists, because the range of knowledge needed at any new solution hole may not be that of the experts employed in the outdated solution. The solution moves, but the knowledge of the experts may not necessarily move with it.

In all specialist areas of e-commerce there is too much to know and too many technological advances to continually keep up with. Any particular solution requires a fair amount of expertise, so to be really an expert, the expert is forced into being confined to a restricted range of technology. This makes experts vulnerable if their areas of speciality have become outdated or superseded by a new technology. In the new hole in Hilbert solution space, where the preferable solution is to be found, it may need some brand new thinking that is outside of the original designer's range of expertise or knowledge. This may make it impossible for the original expert to be a dimension of any new solution.

What do you do when your main competitor uses an expert who is a specialist in a newer and superior technological development? Do you pay your current expert for 'on the job' training? Is your project going to be the experimental model for your expert to learn how to change to another area of expertise? Do you wait for your expert to become expert in new areas of technology before you make a competitive move? Maybe the consultant or expert you use will have many other clients, clients who aren't pressured enough to go for a newer technology. Your expert may then not see any great benefit in changing his or her knowledge base and expertise to suit you.

All these factors make it totally inefficient to carry a group of experts around in Hilbert solution space with you. It is far easier to go to a place where the experts you need are already in place. If an e-business or e-commerce solution is visualized as being at a point in Hilbert solution space where the dimensions are people, it is easy to see how moving around in that space is about changing the people involved in the solution. In the bricks and mortar world of the Industrial

Age this isn't a practical way to think, but in the Internet environment of the Information Age it is the only way to think.

Yvan mentions the problem of there being too many possible strategies to have to investigate before arriving at the best solution. There aren't. What he means is that there are too many possible solutions. Each hole in Hilbert space is a different solution. The trick is to use a single strategy to find the best hole or point in the Hilbert solution space. This will be the place where just the right combination of contacts are to be found, the dimensions of this place being specified by a list of names.

This, then, answers Yvan's second problem: a strategy for an efficient e-commerce solution shouldn't involve establishing permanent fixed relationships with experts or advisers. This is one of the big paradigm shifts that e-business and e-commerce will require. This is at odds with all conventional thinking in the Industrial Age and, emotionally, does not seem right. But as we shall see, the logical and emotional objections disappear when we start to apply game theory to Internet communication strategies.

A few days after Yvan sent that post to the table in the virtual café, he sent another – after having given some further thought to the implications of using the Hilbert solution space model:

> While reading a magazine lately I was struck by the title of an article: 'Internet access WANTS to be free'. It struck me because it precisely describes what Peter says when he writes 'with a bottom-up approach a system designs itself'. Also, I could connect it to what I have read this summer.
>
> My reading was about the conception of goals or goal-driven systems. 'Goal' has many complicated meanings. A goal-driven system does not seem to react directly to the stimuli or situations it encounters. Instead, it treats the things it finds as objects to exploit, avoid, or ignore, as though it were concerned with something else that doesn't yet exist.
>
> When any disturbance or obstacle diverts a goal-directed system from its course, that system seems to try to remove the interference, go around it, or turn it to some advantage. For example, if you climb a hill and throw a ball down you may have the impression that the ball 'WANTS' to go down while trying to go around, exploit or avoid any obstacles in its path.
>
> Looking at the ball we could say that it appears to have some representation of some outcome (a goal: to reach the bottom of the hill) and a mechanism (a will)

to make it persist until that outcome is achieved. Of course, in this simple case the impression of intention is only in the watcher's mind. A complex system may produce a random fluctuation that may persist long enough and drive with it a representation of some outcome. And it is where we must be alert because this may drive the next big trend.

Apparently the next big thing will be a tidal wave of free Internet access. It is said that the big portals are failing. Originally, there were just a few portals like Yahoo, Netscape and MSN, and these guys are still among the biggest. But now everybody's getting into the act. There are literally thousands of portals out there, with new ones emerging every day. Internet content providers have always dreamed of creating a TV-like captive audience that can be force-fed advertising.

That was the goal of push publishers, and that's the goal of portals. But offering free content and e-mail doesn't attract enough eyeballs any more because now everybody's doing it. With more Web options to choose from, the big portal companies are losing customers. That's why the rich portal vendors will find a way to blow away the poor ones by partnering with ISPs to offer free or nearly free Internet access.

To me, this is an example of a system that designs itself because this new wave has emerged from the intense competition among the players and we could not have predicted it.

Yvan, as a senior systems analyst, is realizing that there isn't much you can do to design your way around an environment as complex as the Internet. There are too many unpredictable events. He has come to the conclusion that the system is being goal driven. Once given a goal, the system will automatically find its way over the hills and valleys to its own solution: its own best hole.

You control a system by not controlling it.

This gives us another paradox. You control a system by not controlling it. You just set a goal and let events take their course. This is like another of those infuriating, enigmatic conundrums you find in Zen philosophy. It just seems too ridiculous to have any meaning.

Let's invent another little analogy. Imagine you are visiting a strange and exotic country that no one had ever visited before. Your goal is to find and photograph the most beautiful building in the country. It is a very hilly place.

You can imagine yourself lost in a hilly landscape and you wander around asking people where you can find the most beautiful building. You don't know what is over the hills but someone you meet might know. As with asking your way around a real place, you can't expect every stranger you ask to know the exact location you want to find. They'd probably point you in a general direction and tell you to ask someone else when you get there.

Most likely, you'd be sent to a busy village where there would be many people who are familiar with the locality. You'd ask a few people there. The Internet equivalent would be a special interest group, probably one that was set up to discuss e-commerce. By subscribing to this you can listen in to the discussions and when you start to get a few ideas you begin asking a few questions.

In terms of Hilbert space, you'd be at a spot where there are hundreds of dimensions, people dimensions. A very useful hole. Soon you'd get to know people, you'd make friends. You'd find out who you could rely on, who you could trust for accurate information. Perhaps someone would act as a guide and introduce you to someone else who had a map and could show you the way.

This is the strategy for exploring Hilbert solution space to find the best solution. It's about wandering about in an environment and talking to people who will lead you to others, leading you nearer and nearer to your solution: and the solution is not any specific design, it is the people who have the right knowledge and experience to help you go where you want to go. The trick is: how to do that efficiently in the complex environment of the Internet.

Stumbling around in e-commerce solution space

Let's stop here for a moment to look at some reality. How are people approaching e-commerce solutions without this concept of Hilbert solution space? Two emails, written at the time I was writing this chapter, throw a spotlight on a range of different ways people are interacting with the real world of e-commerce. The first comes from a lady called Jacie, working for a multimedia company in Australia. In a discussion at one of the tables in the virtual café she wrote:

> I've just finished reading Chapter 8 and all the emails I've received over the weekend with their talk of people as objects (as opposed to components in the system, which I think is a more accurate description. I for one refuse to be talked about as an 'object', I don't care what current business practices say...and for the

most part, current business, or should I say 'typical corporate business', practices suck anyway.)

The one thing that kept coming to my mind during Chapter 8 had nothing to do with green frogs and Hilbert space or marbles…all of which make perfect sense to me. No, the thing I kept thinking was how do you communicate this style of working to your team members? How do you get people to throw marbles around without it ending up with them throwing the marbles at you?

Your ending paragraph in Chapter 8 gave me some hope, Peter, that if I hold on till the next chapter I'll start to see some help in 'green frog communication.' But I suspect you're going to talk of the virtual café more than this inter-communication between the observer/designer and the marble-throwers. I know I don't know a whole lot about e-commerce. I don't know a lot about business either as I tend to 'do my own thing' and let others go their own way. I detest office politics; I despise mean-spirited gossip; and I'm far more interested in outstanding results than in process and procedure.

All of this seems to preclude my success in the standard corporate world. But my experience over the past year, limited though it is, has provided some really pointed lessons in what might prove successful in the long run. And it all has to do with communication, choosing the right people to work with, and then really working WITH them to evolve the 'green frog' into something that astonishes everyone. This is why your Chapter 7 was really validating for me.

It has been my experience that your average programmer (or 'marble-thrower') likes to have things neatly laid out in great detail. At least the guys I work with do. For the past two years, I've been 'designing' and helping to program computer-based training and multimedia marketing promos. I've had to develop storyboards, in cooperation with the client or end-user, that I thought were incredibly detailed.

I then worked with the guys in 1) action (someone created a graphic or coded a piece); 2) observe (I looked at it at their request); 3) communicate (I provided feedback…yes, that's it; or, I wonder if you could try this). I thought we were really going to go somewhere, create really cool stuff, become the best of the best.

Then it happened with one particularly visible project that my rosy picture exploded in my face. I provided feedback. The programmer went ballistic. He sent an email, copying it to my supervisor, that in effect accused me of not giving him the details he needed to do his job (this despite the fact that I had sat with him for two to three hours going over the damn storyboard to make sure he 'clicked into' the vision and showed him samples on the Web of effects I wanted to simulate).

He then outlined a list of 14 items he needed precise detail on which included rgb values and pixel counts and exact step-by-step descriptions of every animated effect, etc., etc... I emailed back that I could do that, but I'd have to create the effect myself in order to give him that much detail, which was true. He threw something at my desk; I yelled at him for that; he 'quit' (and then sheepishly begged for his job back the next day).

Our manager sent the whole team to a teambuilding seminar that focused on communication...how different personality types need to be communicated with in order for communication to really occur. In these sessions, we all learned a lot of really interesting things. But one of the things that came out was that of the five people, I was the only one who was markedly 'different' in terms of my core personality. Everyone else was high in steadiness...meaning that they like process, step-by-step procedures, proven methods, the status quo.

When you communicate with someone like this you have to have all your ducks in a row. You have to be calm, procedural, give them detail and facts, and give them time to absorb the facts and determine a plan of action before you start looking for results. (It was also interesting to note that 40% of the population is high in steadiness.) I was the only one low in steadiness and high in dominance...meaning that I challenge the status quo, drive for results, am innovative and creative etc., etc.

I also need people to get to the point. Say what you have to say. Don't detail and outline it, I can fill in the blanks. Give me what you're looking for and then let me find a way to get you the result you need. Above all, don't tell me HOW to get the result. Trust me to get the result you want when you want it, and I'll succeed every time or be able to tell you why I didn't. (Another note of interest is that only 18% of the population is like this. I'm also the only female, except for my manager. I'm not sure what that has to do with everything, except I do feel the guys never really listen to 'cute little old me.' But as I learned, my natural communication style is markedly different from theirs and, in order to be really 'heard,' I need to do some serious adapting.)

All this learning on communication promised to help us achieve some radically better results, until I started to really listen to the unspoken currents running through the team. I realized that, given the personalities I was working with, the only one who would ever really change would be me. I didn't see how these procedurally minded fellows would truly be able to adapt except over a rather long time. And I didn't see how, given their need for detail and plans, we as a team would ever be able to achieve anything spectacular. Sadly, after having helped build up the team from nothing, I had to admit defeat and accept our end as a growing entity with a hopeful future. Personally, I think the team will be dissolved within a year.

But then something else happened at the same time...

I had been left, after our teambuilding exercises, feeling very much the odd man out and the cause of everyone's woe. On one hand, I was told I didn't give enough detail. In the same breath I was told I was too controlling. But while my work with the 'team' dwindled, I got more work from the marketing department. And it came out recently that the key marketing individual I work with (another woman, incidentally, with whom I had worked in the design of the visible project I got beat up on) had the same problems working with the guys on my team as I had. And that she was coming back to our group not to work with the 'team' but to work with me...because I listened to her; I worked WITH her; we created things on the fly together, sitting in the same cube.

Everyone else says she's riding on my coattails. That I do all the work and she just sits there. But what I see is very different...sure, I'm helping her look good. But I get to work on cool stuff. And she has really good ideas. And it's a pleasure working WITH people instead of fighting, and coming out with stuff that has potential! And my manager is happy because I'm 'bringing' high-profile work to the team, helping her look good and keeping the team in existence.

The guys on the team just had a way of taking the storyboard and shutting out the designer and the designer's feedback. They threw marbles...but then never wanted to hear whether the marbles were near the hole or not. They didn't want to be told that. They thought they were smarter, more knowledgeable about programming, that they should be the ones telling which marbles were good or not, and we should just shut up and mind our places.

After reading your book, I want to try doing stuff without a storyboard...just a goal and a vision which, according to the guys, is all I ever gave them anyway. But can you imagine what havoc that would wreak? Everyone would be down my throat. But I could do it...if I worked on my own and got to pick out my own team. And I know the product would blow everyone away.

So the programmer threw marbles regardless of our feedback. He put in extra amounts of extraneous movement because he thought it was cool, and only when the customer saw it and complained about all the extraneous movement did he take it out...And when he complained about the extra work and how dare the customer be allowed to have that much say so late in the day, I pointed out that the result ended up nearly identical to our original design. So why hadn't he listened to our feedback...we were his line to the customer? Because we were younger, newer to multimedia and programming, because he was the 'expert'.

Unfortunately, I don't think all the communication skills in the world can counteract that core prejudice of 'experts' against 'upstarts', especially in a corporation where you're lower on the totem pole. The only way 'experts' will bother listening is if you're the big boss. Because then they'd know if they didn't listen, you'd fire them.

Without an abstract model to measure this scenario against it seems just another typical story of personal friction within a company. Not knowing the people involved it's hard to take sides. However, when viewed within the context of Hilbert solution space the situation becomes very clear. Jacie has a brief from her client. It's put into the form of a visionary goal. It needs a solution.

Jacie isn't free to get that solution anywhere in a solution space, she is forced to go to a point in space where the dimensions are people that cannot provide the right solution. The solution she is looking for is somewhere else where the people dimensions are different.

Because the strategy of her company is to have an in-house design team she is stuck with those people dimensions, together with their limited range of knowledge, ability and attitude; these don't extend into the ideal position she'd like to be in, in her solution space.

Seeing this scenario within the abstract environment of Hilbert solution space, it becomes perfectly obvious that for Jacie an in-house design team is a severe handicap. But it is probably also a handicap for the members of the design team themselves because they are being forced to work outside their range of speciality to become 'Jack of all trades and master of none'. In this way Jacie, reflecting the demands of her clients, is not a suitable dimension for the ideal solution in their solution space.

Far better if the design team were freelance and could offer their services to more suitable clients. Far better for Jacie if she could search around in her solution space for some outside contractors who could more suitably provide the solutions she is looking for.

A different perspective was provided in a post to an Internet e-commerce talk list in a thread entitled 'An insight into e-commerce'. This had developed into a discussion about the role of management in e-commerce. I'd posted the following:

> I don't see management and managers (in the normally accepted sense) being applicable to e-commerce solutions. Also, teams and team leaderships are likely to take on different forms.
>
> The reason I have for saying this is because it isn't economical or efficient for e-commerce solution providers to pay technologists to learn on the job. With digital technology, software packages and e-commerce strategies changing so rapidly, the necessity for so much on-the-job learning cancels out the advantages of maintaining a permanent team that can be managed.
>
> With communication on the Internet so efficient, it is much easier and cheaper to find and hire several specialists who will be expert in various parts of an e-commerce solution that has to be put together. This suggests that there will be teams held together by association rather than employment. As such, leadership will need to be inspirational rather than managerial.
>
> Choosing one or two specialists carefully, they will come with sufficient expertise to provide ideas and suggestions as to what other areas of expertise they should be joined up with. In this way, an e-commerce solution should be virtually self-constructing, much the same way as genes come together in the genome of a cell. This will not need any management and, surprisingly enough, little or no planning.
>
> This is based upon using an object-oriented approach to e-commerce solutions. This approach works perfectly well for constructing complex software systems and I see no reason why it shouldn't be applicable to e-commerce solutions.
>
> In this radical view of management and planning, I'm excluding any activity on the bricks and mortar side of a product or service being provided. For example, if you are marketing health products you'll need traditional managers, teams and leaders to make, pack and despatch the product. The e-commerce side is concerned with product design and marketing. It is in these areas where I think we'll find many dramatic changes in strategies and techniques.

There were a few posts for and against this proposition; one suggesting that Web sites should be designed in much the same way as movies are made. Randy, an experienced e-commerce consultant, wrote in response:

> I see companies needing to get to the Web quickly, so they hire an organization to get them there, giving their own people a bit of maintenance work to do. They end

up with a site that fits the expertise of their contractors, and meets a short-sighted snapshot of their needs. It's a decent answer to some of their needs, but it's only a small piece of a solution.

Granted, with short time requirements, you can't do much better. But you can do better. You can have people who understand the company and can think further than the 'requirements' work to design not just a set of requirements, but a long-range plan of services and maintenance. You can involve your own people in learning the new technologies and the site design, and give them some of the longer-range pieces. They can take over the development not just of the site, but of developing the site's potential – collecting customer feedback as well as feedback and ideas from the rest of your organization.

I see lots of sites serving the marketing and e-commerce needs of companies, but they serve customer needs poorly – they seem to have had their requirements built by bureaucrats and business people who are under pressure. This is a start for building a Web presence, but is small-minded. Consultants will go on to their next project. The people responsible for your site should care about and be immersed in your customers' and your business' needs.

A movie is a great example of a static, very expensive, and narrowly-useful product. Lots of effort goes into its production and marketing and launch, and then it's over. After that, it follows a pretty well-understood life cycle. That's not what you want for a Web site and a business. The problem with high-production-cost items is that they're all glitter, anticipating a certain audience. There's no flexibility engineered in. They're built on one artist's (or committee's) idea, not made to adapt to evolving business conditions.

A Web site should be a very, very flexible thing. There are many different products to use and approaches one can take. The tools are very young. The art of building sites is very young too. Pretty much anything you build will need ongoing work and analysis to be worth anything and you should count on it being obsolete soon. You have to build in-house expertise, learning not just about your site for maintenance and changes, but also keeping up with evolving technologies.

Randy's post describes what is happening far too often to companies who are keen to get into e-business or e-commerce. They have little or no knowledge themselves and they put it into the hands of a consultant to get them their first footing. In principle, this is not a bad idea because they are entering the game.

They are like the poker player who sits down to play and puts money in the kitty to get a first deal of the cards.

Unfortunately, many expect the consultant to set them up to be expert players from the word go. This is impossible. The consultant would have to know not only all there is to know about e-commerce but also everything there is to know about the client and the client's customers. In any case, the consultant is producing an optimum solution from his or her own solution space and not from the solution space of the client.

Realistically, the consultant can only set a company up to play the game and explain the rudiments of how to play. It is unlikely that the consultant could represent all the people and knowledge that would need to be present at the company's ideal solution point in their solution space.

Randy suggests that a company should build their own in-house expertise: 'learning not just about your site for maintenance and changes, but also keeping up with evolving technologies'. This is not, however, a realistic proposition if it is taken as meaning the in-house staff should literally get to know all there is to know about the changes that are taking place. More practically, it means establishing a place in the solution space where they are in contact with the right combination of sources that will keep them informed and provide them with appropriate expertise on demand. Chief among this organized feedback will be the viewpoints and expectations of the company's clients or customers.

Strategies within a solution space

Bottom-up strategies must always start with a green frog. It might not be immediately apparent how a green frog can appear in Hilbert solution space when the dimensions are people. The trick is to realize that the green frog is not literally a green frog but symbolic of a starting position in Hilbert solution space.

In finding the appropriate values for a set of emotions in the software discussed in the last chapter, the green frog was a set of random values. If you are searching Hilbert solution space for a solution in terms of people (i.e., the most appropriate set of contacts), you would be unlikely to start by randomly choosing a handful of people. You already know lots of people; you already have a number of contacts. These are your green frog: the point in Hilbert solution space from where you begin moving towards a better solution.

Jacie's green frog is the people in the company she works for. It's her starting position. She finds the position in the people dimensions of her solution space unsatisfactory. She has to employ a bottom-up strategy to improve upon this position.

Randy talks of companies choosing contractors to build Web sites for them. The contractors are the companies' green frogs. It's their opening play in the game to find an appropriate and successful e-commerce solution. Randy suggests companies should have flexible Web designs so that they can move their Web site into a better position in Hilbert solution space. If the dimensions of the solution space are people, this means expanding or changing the people whose views and experiences can make changes to the design.

If you have the mental agility to change the dimensions of Hilbert solution space in your mind, you can see it in one paradigm as a space where the dimensions are components of an e-commerce system; you can then switch paradigms to see the dimensions of Hilbert solution space as people and then you can change the dimensions once again to see the dimensions as ideas.

Each of these paradigms would see the ideal e-commerce solution described in different ways. In the component-dimensioned Hilbert solution space the solution would be described in terms of server configurations, bandwidth, Web site design, CGI scripts, databases and all the various technological components that go into providing an e-commerce solution. In the Hilbert solution space where the dimensions are ideas, the solution would be described in terms of ideas and concepts. In the Hilbert solution space where the dimensions are people, the solution would be described as a list of people who contribute in some way to the design solution.

As it is virtually impossible to find an efficient strategy that will be able to keep track of the constantly changing technological possibilities available, a strategy to search with components as the dimensions is not very sensible. Similarly with the dimensions being ideas, there is no way to keep abreast of all the constantly changing ideas that are continually appearing. This leaves the only practical strategy to adopt as defining the solution as a place described by people.

This makes a lot of sense because components and ideas are basically information. Searching through Hilbert solution space for solutions described in these terms involves dealing only with information: non-intelligent dimensions. Information has to be sorted and filtered. A judgement has to be made on values and relevance. This is far too complex for algorithmic methods, even if the methods include software employing artificial intelligence.

There is no computer system better than a human brain for doing this kind of information sorting, so the best strategy must be to use people to filter, sort and give judgement on any information, which is why they are the preferred dimensions to have in a solution space for e-business and e-commerce. They are the ultimate in effective components in any intelligent system that involves decisions in a complex dynamic environment. After all, this is what human brains have evolved to do.

Hilbert solution space with people has intelligent dimensions where you can be dealing not just with information but with information that is filtered and selected. This greatly reduces the amount of information that it is necessary to deal with in the searching process. In other words, it is more efficient to think in terms of people than technology or ideas and concepts because you are dealing with knowledge rather than information.

A Hilbert solution space where the dimensions are Hilbert solution spaces

A Hilbert solution space where the dimensions are other Hilbert solution spaces? That seems a thought to fry the brain cells. Yet it is really quite simple to understand. If somebody asks you to solve a particular e-commerce problem, it may be that you will not be able to provide a solution because you haven't sufficient knowledge. To come up with an answer you may have to ask somebody you know – one of your contacts – for information or advice.

In doing this, you have used one of the people in your current position in Hilbert solution space: one of the people dimensions. You can visualize this as you being in your solution space with lines radiating out from you – to all the people you are in contact with. Every one of your contacts, like you, will also be in their own private Hilbert solution space. They can also be visualized as having lines of communication stretching out from them to all their contacts. These other contacts will also be in their Hilbert solution spaces connected to their contacts ad infinitum.

A little thought soon tells you that when you ask somebody to solve a problem for you, it may involve many other people as one person asks another, who asks another, etc. Out of the network of communication that is initiated by a problem you might ask about, will emerge an answer that can be rapidly transmitted back to you.

To the person who asked you to supply an answer to their problem, all the networks of others who were involved in providing that solution are invisible. It is you who gets the credit because it comes from your solution space. You, then, as a dimension in somebody else's Hilbert solution space, will seem to be a very valuable contact to have.

If we now see this in terms of my London doctor, he was a very valuable dimension of my solution space because if I had any personal health problems I could go to him. He, with his extensive range of contacts of specialists and surgeons, was an important contact and once having found him I'd have no further need to go searching in other directions in the field of health.

This can also be related to the sociogram of Chapter 4. Each of the doctors linked into the communication network that was established in the region would likely have access, directly or indirectly, to the knowledge and experience of all the others. Any patient going to any one of the doctors in the region could, in theory, receive the combined expertise of all the doctors. Such a system is not really practical in the world of bricks and mortar but in the world of the Internet it is the norm.

Returning to the scenario painted by Randy, you can open out the dimensions of any consultant who sets up an e-commerce solution for a client, to reveal the people dimensions he or she represents. Consultants are only as good as the knowledge they can apply to the task at hand and this must include the knowledge of their contacts. Just like my London doctor, consultants will have a range of specialists to draw upon. The consultants then will be as good as this combined expertise.

The probability is that a consultant who gets a company onto the first rung of the e-commerce ladder is probably a specialist at just that: getting people onto the first rung. To the client the consultant may serve no other purpose than being the green frog. It is unlikely that the consultant will have sufficient range of speciality contacts to get a client much further, especially if the client is in a competitive situation. It will really then depend upon the company itself to find its own way around its own solution space. This requires not technical knowledge but expert communication strategies.

The game then becomes one of finding the best position in the solution space where the best range of contacts are to be found. This cannot be discovered by chance; it has to be discovered by employing a bottom-up strategy that discovers the right combination of contacts gradually. From the green frog, you have to move progressively nearer to wherever the bottom-up strategy takes you:

towards finding the right combination of people who can provide the most appropriate advice and expertise.

Emotional anomalies in Hilbert solution space

By far the biggest resistance to the idea of object-oriented thinking, Hilbert solution space and bottom-up strategies are a result of instinctive, negative emotional reactions. They don't feel natural. They seem cold and calculating. People don't like to be treated as disposable objects. Common sense tells us that people who treat other people without any consideration for their feelings are unlikely to be able to build cooperative associations and create teams.

This can be evidenced from Yvan's post when he is concerned about the breaking off of a relationship with an expert who is engaged to work on a project. Jacie also indicated her disapproval when she started her post:

> I've just finished reading Chapter 8 and all the emails I've received over the weekend with their talk of people as objects (as opposed to components in the system, which I think is a more accurate description. I for one refuse to be talked about as an 'object', I don't care what current business practices say... and for the most part, current business, or should I say 'typical corporate business', practices suck anyway.)

In another post to a table in the virtual café, Elias wrote:

> There is a growing objectification or commoditization of the individual as the book progresses...a bleeding heart liberal (I guess that's me, before anyone gets the wrong idea) might find that a bit uncomfortable.
>
> ... Peter seems to be used to treating people's 'production' as a resource, while a lot of the participants in this café are rather more used to DOING the production...so the later part of the book highlights the (I consider) almost inevitable (unless we can change the current business model) decline into competitive squabbling over available work for an ever-shrinking number of final delivery channels...creative endeavor reduced to commodity...
>
> He describes the services of his previous employees...Peter (obviously) ran businesses, and puts things in a certain way which reflects this...there will be a number of people in the online community (and therefore, one assumes, in the café) who believe that the WWW is capable of transforming the marketplace and instituting a bloodless revolution...to that mindset, Peter is an apostle of doom...

We, as producers, are being turned into farm produce...the farmer is the guy that rakes in the money, and determines what will grow...that probably disturbs a large section of the creative community...Later, the farmers get done over by the bulk buyers (supermarket chains) and they are commoditized in their turn...the only way to stop it happening, as far as I can tell, is to make loose associations and compete directly with the bulk buyers from the outset (they can't move as fast)...while the creative control is still in the hands of the people doing it...The alternative is Wal-Mart for code fragments and graphics...Uh oh...sounds a bit like Marx.

Another poster, Steve Howard, responded to Elias's post:

In these modern 'liberal' times, there are laws against indiscriminate hiring and firing. If you take offence at Peter's viewpoint, where the employee is just a component, then you should maybe reconsider. He is merely putting into words a basic business fact.

Elias answered:

Not if you are freelance...which is what Peter's production model is heading towards (as far as I can tell)...

I was not talking about taking offence (I basically agree)...I was acknowledging that if one were reading the chapters sequentially, this 'fact' is becoming more firmly outlined as the book progresses...and this could cause a sense of ill-ease in reading the text, if one had not noticed or considered this 'fact' previously...

These posts are typical of many negative reactions to the ideas inherent in the paradigms of object-oriented thinking, Hilbert solution space and bottom-up strategies. Many see this thinking as cold and clinical: devoid of any human emotion or consideration for other people. But this is only as it appears to be in the conventions that have evolved in the pre-Information Age.

Controversially, the CD-ROM 'How God Makes God' describes the way in which emotions have probably evolved over time to cause us to act in ways that are most favourable for survival and reproduction. In this view, it does make sense that emotions have evolved that induce us to form groups and associations for the purpose of cooperation. However, these emotions will have evolved to deal with local and physical associations and relationships between people; they will not have evolved to promote or support any of the quite different kinds of associations and relationships that can now occur in the communication environment of the Internet. This is readily apparent on discussion lists, where the lack of visual and auditory clues can easily cause comments to be totally misunderstood, leading to bitter and heated exchanges.

Besides the possible emotional biases, the protocols and conventions of regular business and social ethics often conflict with the kind of interactions now possible on the Internet. As Jacie's management team-building seminar indicated, training is geared towards the associations and group behaviour of the type suited specifically for the Industrial Age. Team building is based upon the idea of individuals adapting their behaviour to fit in with others. Mavericks and eccentrics are not encouraged. Relationships are associated with stability and permanence. Group cohesion and team spirit are all-important. Groups have standards and set protocols.

Although much of the essence of this applies in the communication environment of the Internet, it takes on radically different forms. Of course associations and close cooperation are important. Of course long-term stable relationships are necessary. But the way this takes effect in the communication environment is totally different from the way it works in the world of bricks and mortar.

To understand how individual and group ethics and behaviour can be so radically different in the Information Age, yet still adhere to the basic tenets imposed by reasoned good behaviour and emotionally acceptable conduct, needs a radical paradigm shift. Without this paradigm shift, no one can function efficiently or feel comfortable in the Information Age.

It is to this area that we go in the next chapter, when we deal with game theory and communication strategies.

Strategies for competition and cooperation

Part 4 looks at how to play competitive games of cooperation on the Internet. The conceptual model is taken from the works of the great economist, Lord Keynes, whose deceptively simple model of the business world led to the recovery of the world economy after the Second World War.

The realization that the game is about competing for cooperation sees the Internet as a place for people to use strategies to make contact with others and build up strategic relationships.

This part also looks at the efficiency of a managed team in the environment of the Internet. It shows that although a managed team is the most efficient organizational structure in the bricks and mortar world it is not appropriate for the environment of the Internet.

Chapter 10

Competing for cooperation

Choice and competition

If any phrase could sum up the difference between the Industrial Age and the Information Age it would have to be 'excessive competition and abundance of choice'. Access to the Internet can provide an overwhelming range of options for information, entertainment, commodities, education, products, services, employment, employees, business contacts, friends or indeed anything else that one could conceivably want.

Anyone who has traded in commercial markets knows that abundance of choice promotes intensive competition. Customers, clients and users have the upper hand because there is more than enough for them to use or consume. Suppliers have to compete with each other for clients' and customers' attention, time and money.

This will apply to every segment of e-business and e-commerce. Small enterprises and sole traders and artisans will be exposed to worldwide competition. Technical specialists, writers, consultants, educators, trainers, marketers, graphic designers, programmers and almost every niche one can think of will find themselves offering their services in a highly competitive environment.

Larger group formations, such as retailers, manufacturers, developers, wholesalers, marketing companies, educational and training establishments, solution providers, Web site builders, Web hosting companies, Internet service providers will all find competition in the Information Age much fiercer than any competition found in the Industrial Age. They will be in competition not only to find customers and clients, but also to find and obtain the services of the most competent and knowledgeable experts and specialists.

In this fast-moving, highly competitive environment, to stand still will be to wither away and die. This will make it imperative for everyone, whatever part they play, small or large, to become skilled in the arts of communication and competitive game playing.

In the Industrial Age, geographic location, physical separation and lack of communication bandwidth restricted most business and commerce activity to regional localities. Now, in the Information Age, these barriers are rapidly disappearing. It's now as easy to hire a team of programmers in the back streets of Delhi as it is to have a local dedicated design team. Artwork and graphic design services are no longer restricted by the need to physically see content or have face-to-face discussion. Without this necessity, clients will find it just as easy to scout around the world to arrange suitable graphic design solutions at competitive prices.

In the Information Age, it may not even be necessary to engage experts for the technological work involved in much of e-business and e-commerce system design. There are numerous template solutions available, covering all kinds of technical needs. Many of these ready-built solutions will require little more than point and click operations to set up, so setting up Web sites and e-business solutions can be no more complicated than learning to use a word processor.

Thousands of different companies have created e-business solutions for themselves and then find they can parcel it up for others to use. This allows anyone from entrepreneurs with small start-up companies to managers in traditional Industrial Age corporations to get into an e-business situation immediately and cheaply to start experimenting.

In the Industrial Age, it was an expensive and lengthy process to set up a retail trading operation. Today, in the Information Age, you can set up an e-commerce retail Web site for free, complete with shopping carts and financial transaction facilities – all in a matter of minutes. It is as easy to install your own graphics and animations into a department in your own Web-based store as it is to put a picture into a word processor document. Any expertise or speciality knowledge that is required is usually only an email away if you have the right friends or contacts.

It is in the area of integrating existing Industrial Age businesses with the Internet that many important competitive battles will be fought. Internet communication strategies will need to be devised to enhance core businesses. The Internet and various forms of Web-based interfaces will be used to get customer or client feedback. They will be used to attract new customers and enhance customer loyalty. New strategic alliances can be formed via Internet and Web communications; complementary operations and services can be integrated or merged.

Industrial Age companies will not necessarily treat the Internet as a way of creating completely new business operations. It can be used as an aid in the distribution process, checking and tracking order processing from customer order to order delivery. These communication processes can be displayed on the Web for customers and clients to see for themselves how their orders are being dealt with. This will enhance customer confidence and give more credibility to a company. How much more assured will customers be if they can readily inspect the flow of order processing? Not only theirs, but others as well.

Email communication strategies and Web-based information sources will be used to back up real-world sales teams. There is no reason why this sales information flow shouldn't be open to public inspection. Why not let a customer or client see the information being channelled to sales teams? Isn't it designed to get to them anyway?

This is the Communication Shock of the Information Age. A new openness and transparency; a world where business deals and acts of cooperation and collaboration can be set up between different parties from all over the planet easily, quickly and cheaply. The implications of the removal of communication barriers are hard for the Industrial Age mind to grasp. Most managers and permanent employees will be replaced by communication specialists who will be dealing with complex networks of personal contacts, with layer upon layer of middlemen.

All businesses then, whether they like it or not, will be forced to employ suitable Internet strategies. These will have to be based upon sound foundations: the ability to communicate with people and to both cooperate and compete with them.

Games of competition

Competition is not something that can be formulated: if there is a known way to win then there can be no competition. Competition is about playing strategic games and these games come in two different forms: zero sum games and non-zero sum games. Distinguishing between these two types of game is absolutely vital in order to be able to devise a suitable strategy for e-business or e-commerce.

Zero sum means that if you take away the losses of the losers from the winnings of the winners the result is zero. In other words, winners win what losers lose. But not all games are zero sum games. There are games where winners win more than the losers lose. There are games where losers lose more than the winners win. These types of games are called non-zero sum games because if you take away the losses of the losers from the winnings of the winners the answer is not zero. Non-zero sum games include games where all the competitors lose, or all the competitors win.

Most people think of all competitive games as zero sum games, where the winners win from the losers, but in the world of business, especially e-business, these are the games to avoid. Seeing business as a non-zero sum game is another of those counter-intuitive notions, another paradox. How can someone gain if that gain is not at the expense of someone else? Solving this conundrum is the key to creating successful e-business and e-commerce strategies.

The enigma seems to be 'where does the money come from if there can be more gains than losses?'. To see how this can be, let's first take a look at the type of non-zero sum game that produces more losses than gains. In most of the poker clubs run in London during the 1960s, the clubs made their profits by taking a percentage of the money bet at each hand. A croupier would be responsible for dealing all cards and organizing the betting and at the end of each hand would remove 5 per cent for the house before passing the winnings to the player who'd won the hand. Although this was quite acceptable to the players – as only the winners appeared to be paying – the reality was that this was gradually draining money out of the game.

After long poker sessions, which could last for perhaps 12 hours or more, it wasn't uncommon for every single player at the table to be losing. The continuous drain on the money in play would have siphoned practically all the money into the coffers of the house. This same situation exists in casinos that run roulette. Here it is not so obvious that money is being siphoned off by the house because it is veiled by the laws of chance. Some people actually think that it is possible for a casino to lose, but the statistical probability of this happening is probably less than the chance of getting struck by lightning.

If a game of roulette runs with a single zero, the house will be siphoning off one thirty-seventh of the punters' bets at every spin of the wheel (on average). With an efficient croupier, this can amount to almost twice the average amount on the table at each spin going to the house each hour. If you want to check this out with some maths, just calculate what one player, betting $37 at each spin of the wheel, is likely to be losing after an hour's play of 60 spins. If the house is on average taking one thirty-seventh of each stake, the poor gambler would probably be losing about $60 an hour (on average), whatever system he or she is playing.

If you include the house take, both the poker and the roulette games are zero sum games. But if you look at the house take as an unavoidable overhead (the players having to pay to be in the game), then the players are in a non-zero sum game where their total losses are greater than their total gains.

Imagine, now, a poker session where the house, instead of taking out 5 per cent from the kitty, adds 5 per cent to each kitty before passing it onto the winner. Imagine a game of roulette where the zero acted like a wild card and everybody won when the ball landed in the zero slot. If you exclude the house, this would be a non-zero sum game for the players where total gains exceed total winnings.

Which type of game is it preferable to be in:

1   A game where the house takes a percentage of the stakes?
2   A game where the house lets the players play for free?

3   A game where the house adds some money to each bet made?

You'd have to have something wrong in the head not to prefer option 3, so wouldn't it make sense to make sure you played in option 3 games rather than the other two? How, then, do you recognize an option 3 game in e-business and e-commerce? How can you find a competitive win-win game where the gains are more than the losses? The trick is to understand where that extra money is coming from and how it is getting into the game.

The CD-ROM 'How God Makes God' features the Sun and the Earth having a discussion as to the nature of the life forms that have appeared on the Earth's surface. The method they use to find out about the human life forms is to listen in on various conversations. They are particularly puzzled by their observations that the human life forms have emotions that unconsciously motivate them towards particular patterns of behaviour.

They are also intrigued when they discover humans are interested in making money and are surprised when they find out that many business associations end up with everybody gaining from the association (a win-win, non-zero sum game). They resolve this mystery when they overhear a conversation where they discover that making money is the way in which humans have evolved to become increasingly efficient at using energy:

'What are you thinking about?'

'I am not thinking. I am reprogramming my brain.'

'Reprogramming your brain?'

'Yes, I have just learned that money can be equated with energy.'

'That's fairly obvious. You can buy things that you'd otherwise need energy to get for yourself, but why should you need to reprogram your brain?'

'Because all my previous associations with money had not registered that connection. Without that connection, between money and energy, my thinking will be sloppy when I am making financial judgements.'

'How do you reprogram your brain then, to equate money and energy?'

'Well, you have to rethink everything you have learned about money and substitute energy for money or value.'

'Give me an example.'

'Okay, this is the way my reprogramming thinking goes. In a commercial situation most of the people involved appear to be trying to gain money or value. If money and value are seen as amounts of energy, successful businesses making money are effectively winning energy. This must mean that business can be considered as a game to win energy. If the game is a "non-zero sum" type of game, a game where everybody can win, there must be energy being introduced into the system somehow.'

'Energy being put into the system?'

'Yes, if all the players are winning energy it has to come from somewhere.'

'Where from?'

'Oil is being pumped out of the ground at an energy cost far less than the energy in the oil. This will introduce energy into the system. Similarly with gas, coal, hydro and nuclear power. This is one of the reasons why economic activity can be a "non-zero sum" game with more winners than losers.'

'Wait a minute. This does not fully explain money making. People were making money long before these energy sources came into being. And money can be made when a prime energy source is not involved; the service industries for example.'

'You are quite right. Introducing energy into a system is not the only way to create "non-zero sum" games. People can also benefit from most commercial situations through energy being saved. Most business profits arise through the sharing of energy that has been gained through doing or making things more efficiently.'

'I don't quite understand.'

'I'll give you an example; is it necessary for you to go to farms all over the country to get your food?'

'No. I get my food from the stores.'

'This must mean that your local grocery store together with other middlemen collect all the food for you; arranging for everything you need to be brought to one single convenient place for you to collect. This saves you a lot of time and a lot of energy. Not only do they do this for you but they also do it for everyone else in the area.'

'I see, because they do everything in bulk they can do it more efficiently?'

'That's right; if you can imagine all the energy saved by you and all the other shoppers not having to traipse about all over the country to get your food you can see that the energy saving is enormous: far larger than the energy required by the store keeper and the middlemen who organize everything.'

'And the profit?'

'You and the other shoppers do not mind giving up a little of your saved energy to pay for this benefit so the store keeper and the middlemen can cover their costs and make a profit. Now can you see how everyone can benefit from saved energy?'

'I must admit that it is an interesting way to look at things.'

'The value to me is that it gives me a way of looking at how to make money. Money does not have to be made through taking it away from somebody else. Money making does not have to be a cut and thrust game between antagonists who try to take from each other. It can be a "non-zero sum" game where everybody can win and nobody need lose. The game of making money need not be about taking other people's money: it can be about trying to be more efficient and profiting by saving energy for people.'

'So making money need not be a battle of wits: it is a thinking game?'

'Yes, thinking up more efficient ways to save energy for people.'

After hearing this conversation, the Earth and the Sun go on to find out that energy is effectively created when people cooperate with each other. They come to the conclusion that cooperation is the main mechanism that saves energy and it is cooperation that is effectively the main source of wealth creation for human life forms. Here is another of the conversations they overhear:

'How is it that such an intangible thing as cooperation can produce a tangible thing like wealth?'

'Cooperation has the effect of increasing the efficiency of doing things. Increasing the efficiency is the same as making more time. The time that is saved or made, depending upon how you choose to look at it, is available to do other things such as creating luxuries and wealth. If there were no cooperation at all, the human race wouldn't have the time to create any wealth. Everyone would need every scrap of time available just for basic survival.'

'Give me an example.'

'Imagine a jungle where all the natives who live there have never learnt how to cooperate with each other. Suppose each of these natives makes an axe for himself to be able to cut down trees to build a house. Each makes his own spear for hunting and each casts his own individual iron pot for cooking.'

'I see, if they cooperate and share these items they need only make one of each?'

'Right, and the time they saved could be used to make something else.'

'So in effect those who cooperated could become wealthier than those who didn't because they would have extra time for making additional luxury goods or whatever else might be considered as wealth.'

'They could cooperate by specializing as well. If one was a good hunter and did all the hunting, another was a good builder and did all the building and the third was a good cook and did all the cooking they would all have plenty of well-cooked meals and live in well-built houses with all sorts of little extra luxuries that could be produced in the time they saved by working efficiently together.'

'They would certainly appear to be wealthier than natives who never cooperated together. So if cooperation is the key to creating wealth it must be the key to making money?'

'That's right.'

The Earth and the Sun then go on to discover that humans are not identical to each other in many different ways: physically, mentally and emotionally. This leads them to conclude that these differences are not just spurious effects of the reproduction process, but are more likely to be an evolved variance that makes it imperative for humans to cooperate with each other.

The argument is that by nature maintaining a difference between individuals, humans are forced to cooperate with each other in order to be able to compensate for any inadequacies they are born with. This cooperation is seen by the Earth and Sun as being instigated and reinforced by evolved emotions that are soft-wired into their brains. This is how their conversation proceeds at this stage:

'I can understand now how this mass of human life forms gets to succeed. Each of the life forms is slightly different from the others. By combining their various attributes they can use energy resources more efficiently.'

'So you think it is this cooperation between the life forms that is the source of their wealth?'

'It would seem to be, but that presents an enigma.'

'What do you mean?'

'Well, if the life forms' emotional devices are encouraging them to compete with each other for resources, how does it also get them to cooperate with each other?'

'I see what you are getting at: competition and cooperation would seem to require conflicting emotional directives.'

'Let's see if we can get some information to solve this puzzle.'

Indeed, this is the enigma. Humans have evolved to be competitive but also to be cooperative. These tendencies seem to require mutually exclusive behaviour. But it is the resolution of this paradox that leads to the formulation of efficient and effective business strategies.

Competing for cooperation

In almost every area of social and business life, communication skills are essential. This is recognized by nature and we have evolved a huge repertoire of different instincts, emotions and involuntary muscle movements that help us to communicate with each other both consciously and unconsciously; implicitly and explicitly. Somewhere, buried in our genetic make-up, is an inbuilt strategy that makes it instinctive for us to make friends, form groups and collaborate and cooperate with each other.

Evolutionary biologists have a simple explanation as to why we have evolved sophisticated instinctive strategies to communicate and cooperate: it is that people in a group have a massive advantage over lone individuals in the competition for survival and reproduction. This is why 'group forming' instincts and emotions have been preferentially selected by the evolutionary process.

Evolutionary biologists explain the advantage of groups by extending the concept of fitness (to survive and reproduce) to include the fitness that is imparted by an individual to his or her associates. They call this 'inclusive fitness'.

When I first came across this in O. E. Wilson's book, *Sociobiology*, I was confused because the value of inclusive fitness wasn't taken as the increase in fitness given *to* an individual *by* the group, but as the increase in fitness given *by* the individual *to* the group. It seemed that the evolutionary biologists had got it the wrong way round; surely, I thought, the group must impart increased survival value to the individual.

It was only after further reading that I found out that, in the case of humans, the prime survival unit is not the individual but the group. The pragmatic selection processes of evolution were selecting for groups rather than individuals. This is not an understanding that comes intuitively.

Nature sees the individual as simply a component of the virtual object that is being selected. The fitness of any individual doesn't count for anything if the combined fitness of the group the individual belongs to is below par. It was a sobering thought: understanding that we are each no more than a statistical part of some virtual whole that nature is more interested in.

Being aware of this subtlety of the inclusive fitness paradigm is a distinct advantage in business because it provides an important Zen-ness: the right mindset to form strategies and make decisions. It alters the emphasis to realize that the game is not about what the group can do for you but what you can do for the group. This provides another of those paradoxes that are counter-intuitive: the way to succeed is to give advantage to others.

This mindset is totally appropriate for the Internet and should be the fundamental tenet of all e-commerce and e-business solutions. Not because it is a nice thing to do, but because it is advantageous. Making a play that increases a bond to a group can be far more valuable than a play that secures a personal advantage.

However, just making these statements is empty rhetoric unless there is some substantial reasoning to back them up. For me, this came while I was working in the City of London writing the correspondence course on investment. It happened as a consequence of a series of discussions I'd had with the head of the investment company who was a keen advocate of sound monetary policy by government.

His pet hate at that time was government policies based upon the theories of John Maynard Keynes, the brilliant economist who'd been responsible for the Bretton Woods agreement that resulted in the stabilization of the economies of Europe after the Second World War. To a monetarist, Keynes' views are anathema because they involve deliberately introducing an element of inflation into the economy.

I wasn't at all convinced that this wasn't a bad thing, so this head of the investment company loaned me a book that was a critique of Keynes' major work, *The General Theory of Employment, Interest and Money*. I forget the name of the book he gave me, but what it contained was an excerpt from Keynes' book that provided one of the key concepts upon which Keynes based all his theories. Figure 10.1, taken from the CD-ROM 'How God Makes God' (where this theory is explained by way of interactive games), shows what I found in that book.

At first, I balked at this mathematical arcane language. It seemed beyond the comprehension of normal mortals. But I was intrigued because here was this great economist giving us one of the fundamental core concepts upon which his thinking was based. So I decided to persevere and try to find out what it was actually saying.

Now if for a given value of N the expected proceeds are greater than the aggregate supply price, i.e. if D is greater than Z, there will be an incentive to entrepreneurs to increase employment beyond N and, if necessary, to raise the costs by competing with one another for the factors of production, up to the value of N for which Z has become equal to D. Thus the volume of employment is given by the point of intersection between the aggregate demand function and the aggregate supply function; for it is at this point that the entrepreneur's expectation of profit will be maximised. The value of D at the point of the aggregate demand function, where it is intersected by the aggregate supply function, will be called 'the effective demand' ....

....................This is the substance of the General Theory of Employment.

Note: D = Demand price for labour.
       Z = Supply price for labour.
       N = Quantity of labour.

Figure 10.1 The General Theory of Employment

I divided this description up into small parts and examined each separately, putting them into everyday language. When I'd finished, I was amazed by what I found. It was like digging up a dirty old blackened stone from the garden, cleaning it, and finding it was made of pure gold. This is how the translation turned out:

Now if for a given number of employees the employer is making a profit (i.e., the value of what the employees produce is greater than the amount needed to pay them), there is an incentive for the employer to employ more people; if necessary, offering higher wages: competing with other employers to get workers. All the employers will compete with each other to get as many employees as possible by offering higher wages than each other. This they will do until it is no longer profitable to employ any more (i.e., employers will keep competing with each other to employ more people until they have driven up the amount they are offering in wages to the point where their total profits start to fall). There comes a point when it does not pay to hire any more workers and at this point wages will be at their highest.

... this is the substance of the Theory of Employment.

In isolation, this seems a rather bland series of statements of the obvious and at first glance it doesn't seem possible that this could form the core paradigm that had produced Keynes' widely acclaimed, major contribution to economic theory. It simply seems to be saying that employers will employ more people if it is profitable to do so and if it is profitable they will compete with each other for employees. Big deal! It seems incredible that such a simple and obvious observation could form the basis of what is regarded as one of the most renowned works in the whole history of economics.

Fortunately, at that time, I was extremely interested in game theory and was reading a book by Thomas C. Schelling called *The Strategy of Conflict* (1960). Schelling had become famous as one of the main advisers to Dr Henry Kissinger during the Cuban missile crisis in the early 1960s when the American government had played out a nail-biting game scenario with the Russians to stop them building missile sites in Cuba.

The essence of Schelling's book was that international conflicts should be put into a game theory framework, such that promises, threats and counter-threats could be described in the form of a pay-off matrix. The idea was that every unfavourable move possible to an opponent could be countered by making that move less attractive to the opponent than some other alternative that would be tolerably acceptable.

His basic proposition was that you could influence the way people acted through changing the pay-off matrix of the outcomes of actions. Schelling observed that the adjustment to the pay-offs, as seen by an opponent, could be made through two tactics: promise and threat. By making a promise of some reward, if an opponent did something you wanted them to do, they would be more inclined to do it. Similarly, a threat – that something unpleasant would happen to an opponent if they did something you didn't want them to do – could be used to influence them not to do it.

Schelling's strategy was to devise ways in which it could be arranged that there was a pay-off matrix that could provide a solution that would be suitable for both sides: a compromise where the outcome was not necessarily the best for either side but provided an acceptable second-best solution for each.

The eureka moment for me came when I made a connection between the core paradigm of Keynes and the game theory approach advocated by Schelling. I'd read somewhere about Keynes' interest in game theory. Suddenly, I could see what Keynes had been explaining. He wasn't stating the obvious at all. He was saying that business was a game and the game wasn't focused on the obvious (i.e., competing for money), it was focused on getting employees. The paradigm shift therefore is not to see business as a game of conflict for money but a game of competition for cooperation.

If a profitable situation arises, employers would be in a win-win situation, but only if they could get employees. Employees would also be in a win-win situation because employers would be in competition with each other and have to pay them more and more in order to win their cooperation.

Keynes' insight was to see that by creating enough profitable situations (by increasing the money supply), labour would be at a premium and employers would be forced to bid up the amount they'd have to pay their employees to attract and keep them. With full employment and employees achieving maximum earnings the economy was bound to be buoyant.

Here then is another counter-intuitive paradox: business is a game where you compete for cooperation. Employers are not in a competitive situation with their employees, they are in a competition with each other to acquire cooperators. Employees are the objects of desire and are keenly sought after and competed for wherever a profitable situation emerges.

Applying Keynes' thinking to e-commerce

The idea behind Keynes' recommendation of increasing the money supply was to allow more non-zero sum situations to be created. Arguably, these increased opportunities are created at the expense of people who have savings, but as most savings are invested into these newly created opportunities the gains and losses are not easy to determine.

The actual gain of Keynes' strategy comes as a result of the whole economy becoming more efficient as an increasing number of people are employed and their employment effort is used more efficiently. This again is another paradox. Why should employees work more efficiently if there is a shortage of labour and they are in high demand?

The answer is that entrepreneurs and big business employers will have to compete more expertly to acquire their cooperation. They will have to pay them higher wages and this they can do only if they are directing the labour efficiently. The net result is that entrepreneurs and employers will have to look for the most profitable areas of trade and commerce and this must be where the greatest improvements in efficiencies are to be found. Any employers stuck in a business that isn't increasing efficiency in some way will not be able to make enough money to compete successfully in the labour market.

Note: This Keynsian view is in sharp contrast to the views of many post-Keynsian economists who recommend maintaining a pool of unemployment to force workers to work more efficiently in order to maintain their jobs. It is also in contrast to the monetarists who want to keep the money supply constant.

Seeing e-business and e-commerce in this Keynsian way, it is not hard to see the potential for huge profits in e-business and e-commerce because the rapid advances in computer and communication technology offer ample opportunities for increased efficiency over Industrial Age techniques and methods. Increased efficiency means saved energy and this energy thus becomes available to be shared in non-zero sum games. The winners in these games are going to be those who most effectively learn how to seek and obtain reciprocal acts of cooperation.

The primary game then is not so much looking for profitable situations (these will be in plentiful supply), the real game is in competing for cooperation. This brings us back once again to communicating and dealing with people.

The value of an act of cooperation

If we use a game theory approach to gaining cooperation, similar to the way Schelling approaches situations of conflict, we can think of using two possible tactics: promise and threat. The promise is essentially, 'If you cooperate with me you will get a reward' and the threat is 'If you don't cooperate with me you will suffer a penalty or loss of some kind.' As the goal is to get cooperation, any threat involving a penalty would almost certainly backfire, so the only valid threat that can be made is the loss of some kind of future cooperation and the rewards that might go with it.

Game theory gives us a very simple framework in which to view an act of cooperation. Each potential cooperator has only two choices: to cooperate or not cooperate. For an act of cooperation to take place, each must be able to see a clear benefit in a decision to cooperate over a decision not to cooperate.

Despite the apparent simplicity of this decision framework, valuing the relative merits of cooperating or not cooperating is far from straightforward. This was not nearly such a problem in the Industrial Age because of the slower rates of change and the reduced level of competition. The traditional Industrial Age business environment allowed more rigid and more permanent associations to be established, where it was relatively easy to see the potential benefits of any association or act of cooperation.

In a rapidly changing world like e-commerce, technical competence and experience have transitory values. A sound and well-established expert in one situation may be totally unsuitable for a similar situation at a later time. Rapidly changing technology can create reputations in weeks and who is to know how long their expertise will be in vogue as technologies and favoured competitive strategies change? Worse still, who is to judge the value of an association or act of cooperation when the judgement involves assessing the abilities of someone where you have no way of truly measuring their worth?

As problematic as judging the value of an expert's cooperation is the corollary: how can an expert or a specialist provide proof of their value to someone else? Maybe you can work out the value of somebody else's cooperation to you, but this information is purely academic if they see little or no value in having an association with you.

This yields another paradox: the Internet provides a perfect environment to offer ample choice in partners for cooperation. It is a perfect environment to communicate with potential cooperators. Yet, it is almost impossibly difficult to make decisions about who to cooperate with.

To resolve this paradox, we need some Zen-ness: a mental model that will enable us to make shrewd judgements. We need to have some way of approximating the possible value of an act of cooperation before it takes place. We need to know how to get somebody else to see the value of us cooperating with them.

For such a model we can do no better than go to the masters of game theory in conditions of competition and uncertainty: the professional investors. Although they may seem far removed from the problems of establishing acts of cooperation in the Information Age, at an abstract level they are coping with an identical situation. An act of cooperation involves a time commitment or a financial commitment. This is an investment. It makes sense then to look at how the professionals in the more experienced world of investment handle the valuations in their world – which is just as changeable, competitive and uncertain as the world of e-business and e-commerce.

We can use the models used by professional investors because we can readily translate time invested and energy expended in an act of cooperation into a monetary sum. Employees generally work for a salary, subcontractors and contractors work for a fee, companies will make a charge and entrepreneurs will want a profit. All these values will be based upon a combination of a number of factors but each will include money going direct to people, money for overheads and money for research and development. It doesn't matter how the relevant values are assigned, they will all boil down to a rate of payment for time, i.e., so much per hour, per day, per month or per annum.

Professional investment managers know how to deal with rates of money spread over time. They are used to looking at incomes and converting them into lump sum values. They are equally adept at converting lump sum values into incomes. It is the ability to perform these tricks expertly that gives professional investment managers their skills.

The key to making these investment valuations is in using relative values instead of absolute values. This is because there are so many unknowns and uncertainties involved in the value of a future income that it is impossible to work out with any degree of certainty a precise value. So, the professional investor will have in mind a base value to which all other incomes can be compared.

For professional investors, the base value of an income is the current value of a pure income that is almost certain to be paid. This value can be obtained by looking at the price of annuities that are issued by issuers who have virtually no chance of running out of funds.

Note: annuities are guaranteed perpetual incomes that are bought for a lump sum of money.

There are many different companies and organizations that will offer such incomes. Usually the safest are backed by large and established finance houses or stable governments. Once arranged and paid for, these incomes can be traded just like any other commodity and they will have a value depending upon the credibility of the prime issuer.

For example, an annuity of $10,000 per annum will have a higher value if the issuer is the Bank of America than if the issuer is a little-known offshore trust. Once you know the current rate for a '(near) hundred per cent safe' annuity – such as the Bank of America – you can value all other annuities by discounting for any risks. For a little-known offshore trust, you discount for the risk of the income not being honoured.

Say an offshore trust offers an annuity of $10,000 per annum. This would be judged by a professional investor as having a risk associated with it. The professional investor will investigate the credentials of the issuer and may judge that there is a 20 per cent chance that the issuer will default on this promise to pay a fixed income in perpetuity. Professional investors are not put off by this risk because they will be dealing with many annuities and so will be able to spread the risk.

If the same annuity of $10,000 per annum is offered by a safe issuer for say $200,000, the professional investor will discount the risk by valuing the offshore trust's annuity at 20 per cent less than the safe issuer's price. Thus the value of the offshore trust's offered income of $10,000 per annum would be seen as being worth $160,000. In this way, the investor will discount the risk, so that, effectively, the value of an offshore trust's annuity will compare favourably to that of a safe annuity. If the offshore company offered their promise of $10,000 per annum for only $150,000, the professional investor might well see this to be better value than the near hundred per cent safe investment.

The value of the safe annuity is constantly changing with the average of total market expectations. It will be discounting all the factors involved in expectations regarding the stability of the currency in which the income is arranged. It will also be discounting all the factors that reflect the general view as to inflation and the state of the economy. By using relative values, professional investors don't have to worry about any of these aspects because they will be common to all annuities. So, the only calculation needed to value any particular investment is to discount the risk factor against the value of the perfectly safe annuities.

Abstracting this principle across to arranging acts of cooperation through the Internet, the vital considerations become clear. Any act of cooperation has a value that is not absolute but is dependent upon the risk factors being discounted by the parties involved in the contemplated cooperation. This value is relative to the current going rate for a known and proven cooperator.

The skill then, in being able to effect acts of cooperation, is not only to be able to value the other party's cooperation to you, but also to be able to estimate the value of your cooperation to them *as seen from their point of view*. It is this matching of valuations that is vital to any proposed cooperative association.

Allowing for risk in contemplating cooperation

As we have covered in previous chapters, all business solutions will best be arranged by splitting up e-business and e-commerce solutions into as many different modules as possible. This will allow risks to be spread and at the same time facilitate the maximum of information and knowledge being brought to bear on the solution.

These modules can be treated as objects that include the designer, so instead of having to deal with the technology involved in the module, it is only necessary to deal with the module's interface: a person. Thus, to arrange for the modular components to be incorporated into a total solution, a solution builder will have to set up many different arrangements of cooperation with a number of different people.

The solution builder is now in the same position as the professional investor. The solution builder will be effectively buying a number of incomes. These incomes are in the form of a promise to commit time to provide a module that will respond appropriately to messages that are sent to it from other parts of the solution. The solution builder will have to give a value to each module designer's promise to build the module he or she is responsible for. The designer, on his or her part, has to specify a price for his or her expertise in the same way that an offshore company might ask a price for an annuity it is offering.

The difficulty is immediately apparent. What are the risk factors involved that will be used to discount the value of the expert's offer to build the module? The solution builder cannot hope to make a perfect choice of expert for every module, so there will have to be a discount built into the price to arrange either for duplication, or for unsatisfactory modules being replaced. The expert on the other hand has to allow for the risk that his or her work will be paid for at the end of the day.

 From the solution builder's point of view

The solution provider, having access to the Internet, will have an over-choice of possible experts for each module. How is the solution provider going to choose which experts to use? How is the solution provider going to be able to judge the risk factors?

The solution builder will not be able to be familiar with all the technical aspects involved in a required solution, not least because it is unlikely that he or she will be aware of them. Instead, the solution builder will have to be an expert in Internet communications because the only way he or she is going to know what modules to include and what experts to use is going to have to come through trusted advice and recommendations.

The solution builder will have to join special interest groups, get advice from other experts whose opinions he or she trusts, be aware of what is happening in his or her own industry in respect of Internet and Web activities and know what his or her competitors are doing. Above all, the solution builder will be part of a constant feedback loop between the end users of the solution and the evolving design.

All this information is liable to be obtained through using suitable Internet communication strategies. Through various sources, the solution provider will be able to get a broad idea of the kind of cooperative situations that need to be set up, the expertise needed and the kind of money that will be involved. The solution provider will be doing all this through communications with people.

Of course, experienced solution builders will have built up a list of experts and specialists that they have used before, but even so, the rapidly changing world of e-business and e-commerce will necessitate that they constantly be on the search for more. All solution builders, then, will be open to establishing new agreements of cooperation. Recommendations from trusted sources will count for much, but so also will tangible evidence.

A solution provider will be particularly responsive to recommendations from experts already working on a solution if, as is likely, the design is based upon a bottom-up approach. Needs arising out of emergence and end-user feedback, as the design progresses, will throw up all kinds of requirements for specialities and new kinds of expertise. In this way a solution builder will not so much be designing a solution and then creating a team to build it; the solutions and the team will be self-constructing: evolving of their own volition in direct response to the system requirements.

Using all the communication possibilities available to create the right mix of people to build the components for an e-business or e-commerce solution, at the end of the day the solution builder will still be investing in uncertainties. However, like the newsagent designing a newspaper delivery service, like the professional investor creating a portfolio of investments, none of the components can be guaranteed to be a perfect choice, so the solutions builder will spread the risk by discounting values and build in adequate redundancies to compensate for any failures or shortcomings.

From the expert's point of view

The strategy of experts or specialists will be quite different from that of the solution builder. They are selling and not buying. They are in the position of the offshore annuity issuer. They have something to offer but its value is going to be highly dependent upon the credibility perceived by a solution builder. Not only must their credibility be high, they must also be able to make solution builders aware of their services.

This is no simple problem to solve. This is similar to the problem the solution builder has when designing a solution to attract, satisfy and retain clients or customers. The world of the Internet is alive with possibilities to make appropriate contacts but unless you have an appropriate and active strategy for communicating you might as well be dead.

As with annuities in the world of finance and investment, there will be some base value for the services an expert or specialist provides. Through suitable email discussion it shouldn't be difficult for an expert or specialist to work out the range of different rates that he or she can charge for his or her services. However, just as with annuities, the base value will be variously discounted by solution builders.

It is common for experts and specialists new to the Information Age to be totally oblivious to the discounting that will apply to their offers of cooperation. They may quote what they see as a fair and reasonable rate for a job and be totally bemused as to why they get so few takers. They seem to lose all perspective as to how their offer might be judged against all the other alternatives a solution builder might have in this communication environment. They'll feel aggrieved that their expertise is so often spurned.

However, if they stop for a moment to look at the situation from the solution provider's point of view they can start to work out a strategy to obtain a suitable number of cooperative deals that will give them the returns they are looking for.

Let's stop for a moment to consider what factors might be involved in an expert's or specialist's strategy when looking for cooperative deals in the Information Age. Firstly, they'd need to decide whether or not they want to be an independent expert or whether they'd sooner be part of a middleman's team.

If the latter, they will have little need to deal with solution builders and will be concentrating on building up contacts and speciality expertise that fits in with the requirements of the group they belong to. Normally this would be the ideal way for a technologist who is starting out, where their employment would be more in the nature of an apprenticeship where they would be able to gain experience and learn from other members of the team.

More practically, the more ambitious expert will soon realize that the real efficiencies and progress in e-business and e-commerce solutions are being made by solution builders who don't use Industrial Age-type teams. Flexible team-building strategies that create teams on the fly in response to particular situations are liable to be more effective and more efficient and so be able to command the higher rates of pay.

This is a big jump for somebody who has been used to working in a permanent team where there is a regular, though modest, salary arrangement. Besides the need to establish contacts to keep up to speed within their own area of expertise, they will have to find and maintain a list of contacts who will be able to hire them to work on solutions.

In a world of object-oriented design techniques, there will be no such thing as permanent or long-term contracts: all jobs will be in and out fast. That is the expert's value to a solution builder in the Information Age: short-term hired experts can efficiently apply their expertise where and when it is needed. This will obviously require the experts to build and maintain quite a number of contacts so as to ensure a regular supply of work.

This is not something that will happen just by entering details into some kind of directory. Without some form of recommendation, or word of mouth reputation, an expert or specialist is about as employable as a green frog.

Starting from the position of a green frog, experts will have to negotiate around their Hilbert solution space until they find a position where they have sufficient contacts who are aware of and appreciate their capabilities. This place in Hilbert solution space can only be found through a bottom-up process, which means starting slowly and gradually moving towards that desired goal.

The most difficult problem to overcome is the start. Without any track record or any contacts there can be no work. With the probability that an expert's or specialist's services will be heavily discounted for value without a proven track record, experts will have to start by pitching their charges at a very low rate, maybe even providing them free of charge to get a foot on the first rung of the ladder.

The experts will have to create a suitable communication strategy that will bring them in close contact with other experts who are actively working on e-business or e-commerce solutions. They will have to establish a rapport, exchange emails. They will have to keep up with the constant evolutionary changes that are occurring in their own area of speciality as well as the broader area in which their services would be applied.

There is no alternative for experts other than to ensure that they have a suitably efficient communication network that keeps them informed and maintains their presence in the community where their services might be needed. Their chosen expertise or specialist knowledge will not be sufficient in itself; it must be supported by a continuous communication infrastructure that keeps them actively in the game.

At first thoughts this would seem to put the expert in a lone and isolated position, but in the world of the Internet this can be very far from the truth. Think back to the sociogram of Chapter 4. Think about how all the doctors were linked in various different ways through lines of communication. Now consider how an expert might fit into a far more complex sociogram on the Internet.

The fact that an Industrial Age-style team is redundant in the Information Age does not imply that there is nothing to replace it. Quite the opposite, there is a far better and more efficient form of association available: the virtual team that has the advantage that an expert can belong to many virtual teams and all at the same time.

Experts are only alone and isolated if they don't make the effort to create their own communication infrastructures that link them to other experts and specialists. Just as components in an object-oriented design strategy can be mixed and matched in a variety of ways, so can experts and specialists. If one expert gets work on an e-business or e-commerce solution there will be a need for others, so the engaged experts can recommend their contacts.

In this way, what would appear on the surface to be thousands and thousands of isolated and independent experts is actually a sea of experts who can rapidly self-organize into special project teams to tackle any kind of competitive situation that an e-business or e-commerce solution might turn up.

It is this ability to self-organize that provides the power inherent in networks of Internet-connected experts and specialists. As solution builders start to become aware of this phenomenon they will capitalize on the power to build highly competitive and adaptive structures to outwit and outsmart the competition. These self-organizing virtual teams will be able to create solutions far better than could be devised by any pre-planned formulated approach.

The experts and specialists, then, will be relying as much on their communication skills and strategies to create a position in these networks as they will on their expert skills and knowledge. Once again, even for experts and specialists, success will be totally reliant upon appropriate strategies for communicating with people.

Chapter 11

The Industrial Age concept of a team is not appropriate for collaboration on the Internet

Why there are no examples or case histories

After I had written the previous chapter, I sent it out to the readers in the café with a note asking what they were expecting or would like to see in the final chapters. I explained that I intended writing the ending of the book like the ending of a detective story, where all the clues spread throughout the book could be brought together to produce a conclusion.

The most frequent requests were for some real-world examples of e-business or e-commerce that would show how the ideas in the book were being applied. This was something my publisher had also been asking for. Unfortunately, I couldn't oblige because the book isn't about procedures or methods, it is about concepts and ideas. These aren't tangible elements that can be put on show; they are elements of the invisible frameworks that lie behind strategies. Such frameworks would be in the minds, not the actions, of strategists. Unless you can actually get into the minds of everyone involved in a solution, you can't really say how it happened.

This is why I have stuck rigidly to my personal experiences because I know all the details and the reasons why things happened. Sure, it needs a little abstraction to map the concepts across to e-commerce, but this is what the book is about: getting at the abstractions so that they can be applied as a kind of streetwise Zen-ness. This allows e-commerce business people to work at the leading edges of the expanding world of digital communications and be able to make shrewd decisions that are not logically obvious. Once the Internet settles down to where things can be formulated and written up as procedures and case histories, all the great opportunities will have long since passed.

Apart from this reason, I'd already made a decision at the beginning of the book to avoid case studies or examples of any Information Age business solutions because it was reasonable to assume that they would be out of date by the time people came to read the book. This had been patently obvious from my reading of other e-commerce books. Some of the examples I'd seen used looked ridiculous by the time the books got into print. The production time cycle of a book takes centuries measured against the light-speed world of the Internet.

E-business and e-commerce books are really only suitable for explaining fundamental concepts. In this fast-moving world, past examples are seldom helpful because trying to play 'copy cat' or 'catch up' isn't a good strategy. The only way to play the game is to get out in front and stay there and, if you do get behind, you play leap frog. At this stage of the Information Age, looking at what others have done in the past is likely to be counter-productive. What we need are conceptual tools that allow us to look ahead.

The puzzling post

One post did surprise me though and made me think much more about the implications of the Information Age. This was written by Yvan Caron, the Canadian systems analyst whose comments and observations I always value:

I read the new chapter and I found it interesting. I really like the passages that were taken from your CD 'How God Makes God'. When I think about your different models that you propose such as Hilbert space, game theory and competing for cooperation I feel that you take great care to explain them in a straightforward manner.

However, I do wonder why do you put so much energy to explain what seems to me just plain common sense. For example, when you say that 'It was only after further reading that I found out that, in the case of humans, the prime survival unit is not the individual but the group'. In some way this chapter and the previous one present many ideas but you use somewhat a scientific language to express these common sense ideas as if they were new or mysterious. I think that we all know that it is not what our country can do for us but instead what we can do for it. In some way this summarizes the essence of Chapter 10 and I heard it many years ago from a previous president of the United States.

Also, it would be nice if you could present some initiatives that are being done on the Internet in order to manage projects in a distributed world. Particularly when you describe what should be the behaviours of the solution builder. I would recommend that you read…

Yvan then provided URLs to several Web site articles that gave quite detailed analysis of various other strategies and approaches being used for e-business and e-commerce solutions. I was quite surprised when I read them because they weren't just alternative approaches he was pointing to, they were approaches that were diametrically opposed to everything I'd written in the previous chapters of the book: they were written from the mindset of Industrial Age paradigms.

Having respect for Yvan's opinions, I wondered how it could be that after reading through and seeming to follow and agree with all the chapters in the book so far, he'd seen these alternative approaches as practical and viable. For an author, trying to explain fundamental concepts, it is quite worrying when a reader seems to have lost the plot altogether.·

The clue to this perplexing anomaly was his rapid dismissal of the 'scientific language' I'd used to explain what seemed to him to be common sense notions of a group. Suddenly it clicked. His idea of a group in the corporate world was totally different from my idea of a group in the Information Age. He was automatically associating a group with the concept of a group that is pro-grammed into the mindset of the Industrial Age: more usually referred to as a team.

Isn't the formation of a team a key concept of every management training course? Isn't this concept taught to every Industrial Age manager and executive as the basic work unit for all strategies? No wonder Yvan was seeing the group as a common sense issue that needed no special elaboration. He'd been there, done that and got the T-shirt. Why bother to re-examine the idea of a group when it has been so extensively and exhaustively covered over many decades of corporate experience and learning?

However, the concept of a group in the corporate world is a very special type of group: it is a managed team. As far as I am concerned, the managed team is a totally inappropriate type of group for the Information Age. My idea of a group is quite different, I'm thinking of a more natural type of group: a leaderless group, where the bonding comes through mutual group member advantage and not as an artefact of carefully orchestrated design. I then looked more carefully at the Web pages Yvan had referred to.

A group does not necessarily imply a managed team

The articles were very detailed, with numerous case studies and examples of the work being carried out by various solution providers. The first thing that came across was the sheer size of the universal effort being put into finding ways to utilize digital communication technology. Billions of dollars were being spent. The articles provided ample evidence that most big corporations of the Industrial Age are fully aware of the opportunities and challenges of the Information Age. It was clear that most corporations seem to fully understand that they will have to reorganize their work practices to take advantage of the benefits the Internet can offer.

The problem was, these articles were advising strategies based upon the paradigms and structures that had evolved before the Internet came into being. They were all variations on the theme of putting top-down, planned solutions into place; in effect, applying the concepts, methods and practices of the Industrial Age to the far different environment of the Information Age.

At another table in the café, a developer of sophisticated plug-in units for multimedia solutions, Vahe Kassardjian, who was actively working at the cutting edge of communication technology, sent in another email:

I find this book very convincing, mostly because I have personal experience in the industry. I am not sure that people of more traditional industries, mostly people from corporate cultures, would buy Peter's advice. The first chapters of the book efficiently demolish the traditional approach. The last chapters are not as convincing. They look academic. Probably because they don't contain as many real-life examples and counter-examples as the first chapters. I wouldn't know how to fix this, though. Should I expect a Zen ending?

Vahe was also recognizing that these concepts would not be readily integrated into the minds of Industrial Age managers and executives. It took me back again to the time I'd encountered those first electronic components in the research establishment. I'd spent months learning all the theory, but when I came to the reality, I was at a total loss as to how to apply this theory to a real-world situation. Perhaps this was the problem here? Perhaps Yvan could agree and understand all the theoretical considerations but not be able to map them across to the more complex real world? Was this because of the different way he conceptualized a group?

Vahe asked if he should expect a Zen ending. He meant it humorously, but it was exactly how I'd planned to finish up. Well, not Zen exactly, but the idea incorporated in Zen philosophy is where you use mental tricks to get away from ingrained and deeply seated dogmas and attitudes to allow you to look at problems in a fresh light. This is also the scientific approach: putting things into an abstract theoretical framework allows you to look at problems in a new and different way that is not influenced by previous learned stereotyped ideas. The Zen technique is simply a way of escaping from conventional thinking.

This is what Keynes had done. He'd managed to put the crux of the economic problems into a mathematical abstraction that allowed him to see the solutions clearly. As we saw in the last chapter, the complicated mathematical treatment amounted to little more than common sense, yet not only did this abstraction help Keynes provide a solution for the European economies after the Second World War, it also helped make a fortune in the stock market for Keynes' college when he advised them on investment strategies.

I decided to read the articles through once more. I wanted to look at them in terms of the different ways of conceptualizing a group. After all, I was no theorist or academic: I'd spent most of my life in the pragmatic, nitty-gritty world of harsh reality and wasn't easily fooled by airy-fairy theoretical considerations.

Examining the Industrial Age's approach

Going through the articles again more carefully and making notes as I went along, I saw how a typical Industrial Age strategist would view the use of the Internet. These can be summarized as follows:

1 The business approach to e-business and e-commerce must be by way of projects. These are the principal units of organization.

2 Projects are the structural framework for implementing all initiatives, progress, growth and change.

3 Projects are run by teams: to do feasibility studies, create business strategies, develop new products, devise imaginative marketing schemes, plan expansion, think out suitable training and educational programmes.

4 The Internet provides a wonderful opportunity to create collaborative tools to manage teams and assist these teams to manage projects.

5 For a team to use the Internet there will be a need for new project management tools that will assist and coordinate enterprise project-based collaboration.

6 All procedures, methods and tools must be carefully evaluated, selected and deployed.

Every one of the software systems described in the articles referenced by Yvan assumed projects were based upon well-thought-out, fully detailed plans. The systems recommended were mostly based upon a virtual workspace that concentrated on planned goals, monitoring every step of the progress, setting standards, detailing documents.

Reading through each article, I kept coming across such expressions as: proper planning, clear, concise performance targets, consensus-based decision making, support for standards, clearly identified goals, defining shared goals, the means to achieve goals, tracking progress towards goals, project control and reporting, development of work breakdown structures, resource assignments, estimating and project scheduling, reporting of effort to date, current financial variance from the initial baseline, work flow designations, document handling, the flow of work, common documents, scheduling based on resources, viewing personal and group schedules and commitments, maintaining a data repository for projects.

Can you just imagine such a system working reliably in the chaotic and competitive environments of e-business and e-commerce, with new technology and new techniques constantly throwing these plans into disarray? Yet these were serious propositions, by advisers to big corporations who were spending millions of dollars on such schemes. Any increase in efficiency offered by digital communication technology would surely be wiped out by such unrealistic approaches to complex systems. As a croupier at one of the poker games I played at used to say when somebody made an unprofessional play, 'I wish they'd come and play a private game of poker with me in my front room.'

All the software systems for organizing projects described in the articles – variously named groupware, teamware and knowledge retrieval – were based upon the Industrial Age concept of a team. This is so fundamental to all Industrial Age strategies that it is probably impossible for many corporate managers and executives to imagine a world where the managed team is not the most efficient structure. Thus, many of the software solutions were particularly concerned with leadership, people problems and team spirit.

The common theme seemed to be that technology is important, but human management is more so. People must be motivated and rewarded for collaborative efforts and the project results. Consideration must be given to human and business motivation. The articles warned of the dangers of personal politics endangering team cooperation and collaboration. The software packages included various built-in mechanisms that supported and encouraged desirable behaviour. All the articles emphasized the importance of psychological issues, warning that ego or emotional factors would be likely to complicate matters.

Extrapolating from the concerns and problems with people issues in the conventional, bricks and mortar world, the articles predicted that these issues would be even more of a problem in an e-business environment, where the members of virtual teams would be geographically separated. Their solution was to call for new codes of behaviour, encouraged by financial rewards and other inducements of personal and career opportunities for advancement and growth.

The articles emphasized a backup need, for all the software solutions they were recommending, that would encourage staff to be hard working, focused and dedicated. It was seen as essential for project leaders to pay attention to people's personal needs, provide adequate training support and coaching. Most of the recommended software packages had provisions for the electronic implementation and support for various psychological methods of people manipulation.

As I read through all the articles, I came to the conclusion that they were not really about having a competitive approach to e-commerce and e-business. It seemed to me more like lists of all the kind of things you would need to put into a sales pitch to sell a multi-million dollar scheme to a gullible corporate management who had no first-hand knowledge of operating in the digital world.

It all sounds so plausible. That is, until you start to think about how such a team-based project might compete against an Information Age communicator who is able to create a group of experts on the fly; able to reconfigure a group of specialists to meet any contingency; respond instantly to any new technological advances or surprise moves made by the competition. Without the need to have to manage, motivate or train anyone, the Information Age communicator will be able to run rings around any managed team.

The idea of an unmanaged group, where there is no concern for people issues or human welfare, must seem utterly bizarre to an Industrial Age mindset. It doesn't seem workable and goes against everything that has ever been written about groups in all the managerial training manuals. However, this is a phenomenon that is going to dominate the organizational structuring of Internet-based businesses.

Although the managed team will still be ubiquitous and an essential element of organization in the Information Age, its functioning will be confined to specific tasks and geographic locations. It will feature mostly in the physical areas of e-business and e-commerce, outside of the periphery of the Internet.

Conventional management techniques are not portable to a highly connective environment, so the role of the managed team will stop at the boundary of the Internet. The Internet is the domain of unmanaged teams. Rather than lead and initiate e-business and e-commerce solutions, the managed teams will follow. As bizarre as this must seem to the Industrial Age mind, the prime objectives of the managers of managed teams will be to follow the directions and initiatives provided by unmanaged groups, where at times they might even appear not to have a leader.

It is this strange state of affairs that we shall be investigating in the remainder of this book.

An event-driven system

After writing the above, I sent it to Yvan Caron for his comments to make sure I hadn't misread his post. This is the reply he returned:

> Just after I had sent you my comments regarding Chapter 10, for a brief period, I felt a bit guilty. I had the following picture in my mind: it was like if I had thrown an obstacle in front of your bicycle while you were moving towards the finish line. I knew that something was missing in your book but just could not put my finger on it or find the right words to express it in a clever way and with delicate distinction.
>
> After reading your start to Chapter 11... I think and I recognize that I am influenced largely by the mindset of the company for which I work. All our work revolves around an integrated suite of state-of-the-art methods, processes, techniques and tools to help us as consultants to manage large-scale, risk-prone projects.
>
> These methods are an integrated, dynamic, fast-moving, and cyclical approach for delivering and maintaining information systems while controlling project costs. This is achieved by: providing an explicit and visible process through the use of deliverables which enables managers to control development projects or maintenance activities; enabling reuse of processes, concepts and deliverables to increase productivity and mobility of project teams; focusing on usable, flexible, and maintainable business solutions that are delivered on-time and within budget; defining clear roles and responsibilities for the professionals involved in a project and providing guidelines to decrease the time they need to become proficient in their tasks.
>
> These processes are captured, structured and embodied today in our knowledge management system. Since everything revolves around the production of deliverables, managers know how much they will pay for each of these deliverables. I think this is one of the key reasons why I was shocked while reading Chapter 10. I just could not figure out how we could act as a responsible solution builder if we had no metrics to guide us.
>
> But the distinction you now make in Chapter 11 is important because it helps us to understand what was previously fuzzy in your writing, namely: the distinction between my idea of a group in the corporate world from your idea of a group in the Information Age. It is important because this distinction will surely influence the metrics that we will have to discover in order to control project costs.
>
> If you can find a way to explain how you will control project costs using a bottom-up approach then it would be easy to convince not only entrepreneurs but big corporations also.

With this post, Yvan had highlighted the chasm between Industrial Age thinking and Information Age thinking. He'd finished up by asking, 'how will you control project costs using a bottom-up approach?'. It still seemed inconceivable to Yvan that you needn't worry about monitoring and controlling costs with an Information Age solution.

This can only be understood in terms of another paradox. You control the costs in an Information Age solution by not controlling the costs. Isn't that a statement worthy of any Zen master?

The paradox is resolved by understanding that Industrial Age projects have a reasonably predictable environment to work in. There may be constant change, there may be intense competition, but systems are designed to work within a known or estimated range of predictability where there are adequate tools, techniques and methods to cope with the variables. Any possibilities of sudden, unpredictable, or totally disruptive disturbances are treated as events to avoid rather than be planned for because regulated and controlled systems are highly vulnerable to changes of a chaotic nature. In the Information Age, chaotic and disruptive changes cannot be avoided; they are the norm rather than the exception.

> In the fast-changing, chaotic environment of the Internet, the controlled and regulated systems of the Industrial Age are like the *Titanic*.

An excellent example of a carefully planned system going wrong due to a chaotic disturbance is the *Titanic*. All the most up-to-date technology in the world had been used to create an unsinkable ship. What happened? On its maiden voyage it hit an iceberg and the collision caused a rupture that was outside of the anticipations of all the design considerations. The unsinkable ship sank.

In the fast-changing, chaotic environment of the Internet, the controlled and regulated systems of the Industrial Age are like the *Titanic*. They are vulnerable to the continuous flow of new icebergs being created by the rapidly evolving technologies. A sudden new development could crack a carefully planned system wide open. One has only to read through the records of various multi-million dollar corporate cruises into the world of e-business and e-commerce to see ample evidence of this.

Some corporations see increasingly sophisticated techniques of control and regulation as the answer to the problem of chaotic change, but this is a brain-dead way to go. The solution lies in abandoning any thoughts of control and regulation altogether and going for a self-regulating system.

Self-regulating systems, to anybody used to regulation and control, are difficult to understand and believe in. For this reason I'll take some more examples from my experiences in the world of bricks and mortar to explain the underlying basis of such systems. We can then abstract out the general principles and map them across to the environment of the Internet.

A planned approach to the fashion business

My first excursion into the world of fashion and designer clothes seemed to be progressing beyond all expectations. The Street Theatre designs were in every magazine, more and more of the multiples wanted to provide concession space for us to trade. There was only one problem though, I didn't have enough money to finance any major expansion. Like all rapidly expanding businesses I ran into the problem of cash flow.

I had a word with my accountant and he brought to my attention a new scheme the government had just announced that had been set up to help entrepreneurs in my position. It was called the Government Guaranteed Loan Scheme. It was an excellent scheme devised by the Thatcher government to help business people who needed capital for a business venture but didn't have sufficient collateral to obtain funding from the banks. The idea was that if a bank thought a business venture looked viable the bank could ask the government to guarantee 85 per cent of any business loans they provided. This greatly reduced the bank's exposure to risk and allowed them to make loans on promising enterprises that they'd normally have to turn down.

I spoke to my bank manager, who was now quite familiar with my somewhat unconventional approach to business, and he agreed that my case was the kind of situation the Government Guaranteed Loan Scheme had been intended for. He said he'd certainly recommend that I should be given this facility.

Knowing that the Government Guaranteed Loan was decided solely upon the recommendation of the bank, I went ahead and started to set up retail units and order all the necessary fabrics and arrange for the manufacturing. Then fate took a hand. My bank manager was promoted to head office and in his place came a conscientious new manager who wanted to see my operation.

When I took him around to my workroom, he wasn't at all impressed. All he could see was a bunch of trendy-looking people who didn't look as if they'd done a day's work in their life. When I introduced him to Boy George, fully made up with dreadlocks and wearing a ladies' dress and high heel shoes, he nearly had a fit. The very next day I had a formal letter from the bank to say my application for a Government Guaranteed Loan had been rejected.

I was then in deep trouble. I was already committed to much of my programme so I hurriedly went to a new bank and asked them if they'd consider giving me a Government Guaranteed Loan. I told them what I'd achieved and showed them all my trading figures and although suitably impressed they told me that before they could proceed I'd have to provide a detailed business plan, a cash flow and a profit and loss account.

I consulted my accountant and he suggested that I buy one of the new Apple II computers that were just beginning to arrive in the UK and use a program called VisiCalc. This VisiCalc program was the first-ever spreadsheet and is reputed to have been the program that made Apple Computers the success it became and established personal computers as a serious business tool.

The VisiCalc spreadsheet was the perfect modelling environment for my business. I set out all the weeks over a two-year period, and entered the 18 retail units I planned to run. I put in values for the weekly overheads. I multiplied these by the necessary numbers to get the required turnover to cover costs and show a profit. From these numbers I could calculate the sales and manufacturing targets.

As I got the hang of using the spreadsheet, I set it up to model various trading scenarios with different sales volumes. I made adjustments for seasonal variations; calculated the manufacturing schedules and the cash flows. I built in various rates of progress, allowed for the possibility of sales falling below expectations, allowed for clearance sales at the end of seasons. Through playing around with the formulae available to the spreadsheet I could simulate all known possibilities and variables and incorporate a variety of appropriate contingency plans.

When I'd finished and presented this plan to the bank manager he told me that it was the best and most thorough proposal for a loan he'd ever seen in his many years' experience as a bank manager. He had no hesitation at all in putting me up for a loan.

Unfortunately, my excellent business plan hadn't allowed for the long time it would take to get the application through and the money made available. It hadn't allowed for the fact that my manufacturer would take on other clients while I was waiting for the money. It hadn't allowed for the fact that all the concession units I'd arranged would be repositioned to the back of the stores when the stock didn't arrive on time. It didn't allow for the fact that when the money arrived and the stock was ready for sale it would be at the end of the season when all garments were on sale.

To say I'd got off to a bad start would be to put it mildly. But it got worse. Although I managed to struggle through and get into the next season with a new range of designs, I'd made the mistake of using a team of conventional designers instead of using customer feedback for design initiatives. This seemed perfectly logical at the time because the sales units I'd opened were scattered all over the country and it was impossible to get information about what was fashionable in every area. But I figured we were so high profile, with our designs in all the fashion magazines, that we could lead the fashions instead of following them.

Big mistake. What my sophisticated designers thought were very clever and trendy designs looked ridiculous in the eyes of the trendies in the clubs who, at that time, were all switching to the new fashion of punk clothing. The smart-looking outfits we were making were being outsold by bits of black rag, strung together with safety pins and zips.

Before I could rectify the position, I was caught out by the catch-22 of the Government Guaranteed Loan Scheme. I'd spent around eight months running without a profit. Although I hadn't actually made a trading loss, employment taxes for the staff and the (then) 15 per cent sales tax had mounted up to a total sum, owed to the Government Inland Revenue Department, of twice as much as I'd borrowed from the bank. Faced with an impossible situation I had no alternative but to wind up the company and go into liquidation. So much for forward planning and carefully thought out designs.

Mapping this situation across to e-business and e-commerce, it isn't hard to spot many parallels:

- the expensively constructed Web site that ends up without any customers;
- the negative cash flows as teams of experts work in vain at redesigns;
- pre-planning to bring about a solution that is out of date before it is in operation.

The real killer though is the mounting losses through overheads as a team struggles to cope with an ever-changing situation. I still cannot believe how I was sucked into a situation where I'd given up a highly flexible, low-cost system and replaced it with a ponderous, slow-reacting organization that carried fatal overhead penalties.

Feedback from a rich source of information

Back to the square one position, with no capital and a highly flawed credibility, I knew I'd have difficulty restarting. Fortunately, the reputation of Street Theatre's success carried some influence and I was invited to take a sales unit in a new, high fashion, market-style store that was opening up in Kensington High Street. It was the early 1980s and London was regarded as the leading fashion design capital of the world and sported hundreds of new trendy designers. Most of these up and coming designers were invited to take sales units in this new, market-style store named 'Hyper Hyper'.

The store was an immediate success; the presence of so many fashion designers under one roof was a great attraction. However, for each individual designer it was a highly competitive situation: their creations had to be chosen by customers who were choosing from among a vast selection of other designs. For me, it was an even greater challenge because I'd lost all my information infrastructure of designers that had worked so well at Street Theatre. I found myself in the midst of over one hundred of the most creative designers in the world and had to compete with them for sales.

I was still working with the experienced dressmaker who suggested that we made a range of classic evening dresses. This didn't require any special design flair or knowledge of current fashion trends. Unfortunately, these dresses were lost in the vast range of other possibilities being offered by the other designers. Sales were pathetically low. To help pay the rent and overheads, I brought in a small jewellery counter and started to sell pieces of costume jewellery to go with the dresses.

It was then that I realized what an opportunity I had. I'd lost my contacts from the London club scene, but because of the draw of the many exciting designers in Hyper Hyper, all the trendy London club people were coming to this high-profile store and walking right past our costume jewellery counter. All I had to do, to find out what the latest fashions were, was to observe all the fashionably dressed people who were passing by.

Not having the resources to build up a range of dresses, I concentrated on the costume jewellery. The trick was to pick out the fashion leaders from the fashion followers. With the help of the sales girl and the dressmaker, we 'spotted' various fashionable trends in jewellery accessories. There was no possibility of being able to manufacture these items, so I went to the fashion wholesale area in London where many middlemen were dealing in costume jewellery. At the time, most of these specialist wholesalers were located in and around Berwick Street, just south of the main London shopping area of Oxford Street.

By diligently searching through the stocks of all the wholesalers, I could find items of costume jewellery that corresponded to the fashion items I'd spotted the fashion leaders wearing. The fashion leaders who visited Hyper Hyper at that time included many famous pop stars, movie and television personalities and even Princess Diana – who at the time was living just a few hundred yards from the store, in Kensington Palace.

It wasn't long before our jewellery counter started to attract attention. Even the fashion leaders themselves started to recognize that we were stocking the latest fashions and pretty soon we had a string of regular customers.

The items that sold, we replaced with identical items from the wholesalers. Those that didn't sell, we sold off at cost. In this way the overall, high fashion quality of our jewellery counter got better and better. Also, we found there was no longer any need to have to rely solely on spotting what the fashion leaders were wearing. They started to come to us, asking for things they wanted.

Very soon, the fashion magazines found out about our costume jewellery counter. Fashion editors and their assistants were constantly visiting Hyper Hyper to borrow clothes for fashion shoots for their publications. Invariably, they would need some high fashion jewellery accessories to go with the clothes. They would come for these accessories to our jewellery counter and we found ourselves in more fashion magazines and with more credits than any other designer in the place.

Not only did the jewellery sell well, by association, the customers were starting to look at the dresses. It seemed reasonable to them that if this unit was selling the most fashionable and up-to-date jewellery it must also be selling the most up-to-date and fashionable ladies' evening wear. It wasn't long before our evening dresses were being worn by all kinds of pop stars, movie and television personalities and began appearing in the pages of all the top fashion magazines.

All this, with no planning, virtually no overheads and no organization. It was an event-driven, customer-designed system that was self-organizing. A solution created as a result of an evolutionary design strategy.

Mapping across to the Internet

It might seem that my experiences in Hyper Hyper have only a vague relevance to e-business and e-commerce. This would be the case to anyone who hasn't acquired the knack of abstracting the essential details from a situation and putting them into a form where the crucial elements can be mapped across to other environments. If you know the trick, the essential essence of the Hyper Hyper success can be applied to the Internet.

Using the modelling environment of Hilbert space, you can say that this whole episode in my business life can be described by two solution points in a Hilbert space, where the dimensions are people. This abstraction would proceed as follows:

Problem 1 – the design-side strategy

How do I succeed in a highly competitive environment where I'm competing against highly expert specialists?

Solution

Find a place in Hilbert solution space where there are lots of people who will be able to give you all the appropriate information.

Result

Hyper Hyper is the optimum place to be in Hilbert space because it is the spot where the people dimensions are most appropriate to supply the necessary information.

Problem 2 – the supply-side strategy

Having got a solution to the design-side information, how do I arrange to find a suitable product?

Solution

Find a spot in Hilbert space where there are a lot of different people who have the kind of products that are being pointed to by the people in problem 1's solution space.

Result

Berwick Street and the surrounding area is the point in Hilbert solution space where the people dimensions are most appropriate to supply the products.

The whole situation is now transferred to a simple model in your head. Two solution spaces, one feeding information to the other. This can now be applied to any situation where there is the kind of problem that involves what to do and how to do it. Let's now take each of these solutions in turn and apply them to the Internet.

The design-side solution point in the Internet environment

The Hyper Hyper situation may seem unique in the world of bricks and mortar but in the Hilbert solution space of the Internet – where all the dimensions are people – such a situation is far from unique. Defining a solution as a place where it is possible to get maximum information from a group of people, it can readily be seen how Internet Special Interest Discussion Forums provide many such points. There are tens of thousands of these groups in operation, each with a unique group of subscribers and each with a unique subject matter. Hanging out in any one of these email discussion forums is the Internet world's equivalent of hanging out in Hyper Hyper to see what the fashion leaders are wearing.

Now, as unlikely as it was for me to become successful in the highly competitive world of fashion, it seems equally unlikely that I could become recognized as an expert in multimedia programming. Yet, I managed to do it, simply by finding the appropriate point to hang out in the Hilbert solution space of the Internet.

The group as an information source

After starting a family, I decided to retire from the hectic life of the ever-changing and highly competitive London fashion scene to find a new, more sedate business interest. My acquaintanceship with the Apple computer had alerted me to the potential of a whole new world of possibilities that seemed to offer just the kind of lifestyle I was looking for. It appealed to me to work from home with no pressures and not have to spend several hours of each day negotiating London traffic. My assessment was that CD-ROMs were going to be the next big thing and this seemed an ideal project to work on.

I moved away from London, into the countryside, to work on the CD-ROM 'How God Makes God'. In the four years it took to create the CD-ROM and then for it to became apparent that the market hadn't materialized, I'd used up most of my capital and lost nearly all of my contacts. Once more, I was into familiar territory: back to square one.

I could have returned to London, but by then I'd discovered the Internet and seen the light. The World Wide Web seemed to me to be the ultimate marketplace and I wanted to play in this exciting new game I'd found. The problem was I couldn't see any way in. I didn't have the knowledge, the contacts or the money.

Then, a friend of mine rang to tell me that a publisher's agent was looking for somebody to write a book about programming in a multimedia authoring package called 'Director'. He'd known I'd made the CD-ROM using this program and thought I might be interested. I was, but the problem was that I'd actually developed the CD-ROM using another program called HyperCard and only at the last moment converted it to the Director format. In other words, I'd had only a very brief exposure to the Director programming environment and was a complete novice.

However, remembering my experience with writing the course on investment, I thought I could write the book as a learning exercise. My learning process could then be passed on to others who would also want to learn how to program multimedia projects. I made a proposal, it was accepted and I then set about writing the book.

As it happened, at this same time, Macromedia, the developers of Director, suddenly brought out a radically improved version of Director. It included many additional commands and features, new and quite sophisticated list structures and introduced special facilities for using object-oriented programming techniques. This was a completely different ball game: presenting a far more difficult task than I'd bargained for.

I was in a fix because there were no books to refer to at that time. I then discovered that some of the more dedicated users of the Director multimedia authoring package had got together and set up a Special Interest Group Email Discussion Forum on the Internet called Direct-L. By subscribing to this forum, I found myself in the company of several hundred people interested in learning about programming Director. They ranged from novices to dedicated expert programmers.

I'd hit upon the perfect point in Hilbert Internet solution space to find out all I needed to know to be able to write a book on multimedia programming. This was the Internet equivalent of Hyper Hyper; it was a people place, a place where I could learn and get information to design a book on programming multimedia. It was a place where I could find out what people wanted to know and learn when using the Director multimedia authoring package.

At first, I was in awe at the expertise I encountered in this group. I daren't mention I was writing a book on programming because I had to start off by asking the most elementary questions. Cautiously and nervously I began to take an increasingly larger part in the discussions. My knowledge of Director and the programming language (called Lingo) increased by leaps and bounds.

It was a revelation to me that I could so quickly learn to communicate and tap into the minds of some of the people at the cutting edge of multimedia technology. I could learn directly from the experts. Not just through passively reading, but by active participation and discussion. The experience took me right back to my days at the Radar Research Establishment at Great Malvern where I had learned so much simply by mixing with the scientists.

Here, I thought, was something really different from the conventional world of information and learning. As I asked questions of those who knew more than I did, and answered the questions of those who knew less, I came to the conclusion that this was a potent and potentially powerful phenomenon. And it was exclusively a manifestation of the Internet.

What struck me particularly was the way in which it provided information on demand: on a need to know basis. Needed information was being provided through an intelligent interface: a group of humans. Indexes and search engines are often useful but very limited in the help they can give. They don't cut directly to individual specific problems, they don't prompt the asking of different questions or provide answers to questions that are needed but not asked. This amazing manifestation of the Internet, the Special Interest Group Email Discussion Forum, was doing just this: providing intelligent usable knowledge as opposed to mere information.

It meant that anyone could tap into this source from any starting point of interest or previous learning. Any member of the group could expand on their unique current knowledge; building upon it with a bottom-up strategy by adding new modules of knowledge a piece at a time. There were no fixed methods or list of things to know, everyone could tap into this pool of knowledge in any way they wanted, to create and form their own niche that could be quite different from any others.

As the months went by, I came to understand how this discussion forum was being used in different ways by different people. What had initially appeared to be a single narrow-based subject turned out to have innumerable variations. It seemed that everyone was using the Director authoring package for a different purpose and had links to all kinds of other interesting areas of digital communication technology.

I'd been very impressed by the seemingly altruistic and generous help provided by some of the members of this Direct-L forum. Every day, day after day, some of them were selflessly answering questions, giving advice and explaining all manner of technicalities. It was only after I had private email correspondences with one of them that I discovered this was not always as altruistic as it seemed. This particular correspondent told me it was the way he got most of his leads and contacts for his programming contract work.

The penny dropped. The success of this forum was not so much a mutual display of generosity and goodwill: it was providing a very practical and valuable service. The people who were giving were getting even more out of it. It was a win-win, non-zero sum game where everyone was benefiting. This particular point in Hilbert space with its people dimensions was an optimum point for many people: it was a knowledge-generating machine that everyone could feed from. Even more of a surprise was that this knowledge generation system was perpetual and self-organizing. It was being driven by needs that were continuously being satisfied – and the fulfilment of those needs was being rewarded.

Having realized that this forum was being driven by fulfilment and reward, I started to look for other motivations of the more active members. The more I looked the more I found. It then gradually dawned on me that this was not just some ancillary by-product of a multimedia authoring application, it was its main driving engine. The discussions on this forum were feeding straight back into the design. Further, it was not only an engine influencing the design of the Director application, it was an engine that was having a substantial influence on multimedia in general.

This indeed was a revelation. Here was another phenomenon unique to the Internet – a discussion group of customers that was driving a product and influencing a whole section of industry. Sherlock Holmes would certainly have seen this as a case for investigation.

As I began to see the further implications of this observation, I became more and more interested and intrigued. I experimented and found that any attempt to steer the forum off subject was met with fierce resistance. This was not an organized or premeditated resistance; it was a spontaneous reaction from forum members to keep the email posts strictly confined to the subject of multimedia in general and the Director authoring package in particular. It seemed to be a self-regulating system, obeying strict rules without any formal or recognized authority.

Many of the Macromedia staff employees were posting to the Direct-L forum. With some, it even seemed to be their full-time job. Surprisingly though, although these employees were always trying to dominate the forum, Macromedia neither owned nor controlled it. The forum seemed to have a life and an independence of its own.

It was very apparent that the postings by the users of Direct-L were having a large influence on Macromedia's product and marketing strategy. Direct-L represented the opinions and the reactions of hundreds of different users, covering a wide range of applications and computer platforms. Although the constant barrage of niggles and complaints must have been a thorn in their side, it was helping Macromedia to produce a far better product than they could ever have hoped to provide by relying solely on their own design initiatives and in-house testing facilities.

As the numbers of the people on the Direct-L list grew, so did its power and influence. It had started out as a small group of enthusiasts trying to learn from each other how to use a product and had evolved into a self-organizing entity that was beginning to dominate the design of the product.

The Midwich Cuckoos

In a way, this phenomenon of the email discussion forum manifests a metaphysical effect similar to that enjoyed by the alien children in John Wyndham's book *The Midwich Cuckoos*. The spine-chilling story of *The Midwich Cuckoos* has been portrayed in a couple of movies, the most notable of which was the 1960s version entitled *Village of the Damned*. In this story, all the women in a village suddenly become pregnant and it turns out that each has been impregnated by an alien force that means to take control of the Earth.

As all the implanted alien children grow up, it becomes apparent that they have several supernatural powers that give them powerful advantages over the villagers. Not least among these supernatural powers is an ability to telecommunicate their thoughts to each other. In essence this meant that what one alien child knew the others would also know. In effect, they had a common mind.

Such a power gave the alien children an overwhelming advantage in their conflict with the villagers. At the time John Wyndham wrote this book, it was inconceivable that humans would ever evolve a way to acquire this power themselves. Yet, this is almost exactly what Special Interest Internet Forums are achieving. These manifestations of the Internet allow a group of people to have a common mind, such that what one knows everyone else can know as well. This has very significant implications for the future of e-business and e-commerce strategies.

Even more remarkable than the ability of the Internet to provide the metaphysical effect of a common mind is the significance of these special interest group forums on the structure of the business model. Up until the Internet, the way to design a product to satisfy client needs adequately was through market research techniques that interrogate potential customers to determine their requirements and preferences. This is basically a static process where results are analyzed and appropriate conclusions drawn.

Internet forums, such as Direct-L, provide a dynamic environment in which to assess client needs, preferences, reactions, acceptance and satisfaction – potentially a far more effective technique than the classical methods of market research. It costs nothing to run and is self-perpetuating and self-organizing.

Not only can these Internet forums replace the need for conventional marketing research strategies, they can also replace the need for design initiatives. Product design can be taken out of the hands of product developers and independently provided by the customers.

It seems that a bizarre and emergent effect of the Internet is to create a situation where customers design their own products. This is one of the unpredictable outcomes of a dynamic complex system. Its ramifications for the future of business procedures and strategy are inestimable.

From an entrepreneur's point of view, from a solution provider's point of view, from a corporate strategist's point of view, from a middleman's point of view, from an expert's point of view: simply becoming involved in one of these forums provides exactly the same kind of business creation information as I found in Hyper Hyper.

Chapter 12

Communication strategy

The supply-side strategy

In the last chapter, we saw how an information source could be seen as a collection of people at a solution point in a solution space. This point was exampled as a costume jewellery counter in Hyper Hyper and the people providing the information were the customers and the passers-by. It provided the solution to the problem: 'what is required?' This retrieved information could then be used as the desired goal in the 'how to get it' part of the strategy.

To reach this goal, it was necessary to move to another point in solution space to communicate with a different group of people who could provide a solution to the problem: 'We know what we want, but how do we get it?'

In the far simpler and more stable environment of the bricks and mortar world, these supply-side solution points often take on a physical reality. In the case of the costume jewellery counter in Hyper Hyper, the supply-side solution point had manifested as a geographic location: an area around Berwick Street in London where many wholesalers of costume jewellery had set up in business. At the time, there were probably around one hundred different wholesalers in and around Berwick Street, each providing various types of fashion accessories and all run as entrepreneurial enterprises in competition with one another.

Despite the competition, Berwick Street provided an overwhelming benefit to these wholesalers because, not only was it a place to sell from, it was also a place to get the information as to what to sell. Just as Hyper Hyper provided a solution point for me to know what to buy for my jewellery counter, so Berwick Street provided a solution point for all the wholesalers to know what to get from the manufacturers to supply to the retailers.

The people providing the information at this Berwick Street solution point were the retailers themselves, who would go there by the hundreds to buy for their customers. Each retailer arrives knowing what their own customers want and passes this information on to the wholesalers by buying and asking for particular items. This allows the wholesalers to acquire up-to-date knowledge of the current fashion trends on a large geographic scale. In essence then, the wholesalers in Berwick Street have positioned themselves at a physical solution space where they can find out exactly what to order from the manufacturers.

From this we can deduce that commercial strategies of the wholesalers also have to have two solution points:

1   to get information as to what the retailers want to buy; and

2   another solution point to let them know where they can get it.

The first solution point is provided at their sales location in Berwick Street, but the second solution point is more problematic because it doesn't occur at any single geographic location. Costume jewellery manufacturers come from all parts of the world.

To make contact with these manufacturers, the wholesalers will have to seek them out. They will need to go to international trade shows; visit individual factories or workshops; travel to many places in the world where there are concentrations of costume jewellery manufacturers. Most countries and big cities have speciality manufacturing areas. These are usually the smaller manufacturers who can't afford to display their products at the trade shows. They tend to concentrate in the same physical area for the same reason wholesalers congregate in and around Berwick Street: because it provides a more efficient supply-side solution point for the wholesalers to visit.

Looking at this complete system as an abstraction, it would appear as thousands of solution points with information flowing between them: a complex network of interconnected nodes. The information starts from the customers, feeds through to the retailers, then on to the wholesalers from where it goes to the manufacturers who use it to decide what to make. The information reflects customer requirements and then feeds back again as a desired product. It is a system of constant, backwards and forwards information flow. A seemingly chaotic pattern of activity, yet all part of a dynamic, continuously adapting system.

Of course, there are many original design initiatives that enter the system, but these are unpredictable, random events that sometimes do and sometimes don't create chaotic instabilities of demand and supply. No serious trader bothers to look too closely at the origination or reasoning behind these creative efforts; they are treated simply as statistical noise that business strategies have to allow for.

The product here is fashion costume jewellery, but looking at the abstraction of this system – the information flow from the customers to the basic product manufacturers – would see this same model applying to almost every possible commercial system.

To map this system of information flow across to communication strategies needed for e-business and e-commerce solutions, we need only see beyond the physical substance of metals, glass and plastics to the real purpose of the jewellery: as a fashion statement. In this abstraction, the jewellery is not thought of as a work of art or a piece of technology but as a message that the wearer wants to broadcast.

At one level, this message advertises the wearer's taste and fashion sense, but at another level the message is proclaiming the wearer's identification to a group and even his or her position within a group. Using this abstraction, rather than the physical reality, would see the fashion jewellery business as one of dealing entirely in messages: messages in a state of chaotic change as trends and fashions reflect the constantly evolving nature of groups and their hierarchical structures.

With such an abstraction, you can quite easily map this physical trade in costume jewellery across to the Internet because the Internet is also about dealing with messages.

The dynamics of the middleman

The strategy of the jewellery counter was quite different from the strategies of all the other designers in Hyper Hyper because it didn't use its own managed team for the supply-side of the business. Instead, it relied upon a network of middlemen: a flexible structure that could call upon the expertise, initiatives and capabilities of hundreds of people.

To understand how this works, it is necessary to take into consideration the practical restraints and limitations that are determined by time and money available. As already mentioned, there were something like one hundred different wholesalers in and around Berwick Street and there were hundreds more all over the country, not to mention the untold thousands that were located in different places throughout the world. This meant that I had to be selective, limiting my sources to only a very small sub-section of all the possible sources available.

A far greater limitation, though, was the amount of money I had available for buying each week. This even further restricted the number of wholesalers I could buy from. There is a similar restriction in e-business or e-commerce situations, where each end consumer is restricted not only by available selection and time but also and mainly by the money available to spend. What the end user has to spend on has to be carefully selected and in the environment of the Internet there is always overwhelming competition for a spender's time, attention and money.

Abstracting this procedure over to information exchanges and communications strategies would see similar practical limitations in the form of the time it takes to access the sources and absorb the content. Email correspondents need writing to, replies have to be read. Web sites need visiting and the content downloaded and looked at. Search engines throw up many possibilities that have to be investigated.

These pragmatic considerations can influence the supply-side of the equation far more than the relative quality of the content. Almost invariably, the supply-side quest is not for the 'best possible' because there isn't enough time to find the best. The most efficient search strategy looks for 'good enough' and then stops searching.

So, whether it's products, services or information, the main criterion is going to be the efficiency by which 'good enough' can be obtained in the time available. Forget 'best', that is not a practical consideration.

Note: When I first drafted this chapter and sent it out for discussion, Sheelagh Barron, an information researcher for the film industry, wrote about this sentence:

This worries me. If the benchmark becomes adequate/good enough it inevitably leads to dumbing down. 'Good Enough' should be a reluctant last resort not a target...

Although this would be a commendable attitude to have in the Industrial Age, it is totally inappropriate for the Information Age. The reason is: there is always too much to know, too many different alternatives, too much that is unknowable and on top of that anything that is known is liable to change. This makes it totally inefficient to have a strategy to look for the best because the search space is far too vast. You could go on for ever looking for the best or some kind of improvement on what you already have. Where do you stop?

The obvious stopping place is where you have something that is 'good enough'. This need not imply that it is a mean compromise. 'Good enough' depends upon the strategist's definition, which might well be defined as something that puts them way ahead of the competition. This is the same kind of strategy that professional investment managers use. They don't waste their time trying to find a definition of a perfect investment opportunity, they look for investments that are better than others available; it's a relative, as opposed to an absolute, best choice.

This can be appreciated if you consider searching in a Hilbert solution space that contained every person in the world. For example, say you wanted to find the best six people to advise you how to decorate your house. Common sense tells you that it would be impractical to search the whole world for the best six, so you'd choose six who were the best you could find in a reasonable amount of time.

Everyone who gets married adopts this strategy. People don't go around searching the whole world for the person who would make them the best marriage partner. They make the best choice out of what is available in the time and the geographic area it is practical to search in (this strategy is probably reinforced by evolved emotions that make it likely that people 'fall in love' with somebody within a limited range of choice, eliminating the need for any extensive search and selection procedures).

Keeping up with technological changes

When buying stock for the costume jewellery counter, the usual practice for the weekly buying was to have a quick look around to see what the various wholesalers in Berwick Street were stocking. Then, I'd make a mental list of those that seemed to have the kind of items my Hyper Hyper customers had been asking for. Having made this list, and putting it in some order of preference, the procedure would be to work through this list until the week's buying money had run out.

Effectively, this selection of wholesalers was equivalent to creating a 'virtual design team' on the fly each week: made up of the wholesalers who were currently right on the ball with what my customers were wanting.

I didn't have to know much about any manufacturing techniques; I didn't have to worry about team spirit; arrange training; deal with conflicting egos or provide a variety of rewards, incentives and inducements. My virtual team of designers/suppliers simply supplied whatever goods my customers wanted: on demand, hassle free and whenever I wanted them.

In the fashion business, as in digital technology, trends tend to come and go quickly and unpredictably. This constant flux I could easily cope with by using this strategy of varying the wholesalers I bought from. I bought from six or seven of them each week, but it was never the same wholesalers every time.

What would happen is that as trends or fashions changed, the wholesalers would vie with each other to get new designs from their manufacturing contacts to correspond with the changes. Some wholesalers would be quicker at spotting a trend than others and would usually have the lion's share of the new business for the time that fashion lasted.

The way the dynamics of the system worked was that the wholesalers who were benefiting from a current trend or fashion were too involved with their busy trading to be ready to take advantage of the next change of fashion when it came along; their buying money would be committed and they'd be locked into manufacturers who were geared up for the currently popular fashion.

This invariably meant that any change in trend or fashion was catered for by other wholesalers who weren't so busy. These less busy wholesalers and their manufacturing contacts would have had the time and resources available to explore other possibilities and would be in a better position to act when the fashion changed.

This made it easy for me to keep up with new trends and sudden fashion changes because, in the parlance of the time, I would only need to find the wholesalers who were 'hot' and buy from them. In this way, my virtual team was constantly changing as the wholesalers were engaged in a continuous cycle of leap-frogging over each other as they vied with each other to be the first to bring out any new fashion trends.

Such versatility just wasn't available to the other retailers in Hyper Hyper. They had managed teams that had limited knowledge and capabilities. Changes in fashions and trends often presented them with lengthy and expensive redesign procedures in order to catch up.

Mapping this across to e-business and e-commerce solutions, the parallels between the changing fashions in costume jewellery and the changing trends in technological developments are quite obvious. In such a changing environment it makes a great deal of sense to have virtual teams of specialists that can be put together on the fly to deal with any technological issues. Only in this way can the emergent changes due to technological developments be handled efficiently.

Experts and specialists in technology, like the costume jewellery wholesalers and manufacturers, can easily become locked into areas of speciality while their expertise is hot. This makes it likely that they will be unprepared when trends change. Experts and specialists need a learning curve and explorative time before they can properly leap onto the next bandwagon. They can't do this if their time is fully taken up with contracts using the passing technology. It does seem reasonable, therefore, to suppose that the expertise of all specialists will run hot and cold and it will be up to the skill of the people who hire their services to spot which state they are in.

Looking at e-business and e-commerce in the light of this model, it would seem that the best strategy is to go for virtual teams rather than permanent teams; they are more flexible, can rapidly adjust to changing trends and emergent situations, and there will be no need to manage or to worry about people problems. The overheads will be practically zero. This then makes a strong case for conventional managers to be replaced by specialist com- municators who will be able to keep track of a pool of expert services and choose from them according to how hot they are at the time they are needed.

The strategy of the producers

I wasn't alone in the strategy of employing a virtual team to keep up with the changing fashions. The wholesalers were also using this same strategy to acquire products from their manufacturing contacts. Like me, they had access to a number of sources of costume jewellery supply – the manufacturers – who were in various states of readiness. They could shop around these sources to obtain what the market demanded at any particular time.

By using various combinations of different manufacturers on demand, the wholesalers had a virtual manufacturing capability that could flexibly respond to the rapidly changing demands of fashion. It carried no overheads and didn't involve any people problems. This allowed the wholesale operations to be run as small, proprietary enterprises, mostly family concerns. Despite their small size, they had vast turnovers that would be the envy of many larger organizations.

The most vulnerable to changing trends and fashions were the core businesses of the costume jewellery manufacturers. They didn't have quite the same scope for flexibility as the retailers and the wholesalers because their businesses relied upon expert craft workers and speciality plant and equipment. They were forced to work as permanent managed teams with the associated needs of having to keep people happy and motivating them.

However, the constant ebb and flow of the changing fashions and the irregular demands on their products made it impractical for costume jewellery manufacturers to extend the principle of managed teams too far. Of necessity, they had to keep their core business as small as possible, because the changing fashions could see them working at full stretch for a few months and then finding the business dropping off to practically nothing. They couldn't afford to keep on permanent large teams in such conditions because the overheads would kill them off in the quiet spells.

To keep their overheads down to a minimum and yet still be able to take advantage of the rushes when they came, the manufacturers had to have a very flexible employment strategy. Usually this involved concentrating their manufacturing capability around a narrow but essential niche speciality and making use of other speciality workshops to carry out parts of the work they weren't equipped to do themselves.

They would also maintain contact with a host of out-workers who could be employed temporarily, on demand, to work at home on repetitive tasks that required little training. In this way, the manufacturing companies could work with a very small permanent team, keep overheads to a minimum, and yet still retain a capacity to expand production at a moment's notice.

Fitting into this pattern of business, many of the manufacturers used their quiet times to develop new products or explore new techniques and methods of working. This enabled them to be in a good position to benefit from the next emerging fashion trend when it came along.

Looking at the structure of these highly adaptable manufacturing concerns would see the main framework as being a communication network driven by information. Manufacturers would be like central hubs, communication linked to a range of complementary manufacturing facilities and a number of wholesalers. They can be seen as systems that are being fed by information flowing from the customers, via the retailers and the wholesalers.

Such systems have direct parallels in e-commerce and e-business. Many middlemen interpret customer demands and organize technology to satisfy them. This invariably involves a chaotic and continuous redeployment of effort and resources as competition and technological changes keep moving the goal posts.

Prime technological developers and contractors are very vulnerable to the changing technological trends. They can easily expand on the basis of being expert in one particular area of technology only to see the business fall away rapidly as this technology is superseded by something better.

Just like the costume jewellery manufacturers, the more sensible prime contractors and producers maintain a relatively small staff of communicators, who keep in regular contact with pools of different kinds of experts and specialists. These experts, working from home or in small studios situated perhaps anywhere in the world, can be quickly assembled into a virtual team when the need arises. This is the only way that rapidly changing technology and competition can be successfully handled in the chaotic environment of e-business and e-commerce.

The need for teams to be created on the fly for temporary periods makes it impossible to apply the Industrial Age concepts of organization and managed teams. It is far more efficient to use object-oriented methods of organization, where virtual team members can be treated as objects. These people objects can be given messages to which they respond by carrying out appropriate functions to satisfy the system requirements.

To the mind of an Industrial Age thinker, this scenario will seem cold and heartless; a robotic system that has no considerations for human emotions. But is it? The various businesses that have evolved to cope with the similar continuously changing environment of the fashion industry are run in just this way. But they are not noted for their cold robotic atmospheres.

Limitations of the managed team

It must be very perplexing, for managers and executives trained in the ways of the Industrial Age, when they find that conventionally managed teams are not very efficient when working in the environment of the Internet. They will know that properly managed teams work well in the bricks and mortar world. They might even see them working efficiently in the bricks and mortar side of e-business and e-commerce solutions. But as soon as any activity involves using the Internet, the managed teams of the Industrial Age appear to be inefficient and dysfunctional.

Why this problem seems so enigmatic is because Industrial Age thinking sees the managed team as the basic structure to be used throughout the whole hierarchy of any system of organization. At the top, a commander-in-chief effectively manages a team: a board of directors. Each director manages his or her own team: a team of key managers and executives who are responsible to them. Each of these key managers also has their own departmental teams to manage. This hierarchy of teams stretches right down from the top through to the bottom of the organization so that the whole edifice becomes a hierarchy of teams. Effectively then, it is a system made up of teams of teams, where every team (except for those at the bottom of the hierarchy) consists of people who are backed up by a team.

In such a system, everyone in the hierarchy is being pushed and supported by people below. Managers and executives become increasingly more powerful and functional the higher up the hierarchy they are. Even incompetent managers can retain their places in such hierarchies because they can do so on the backs of those below them. This channelling of information and effort into a common goal has proven to provide great power and stability in the Industrial Age.

Now imagine such a hierarchical structure suddenly having everyone in the system connected to the Internet. Information and knowledge need no longer be channelled exclusively upwards and in steps of one hierarchy at a time.

Information can go in all directions; anyone can bypass the usual communication channels. This can throw the established communication system into disarray. External communications will also be affected; instead of the system being linked to the outside world through a few controlled outlets, everyone will have their own independent connection.

This would not be a trivial change to the system. It would be a major transformation. Almost every way in which the system is controlled and managed would be affected. Not only would the controls and management be affected, the system would be likely to function in a totally different way, perhaps throwing up bizarre side effects.

Employees will have knowledge and value according to how effectively they can communicate in this linked communication environment. Knowledge, and the power that it brings, will no longer be determined by procedure and precedence. Managers, who normally go to meetings armed with all the knowledge of the people below them, will begin finding that this information is already known to everyone else by the time they arrive. There will be a great reduction in the value and effectiveness of physical meetings. This could greatly weaken the hierarchical structure because the phenomenon of 'the meeting' provides the focal points that stabilize it.

More alarming for the Industrial Age organizations is that connectiveness will allow employees skilled in the art of communicating by email to emerge from the ranks to usurp control from designated team leaders. Such emergent leaders might have goals far removed from the goals of the appointed managers.

It doesn't take much thought to realize how connectiveness by way of the Internet can totally disrupt a hierarchical system of managed teams.

The alternative to a managed team

The possibility of replacing managed teams with something else when competitive pressure necessitates using the Internet is seldom considered. And the idea that a managed team should be replaced by a virtual team, where people are employed on a temporary basis and treated as objects, seems unthinkable.

The reaction to these object-oriented solutions is not so much on the grounds of logical reasoning, but a reflection of an instinctive awareness that people don't want to feel vulnerable or isolated. It is based upon a conception of people wanting to feel safe and secure. It is a recognition that people need to feel wanted and looked after. Any system that creates negative emotions in these respects is seen as being unrealistic and unworkable.

However, the connectiveness of the Internet brings about a new way of thinking about groups and what separation from a group implies. The reality of the Internet is that there is no real separation between people: everyone is permanently connected to each other either directly or indirectly. This makes it impossible for anyone to be lonely or isolated unless they actually choose to opt out of the connectivity.

Outside of the environment of the Internet it takes much effort to become a member of a group; it is impractical to belong to many groups at the same time; being dropped from a group is a traumatic experience and to join a new group involves a wretched process of finding new contacts, making new friends and building new relationships.

Things are very different on the Internet. It is incredibly easy to join a new group. In fact it is easy to join many different groups all at the same time. By being actively involved with many groups, the temporary dropping out from one of the groups is not a serious problem; there are many others and, unlike the world of bricks and mortar, it is easy to drop out of a group for a while then drop back in again later.

It is this ability to be sociably mobile, to move easily in and out of groups, that makes the Internet such a different environment from the environment of the physical world of bricks and mortar. This ease of mobility takes away the pressures normally associated with belonging to a group. Nobody is forced to stay in groups where they don't feel comfortable. They don't have to stay in situations where there are incompatible goals or conflicts of personality. It is so easy for anyone to reposition themselves in this people space to be where they feel most comfortable and productive. In other words, people can move around until they find a nice group of people to socialize or work with.

This is what is so hard for the Industrial Age mind to come to terms with: people don't have to be stuck with the particular group of friends and colleagues that chance, geographic location or an occupational environment forces upon them. Anyone can simply adjust their position in the Hilbert space of the Internet to go where it suits them best.

The managed group of the Industrial Age corporate world is purposely designed to play upon the emotions of human instinctive needs for a group: forcing them to pull their weight; forcing them to conform and get along with other people; making them feel bad if they are not a member of the team. Billions of dollars have been spent on psychological techniques to get group members thinking this way. This is why any other method of organization seems so strange; it is because the corporate idea of a managed group has been conditioned into every employee as a way of life which has no viable alternative.

Outside of the corporate environment of the Industrial Age, the psychological pressures to maintain group adhesion and induce team spirit are seen as a kind of emotional blackmail and employment as a form of emotional slavery. The near infinite choices available in the world of the Information Age don't facilitate this kind of emotional pressure. People are too free to move on. This is not any kind of Utopian dream, it is a reality brought about by the connectiveness of the Internet.

Strangely enough, most people find such freedom scary. They like to be managed, they like others to take over responsibilities for them. So how is an object-oriented organization going to work if so many people prefer regulation and dependence? The answer is that they can have freedom, regulation and dependence all at the same time. These are just more of the paradoxes of the Information Age: you can be controlled and managed without having to sacrifice freedom; you can exercise discretion without having to bear responsibility.

These paradoxes are resolved by the connectiveness of the Internet environment, which allows people to be continuously in contact with others. The very nature of the connections ensures that everyone is reliant upon each other, yet, just like the Internet itself, breaking any single link is not fatal and most times it is not even regarded as an inconvenience.

The paradox of the unmanaged team

It is not easy to conceptualize a system of organization that is based upon temporary unmanaged groups where everyone has so much freedom and autonomy. The instinctive reaction is to ask how you can get members of an unmanaged group to obey rules that enable them to cooperate with each other. It seems quite beyond the imagination to visualize a group that is not held together by rules. Yet, rules are the manifestations of management and if a group is not managed, then, by definition, there can be no rules.

> Rules are the manifestations of management and if a group is not managed, then, by definition, there can be no rules.

Just imagine if I'd gone into my wholesalers in Berwick Street and said to them, 'Right, before I start buying I want to sort out a set of rules to define how we are going to work together.' They would have thought I'd gone crazy. Yet these wholesalers were members of a group, a virtual group, a virtual team: my virtual team of buyers.

The unmanaged group isn't held together by rules, but by benefits of mutual advantage. In other words, an unmanaged group of autonomous decision makers will work together only if it is in each of their interests to do so. It is the benefits of cooperating that hold an unmanaged group together, not any rules. Where do the benefits come from? As we saw in Chapter 10, benefits can manifest spontaneously from cooperative activity that increases efficiency. These are the profits that emanate from a win-win situation.

Having established that mutual benefit holds groups together, it becomes pertinent to ask certain questions:

1 Who is going to initiate such groups?
2 Who will be the one to identify a win-win situation where cooperation produces benefits?
3 Who is going to decide who is in the group and who is not?
4 How does anyone get invited to take part in a win-win situation?

The first three questions have the same answer. It is going to be an initiator: someone who is able to identify a win-win situation where cooperation can produce benefits. However, it will take more than just recognition, of the win-win situation to form a cooperative group. The initiator will have to provide enough evidence that profits will result from a proposed cooperation before anyone else will cooperate.

Even if an initiator can recognize a win-win situation and be able to produce the evidence that profits will result, the initiator will still be a long way away from being able to bring about a cooperative group. The initiator will still have to:

a know who to contact;
b get enough of their attention so they listen to the proposition;
c have sufficient credibility to be convincing.

The fourth question has similar communication hurdles to overcome. Everyone would like to be invited into a situation where cooperation can create wealth for everyone involved, but to get invited into such a win-win situation you have to have some valuable quality or asset that is needed by the group. Nobody wants to be in a cooperative situation with people who aren't able to pull their weight.

The people initiators are most likely to want to bring into a win-win situation are people with money, special skills, contacts or communication abilities. But just like the initiator, it is one thing to have a valuable asset and quite another to be able to inform and convince other people that they are available. The people who have assets and want to get into win-win situations must:

a   know who to make aware of their assets;

b   get initiators to investigate their assets;

c   have sufficient credibility that their assets can be valued at their true worth.

Looking at the two positions of the initiators and the asset holders, they require almost identical communication strategies. They have to find suitable contacts, get their attention and convince them of their credibility.

It might seem strange to struggling artists or programmers that they are in a similar position to an entrepreneur or a financier but the reality is that everybody needs other people and the right kind of people have to be found, cultivated and convinced. This requires a communication strategy: a strategy that is optimal for getting other people to cooperate with you.

This then is the paradox of the unmanaged team: everyone wants to be in one but it is difficult for people to get together to form one. The solution is through everyone involved being able to adopt a suitable communication strategy. In this way, win-win situations and unmanaged groups will form spontaneously.

Mapping the unmanaged team across to a people space

Examining the details of examples and case histories of win-win situations and unmanaged teams is helpful only if you want to copy the same situation. To be able to find new situations, create them or take part in them, it is necessary to have an all-purpose, mental model that can apply to any situation.

This needs the Zen-ness that has been mentioned several times in this book: the mental model that allows us to be at the right place at the right time and make the right decisions. To create such a model, we need to start with a basic abstraction that can visualize an overall commercial system. From there, we can move on to appropriate communication strategies that can be used to form or take part in any kind of cooperative group.

When buying costume jewellery for the counter in Hyper Hyper, I had been creating an unmanaged team of people every time I went to Berwick Street. These virtual teams were formed on the basis of people taking part in a win-win situation: taking part in a process of supplying costume jewellery that people wanted. We were all profiting from this strategy.

First, consider the people who were invited in. They were wholesalers, and as wholesalers they were representatives of other virtual groups: i.e., the manufacturers. This structure is similar to the structure of the groups of managers in the hierarchical system of managed groups in the corporate world. The power of each person in the group is based upon the pyramid of groups below them. In the case of the wholesalers, their power is based upon the power given to them by virtue of their relationships with groups of manufacturing contacts.

The corporate system is based upon managed groups, the costume jewellery buying system is based upon unmanaged groups. In the corporate system, the groups have a relative permanence and people are trained, coerced, manipulated and provided with rewards and incentives. In contrast, unmanaged groups are temporary, and come together simply as a result of sharing in the profits emerging from the common business activity. Each type of group comes together because the people in them can directly contribute in some way.

Another difference between the two types of group is the need for a group leader. In the corporate world of managed teams, great emphasis is placed upon the role of leadership. Countless training manuals try to define this ephemeral quality, even though nobody is really sure if people are born to be leaders or whether people can be trained to be. Probably it is a bit of both, but the essential point here is that leadership, in the context of a managed team, is a quality that is usually equated with management. So, does an unmanaged team need to have leadership?

This question is at the core of understanding how complex systems work. It is also at the core of understanding how to create viable e-business and e-commerce solutions. To get at the root of the problem, consider the definition of a leader: it is someone who leads the way. This is a great thing for a group to have, but only if the leader can lead effectively. If the group is working in an environment where the right way can be judged or calculated in some way, good leadership is realizable. But what if it isn't possible to find out the correct, or even the best way? What value does leadership have then?

This is the situation that exists in the chaotically changing environment of the Internet and is the crux of the difficulty in creating e-business and e-commerce solutions. The rapidly changing technology, the ever-increasing amount of information available, the plethora of fast-adapting competition reduce the value of leadership to a point where leadership can actually become a handicap to a group. This implies that the type of group that would be most appropriate to cope with the chaotic environment of the Internet should be leaderless.

To the thinking of the Industrial Age, with their systems based upon managed teams, the idea of a leaderless group is an oxymoron: a nonsensical concept that is a contradiction of terms. However, let's apply this thought to the unmanaged groups formed in the costume jewellery business strategy. Was there a leader in these groups?

After the jewellery counter had been going for a while I became interested in other things and, to save having to spend time in Berwick Street, I gave the job of buying the costume jewellery over to the girl who was running the jewellery counter. She had direct access to the customers and knew even better than I did what they wanted. She bought the stock in exactly the same way as I had.

The arrangement worked extremely well, yet by no stretch of the imagination could she be regarded as managing or leading these virtual teams. She was simply playing a role in a series of different unmanaged teams that manifested each week as a direct consequence of what customers wanted. She didn't even have to choose the wholesalers – the members of the virtual teams – these were chosen for her by her customers' requirements. They were not being selected according to her judgement, but because they had the stock her customers needed. She didn't have to lead the activity of the wholesalers, but simply pass information on to them that she herself had received from her customers.

These virtual teams that were created each week for the purpose of buying jewellery were thus unmanaged and leaderless. They were virtual objects that were responding to messages emanating from customers with a need to communicate messages to their peers. Each of the unmanaged, leaderless groups was a virtual object, each made up of other objects that were also virtual objects.

Although many of the virtual objects involved in this complex system of communication were managed teams, the system itself consisted of unmanaged, leaderless teams. Whether managed or unmanaged, each team or virtual team is represented in the system by a human. As the team or group that each person represents can be treated as an object, the person representing that team or group can be treated as an object. In this sense, the system consists of people objects that exist in unmanaged, leaderless teams.

Taking this abstract view of the system, all activity can be described in terms of the linking together of two solution points in a solution space. One point is where people are saying what they want and the other is where people are saying they've got it. In this way, the system can be viewed as a complex environment of inter-linked groups brought together and driven by customer demands.

Such a system consists of nothing but people and communication messages and can be mapped across to a Hilbert solution space where the dimensions are people. With such an abstract model in mind, the whole of any e-business or e-commerce enterprise can be modelled as a network of communicating people and any business plan reduced to that of strategies of communication.

It is this trick of abstracting away from the actual details of a real-life situation that can lead to the seemingly mystic quality of Zen-ness. With such Zen-ness it is possible to create appropriate communication strategies for any kind of e-business or e-commerce project.

Chapter 13

The strategy of the individual

A new perspective for the individual

In 127 AD, the Greek astronomer, Ptolemy, developed a theory of the Earth being at the centre of the universe with all the stars and planets moving around it. For hundreds of years this was assumed to be correct, but it caused much head scratching when it came to working out the movements of the planets. These appeared to take bizarre paths through the heavens, which defied all logical explanation.

Then, in 1543, a book by Nicolaus Copernicus, a Polish church official, revived an ancient theory that the Earth and the planets were moving around the sun. This repositioning of the centre of rotation threw a whole new perspective on the way in which the planets moved. It made much more sense and led to the German theorist, Johannes Keppler, being able to describe accurately the exact elliptical motion of planets which in turn allowed Isaac Newton to deduce the laws of gravity.

A somewhat similar effect occurs in the transition from the world of bricks and mortar to the world of the Internet. In the Industrial Age, the company is at the centre of a business system. The group is at the centre of its members. Individual people circle around the group and the groups circle around the company. In the environment of the Internet, the perspective is quite different: individuals are at the centre of their own universes and can function quite independently of any particular group or company. Thus, as far as any particular individual is concerned, the world is circling around them.

This change in perspective puts the onus on each individual to make their own connections to the rest of the world. If they want to benefit from the freedom that the Internet provides, they must be able to make their own contacts. In other words, the downside of freedom is that the normal social and business contacts provided automatically in a restricted environment are not present in the free environment of the Internet. Each individual in this environment of free choice has to create their own circle of friends and contacts.

This is a very different state of affairs for anyone used to being in a managed team. They'll find it is not an easy or natural transition from the world of bricks and mortar to the world of the Internet. There are many adjustments that will have to be made; there are communication techniques to be learned. Making contact on the Internet requires positive action necessitating a purposeful and sensible strategy.

In the world of bricks and mortar, a limited variety of contacts are nearly always at hand. From the day everyone is born they are placed into a ready-made group of contacts: a fixed family circle; a local neighbourhood. They will go to a school where there is a ready-made group of people of their own age to become friends with. Leaving school to go to university, the armed forces, a job of work – all provide a ready-made social scene. Most people can go through the whole of their lives without having to start from scratch to create their own contacts to form a social or business environment of their own making. On the Internet, this is the first thing you have to do.

When social and work environments provide a ready-made group of people to mix with, the emphasis is on fitting in, accommodating other people. The environment of the Internet is the exact opposite of this: nobody is forced to fit in with people they don't care for because they can just move on. They don't have to tolerate people or accommodate their foibles or behaviour because there is an almost infinite choice of other people and groups to associate with.

Moving on is easy because finding new friends and contacts in the connected world of the Internet is many orders of magnitude easier. It is also far less stressful, because anyone making an error of judgement in their social behaviour can learn from the experience and start again. In many ways, the environment of the Internet is much like going to a new place for a vacation: people are a bit nervous at first because they may not be used to making new friends, but as everyone is in the same boat, they are highly receptive to establishing new associations and the social atmosphere is far less closed or guarded than in long-established communities.

The key to understanding the communication environment of the Internet is to realize that the rules of social interaction are different from those in the world of bricks and mortar. Then, it is simply a matter of devising a suitable personal strategy for communication. It is to this area we go now.

The essence of game theory

If you sat down next to somebody in an airport waiting lounge and asked them to be your friend and give you a hundred dollars they'd probably move away and find somewhere else to sit. If on the other hand you told them that you'd just heard from your pal at the reception desk that there was going to be a delay to the flight you'd be likely to have no problem in striking up a friendly conversation with them.

These are common-sense predictions as to the outcomes of two initial communication exchanges. If a variety of initial approaches could be tried out and analyzed, some general rules might emerge to enable you to work out a general strategy for getting friendly with people in airport waiting lounges.

This is the way game theory works. A number of tactics are tried and from the results of these attempts some general rules might emerge that can be used in a 'rule of thumb' strategy that will lead to a reasonable degree of success in similar circumstances.

This is the essence of the Zen-ness that has been mentioned previously in this book. The rules that emerge are not hard and fast rules that work every time, they are 'best guess' tactics that are likely to give the best results over a period of time.

All strategic game players must acquire this knack of seeing situations as if they were likely to be repeated often – even if they aren't. This is the only way to achieve success in conditions of uncertainty and competition. It's a simple mental trick to think of yourself as having to decide what play to make if you had to use a single play in one hundred identical situations. The question to be answered is, 'What play would be likely to be right the most times?' This trick allows you to make a statistically optimum choice. This is the essence of game theory and is the Zen-ness that makes it appear to others that successful players seem to have all the luck.

Using game theory as an abstract modelling environment, it can be used to devise a suitable strategy in any competitive game-playing situation where there is uncertainty and unknowns. The environment of the Internet is just such a situation: where the game is to compete for cooperation. A superior strategy here would see the user of the strategy being a likely winner to secure the cooperation of others and thus be able to participate more successfully in collaborative ventures to create wealth.

A strategy for seeking cooperation

Whether an entrepreneur, a solution builder, a contractor, a middleman, a consultant, an expert or a specialist, it will seem a daunting task for anyone starting out in the Information Age to have to build up their own network of contacts. There are so many people, so many choices. Where do you start? How do you get people's attention and interest? How can you find and maintain a permanent network of active contacts? How do you get people to cooperate with you?

This is where it is necessary to have Zen-ness: a conceptual model that helps you to become streetwise on the Net. Such a model comes from a unique experiment proposed in the late 1970s by the political scientist Robert Axelrod. He invited contestants from universities all around the world to take part in tournaments where computer programs would compete against each other to win points according to how successful they were at cooperation. The tournament took the form of a continuous series of plays in a game situation called The Prisoner's Dilemma. This is a game, due originally to Merrill Flood

In the simplified version of The Prisoner's Dilemma chosen for the tournaments, programs continually interacted with each other on a round robin basis where they decided whether to cooperate or defect. Points were awarded according to the decisions made.

Calling one program A and the other program B, points were awarded as follows:

1 If program A decides to cooperate, it will get 3 points if program B also cooperates, but 0 points if program B defects.

2 If program A defects, it will get 5 points if program B chooses to cooperate, but only 1 point if program B defects.

As the programs are not allowed to communicate, to program A it looks as if the best policy would be to defect as there seems to be a statistical advantage if program B's decision is an unknown.

However, this situation would look identical to program B, so if they both made what would seem to be the best decision they would continuously each decide to defect and continuously each receive only 1 point at each play. Clearly, it would be much preferable if they could somehow come to an agreement to cooperate whereupon they would get 3 points every time.

Figure 13.1   The Prisoner's Dilemma

and Melvin Dresher in about 1950, which depends upon the participants cooperating with each other in order to get the best results.

For readers who want to go through the mechanics and details of the tournament form of Prisoner's Dilemma, the rules and structure of the game are shown in Figure 13.1.

The computer programs competed in thousands of these Prisoner's Dilemma games with the objective of trying to win the most points. They were not allowed to communicate directly with each other but were allowed to see the results of all previous plays. Some of the programs in the tournament were highly complicated, but the winner was the simplest program of all: a program called TIT FOR TAT. This program would always decide to cooperate with another program at a first encounter. At each succeeding encounter, it would copy the decision made by its opponent in the previous play.

Despite the sophistication of many of the other programs, this simple strategy succeeded over all others in a host of variations of the game. It even succeeded when the designers of other programs were made aware of the TIT FOR TAT strategy. The only superior strategy to emerge was a variation of TIT FOR TAT that allowed forgiveness: where instead of invariably copying a defection, it would allow a competitor to make a few defections before following suit. This improvement on the original program allowed other programs to learn from their mistake of defecting, thus providing another opportunity to cooperate once they had learnt that cooperating was a better tactic than defecting.

Axelrod used the results from these Prisoner's Dilemma tournaments to explain how, in a world of people selfishly looking after their own interests, cooperation could emerge spontaneously (*Note:* Robert Axelrod, in collaboration with the distinguished evolutionary biologist W. D. Hamilton, produced a technical paper, 'The Evolution of Cooperation in Biological Systems'. This paper eventually formed the basis of Robert Axelrod's book *The Evolution of Cooperation*, first published in 1984 by Basic Books of New York with the reprint version published in 1985.)

The original paper, written in 1981 by Hamilton and Robert Axelrod, was an explanation as to how altruism could have evolved. (This was an enigma for many years and was often used to refute Darwin's theories which were based upon survival of the fittest.) Altruism does seem to be self-defeating if used in a competitive environment, but what the tit-for-tat strategy clearly demonstrated was that it could have a profoundly beneficial effect at a group and an environmental level.

Tit-for-tat involves an individual player using the same tactic that an opponent uses in a previous exchange, so if all players start off by being generous, the whole population will soon be continually cooperating with each other. If a cheat arrives in such an environment, he or she will gain from the first exchange (taking a favour without honouring a return obligation), but after that the cheat will consistently do badly.

Axelrod then looked at many different real-life strategies that had similarities to the Prisoner's Dilemma. He studied situations as diverse as biological systems, the behaviour of US senators and trench warfare in the 1914–18 World War. He concluded that this strategy of tit-for-tat emerged spontaneously if there was a strong likelihood of further interactions. He also observed that a strategy of tit-for-tat could emerge successful even if a population of competitors were predominantly using the more selfish strategy of constant defection.

This, it seems, is the key to understanding how to acquire cooperation: an exchange has to be associated with the expectation of many similar events in the future. It is in keeping with the essence of game theory: making a play as if the identical situation is going to be repeated again and again.

Placing a value on relationships

There have been many more experiments with tit-for-tat strategies since 1981. No strategy has outperformed it for success, only a few useful refinements discovered. Such refinements have been based mostly upon forgiving or allowing for misunderstandings or mistakes. This enables fresh starts to be made to a series of cooperative exchanges when they break down.

The most important general outcome of all the experiments, though, is that they can create relationships which have value and this value will increase the longer and more reliably the cooperational exchanges go on. In terms of e-business and e-commerce, this is highly significant because this conclusion can form the basis of communication strategies for developing all kinds of cooperative relationships.

It may help to have a metaphor here, to create a mental model for the understanding of building value into a relationship. As the example in the airport waiting lounge illustrated, relationships involving cooperation have to be started slowly. At the beginning, they can be of an extremely trivial nature with little or no value. However, given perseverance, they can develop into substantial friendships and business associations.

This can be likened to rearing a chicken. At first, the chick has nothing to offer, apart from a cute novelty appeal. As it begins to grow the chick loses some of its cuteness and requires more and more time and effort to keep it alive. It will require more space, make more mess. There may be a temptation to abandon the growing chicken and let it run off into the wild, perhaps allowing a return to buying and rearing more baby chicks that are so cute and easy to keep alive.

However, by persevering, by feeding and looking after the growing chick, it may one day start laying eggs. At this point the relationship will have transformed into an association of mutual benefit: a symbiotic relationship where each is helping the other to stay alive.

Using the trick of abstraction, we can relate this to Internet associations. These take an investment of time and effort at the beginning, but they can blossom into arrangements of mutual exchange that have tangible values to each participant. For chicken food and eggs we can substitute information; this will see an investment in time and effort producing a valuable source of information, help and knowledge.

Using the abstraction trick again, we can say that useful information, help and knowledge have value. Value is readily convertible into money or energy. A regular source of useful knowledge and help can then be equated with a regular source of income. This takes us into the same ball park as the professional investors. Aren't they playing this same game, looking for valuable incomes? Haven't they developed all kinds of strategies for dealing in incomes? Don't they decide value by measuring one income value against another? Don't they look to build up portfolios of reliable and good value incomes?

This trick of abstracting out the essence of a cooperative strategy allows us to map between Internet communications, rearing chickens and investment managing. We can readily swap the concepts from one to another. The abstraction allows us to see the value not only in building up cooperative relationships, but also in being able to build portfolios and compare relative values.

Taking the chicken metaphor further, we can think of a farmer who is earning a living by selling eggs. Imagine this farmer with a hen coop that can hold a maximum of 50 hens; he could be likened to the investment manager with a portfolio of 50 annuities or fixed interest bonds. Some chickens and investments would be better value than others. Also, their values can change.

In terms of the overall value of the farmer's chickens or the investment manager's portfolio, it would make good sense to be trying constantly to maintain or even raise the total value. Farmers would constantly be removing the chickens that were laying the least eggs and replacing them with better layers. As the economic conditions changed, investment managers would constantly be replacing investments that were underperforming with a view to replacing them with better-performing investments.

Abstracting this across to social and business contacts would see an Internet communicator having a finite time to manage and maintain a number of contacts. The returns from each would have value. so it would make sense for an Internet communicator to optimize his or her Internet communication time by dropping associations with the poorest value and replacing them with better value.

In plain words, it means we have only a limited time to spend communicating with people on the Internet and this time ought to be spent as efficiently as possible. Like the farmer with his 50 chickens and the investment manager with his 50 investments, a person with time to spend communicating with 50 email correspondents would need to be constantly replacing the worst performers.

In the world of bricks and mortar, such an attitude would be regarded as unethical. It isn't considered good behaviour to drop friends and colleagues as soon as they are of no use to you. Society norms and instinctive emotions tell you that this is a bad attitude to have. But this is not the world of bricks and mortar; it is the world of permanent connectivity where the temporary dropping of a communication link is acceptable behaviour.

In the Industrial Age world of projects and managed teams, such a strategy could be likened to constantly replacing the poorest performers in a team with more suitable members. Although this would tend to make the team more efficient, replacement of team members in this way would be carried out re-luctantly: out of necessity or in extenuating circumstances. To consider replacing team members frequently and constantly would be unthinkable to most managers and executives of the Industrial Age. Yet, this is the optimum dynamics for groups in the Information Age.

It is this conceptual chasm that most Industrial Age strategists find difficult to cross. Their reasoning is that it takes a lot of time, effort and money to create and build a stable, efficient team where the team members complement each other and work well together. It seems foolhardy to have a strategy that treats an efficient team so lightly and replaces members in such a cavalier fashion. Thus, for both a group in the world of bricks and mortar and a team in the corporate world of the Industrial Age, it doesn't seem right to treat communication contacts in this way.

However, a collection of communication contacts on the Internet can be considered to be a virtual group or a virtual team, much like the virtual teams that were created in Berwick Street for buying costume jewellery. They can be looked upon as virtual circles of friends and contacts, selected temporarily from a wider pool of contacts and friends. By selectively dealing with only a few contacts at a time, it reduces the time, and takes away the pressure, of having to maintain continuous contact with the whole of a wider base of friends and contacts. This allows Internet communicators to have far larger ranges of friends and contacts than is possible in the world of bricks and mortar. As this works for both sides of relationships, far from being an unacceptable practice it is highly beneficial to all.

Likening this to retailer associations with wholesalers in Berwick Street, the wholesalers bear no animosity when they are dropped out of a retailer's weekly buying schedule. They know they can't always have the stock a retailer needs, but they also know they'll be needed again as soon as their stock once again coincides with the needs of the retailer's customers. In this way the wholesalers are not dropped altogether when a retailer doesn't buy from them, they are just returned to a pool of the retailer's contacts that are selected from each week.

This happens on the Internet because it is so easy to make many more friends and contacts than it is practical to maintain a continuous dialogue with. Thus, the best strategy for everyone to adopt is to establish a large pool of contacts but concentrate on just a selected few of them at a time. In the world of the Internet this is acceptable behaviour because everybody is in the same situation and realizes eventually that this is the most effective way for everyone to behave. The ease of communicating and the ability to use computer programs to keep track of communications and relationships make it a far different environment from the world of bricks and mortar, or the managed team projects of the Industrial Age.

From the paradigm of an Industrial Age thinker, this still may not ring true because of the need for people to be able to fit in well together; to have to know each other; to allow for inadequacies and be able to anticipate how others are thinking and working. However, as we have already covered, these consider-ations are completely redundant in an object-oriented world of virtual groups because people have only to be concerned with their own actions and behaviour.

Replacing a team with a network

The jewellery buying for the counter in Hyper Hyper could, in theory, have been handled using a strategy of managed teams. A team could have been used for market research to determine the best jewellery items to buy. What would be the actions of the project leader in such a team? What kind of team would be needed to keep track of the rapidly changing trends and fashions? Would such a team do any better job than an intelligent sales girl behind the counter who could observe and communicate directly with the customers?

The sales girl was a direct communication link in a communication network, a link that led from the customers to the suppliers. There were no special procedures involved in her job, or special training needed. She simply communicated, observed and passed the results on to a supply network.

Now think of the buying side. Once the necessary information as to what to buy is available, why couldn't a managed team be used to buy directly from the manufacturers, rather than go through middlemen, the wholesalers? How would the leader or manager of such a team fulfil his or her role in directing the team? How many team members would be needed to cover all of the manufacturers? How many controls and safeguards would be needed to make sure they were working conscientiously as they travelled around the country visiting manufacturers to find out if they could make the items needed?

Even if such a team were created, what would be the pressures on team members to go to work for a competitor once they had been trained and had familiarized themselves with all the manufacturing contacts? Retaining the loyalty and services of team members would certainly require much work and ingenuity on the part of the team leader.

The switching of loyalties in the world of bricks and mortar isn't that easy, but what about in the environment of the Internet, where making contact and communicating with people is so easy? This brings into question the value of training people and putting them into positions of responsibility. If it is easy for people to switch loyalties as soon as they have been trained, learnt the ropes or know all the contacts, the value of a managed team would disappear. This situation was illustrated in Chapter 1, where all the students who were educated at the research establishment found their education put them in a position to get better jobs elsewhere.

There may be certain practical and logistical restraints to changing employment in the world of bricks and mortar, but in the environment of the Internet the restraints are minimal. It certainly makes it reasonable for a company to think carefully before they hire anyone on a permanent basis for any role in the environment of the Internet; it may make better sense to call upon the services of speciality experts as and when they are needed. Maybe it is not practical in the world of bricks and mortar, but it makes a great deal of sense in the environment of the Internet: the environment of e-business and e-commerce. After all, in any area of fast-changing technology, job changing and the poaching of staff is a fact of life; this is not very far removed from the temporary hiring of specialists and experts.

Compare the strategy of using a managed team to buy costume jewellery with the strategy of a virtual team consisting of the wholesalers. Does it make any sense to retain the same set of wholesalers each week? Doesn't it seem sensible to chop and change the members of this virtual team around as fashions change and the various virtual team members, the wholesalers, run hot and cold?

It makes sense because the virtual team is not really a team at all but a selected part of a vast information network. The interaction with this network is achieved by selecting appropriate nodes. If we replace Berwick Street with the Internet and the wholesalers of jewellery with information providers, we can see how buying costume jewellery was arranged by tapping into the nodes of a vast network of people involved with the manufacture and supply of costume jewellery.

The selected nodes act as the interface to a vast dynamic network of information flow. If this were likened to a complex electrical network, the virtual team could be thought of as a multi-wire socket: each wire to the socket coming from a different point in the electrical network. Connecting to this network is simply a matter of plugging into the socket. The trick in both cases is to make sure that the leads going to the socket are coming from the right places in the network.

If this analogy of a plug and socket is taken further, two sockets can be connected using a connecting wire and two plugs. This is the connection between two solution points in solution space; it can be the link between a demand and a supply. This throws the spotlight onto the sales girl who ran the jewellery counter and also did the buying. She was the connecting wire with a plug at each end. It is here, at this link between demand and supply, that the efficiencies can be realized and the profits made. The trick, though, is to be able to connect the right wires up to the sockets at each end. In the world of the Internet this involves finding the right collection of people to be the connection nodes into an environment of information.

It is this kind of abstract vision that provides the Zen-ness for e-business and e-commerce solutions. This ability to abstract away from the real-life detail is what allows the streetwise to out-pace and out-manoeuvre their competitors. It allows the streetwise to avoid the many pitfalls brought about by confusion with issues relevant only to the world of bricks and mortar.

The fragmentation effect of the Internet

The example of the costume jewellery counter in the world of bricks and mortar represents a very simplified form of network because there are only two levels of organization between manufacturer and customer. But in the world of the Internet, vastly more complexity is involved – necessitating a far larger number of levels. This is because each level is effectively a filter to the information in the level below.

Multiple levels of filter are required, otherwise the intermediaries at each level would have to have more up-to-date knowledge than is possible to either absorb or comprehend. Competition will ensure that intermediaries working beyond their capacity to cope efficiently will be bypassed. This is a reality that isn't appreciated by people trying to cover too large a range of products or services. They spread their resources too thinly and more often than not produce an underperforming solution: a pathological result in the Information Age.

This state of affairs can be appreciated by imagining every manufacturer of costume jewellery in the world having a Web site. Even though it would be easy for customers to go directly to a manufacturer, it would be unlikely because they wouldn't know where to start looking, or know what items are currently fashionable. Retailers can solve this problem of over-choice for the customer because, as with the counter in Hyper Hyper, the selection they can offer will be selectively limited and constantly in keeping with the current fashions.

If the choice of manufacturing possibilities is too large for the retailer to deal with efficiently, the retailer may well go to middlemen who might be spending the whole of their time with manufacturers and be able to filter out a more convenient selection to choose from. Perhaps the number of jewellery manufacturers grows so large that manufacturers have to start specializing in niche areas to ensure a reasonable amount of business. If there were thousands of niche specialists then there would need to be niche middlemen. If there were thousands of niche middlemen there would have to be wholesalers who specialized in niches.

It doesn't take much reasoning to realize that the result of expanding choice on the Internet is going to throw up all kinds of specializations and this, in turn, will lead to layers of middlemen who, between them, create an information network that evolves to optimally satisfy customer needs. Nobody can compete with this self-organizing system; they can only become part of it.

In the world of bricks and mortar, the costs of the middlemen can be quite high. This puts a practical limit on the number of middlemen levels and the degree of specialization. However, in the world of the Internet, the ease of communication and the low overheads allow the cost of middlemen to shrink to insignificant proportions.

If this situation for costume jewellery is repeated for the millions of different types of products and services possible on the Internet, the Internet environment will consist mainly of middlemen, each taking up some niche in a complex network of information. Each of these middlemen will need to be able to create their own demand and supply connection points and each of these points must consist of a number of people. This puts everyone involved in e-commerce in a similar situation; each, like the girl running the jewellery counter in Hyper Hyper, will need to become the link between two sockets. The only difference is that everyone will have to wire up their own socket connections to the network themselves.

On the service side, the situation is similar. Take for instance the design of a Web site. The number of different applications and programming solutions on offer is huge. It isn't possible for any one contractor or consultant to know the full capability of every approach possible; every solution provider, contractor or consultant will be forced to have their own particular favourites.

Each approach will have its own large variety of speciality niche areas that can only be truly appreciated by niche specialists. This necessitates a solution provider, contractor or consultant having to use layers of intermediaries to be able to use any chosen approach effectively. Any solution provider, contractor or consultant that tries to bypass the intermediary levels is likely to underperform with the solution. This will risk both them and their clients becoming vulnerable to competitors who can more efficiently and effectively utilize the full potential of the technology.

Thus, each solution provider can best be thought of as being at the head of a pyramid of middlemen who, between them, can provide an optimum solution, the solution provider being the pipe through which the solution is being delivered.

Creating a profitable hub

The real-life situations covered so far have been dealing with the connections between the information coming from a solution point consisting of customers and a supply coming from a solution point consisting of manufacturers or service providers. In the jewellery example, the whole system of supply to satisfy a chaotic demand for costume jewellery involved three solution points:

1 customers, supplying information and feedback to the retailers;

2 middlemen, acting between the retailers and the manufacturers;

3 manufacturers or product producers, supplying the middlemen.

In the world of bricks and mortar – where physical products are involved, or where communication needs face-to-face presence – the solution points are self-forming. Fashion leaders went to Hyper Hyper and this formed a physical information solution point. Wholesalers grouped around Berwick Street to create a physical solution point for the retailers to buy from. Manufacturers group in physical locations or at trade shows to provide physical solution points for wholesalers to make contact with them.

These physical solution points have evolved as a natural result of a dynamic system's self-organization towards increased efficiency. The system has matured, having discovered its own way of coping with the chaotic changes in fashion. This makes it easy for anyone, even with relatively little specialist knowledge, to tap into this naturally formed system and begin trading straight away.

Having a physical presence at one of the solution points (such as a jewellery counter in Hyper Hyper, wholesale premises in Berwick Street or a stand at a trade fair) makes the creation and maintenance of a business enterprise much easier. Without such a physical presence, it is necessary to create a personal solution point. This must take the form of a list of personal contacts. Such a list is not something that can be acquired easily. It is something that has to be carefully built up, one entry at a time.

It becomes obvious here how silly it is to create a stand-alone Web site that is not at a solution point, i.e., a place where there are no contacts regularly connecting to it. However attractive and creative a site may be in a visual sense, it is totally useless unless it is the interface to a number of people. It is the getting of these people to interact with a site that is the tricky part, not its design. Many people are under the impression that an attractive site will attract people. That is a fatal fallacy. A Web site is about creating a solution point, not creating a technological wonder.

People involved with e-business and e-commerce must each have two solution points; these can be looked at as an input and an output to a person's activity. These solution points can be such that one is in the world of bricks and mortar and the other in the environment of the Internet (Web sites are included in this environment). Alternatively, they can both be in the environment of the Internet. More intriguingly, both solution points can be in the world of bricks and mortar – but connected together with a series of solution point pairs in the environment of the Internet.

Whichever combination is used in any particular business situation, it is almost certain that one or other (maybe both) of the solution points will have to be created from scratch. E-business or e-commerce people will have to find their own contacts and create their own solution points. Invariably, these will boil down to a list of humans: either customers or trusted contacts.

In the world of bricks and mortar, sales people are the people most noted for making use of a list of contacts. In the minds of most people, sales people, and their lists of contacts, are associated only with the sales transaction itself. Few people see these in terms of a communication network. Yet, most sales people are interested in more than simply single sales; their prime interest is in establishing contacts for long-term relationships which will result in a series of sales.

Sales people who are working towards building up a list of long-term relationships will usually expend much energy to build up a relationship of trust before they start to profit from the relationship. Invariably they will use a tit-for-tat strategy where they will open the relationship by cooperating, which will involve giving the contact something – usually in the form of information, help or guidance – and waiting for the contact to respond with a cooperative response.

Many people are wary of this approach and suspect that such a strategy is designed to build up to where a sales person can make a highly profitable sale and then defect. This is a very short-sighted view. It is only used where the sales product is such that long-term customer relationships, or reputation, are not seen to be worth cultivating. This happens almost invariably in zero sum games, where the winners win what the losers lose. A reasonable amount of common sense keeps most people out of such situations.

Most times, sales people are working for continuous, mutually profitable relationships; it is only a short-sighted sales person who works any other way because all the hard work goes into a first sale and, if the customer benefits from the sale, subsequent sales get progressively easier. In a non-zero sum game – a win-win situation – mutually profitable relationships can be maintained indefinitely. These are the kinds of relationships that are most profitable to seek out in the environment of the Internet.

In situations where a sales person has worked to build up a list of personal contacts, the successful continuation of the interactions must be based upon the sales person's ability to create benefits for all concerned: a win-win situation. Such a list of contacts can be viewed as a network, where the sales person is the hub of this network: a hub that is distributing wealth to all the contacts connected to it. The sales person takes a proportion of the wealth created at this hub in the form of commissions or a percentage of the sales revenue.

In this way, it can be seen that a hub can be profitable to everyone who is part of it. This brings about the interesting situation that there can be two major strategies in the environment of the Internet that will both be profitable:

1 To be an initiator and form a hub, or solution point.
2 To arrange to connect to the hubs of many initiators.

The second strategy involves forming a virtual hub that, in effect, connects a single person to many hubs. In this way a person can benefit from many hubs that dissipate benefits without having to initiate any themselves. It is this realization that there are two types of strategy, and that they are complementary, that can lead to an understanding as to how to make best use of the Internet. It is especially powerful if a person is able to make use of the two strategies simultaneously: perhaps one as an input and another as an output, in a business role or a business venture.

Putting the clues together

Part 5 is the equivalent of the final drawing room scene in detective stories, where the detective puts all the clues together. In this mystery, the murder victims have been money and time: wasted on futile attempts to apply Industrial Age thinking to e-business and e-commerce solutions in the Information Age.

The conclusion is not in the form of a set of instructions that can be written down in a bullet point list. It is a mental model that can be used to see the Internet for what it is: a massive connectivity that can be tapped into to vastly increase individual efficiency, power and wealth.

Chapter 14

Inheriting knowledge and skills

A real-world example of a wealth-producing network of contacts

The crucial key to any strategy for e-commerce or e-business is in finding or creating the input and output solution points. These can be seen as two lists of contacts: one representing the demand side; the other representing the supply side. The wealth creation process is in linking these two sides together efficiently. The two solution points can be thought of as containing pointers: one solution point with pointers to people upstream and the other with pointers to people downstream.

Because we can view this as an abstraction, this simple model can be applied to all possible situations. It applies to the expert or specialist:

where one side represents contacts in the world of special knowledge that supplies the information needed to continually update the expert's or specialist's knowledge base. The other side will represent contacts to appropriate people who might have a need for the particular expertise provided by the specialist.

It will apply to the middlemen who will also each need two sets of contacts: one set linking them to the levels of organization nearer the supply side, namely the experts, specialists or the prime manufacturers; the other set with contacts linking them nearer to the demand side, namely the customers and clients.

These nodes and links can be thought of as occurring in a vast, complex network of interconnected people that spans between the prime sources and the ultimate consumers, each person in the network having to find or create their own input and output solution points made up of human contacts.

Places like trade shows, conferences, Internet discussion forums, etc. are easy places to make initial contacts. Quite often though, especially in the environment of the Internet, populations have to be searched and filtered to be able to find suitable people to make up an optimum solution point. This necessitates setting up many mutually cooperative associations, often requiring a lengthy process of playing tit-for-tat to bring the associations to fruitful maturities.

An example of solution point building that readily comes to mind is one that once gave me a regular supply of old fur coats. Old fur coats may seem a long way removed from Internet communication strategies, but bear with it, it's the abstraction that counts. Solution point building is always a first step when trying to move out of the dreaded square one position. After I sold out my head shop business in the early 1970s, I invested all the money I had into a property development at La Manga in Spain. This is now an established holiday resort, but at the time, building had just begun and it seemed an ideal place for an entrepreneur to be investing.

Being an optimist and a gambler, I geared up my money (used it as part payment) to build a shopping mall consisting of 42 small boutiques designed to appeal to holiday makers. Unfortunately for me and my money, the Arab–Israeli war intervened, oil prices were hiked fourfold, the world's currencies went into chaotic turbulence and the tourist industry and the developments that depended upon them were killed stone dead. I lost everything I had in that debacle and found myself back in London with nothing more to my name than an ancient motor car that I'd bought with the last of my money.

Fortunately, I still had many friends in London. One of them loaned me some money and rented me a small trading space in his shop which was located in a side road off Carnaby Street. The condition of the offer was that the space would be available only after the end of September, when the tourist season had ended. As this was in July, I had about two months in which to organize an off-season business.

In many ways, this is very similar to the situation faced by many would-be entrepreneurs wanting to start an e-commerce business from a simple Web site: a small area to trade from, a small capital and no idea as to what to sell. There would be very little passing trade, so unlike the costume jewellery counter in Hyper Hyper, there would be too few people to use as a guide as to what to sell. This meant I had to come up with a very unique, speciality product.

Although I was stuck in a particular demand-side solution point, it wasn't too bad a situation because even though the tourist trade had slowed right down, Carnaby Street is in a highly populated business area. Many people could easily get to the shop if only they knew it existed. However, as passing trade was slow, I knew I'd have to sell a product that was unique enough for people to want to come specifically to the shop to buy it; I needed regular customers and a product so unique that its whereabouts would be spread by word of mouth. Not too dissimilar to the start-up situation faced by many small Web site traders.

Such a product wasn't easy to find. If it were, then it would probably have been stocked by some of the hundreds of other shops in the area which were constantly on the lookout for off-season lines. I needed something that was not easy for other retailers to get hold of.

Going through the various possibilities, I decided upon selling old fur coats. At the time these were quite fashionable, and I'd had experience of selling them before. Also they were a seasonal product with the season starting in October. All things considered, especially the small amount of capital I had available, it seemed a reasonable choice. All I had to do was to set up a system of supply, but this was easier said than done. Old fur coats were such a specialist product that there were no ready-made solution points. There was no equivalent to Berwick Street: a place where many wholesalers would be selling old fur coats.

I knew the only way to get old fur coats was to go around all the little bric-a-brac and used clothing stores. They occasionally had the odd fur or two to sell. There are not many of these but there is usually at least one in every town. I then set out in my rusty old car, to search out these stores.

I divided the whole of the south of England into areas and each day drove around one of the areas looking for these small stores. At each one I found, I'd ask if they had any furs. As this was in July and August 1976, the hottest summer on record, my request was greeted with some amusement, but I told them what I was doing and said I'd be returning the following month to see if they'd been able to buy any in by then.

For six weeks I bought practically no furs at all. I travelled at least 200 miles each day in the blazing heat and achieved not much more than a list of possible contacts. However, after I'd covered the whole of the south of England, I started to return to the stores I'd visited. Some of these had found furs for me. I bought all the furs I was offered, at the asking prices and without any quibble (except if they were asking silly high prices). Each purchase I viewed as the possible start of a mutually profitable, cooperative association. I even bought furs that I knew would be unsaleable in order to establish a relationship.

When I made a second return visit to the stores, some had made an effort to buy in furs specially for me. Again I bought all they had and on my next round of visits, I called only on those stores that had made an effort to get furs for me. By the end of September I'd used up all of the money I'd borrowed.

Fortunately, the furs started to sell quite well and I could start buying again and was able to continue visiting the stores on a regular basis. Several of them were now going out of their way to find furs for me. Soon, I could concentrate on just these and as their confidence increased that I would return to buy all of their stock they began to put more effort into getting hold of furs within their areas. It wasn't long before I could rely on just this handful of suppliers and so reduce my buying time to one day a week.

The essence of this venture has many lessons for e-commerce. I'd simply used a tit-for-tat strategy as I visited and revisited these contacts. Those that responded to my cooperative tactics with cooperation I could build up relationships with. As the cooperative encounters continued they became progressively more beneficial for each of us. I, for my part, was visiting them reliably every week and paying them what they asked and they in return were getting more and more confident and increased their efforts.

The net effect was a system of cooperation where I'd created my own people solution point. In effect I'd built a virtual team of conscientious workers who were searching the south of England for furs for me. There was no need for me to put some complicated reward system into effect. There was no need to motivate them, find ways to make them more efficient or check up on how hard they were working. It was a leaderless system that had evolved out of a tit-for-tat strategy being used by all of the participants.

Mapping the abstraction across to the Internet

It doesn't take much abstraction to realize how many different types of e-commerce businesses could be based upon this simple principle. There are all kinds of speciality products and services that could be sourced in the bricks and mortar world and offered from a Web site. It is a way of bringing the bricks and mortar world into the Information Age.

Although selling old fur coats from a Web site might be unrealistic, it can serve as a useful hypothetical example to explain how this kind of situation can be developed even further. Supposing the Internet had been around at that time and instead of using a space in a shop off Carnaby Street I'd used a Web site. Imagine each of the little shops I'd been buying furs from as having a computer, an Internet connection and a digital camera. Then, every time they bought a fur, they could email me a photograph and give me a price. I could then transfer the photograph to my Web site, offering the item for sale – adding a small mark-up to the asking price for myself as a trading profit.

If an Internet customer wanted to buy, they could pay by making a secure credit card transfer. I would then transfer the money (less my mark-up) to the contact's account together with an address of where to send the fur. I wouldn't have to see the stock or even organize the despatch. All of my activity would amount to no more than a few electronic transfers. In the bricks and mortar world, my business had been confined to the southern part of England because of the amount of travelling involved. In the world of e-commerce I could have contacts buying furs from places all over the world and still this would involve no more than the manipulation of electronic documents.

As my part in this activity would be minimal, my added mark-up to the price could be a very small percentage. This would allow the fur-buying contacts to get practically all of the profit and therefore have no incentive to create a Web commerce site for themselves. Taking a very small percentage is a key element in the success of middlemen in e-commerce business.

The more contacts I could find, the better selection of furs I'd be able to offer on my Web site and this would increasingly add to the attractiveness of the site to anyone who was looking to buy an old fur coat. In this way, I'd be creating what is known as a portal: a front door to a large range of a unique type of product that is not easy to find in the world of bricks and mortar. Such a situation can act as a magnet to attract customers.

If I could build up the number of contacts supplying to this portal faster than my competitors, I would be at an advantage to them. Word will spread that this is the best portal to find this unusual product and the portal will attract further customers. This in turn will make it an attractive place for even more fur suppliers to supply me with furs. In effect, the system would become self-sustaining and self-organizing, attracting its own solution point of suppliers and its own solution point of customers. When an e-commerce system reaches this stage, it is often called the point of critical mass: the point at which it becomes completely self-maintaining. This is the principal aim of all e-commerce solution providers.

Having established a prime portal that has reached critical mass, I can easily keep competitors at bay; with a high volume I could reduce the profit mark-up to a point where it would be uneconomic for any competitors to compete for either my suppliers or my customers. This is a point overlooked by many people trying to set up an e-commerce business. E-commerce is about more efficiently satisfying demand. This nearly always manifests in the form of reduced costs and prices.

Although an e-commerce business may not be practical with old fur coats, the hypothetical situation gives an idea as to how small entrepreneurial businesses can be built up from scratch. It is a win-win, non-zero sum game situation where everyone can gain. It is self-organizing in a way that causes the system to become optimally efficient as overheads and costs become smaller and smaller. Customers will have a wide range of choice and will be buying at best value. This will leave over-priced items unsold. In this way the buyers and the suppliers will have to keep their prices low in order to make sales and this ensures that the most efficient will be doing most of the business.

This natural regulation, resulting in customers having a wide selection of goods at the most competitive prices, is the way systems designed bottom-up evolve towards maximum efficiency. Nobody has to plan it, nobody has to manage it. There are no rules or regulations. The system self-regulates towards a state of maximally efficient service in satisfying customer needs.

Abstracting out the essence of this situation, anyone can create their own supply solution point using the same technique that I used in buying the old fur coats. Starting with nothing more than a green frog, contacts can be acquired one at a time and then whittled down and selected to provide an optimum group of people to provide an ample supply of the desired products in the most efficient way.

 ## Extending the concept to information exchange

Abstracting away from the hypothetical situation with the furs, it isn't difficult to see how this same situation could be applied to costume jewellery. Theoretically, it should be possible to have a portal to cover every piece of jewellery being made. All that would seem to be necessary is to make contact with every costume jewellery manufacturer in the world and display their products on a Web site.

Immediately you think of doing this the problems become obvious. There would be so many possible items to exhibit that the Web site would become thoroughly confusing because of over-choice. Old fur coats, which have been created in the past, represent a fixed and stable product range. Not so costume jewellery, which has an indeterminate range that is in a state of continuous dynamic change. The sale of costume jewellery then, as opposed to the sale of old fur coats, involves not only finding items, but also selecting from a vast range of ever-changing possibilities.

The reason the costume jewellery counter worked in Hyper Hyper was because it offered a filtered selection of all the jewellery made in the world. The selections had been made by the customers themselves as they jointly followed the changing trends and fashions. This counter was not only supplying costume jewellery, but more importantly, the information as to what was currently fashionable.

Earlier, we saw how costume jewellery could be viewed as a form of infor-mation. The trick now is to combine the scenario of the fur-buying business and the essence of the costume jewellery business and substitute information for furs and jewellery. This abstraction sees us looking at how to build up an efficient supply of information that is optimally filtered from a wide range of sources.

Imagine taking time to build up a collection of information providers instead of fur suppliers. Imagine covering various Internet Discussion Forums and looking for contacts in the same way I looked for bric-a-brac shops in the towns of southern England. Imagine using a strategy of tit-for-tat to build up relationships based upon information exchanges. Imagine gradually whittling down and selecting the most appropriate and efficient information exchangers. Imagine the information relationships becoming more and more efficient and usable.

What you would end up with is a number of contacts who would be your links to many different areas of knowledge. They may be spread out all over the world, but you would have brought them all together into your personal Berwick Street of information. It would be a virtual area, full of information suppliers to whom you could go for information every time you had a need. It would be a personal solution point of people with whom you had built up a relationship of trust and cooperation.

The more efficiently you can communicate with and maintain the cooperation of the people on this list, the more extensive the range of filtered information available to you. This will need a means of organization, a conceptual model that will make it easier to deal with many contacts and exchange information with them. For this, we have all the possibilities of computers available to us: enabling the creation of communication strategies that are not possible in the world of bricks and mortar. That is where we shall be going in the final chapter, but before then we need to take one more look at the concept of object-oriented design.

The magic of ancestry and inheritance

So far, we've considered only two of the main aspects of object-oriented design thinking: splitting a situation up into objects and keeping each object self-contained. This allows systems to be created where independent objects pass messages to each other and each responds in characteristic ways to messages they receive. But this is only half the story. The real power of object-oriented design comes as a result of two other features that provide the organization and the efficiency. The first of these is the phenomenon of ancestry and inheritance.

Newcomers to the concept of object-oriented thinking and design are often bemused by a system that appears to have no organization or controls. They cannot see how independent objects, passing messages to each other, can be purposely organized, let alone have the ability to self-organize. The secret is in a characteristic of object-oriented systems known in programming circles as inheritance or ancestry. This describes the ability of objects in a communication environment to be able to pass on a message to another object if it cannot understand or deal with it.

In object-oriented programming systems, all objects are designed with memories. In these memories are listed a number of specific messages that can be acted upon by code in another part of its memory. In this way any incoming message can be compared to this list of known messages and, if it is recognized, a particular piece of computer code goes into action when the message is received.

If an object receives a message that is not on its list, it will pass the message on to another object. The key here is to understand that the message is not passed to the next on the list of the sender of the message, it is passed on to an object that is known only to the receiver of the message. In other words, the message sender sends out a message and doesn't have to be concerned about what happens if the message cannot be dealt with by the object it sends it to; that problem is left to the receiver of the message to solve. At a stroke, this saves the message sender from having to be concerned about any of the details involved in getting an appropriate response. This greatly reduces the amount of complexity that the message sender has to deal with, freeing up more time to spend on the demand side of a solution.

In simple systems of OOPS in computer programs, each object has, in its memory, only a single name and address of an object where unrecognized messages are sent. In computer terms this object is known as its *ancestor*. The passing on of the message to an ancestor occurs within the private shell of the receiving object. This is invisible to any other object, so the sender of the message is completely unaware that the message has been referred elsewhere. This can be thought of as being similar to a television quiz show, where if a contestant cannot answer a question he or she is allowed to phone a friend. If the person whom the contestant phones can give the correct answer it counts the same as if the contestant had given the right answer themselves.

The important point to note here is that the sender of a message is oblivious and unconcerned as to which object makes the response; all it knows is that a message is sent to an object and the response is made. It doesn't know or care that any other object is involved other than the one it sent the message to.

Object message passing doesn't stop at one message referral. If objectA sends a message to objectB and objectB also cannot recognize it, objectB will pass it on to its own ancestor, objectC. If objectC also cannot recognize the message, it might be passed on to objectC's ancestor, objectD. This message passing can go from one ancestor to another until one of the ancestor objects recognizes and responds to the message.

This can be likened to the contestant in the quiz show phoning a friend for an answer to a question and the friend saying 'I don't know, but I'll ask my wife'. His wife might not know the answer either, so she may say, 'Wait a moment and I'll ask the next-door neighbour.' The next-door neighbour also might not know but will ask someone else. The referrals can continue from one person to another until at last somebody comes up with an answer to the question.

In this way, many objects can be tied together in a message path, so it only requires one of the objects in the message path to be able to respond to the message for objectA to appear to respond and so get all the credit. This is why the object that an object passes unknown messages to is known as its ancestor: because the message-passing object effectively inherits all of its ancestor's capabilities, skills and knowledge – not only of a single ancestor but all the ancestors of its ancestors.

Mapping this across to people in the technological world of the Internet, it is as if somebody is asked to produce a complex CGI script for a Web page. They may not even know what a CGI script is but if they can pass this request to someone they know who can do it they can comply with the request. Even if they don't know somebody who can write the script they can ask somebody who might know someone else. If through a series of connections the script gets done and is passed back down the line of communication to the original person who was asked to produce the script, that person would have appeared to have responded to the request.

Similarly with information. If somebody is asked a question or set a problem to solve, they can refer it to an ancestor path and get the information they need or a solution to the problem. Clearly, anyone who has a string of ancestors consisting of all kinds of experts can appear to be a very useful and versatile person to know. Any technical question could be answered, or any speciality function or service provided, as long as it is covered by the expertise of one of their ancestors.

Parenting and child objects

At first thought, the above description of a chain of inheritance seems a very unlikely scenario. Why should a whole lot of experts provide expert or specialist services and let somebody else take the credit? Something about this kind of arrangement seems wrong. However, we now come to the fourth powerful feature of object-oriented thinking and design: the parent–child phenomenon.

This phenomenon is an illusion, created in an object-oriented programming environment, that an object can have any number of simultaneous existences. In computer programs, an object can be duplicated, or cloned, so that it can appear in several different systems or subsystems at the same time. An example might be an object that is a functioning but empty database. Other objects might have a need for such an object to put their own particular content into. So instead of building a separate database for every object, clones are made of one master database and given to every object that needs a database for its own exclusive use. In this way, the master database would appear to be able to exist in many different parallel worlds. In the computer programming world of OOPS this is described as parenting: objects birthing several identical children so that each can evolve differently.

Mapping this idea across to a world of people objects, it can be seen that anyone who has a speciality expertise can, like the database, be available to many people at the same time. In the world of bricks and mortar this isn't practical, but in the communication environment of the Internet, it is easily accomplished. Experts and specialists can appear in the ancestral message paths of many different people all at the same time.

This is widely encouraged because many people would like to inherit the skills, knowledge and experience of true experts, so any real expert can expect to have many people trying to include them in their own ancestral path.

This dramatically alters the perception of the expert. Instead of being seen as being in a single ancestral message path, dependent upon receiving messages from a single source, the expert becomes the centre of a hub of message paths. Each expert is thus at the centre of his or her own universe and at the centre of attention. Being at the centre of a hub of people, who are passing on requests for their specialized services as and when they are needed, is effectively positioning the experts at their ideal demand solution points. The effectiveness of these solution points is dependent upon how many ancestor message paths an expert can tap into.

Notice how this is so different from the organizational frameworks built up with managed teams. In a managed team the expert would be at the periphery of the team and would have to fit in with the team's rules and regulations. In the object-oriented environment, the expert doesn't really need to be in a team at all, but simply allow someone who is already in a team to inherit their expertise. The expert would then be free to concentrate on their own contacts: their personal virtual team that would consist of people at their supply and demand solution points.

In the book *Lingo Sorcery*, I explained the inheritance and ancestor in the object-oriented concept by means of a design for a calculator. A single object is called a calculator but in fact it couldn't make any calculations whatsoever. All it could do was to pass on any calculation instructions to a line of other objects. If a request came for an addition, an object in the ancestor message path programmed to make additions responded to the message and sent the answer back to the calculator object. Similarly, other objects specializing in subtracting, multiplication or division would respond to any message that corresponded to their speciality. In this way, the calculator object received all the calculation instructions and appeared to be making the calculations itself.

Now if you can imagine several other objects called calculator1, calculator2, calculator3... etc., each of these could also appear to be acting as a calculator simply by including the same functional objects in its own ancestor path. In this way, each of the functional objects would be in a complex network where they were each being called into service by each of the calculators as they were needed. The message paths would see each calculator object as being the central organizer of the same set of objects. Each functional object would also appear to be surrounded by the same set of calculator objects asking it to make calculations for them. The enigmatic effect is that whichever object is looked at in the network of communication, it appears to be the central important figure of a whole lot of other objects. In other words, there is no single dominant hierarchy; every object is at the apex of its own virtual hierarchy.

Mapping this across to the world of people connected together by the Internet, it is easy to see how everyone connected to the system can be at the centre of two quite different virtual worlds (input and output solution points): one where they are inheriting the skills, knowledge and experience of others, the other where they are at the centre of a network of people wanting them to help them. This is an extremely potent situation where everyone's particular unique ability can be highly leveraged.

Such a system has immense potential for adaptation and flexibility. Substituting non-functional calculator objects for solution providers and the calculation objects for experts and specialists, it is easy to see how the total system could be infinitely reconfigured to solve all kinds of e-business and e-commerce problems with the utmost efficiency.

Solution providers can concentrate on customers' needs without having to worry about technical details, passing these on to the experts to supply the answers. Experts and specialists could work only in their own chosen area of speciality, leaving the solution providers to find application for their skills. Everybody would be able to concentrate and become more expert in their own particular niches. This would create an even greater demand for their services.

The structure of the connectivity

As soon as this pattern of associations emerges, it starts to explain why the environment of e-commerce is totally different from that of the bricks and mortar world of the Industrial Age. It provides a reason as to why conventional corporate strategies with their emphasis on managed teams are having such a hard time coping with e-commerce.

The leaders of managed teams are having to spend too much time organizing and motivating team members, leaving them little time to concentrate on the overall function of the team. Team members themselves are forced away from individuality and specialization and compelled towards working in sympathetic harmony with other team members. Such an arrangement works well in a physical environment but is very inefficient and unstable in a world of extreme connectivity and multiple specialization.

In the environment of the Internet, project leaders shouldn't be team leaders in the traditional sense. They have to be primarily solution providers and decision makers. Most of their time should be spent on the demand side of their network of contacts where they can act as channels through which demands are being satisfied. Unlike the traditional role of leader managers, they haven't the knowledge, resources or time to train and educate a team because the range of knowledge and expertise that may be called upon will not only be huge but also constantly changing and evolving.

Such solution providers will need to be constantly maintaining and replenishing a pool of contacts who are experts in the various areas that may need to be coordinated into a solution. It doesn't matter if they are odd-balls or unsociable. All that matters is that they are unquestionably expert in their field and reliably produce what is asked of them. Solution providers could not possibly afford to hire such a pool of experts on a permanent basis. It would mean using their time inefficiently. This necessitates creating virtual teams on the fly, as and when they are needed by the demands of the system higher up the demand–supply hierarchy.

The individual experts and specialists, for their part, will not want to be involved in any 'Jack of all trades' employment situation. They will want to be carving out a more profitable existence for themselves as experts in their chosen speciality niche. They will resent any time being spent in areas that have no relevance to achieving and maintaining this aim. The only managed team they will be interested in is the team of helpers that assist them in their speciality service. In this way they will be more like the artisans of the pre-Industrial Age: acting as tutor and inspirational head to a team of dedicated apprentices, who work cheaply for their master in order to learn the intricacies of the speciality before starting out on their own.

Coping with too many experts and specializations

Although it is possible for a solution provider to build up valuable cooperative relationships with a pool of experts and specialists, even though he or she is not employing them full time, there is always the risk that the required experts will be busy on some other project at the time they are needed. However, this is not an insurmountable problem because the solution provider can make an effort to ensure that he or she knows a sufficiently large pool of experts to have overlap or duplication of specialization. This will allow alternatives to be substituted. This is similar to the strategy of the newsagent, who will ensure that there is enough spare delivery capacity to make up for any newspaper delivery boy or girl who doesn't turn up for work one morning.

This requires all solution providers to have a very wide and versatile range of contacts, where all types of expertise and specialization are covered several times over. However, as all experts assembled for a solution have to be trusted to carry out their part of a solution reliably and efficiently, it will need the solution provider to be able to assess the quality of work of a very large number of experts. This could easily become the main work of many solution providers:

searching for, assessing and maintaining contact with a large assortment of freelance technical specialists.

Another way a solution provider might deal with this problem is to go to an agency which specializes in maintaining lists of experts and specialists who can be called upon as and when a need arises. Such services are common in the bricks and mortar world, but can be woefully inadequate in the highly specialized environment of digital technologies, where only an expert can recognize another expert. A curriculum vitae might be a good basis for taking somebody on with a view to long-term employment, but is totally useless for the selection of somebody to be brought in for a fast and efficient specialist function. More likely, a solution provider will not trust an agency, but will seek the advice of a respected contact who is a specialist or expert themselves and has maybe worked with another expert whom they can recommend.

This need for various kinds of expertise at short notice is common to all solution providers who work with virtual teams or outsource some of the work, so it is likely to breed a layer of Internet middlemen who specialize in representing specific categories of experts. These middlemen would then be specialists in their own right: specialists in recommending certain types of experts.

This will generate much Internet communication activity, where solution providers are searching for and setting up cooperative relationships with various middlemen whom they can trust to recommend expert services to them. Correspondingly, there will be many middlemen who will make a speciality of cultivating stables of experts whom they can recommend to the solution providers. In this way layers of middlemen will form between the experts and the solution providers such that the vast range of changeable expertise involved in e-commerce solutions can be comfortably handled in the same way that Berwick Street wholesalers handle the large variability of costume jewellery.

If the use of experts recommended by middlemen is seen in the context of an object-oriented framework, each middleman can be thought of as inheriting the skills of all the experts and specialists they represent (their ancestors). Similarly, the solution providers can be thought of as inheriting all the skills of the middlemen and their expert ancestors. This leads to a conceptual jump that takes you to thinking of the solution providers as not needing to deal with any experts or specialists at all. If the solution is an object-oriented design that is constructed and connected solely through message passing, the messages emanating from the solution provider can go via the middlemen rather than directly to the experts.

Working in this way will see the main activity of a solution provider as an Internet communicator at the centre of a hub of middlemen, rather than as the communicator at the centre of a hub of niche experts. This will undoubtedly allow the solution provider to be less concerned with technical detail and so have more time available for working on higher-level strategic issues.

The arrangement of solution providers dealing with middlemen, rather than the experts, makes sense if it is remembered that a solution provider has only so much time in the day. This time will be far more efficiently used if it is spent with people who have a wealth of inherited expertise, than it would be with experts who each had only a single speciality. This will result in the solution provider being able to apply a far greater amount of expertise to an e-commerce project, effectively making him or her more efficient and capable.

Middlemen, and the relationships they have with the experts, can be compared to the example of the virtual calculators. Just as several calculators can share the same calculating objects to provide a similar calculating capability, so middlemen can represent the same experts. This will promote competition among middlemen for clients and experts, where the most efficient middlemen will be the most likely to succeed. This competitive environment should produce a system that is self-regulating and continuously evolving towards greater efficiency.

A solution provider, working with several middlemen rather than individual experts, will have many other advantages. The middlemen can be chosen such that there is considerable overlap of the expertise available. Besides this, the middlemen will have a broader view of the total e-commerce environment than could be expected from dedicated experts who need to be narrowly focused. By discussing an e-commerce project with a number of different middlemen, a solution provider will have access to a variety of views and opinions. This will greatly broaden the base upon which strategic judgements are made. In this way, the risk of providing a short-sighted or biased solution is greatly reduced.

The middlemen will of course need to take a profit. This they will do by taking a percentage of the expert's fees or adding a percentage to the expert's charge. This profit taking need not be excessive, though, because of the efficiency by which the Internet allows middlemen to work. They will have few overheads and can work with many different experts and solution providers at the same time.

What makes a good solution provider?

If we now take a look at the effective functioning of an e-commerce solution provider in an object-oriented environment, what kind of person should it be? Should it be somebody who is an expert in all the niche areas used in the solutions? Should it be someone who is expert at managing and motivating people? I think not.

It seems more likely that the most effective solution provider will be someone who has a firm grasp on the required strategic aims of a solution, a strategist who can coordinate ideas and people to create and guide an evolving system. The solution provider will need to be thinking mostly in the area of the results side and consider their main role as having to communicate the results and discrepancies back to the experts who can contribute to a correction or a solution.

In other words, the solution provider shouldn't be the designer of a solution, but the feedback loop to a self-organizing system that contains all kinds of novel possibilities for achieving stated goals. In this role as a feedback functionary, the solution provider would need to be an expert email communicator who has many contacts with middlemen and can gather together a large variety of expertise, opinions and recommendations to bring to bear on the problems.

This raises the question as to how you can decide what makes a good solution provider. What would you look for in their CV if you wanted to hire one? It soon becomes obvious that there is no way that anyone can accurately determine who would make a good solution provider until the results of their efforts are proven. Even then, there may be so many unknown factors that a choice between different solution providers becomes almost arbitrary.

This is a very real problem in e-commerce. The choice of a solution provider may not only involve the risk of wasting investment funding, it also has a large bearing on the ability of a company to trade and compete successfully in the e-commerce marketplace. Having a solution provider who is biased towards employing inappropriate technology can result in the loss of millions of dollars. The World Wide Web is full of examples of solution providers having the wrong set of priorities to produce novel and attractive sites that are totally useless for their designated purpose of satisfying specific customer or client needs.

Seeing the choice of a solution provider and the people who advise them and the experts that are selected to work on a solution as all being risk elements, it seems appropriate to use the strategies of investment managers. They offset risk by spreading it. Using these strategies to safeguard against risk, it makes no sense at all to gamble on any single solution provider, or any single solution. Any sensible strategy must be able to break up the risks into different independent compartments and spread the decision making between several solution providers. This will minimize the effect of any errors of choice or judgement, so they can cause only slight setbacks and not fatal disasters.

In the world of object-oriented design, this is not a problem because you can split up all solutions into separate and independent modules. Any error in one need have minimal effects on the others. This situation was described in the virtual house-building scenario covered in Chapter 7. Similarly, the risk of a solution provider having incomplete knowledge or not having a sufficiently large range of specialist contacts could be minimized by using a virtual team of solution providers rather than a single one.

Such a group of solution providers would not be in the form of an organized managed team, but more like the virtual teams created when a group of wholesalers were combined to provide a buying solution for costume jewellery. In other words, a single solution provider is replaced by a virtual team where the members of the team are not permanently employed and are not managed or motivated.

With an Industrial Age mindset this makes no sense at all, but in the object-oriented world of the Information Age it is a highly appropriate solution. The trick is to think of the solution provider not as being a manager of a project, but as the representative of a particular virtual team. In this way you can bring several solution providers together to have the combined power and expertise of all their contacts. If the responsibility of making the right choice of niche specialists to provide a solution is spread among several solution providers, so will be the risks. Also the weaknesses or deficiencies of one solution provider can be compensated for by another.

In this way, it will be more effective and efficient if several solution providers are combined to bring about a solution between them, each providing their individual interpreted feedback to their own pool of niche specialist contacts. In this way they would not be competing with each other to provide a solution but competing with each other to make improvements.

In the Industrial Age, such a system would be unworkable unless every one of the solution providers had the same conceptual model for the solution. In the Information Age, it is the only system that is workable because there are too many possibilities for anyone to be able to decide or agree upon what the optimum solution should be. Using several solution providers acts as a safeguard against the dangers of limited knowledge. There may be disagreements but in an object-oriented system, a module in the solution can be duplicated if there is genuine doubt as to the best type of module to use.

In effect, each solution provider initiates part of the overall solution, but there is considerable overlap. This makes each of them expendable. As they are effectively the representatives of a virtual team of niche specialists, they can also be employed on the same temporary basis as the specialists they represent. Again, this may seem preposterous with an Industrial Age mindset, but in the object-oriented world of the Information Age it makes sense because it will also be beneficial to the solution providers themselves.

In the same way that a niche expert can specialize in a favoured area and a middleman can specialize in a type of expert, so a solution provider can specialize in a favoured niche of an e-commerce solution. This allows a virtual group of solution providers to have complementary inputs as well as providing substantial overlap. This provides a similar solution to the problems of doubt and unknown reliability that the newsagent employs with the newspaper delivery children: using people well within their capacity and allowing overlap to make up for any deficiencies or unreliability.

It might be thought that solution providers would be unhappy with this arrangement, but why should they be if they have a powerful selection of capable specialist contacts? If they have a good pool of specialists to draw upon and are effectively able to bring all this expertise to the table then they will be in demand. And like the experts and the middlemen, there is no reason for them to work full time for the same clients.

In the bricks and mortar world it is normal to hire a team leader, a consultant or a main contractor on an exclusive full-time basis. This needn't be the case in the object-oriented environment of the Information Age because there is no main structural plan and all the components of the system are built up of interacting modules. It needn't be necessary to have either full-time or permanent involvement of solution providers, middlemen or experts.

For the e-commerce client, paying only for part-time involvement would mean being able to utilize the expertise of several solution providers for the cost of a single one. All would be able to add their ideas and experience to the creation of the solution, plus make available the full range of their expert and specialist contacts. The employer would truly be getting the value of many for the price of one.

For the solution provider this is also an advantageous arrangement. It would provide more security because each individual employer would represent a part of their income. Also, working for several employers at the same time would offer a greater range of opportunities for the solution provider's expert contacts. This would strengthen his or her relationship with them.

Although this may seem utterly bizarre to the Industrial Age mindset, it is completely practical due to the ease of connectivity and communication. The model of the employers employing several solution providers to share in the design of a solution and combining resources is virtually identical to the situation of going into Berwick Street and using the combined resources of the different wholesalers to provide a weekly costume jewellery buying solution.

In Berwick Street all the wholesalers represented all their contacts. Their combined resources were better than any individual wholesaler. They provided overlap. They were all employed simultaneously. They were employed on a temporary basis when their contacts were hot. At an abstract level there is no difference whatsoever and that system works perfectly well in satisfying customer demands in a chaotic world of unpredictable change.

Chapter 15

The optimum strategy

 Summing up the situation

The book started with the enigma that large established corporations, despite their vast resources of people, money and expertise, were not making any more headway in exploiting the possibilities of the Internet than start-up companies.

Looking at the effects of newly emerging technologies and the complexity of the Internet itself, it is evident that e-business and e-commerce environments exhibit all the classic symptoms of unstable chaotic systems. These conditions are totally different from the evolved maturity found in most business and commercial environments of the pre-Internet world of bricks and mortar.

There are three major differences:

1   Technology is expanding too fast to keep up with.

2   There is too much information to deal with.

3   Super-connectivity is creating situations that have never been encountered before.

Industrial Age business and commercial strategies were based largely on organization and control. Complexity was dealt with by creating structured and well-ordered frameworks within which reasonably accurate predictions could be made. These frameworks provided foundations for logical and rational decision making.

All this goes out of the window when a chaotic environment is encountered. The methods and techniques that have proved so successful in dealing with the mass markets of the Industrial Age are found to be unsuited in digital communication environments. In particular, structural, top-down approaches are unworkable, planned projects and managed teams are inappropriate.

Looking for alternatives to the inappropriate techniques of the Industrial Age, we have looked for clues in areas of the bricks and mortar world where people have learned to compete in chaotic and unpredictable environments. These were:

1   the world of the professional poker player;

2   the world of the newsagent dealing with unreliable staff;

3   the highly complex world of the computer programmer;

4   the world of creative arts;

5   the risk-taking, competitive world of the entrepreneur;

6   the environment of finance and investment;

7   the rapidly changing world of high fashion.

Each of these areas has characteristics that are present in the chaotic environment of the Internet. By considering the uncertainties, complexities, unknowns and competition that are encountered in these various areas, we have gained an insight into the type of conditions we might expect to have to face in the emerging world of e-business and e-commerce. By examining the techniques employed by some of the professionals in these chaotic environments, we have abstracted enough essence to form the basis of a strategy to cope with the difficult conditions that might emerge in any business involving the Internet.

For such a strategy to be workable, it must be able to make allowances for all the problems that are liable to occur. Here are some of the assumptions it would seem prudent to take into consideration when starting out on the design of any e-business or e-commerce strategy:

1 All potential clients or customers are constantly deluged and swamped with information.

2 Nobody knows all the answers.

3 The environment of the Internet and the World Wide Web is beyond your or anyone else's ability to be able to understand it completely.

4 Everyone is occasionally unreliable.

5 Everybody is mostly too busy for you to be able to get their attention.

6 Most people haven't the time to listen to what you have to say.

7 Whatever you know, there are many more important things that you ought to know but don't.

8 Nobody is going to cooperate with you unless they see there is something worthwhile in it for them.

9 Whatever you know, somebody knows it better.

10 Anyone you want to establish a communication relationship with has only a very limited number of people they have time to write emails to.

11 Credibility and trust are very hard to come by.

12 Whatever you do, there are thousands of others trying to do the same thing at the same time.

13 Sudden and dramatic changes will occur constantly.

14 Whatever you do will be rapidly outdated by new technologocial developments.

15 Whatever you do or say will quickly be known to everyone else.

16 Whatever you do will be copied or bettered by your competitors.

17 All services and products will get progressively cheaper as increased competition, reduced costs and increased efficiency bring prices and profits down to a minimum.

18 Whatever you are offering, there will be a plethora of similar alternatives in the market place already.

19 Nobody can have more than one area of real expertise.

20 The solution you have to come up with is beyond yours, or anyone else's imagination.

21 Whatever technology, programs, tools, methods and tehniques you use will rapidly become unsuitable or irrelevant.

22 Any final solution you come up with will have to be abandoned or radically altered within a very short period of time.

23 Everyone is going to distrust you until you have built up a relationship of trust with them.

24 Nothing is free, even if it seems to be.

With this set of assumptions, it would seem impossible that a suitable strategy could be devised to be able to make a success of any e-business or e-commerce enterprise. However, these same problems are going to be encountered by all competitors. The winners are going to be those who are best able to play the game in spite of all these problems.

What makes the effort worthwhile is that the Internet is an environment rich in non-zero sum games where everyone can be a winner. The increased efficiencies brought about by digital communication technology can create innumerable win-win situations where winning isn't about winning off other players but winning with them. This will involve strategies based upon establishing cooperative relationships with people rather than competing with people for limited resources.

The two elements of a strategy

If the 22 initial assumptions are taken into serious consideration, it rules out the possibility of using any set or rigid plan. The only possible approach is to use a flexible conceptual framework that is forgiving of mistakes, misjudgements and misconceptions. Such a framework is game theory, which allows decisions to be made on the basis of possibilities and probabilities: minimizing the effects of uncertainties and unknowns by spreading risk.

Trying to find e-business and e-commerce solutions through study and learning is futile. There is too much information and most of it is constantly getting outdated anyway. It is even impossible for anyone to know who has the right or wrong information, let alone the right answers and solutions to problems. This makes progress a haphazard affair unless the combined and filtered opinions of many people are taken into account and an allowance made for the probability of some of them being wrong.

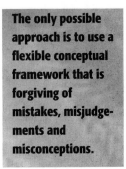

The only possible approach is to use a flexible conceptual framework that is forgiving of mistakes, misjudgements and misconceptions.

We have seen how these conditions are likely to promote the formation of networks of people specializing and interacting with each other. Such systems evolve and grow according to the pressures created by demands. The systems cannot be controlled or planned in any way, but competition will ensure that they evolve towards maximum efficiency of their own accord.

This ability of systems to self-organize towards maximum efficiency suggests that anyone who wants to be a successful player in the environment of e-business or e-commerce should try to find a way to tap into these self-organizing networks – rather than trying to create completely independent systems of their own. This will involve making open rather than closed business systems that will be able to interact freely with the whole of the Internet.

As we have covered in some chapters, an object-oriented approach can view any e-business or e-commerce solution as consisting only of people. In reality, each person may represent some form of media, a process, a piece of hardware, a software program, a bricks and mortar organization or a specialist managed team, but as far as any practical strategy is concerned, all the technical details can be ignored and the strategy confined entirely to dealing with people.

By reducing the environment to one of people communicating with each other, the whole system can be viewed as nodes, people nodes, and lines of communication connecting them together. This reduces the number of elements crucial to any successful strategy to just two: an identifying presence for each node in the network and the network connections to each node.

Giving yourself an identity on the Web

Many people dismiss the Internet as a second-rate environment for communication because of the lack of visual or auditory clues. What they ignore is that judgements in the environment of the Internet are made on quite a different basis to those in the physical world. Certainly there are no facial expressions to read, or appearances to go by, but in the environment of the Internet these are replaced by a far more efficient medium: the Web site.

Anyone with any serious intention of using the Internet for business will have to have their own Web site, whose address they will probably include with their signature at the bottom of all email correspondence. This is their identity. It plays the same role in Internet communications as physical appearance and 'getting to know you' conversations do in the everyday world. Just as people in the physical world will judge a person initially by visual appearance, how they speak and how they act, so in the environment of the Internet, a person will be judged by their Web site.

The logic is simple: in the environment of the Internet there are millions of people to communicate with. To be able to take advantage of this vastness of choice, there is no time to visit them all and use conventional ways to judge them. A method has to be found to make a rapid assessment: to ascertain whether or not somebody's opinion can be taken seriously or whether or not they are going to provide a competitive value for the limited time available for communication.

This may seem a cynical and inhuman way to view the world, but this isn't the world of bricks and mortar: it is the world of high connectivity and infinite multiple choice. It is a world where associations needn't be based upon a broad range of characteristics, but can be confined to very narrow and specific areas. This is not intuitive. In the bricks and mortar world, where contact and communication are difficult to come by, relationships have to encompass a range of different considerations. In the world of the Internet, cooperation can be based upon strictly limited areas of mutual interest. This greatly improves the efficiency of communications.

Efficiency is important because the criteria of cooperative relationships that matter, such as truthfulness, reliability, honesty, credibility or any other kind of trait that might affect the value of an association, can only be ascertained during a suitably long series of tit-for-tat communications. This takes time and effort, so establishing a worthwhile relationship is not entered into lightly. This is why a Web site can be of great benefit, because it can provide an initial basis for deciding to begin a process of establishing a cooperative association.

It should be appreciated that throw-away relationships are a wasteful and inefficient use of Internet communication time. Valuable relationships develop gradually, based upon a growing mutual trust. This is no different from the world of bricks and mortar, where caution is exercised before giving trust, and care is taken not to become vulnerable to any hurtful defections. But once trust is established, both sides will have gained a valuable asset. Building up an association slowly creates stable relationships because only a fool would defect on a relationship that has taken time to develop.

 ## Multiple personalities

Web sites should be efficiently packaged so that all the benefits of establishing a communication contact with the site owner can be quickly and easily appreciated. This is easy to do if there is only a single quality or asset, but if there are multiple assets then the full picture can be confusing. For this reason, it is probably more effective to describe different assets quite independently of each other. Many Web sites guide customers or clients with different needs to different parts of a Web site to prevent them losing interest or exposing them to irrelevant material. This same principle can be used for personal Web sites or by site owners who have more than one area of speciality they wish to offer.

This is particularly important when considering the demand and supply solution points that every individual or business must have. The contacts on the supply side will be quite different from the contacts on the demand side. It makes sense then, that each type of contact sees a different aspect, perhaps requiring completely different sites, maybe even on different servers with different domain names. Such dual personalities are not always possible in the world of bricks and mortar, but in the world of the Internet they are easily arranged – and make a great deal of sense.

The strategy of the expert or specialist

It is quite surprising how few experts and specialists realize the strategic importance of their personal Web site. Yet it is how people are going to judge them when they consider hiring their services. It doesn't have to be an all singing, all dancing Web site (in fact, an over-gimmicky site can be as off-putting on the Web as loud and flashy clothes can be in the world of bricks and mortar). All that is needed is an efficient description of the service or utility that is being made available.

Although it is hard to generalize, if we consider a hypothetical case of a typical expert it will give some idea of the broad concepts involved. Let's take the case of an expert in vector graphics. This is a special type of graphics that provides low bandwidth pictures, animations and navigational maps frequently used for Web pages (Macromedia's Flash products are based upon vector graphics). Although almost any programmer or Web page designer could quickly learn to make superficial use of vector graphics, few designers will have time to become truly expert because vector graphics is just one of many hundreds of speciality areas that are used in Web site design strategies.

The managed team approach would be to get one of the team designers to create a suitable vector graphic when the need arises. This the designer could do, but it is probable that this is not something he or she would be doing all the time. As a consequence, the managed team designer is likely to produce a vector graphic solution more slowly, less efficiently and possibly inferior to a solution that could be produced by a designer who did nothing else but vector graphics.

A busy contractor, seeing a possibility for a vector graphic application in a Web site design, might well consider getting a specialist to produce the vector graphic if he or she knew somebody who could do this kind of work efficiently, cheaply and reliably. The vector graphics specialist, being thoroughly familiar with all the techniques, the pitfalls, the problems and the possibilities in this narrow niche area, would likely be able to produce a vector graphic in far less time than it would take the contractor. This would allow the specialist to charge a good price for his or her time, yet to the contractor this price would appear to be a bargain.

In this way, the contractor would effectively be using an ancestor message path to inherit the skills of the specialist in vector graphics. As far as the contractor's client is concerned, it is the contractor who is the expert in vector graphics. The graphic designer wouldn't worry about being credited because it would be the contractor he or she would want to establish and maintain a cooperative relationship with, not the contractor's client. The better the graphic designer can make the contractor look, the more chance that the contractor will get more work for the graphic designer to do.

If a Web site design is broken up into many little speciality areas, with each area being outsourced to an expert, it is easy to see how a whole project can be created far more expertly and probably at less cost than with an in-house, managed team. This would see the role of the contractor becoming more of a middleman than a manager and able to produce expert solutions with a minimum of overheads. This way of working is possible because of the efficiency of the Internet communication environment, which allows a variety of specialists and experts to be contacted quickly and easily.

The viewpoint of the expert or specialist

This is a reasonably realistic strategy for a contractor, but what about the vector graphic designer and all the other experts and specialists involved? Would it be such an attractive arrangement for them? Wouldn't they each need to have a lot of contractors like this to ensure they had a regular income? How, then, do they get known to a sufficient number of client contractors to build up a critical mass where they can enjoy a continuously full workload?

The solution to this problem is not found by studying what the experts or specialists do but by looking at the way in which the people who use their services work. For this, we can take as a model the doctor I used in London. He was my solution point for health issues because he used a virtual team consisting of dozens of specialist consultants. In effect, this doctor was a channel to a combined collection of specialists and experts who could cope with almost any health problem I was likely to encounter. This is not dissimilar to an e-commerce solution provider who is working with a pool of experts and specialists whom he or she can draw upon to provide e-commerce solutions.

The doctor had spent many years making contact with various medical practitioners at the Middlesex Hospital. He'd visited them at their practices, mixed with them socially and heard their views and opinions of each other. Over the years, he'd managed to assemble a list of contacts that he knew he could trust: confident that he could send his patients to them and know that they would receive the best possible treatment.

This is the way expert e-commerce solution providers will work. It is not what they know themselves that will make them good solution providers, but the work they have put into knowing people they might bring together to provide a solution. This will take time and effort and just like I took time to search for and establish a group of contacts to supply me with old fur coats, so the expert solution provider will search for and establish a suitable group of technical experts who can be called upon to put together a competitive solution.

If the strategy of good solution providers or contractors is to seek out good specialists and experts to add to their pool, then the best strategy for experts or specialists is to find ways of bringing themselves to the notice of these solution providers. This means mixing with solution providers and contractors in list serves (special interest discussion forums), or being prominent in their own speciality discussion forums where solution providers and contractors might be lurking. Being able to take part in discussions will draw attention and if a Web site address is attached to posts then there is every chance that a potential client will take a look.

Drawing attention is one thing, but the question then is, 'Drawing attention to what?'. In the world of bricks and mortar there are discussions, interviews, telephone conversations, etc. These are too slow and cumbersome for the Information Age. There are too many people, too many different types of speciality, too many changes in technological developments. Solution providers and contractors will need a fast way to judge and compare. For this they will go to a specialist's Web site.

Using the example of the hypothetical vector graphic specialist again, the vector graphic specialist could fill his or her Web site with examples of all the different kinds of applications that vector graphic techniques can be used for. Not the technical details, but examples that clearly show the benefits of using vector graphics. People might then go to the site for inspiration and find a novel application that fits in well with their Web site design.

The obvious place to look for superior design ideas is on the Web site of an expert who has a host of examples on show. In special interest email discussion forums, it is very common for people to ask each other about effects and techniques they have seen on a particular Web site. If an example or source is known, people will readily pass on the information, particularly if it can be done simply by providing the address of a Web site.

Up-front with the costs

One of the biggest barriers to initiating a new cooperative business relationship is the uncertainty as to how much it is going to cost. In the world of computer programming and graphic design, prices and costs are always tricky subjects. Design projects seldom go as planned. Bugs, learning curves and customer satisfaction are always major headaches and have to be discounted in the price. These cost uncertainties can inhibit many clients from making contact with an expert or specialist, even though they might have good reasons for wanting to try out their service.

A niche specialist would have an advantage in this situation because the familiarity that comes with narrow specialization can take away most of the uncertainties. This would allow an expert in any niche speciality to provide not only examples, but openly display reliably accurate pricing for doing jobs similar to the examples.

Using the game theory trick of making a decision based upon repeating the same thing one hundred times, a niche expert or specialist would be able to display prices that were very competitive. Even with very competitive pricing, the experts should be able to gain ample reward for their time because of their increased efficiency. The contractors and solution providers, who would be measuring the expert's pricing against the cost per hour of doing the work themselves, would likely see the prices as bargains, even when the prices might include adequate allowances for unknown contingencies.

Such speciality services would be very easy and convenient to use. Solution providers and contractors wouldn't have to negotiate the price and they'd know in advance the kind of product or service they would be getting. Word of such convenient and available expertise would soon spread. It wouldn't take long for a competent specialist to build up a critical mass of contacts, leading to a steady stream of work. And all without the need for expensive or time-consuming advertising.

In the bricks and mortar world, this degree of specialization would be impractical. It is only in the environment of the Internet that such a niche speciality business could work.

Attaching to the network

The second of the two crucial elements of e-business and e-commerce Internet strategy is network connections. This involves creating a suitable hub of communication links from the node into the communication environment of the Internet.

As we have covered previously, the complexity of the Internet environment needs intelligent interfaces between nodes. Only humans can suitably fulfil this role, which means that a Web site cannot be considered a node in its own right, it must connect to the Internet via a human. This may not be obvious. Many people, even some Web site designers, seem to think that Web sites can create businesses merely by their existence. They give very little heed to the myriad people interacting in the hidden background, who provide the all-important dynamic interactions necessary to make Web sites successful.

In reality, a Web site is nothing more than an elaborate catalogue or an automatic order taker. In some cases, it may dispense software or information, acting like a kiosk. It may serve as the front end to a database and a delivery service. It may provide chat rooms and email discussion forums. Whatever automatic functions a Web site may provide in an e-commerce or e-business scenario, it should always be regarded as playing a passive role because the functions will be worthless unless human-to-human communication strategies can get the site working up to a point of critical mass. Even then, it will need a supporting network of human-to-human communication links to maintain that state of critical mass in the face of stiff competition.

Realizing that all e-business and e-commerce is dependent upon human interactions, it becomes pertinent to start thinking about the different kinds of strategies that might be required for making contact with people. As every individual, business or Web identity would have to have an input (demand) set of contacts and quite a different set for the output (supply) contacts, it would seem reasonable to expect that every situation should need at least two quite different kinds of communication strategy.

It would also seem reasonable that the choice of strategies would be dependent upon the kind of business or niche role that was being represented. Surely an expert programmer would need a different strategy to a middleman? Surely the service companies, the application program developers, the contractors, the graphic designers, the hardware manufacturers, the solution providers, etc., would all need different strategies tailored specifically to their individual needs?

And the core business strategists: the people who hire the contractors and the solution providers – what kind of strategy would they need? Surely their strategies would need to be different from those of the myriad ancillary roles that are just a part of the system being put together?

Employees in managed teams might also use the Internet. They could enhance their roles in their organizations quite considerably by having network connections. Would the members of a team need to have a different strategy from their managers or team leaders? Would employees need to have a different strategy from their employers?

Surprisingly, the basic communication strategy for all this vast assortment of needs and purposes would be exactly the same. Whatever type of contact is needed and for whatever purpose, they would each need to employ a similar method of acquiring and maintaining a suitable network of contacts.

This only becomes obvious when it is understood that the true power of the Internet comes from its massive connectivity. This gives rise to the unimaginable complexity of people being able to connect up to each other in a multitude of different ways. The whys and wherefores of communication then become insignificant details, compared to the vastly more difficult problem of coping with the complexity itself.

Dealing with the complexity

The fundamental problem to overcome is the limitation of our human brains to cope with complexity. Human physiology has evolved in environments where massive connectivity has never been present. Humans haven't had the opportunity to evolve any specialized brain mechanisms, or emotional programming, to cope with or take advantage of a massively connected environment.

Fortunately, the human brain and computers deal with the storage and processing of information in very similar ways, so with a little ingenuity, the computer can be used to compensate for the deficiencies of the evolutionary process.

This was the view taken in *Magical A-Life Avatars* where the main theme of the book was that the highly complex world of the Internet would need tools that enhanced the natural ability of the human brain to cope with complexity.

Note: the emphasis is on enhancement, not replacement.

The book used a conceptual model where it was imagined that a single gargantuan library was being used to store every piece of information in the world. The amount of information in this library is beyond the capabilities of the library staff to organize or catalogue properly. Only about 20 per cent is indexed and, as millions of new documents are being added each day, the whole library appears to be totally disorganized.

Entering such a library would be a nightmare. You'd be liable to find so many irrelevancies, discover so much that you didn't know, that any search would probably leave you more confused than when you started. All the information you could ever need would be there somewhere, but the problem is how to extract it efficiently.

In *Magical A-Life Avatars*, it was concluded that going into such a library, searching around for information, would be hopelessly inefficient. The best strategy might be to start by going into the library café and trying to find people who had already spent some time in the library and knew where things were.

Of course, you couldn't expect to find anyone who knew where everything in the library was, but you'd probably find people who knew where information relating to their own particular area of speciality could be found. The trick would be to find someone in the café whose speciality corresponded to the area of knowledge you were interested in yourself.

Immediately, it becomes clear that a strategy to get knowledge will become a strategy for finding people in the café rather than a strategy for finding information in the library. The limitation of this strategy would be the time it would take to find these people.

The trick now is to imagine a library café filled with millions of people. You cannot talk to them all, so you have to start listening in on discussions, talking to people, asking if they know of people who are specializing in the knowledge you are looking for. You might then find there are groups whose common interest has brought them together. One of those groups might be discussing just the sort of things you want to know about. Given enough time, you might find several people who'd have answers to the questions you want to ask.

The problem with this scenario is that there are millions of people and an almost infinite amount of information. As nobody can know all there is to know, the people you find are liable to come up with different kinds of answers. Also through talking to various people, you might find you are asking the wrong questions, or looking for answers in the wrong groups. You might discover new information that completely changes the nature of the problem you want to solve.

Going from one person to another and from group to group you might arrive at a satisfactory conclusion, but it could take quite a lot of time. Far better if you could get all the different people who might be able to throw light on your problem together in one place. This would make it easier to combine and compare their knowledge and opinions. Biases could be ironed out; misconceptions corrected; knowledge gaps filled.

There might be others in this huge café, trying to solve similar problems and using a similar strategy to yourself. If you could only find them, you'd be able to swap notes, and help each other out to save much of the legwork. Wouldn't it be convenient if you could bring them all together at a single table in the café to have a discussion with you?

The goal, then, of a suitable communication strategy, might be to get all the people who may be able to help you with your problems to come together at one single place in the café where they would be conveniently on hand to give you all the information, advice and services you require.

An unrealistic goal? Impossible in a gigantic café of millions of busy people competing with each other for attention? Maybe it would be impossible in the world of bricks and mortar, but in the magical world of the Internet such things are possible, if only you can find the right strategy.

The right strategy would involve seeing this café as a Hilbert space: a solution space where all the people in the café are the dimensions. Gathering a selection of these people together in one spot is simply a matter of connecting to them. In this way, you place yourself at the centre of a communication hub which then becomes your solution point in the solution space.

This effectively allows you to make everyone in the café leave, except for the people you are connected to. These you will have identified as being the most ideal mix of people to help you solve all your problems.

Getting attention and cooperation

Connecting to people isn't easy. Connections have to be two-way to have any value. They are only valid if the person you want to be connected to also wants to be connected to you. This puts a serious restraint on the choice of people you can include in your personal hub of contacts.

An appropriate communication strategy must allow for the fact that everyone has a limited time available to spend communicating. This forces them to be selective. For example, it would be very nice to be able to be connected to the President of the United States and Bill Gates, but it is unlikely that they'd have sufficient incentive to include you as one of their contacts. This would mean that, even if you could manage somehow to send a communication to them, the link would be worthless because they'd probably have no time to read or respond to it.

A realistic strategy for connecting to people must ensure that you don't aim too high with your choice of connections and that you have sufficient to offer the contacts to make you one of the few people they have the inclination and time to respond to. On the other hand, you don't want to aim too low because you also have only a limited time available and you'll want this to be as valuable as possible.

This returns us to the need for a strategy to get people's interest and cooperation. Everybody you'd want to help you with your problems would have problems of their own. The tit-for-tat strategy tells us that cooperation has to be built up slowly. You give a little and they may cooperate and give you a little. You respond back and gradually a valuable relationship is built up. In this café of millions, there will be many others trying to claim the attention and time of the same people you'll want to cooperate with you. Why should they cooperate with you, rather than with the others?

A solution to this problem is to think in terms of object-oriented strategies and the concept of inheritance. People who are valuable to you might be valuable not because of what they know themselves, but what their contacts know. Their value would derive from the knowledge they would inherit from the people they were in communication with. This could appear to make them super-specialists, with a virtual knowledge that gives them status and causes them to be desirable people to know.

To be able to stand out in the crowd and be able to attract the interest of such super-specialists, you'd need to become a super-specialist yourself. This would involve choosing an area of speciality for yourself and then going around assembling appropriate contacts with people you can inherit knowledge from.

This would be the route to achieving a powerful solution point where your communication time would be optimally valuable and productive.

A world of groups

To imagine a giant café, containing millions of people, provides a useful metaphor for the Internet, but the idea of trying to find particular people to talk to in such a place seems a daunting prospect. After all, the café would need to be the size of a very large city, perhaps even the size of a country, to be able to contain all the people using the Internet.

Fortunately, the huge size, and the large number of people, isn't as much of a problem as it would first appear. In large cities, people with similar interests tend to congregate at recognized meeting places. This spontaneously emerging order seems to be a natural characteristic of large populations. An event or particular set of circumstances can associate a physical location with a special interest. Once established, this acts as a magnet to attract others.

This instinctive tendency of large populations to gather into groups of like interests also happens on the Internet. People tend to congregate in various list serves, special interest group forums and news groups. This greatly reduces the problem of finding the right sort of people to make contact with. If you know what kind of knowledge you need you can simply go to an appropriate community where such contacts are liable to hang out.

There are tens of thousands of these online communities on the Internet, but they are easy to find by using search engines or asking around. If you can join at least one email group, you can post a query asking about others. People are extremely helpful in this way and readily respond with help and guidance. A day or two of investigation and asking questions will soon locate, from among the tens of thousands, the groups that are likely to contain just the kind of people with whom you'd like to establish contact.

Communities and groups on the Internet are much easier to join or leave than their equivalent in the bricks and mortar world. There are no formalities to observe. Groups can be joined or left without anyone even noticing. Group members are effectively cloaked in invisibility until they actually make a contribution by posting an email to the group. There is no equivalent to this situation in the bricks and mortar world, so for first-time members it is a novel and highly edifying experience.

Parallel worlds

Even though it may take only a few hours of work to find some promising groups, there is still the problem of the time it takes to appreciate the substance of a group, find somebody suitable and receptive enough to strike up an association with, and then put into effect a tit-for-tat strategy to build up a relationship. In the bricks and mortar world, this would represent a serious limitation to the number of contacts you could reasonably hope to acquire.

Establishing reliable relationships of trust and cooperation can take weeks, months or even years. And to build up a whole collection might take a life-time. However, with the multiple connectivity of the Internet, this time can be reduced by orders of magnitude because it is possible to exist in parallel worlds.

The idea of parallel worlds comes from the imagination of science fiction writers who extrapolate from some of the concepts found in quantum physics.

In the quantum world, it is not possible to measure both the momentum and position of an atomic particle at the same time, so to get around this, particles are thought of as having a probable existence rather than an actual existence. A probable existence is where you don't know where a particle is or even if it is there at all, so you describe it in terms of a range of possibilities.

A simple way to think of this is to consider a clock. Each hand of a clock varies in position over a range of 60 divisions. This gives us a way of visualizing the existence of time because we can visualize all of time's possibilities in terms of the positions of hands on a clock face. However, we don't have to be able to see a clock face, or the position of the hands, to use time in calculations.

Quantum physics does something very similar when it deals with particles. As long as we can describe a model of where particles are likely to be, we can make calculations about particles (in the same way that calculations with time can be made without having to see the hands of a clock).

If we wake up in the middle of the night, it may be too dark to see the face of a clock. Until we turn on the light and actually look at the hands, it could be any of a range of possible times. In this state of not knowing, it can be interpreted that all possible times are in existence and we select one of these times by turning on the light and looking at the position of the hands on the clock face.

Studying a particle with quantum physics is something like contemplating the position of the hands of a clock when you wake up in the middle of the night. You know where it is possible for the particle to be, but without being able to turn on the light to see it, the particle is effectively at all possible positions.

A fanciful interpretation of this mathematical concept, by science fiction writers, reasons that as the world is made up of atomic particles that can only be described in terms of probabilities and multiple existences, then the whole world can be described this same way. This leads to the bizarre conclusion that there might be other parallel worlds in existence and we are only experiencing one of them.

Science fiction writers can let their imaginations run riot with the idea of parallel worlds: speculating on the possibilities of people being able to move between different worlds to enjoy different lives and different circumstances. For example, in one parallel world you might be poor and in another you might be a multi-millionaire. By moving from one existence to another you could go from being poor to being rich. This is like waking up in the night and being able to choose what time you want it to be.

We know of course that in the real world this is not possible, but in the world of the Internet there is something even more spectacular because it is possible to live in several worlds at the same time. Imagine waking up at 2 am, 3 am, 4 am, 5 am and 6 am, all at the same time. There would then be five of you in simultaneous existence. With these multiple existences, you would be able to talk to several different people at the same time. You could attend many different meetings or conferences in different parts of the world on the same date.

Supposing everyone you knew also had these multiple existences. Couldn't you ask them each to send one of their virtual selves over to you for a meeting? They could do this while they were still attending to their own private businesses with their other selves. You could get all of your friends and contacts to send over one of their spare existences to have a big meeting with you to discuss your problems. At the same time, you could send one of yours to help them with theirs.

This is what can be done on the Internet, and it is being able to exploit this bizarre parallel world of the Internet environment that can provide a massive advantage for anyone involved in e-business or e-commerce.

Living in parallel worlds

In the bricks and mortar world, information and knowledge can be gained by attending conferences or listening to and taking part in discussions at meetings. Because of a need for a physical presence, only one of these can be attended and only one speaker can be listened to at a time. This sequential exposure to information and knowledge means that it may be necessary to sit through much uninteresting or irrelevant discussion before reaching anything useful or interesting.

In the world of the Internet, discussion takes the form of email. This makes it possible not only to take part in many discussions at the same time but to be able to tune into or tune out of any of the conversations at will. Not only would you be able to attend different meetings and listen to several people all 'talking' at the same time, you could also hold any number of simultaneous conversations. It would be exactly as if it were possible for you to exist in many different parallel worlds at the same time.

The concept of parallel worlds greatly changes the nature of the gigantic café with millions of people. If you can have multiple existences, you can join in several group discussions at the same time. You can have multiple simultaneous conversations.

If everyone has multiple existences you can get the people you have built up relationships with to send one of their existences over to sit at a table with you. You could have these clones sitting around in different groups, at different tables, discussing different aspects of your problem. Because of the parallel worlds effect, you can effectively sit at each of these tables at the same time.

The ramifications of this are not intuitively realized because it is an experience quite unique to the environment of the Internet. The trick is to use a paradigm shift to see yourself at the centre of many hubs of communication. As an individual, connected to several hubs (i.e., being a member of several email discussion forums and groups), you can act as an intelligent interactive channel between them.

An idea brought up in one discussion forum can be transferred to a different group for qualification or expansion. This allows you to start with a basic idea and by means of steering it through different discussion forums be able to gradually hone and develop that idea to where it can become of practical use. On the way through, you can pick up new ideas, discover interesting branching and maybe even gather together a useful group of fellow cooperators to carry through a project. In this way you can develop and evolve a fresh idea from conception through to maturity.

Not only can you steer an idea from one group to another, you can also take an idea around a number of groups then bring it back to the group where it started. In this way you can create your own feedback loops to take ideas or projects through many generations of evolution.

Not only will you benefit from the development of the idea, but so also will the groups through which you present and pass the ideas. Effectively, by transferring thought and ideas from group to group, the groups are being cross-fertilized with knowledge. As this technique is also used by others, the groups become nodes for all kinds of ideas to breed, develop and evolve.

It is this dynamic, interactive feature of email discussion groups that allows them to be used as tools in the hands of all participants over and above their obvious use as information sources and places to meet and make contact with people.

The private virtual café

Once you click onto the concept of being able to be part of many discussion forums at the same time, there comes the very real problem of information overload. Being subscribed to many discussion groups can easily result in several megabytes of messages arriving daily. It is impossible to read all the messages.

This calls for another paradigm shift that again is only possible in the environment of the Internet: the creation of a personal private café that has all the advantages of the city-sized café but is more practical to use. The shift here is to realize that a computer is not limited to the programs and applications that are designed for it. Intelligent use of proprietary programs or even shareware can create a virtual program of any system you care to imagine.

This requires thinking beyond the applications and deciding for yourself what you want to use your computer for. Your computer RAM space can then become not the holder of applications but a part of your imagination for you to construct whatever scenario you see fit.

Why not then use your imagination to create a personal café that is organized for your own personal convenience. In your mind, think of an empty café: a room full of tables. You add chairs, just sufficient to fill the café with the number of people it would be comfortable for you to maintain email relationships with. It can be five chairs, it can be ten, 20, 50 or even more depending upon the time you want to commit to reading emails and responding to them.

In this virtual café, you can seat all the contacts you have formed cooperative associations with. On the screen it's a list of names; in your mind it's all the people you have got to know and trust sitting around in a café waiting for you to email them. Although discussion will be by means of email correspondence, you can imagine sitting at the tables talking to them. You can use the parallel worlds trick and sit at several tables at the same time, having multiple simultaneous conversations.

You can arrange a selection of your contacts to sit at the same table with you and join in a discussion. This is easily arranged by including several people's names in the 'To' header of your emails. The recipients respond in the same way, by including the same list of names in the 'To' headers of their emails to the table. In this way, a private list serve is created with all emails being sent to everyone at the table. In the world of the Internet, this is analogous to a group of people sitting around a table in a real café and having a discussion.

Because these virtual table discussions are via emails, rather than real-time chat, everyone can respond at their leisure. Also, the parallel world concept can be brought into play again, so you can create several table discussions and take part in all of them at the same time. This can be likened to a chess player who plays several games at the same time with different opponents. Except these wouldn't be opponents, they'd be cooperating friends.

Remember this is an environment of your imagination, so the people in your café needn't even be aware that they are in a café unless you share your imagination with them. As far as they are concerned, you are simply having an email correspondence with them. For you, though, it is a convenient way to conceptualize your communication interface with the complex world of the Internet.

Around this café, you can imagine several virtual doors, each of which is an entrance to a different email discussion group. This is easily arranged in practice by having a file containing the email addresses with subscribe and unsubscribe messages for several chosen discussion groups. This makes it easy for you to pop into special interest discussion forums for short visits, and leave whenever you like. Imagining this as going in and out of doors puts the discussion forums in perspective with the café.

You can go through these discussion forum doors to listen to discussions; take part in them; make contact with people; form relationships with them and then put them into your café. Once you have brought these people into your virtual café, you can go from table to table, speaking to them as you will.

In this way, you can have your own private café filled with lots of people who between them have a knowledge of what is happening in a variety of discussion forums. This gives you the double option of going through one of the doors to a discussion forum or having a private discussion with somebody who is representative of the ideas and thoughts of the forum.

This virtual café then represents your intelligent interface to your real-life contacts and their combined knowledge and experience. You can go to any of the people in the café or you can go through any of the doors into a discussion group to find an answer to a question or a solution to a problem. Using the phenomenon of parallel worlds you don't have to do this sequentially: you can do any number of these at the same time – giving you a dynamic connection to multiple sources of information where you can move ideas around, get new knowledge and get help with your problems.

More importantly, it becomes the way you have wired yourself into the multiple connectiveness of the Internet. It is your way of tapping into its power and using the knowledge it contains in a way you can comfortably cope with.

This makes even greater sense if everyone else in your café has a private café of their own. By virtue of your café you may have direct regular contact with 50 people. If each of these has 50 contacts in their café, you have indirect contact with 2,500 people. If they each have a virtual café with 50 contacts, you have access to 125,000 people – all within three email messages away.

It doesn't need much imagination to see how such connectivity can link the knowledge of every person on the Internet. It is this potential for massive Interactive connectivity that is the exciting prospect for the future of e-commerce and e-business.

Using the café

The café represents your interface to a selected number of people. It is also a convenient way to visualize a solution point in Hilbert space. The people in the café are the dimensions of your solution.

In a previous chapter we saw how to function in the environment of the Internet. It needs two solution points, one for input and another for output. Why not have two cafés then? One to contain all the contacts that are involved in the demand side of your functioning on the Internet and another for the contacts on the supply side. This nicely separates the two sets of contacts and is a convenient conceptual trick to keep them apart.

Solution providers can have one café for their clients and another for the middlemen and specialists they use to create solutions. A middleman can have one café for the solution providers they deal with and another for the experts and specialists they represent. Experts and specialists can have one café for their clients and another for their peers with whom they swap technical knowledge.

A core business executive can create a café to hold a variety of e-commerce advisers and consultants, inviting them in for various lengths of time to give advice or direction and taking part in discussions. An employee in a managed team can create a café of suitable contacts with doors to suitable discussion forums to supply an appropriate rich source of information to help him or her perform well at his or her job.

With a little imagination, anyone can use the concept of the café to power-assist any personal job or enterprise they undertake, both in the virtual world of the Internet or in the real world of bricks and mortar.

Epilogue

The most efficient: top-down or bottom-up?

As the reader may have gathered, this book was written in true bottom-up style. Starting from an arbitrary point, and letting the book evolve as a response to feedback and inspiration, it took unpredictable directions and came to conclusions that were even a surprise to me.

It thus serves as a real-life example of the creative strategy described in the book itself. Another paradox: a book that describes its own strategy for creation.

To put this into perspective, the writing had really been born in the tangible world of bricks and mortar. The physical world of book publishing is a conservative industry that invests in formulated plans in the form of detailed book proposals where the content is fully specified before it is written. These comprehensive proposals are needed to gain the marketing and financial support necessary before a book deal can be finalized.

Although the acquisitions editor was aware of the way I would write the book, a detailed table of contents had to be supplied as part of the proposal. This could only be approached from a top-down perspective. After thinking carefully about what I thought the book should contain, I wrote down a list of chapters and subheadings to include all the points I thought might be important and likely to be covered.

It looked impressive, but I never once looked at it again until the book was completely finished. Then, when I had written the draft of the final chapter, I read through the list to check to see what things I might have missed. Reading all the subheadings, and ticking those that had been covered, I was surprised to find that the seemingly directionless bottom-up approach had covered every single point in the first half of the proposed chapters. The book had apparently produced exactly the same result as if I'd used a top-down approach: with one exception, exactly halfway through the original list the ticking stopped. The book had covered only half of the content I had originally thought would be necessary.

At first, it seemed that the bottom-up approach had been inefficient. I then realized that by working with the feedback from the café I'd been able to cover points I would probably have missed with the planned, top-down approach. I'd also been able to add additional explanation where aspects weren't clear and provide duplicate explanations to cover more than one viewpoint. More importantly, I'd included topics and conclusions that I had no idea existed when I'd written out the initial proposal. It was this additional material that had accounted for the apparent loss in efficiency.

What it proved then is that the top-down approach might only give the illusion of being a more efficient way to produce a product or solution. Actually, it was less efficient because it would likely result in an inferior or limited product.

A follow-up book?

Stopping half way through a proposed list of contents isn't as odd as it seems. The first half of the original proposal concentrated on abstract thoughts and ways of thinking about the problems associated with the complexity of the Internet environment.

In stark contrast to the first, the second half is concerned with more practical issues: putting the ideas into practical effect in real-life situations. This is a sharp division and justifies the original proposal being split up into two separate books. The publisher agreed and immediately accepted a proposal for another, follow-up book based upon the second half of my original proposal. The provisional title is to be *The ultimate game of strategy – finding a personal niche in the world of e-business*.

Continuing with a follow-up book will allow me to go deeper into the mechanics of game theory; make practical use of the café for imaginative communication strategies; join and create networks of cooperators and collaborators; introduce the concepts of evolutionary biology into the design of dynamic Web-based systems; explore the use of powerful Web site design software packages; and investigate the strange phenomena of hubs and portals.

More interestingly, it will give me the opportunity to write about the mechanics of creating a real-life e-business from scratch and record its step-by-step progress. For both me and the readers, it will be an opportunity to explore the challenge of starting from a square-one position, but with the advantage of having a powerful set of conceptual tools to enhance competitiveness.

The progress of this new venture and book will be detailed on my Web site at: *www.avatarnets.com*

Peter Small
January 2000

Appendix

The café

For me, the most edifying experience of writing this book has been the success of the virtual café, which was used to get feedback as I wrote each chapter. It was devised as a solution to the frustrations I'd had when trying to develop new ideas within the environment of Internet email discussion forums.

Internet email forums are without doubt the most exciting and revolutionary phenomena to emerge from the Internet. Groups of hundreds of people join to meld minds, share knowledge and transfer information. Anyone belonging to these groups taps into a dynamic information service, a continuous, up-to-date news bulletin, a fountain of ideas and inspiration. Without doubt, the membership of such email groups bestows upon any individual a massive competitive advantage – even when working in the conventional world of bricks and mortar – because they provide a virtual backup of hundreds of advisers and assistants to help them with any problems they encounter.

The most useful and valuable are the email forums that are narrowly focused around a single theme: a specific area of technology; a computer application environment; a business niche; a hobby or an interest. These forums tend to be self-regulating, with strong pressures brought to bear on anyone deviating from the main subject theme. This self regulation improves the information to noise ratio, allowing useful knowledge to be transferred with better efficiency.

The essential and valuable feature of group self-regulation has a downside though: the regulation that is so effective at reducing noise also excludes any attempts to extend the envelope of the group's activity. Radical ideas and new directions are quickly crushed out of existence just as ruthlessly as inconsequential drivel. This is as it should be, as most of the ideas and directions introduced into list serve forums do tend to be inconsequential drivel anyway.

There are Internet forums that do try to cater for speculative ideas, but they soon become either too noisy to make it worth the time to read the contributions, or dominated by a small clique who confine the discussions to within their own area of opinion. Usually, such groups need a regulator to control the postings. But, by definition, contributions that are confined to the limitations of whatever a regulator regards as interesting defeats the purpose of having a group free to explore speculative ideas.

My experience of trying to explore new ideas within Internet discussion forums has been far from satisfactory often ending up in flame wars and sometimes even getting me thrown off of lists. It was no better when I started my own email discussion forum after writing *Magical A-Life Avatars*. There, I was in a position to set the subject area (which was to explore the open source potential of multimedia run time engines to create intelligent agents). Yet, the combined efforts of a few determined posters made it impossible for me to have any real influence and the discussions took off in a direction quite different from what I had in mind. In trying to bring the discussion around to the original intention, I was hounded out of my own discussion forum.

The problem appears to be that everyone has built into their minds a personally unique model of the world with which they interpret events and information. They like new ideas to slot easily into this framework of thought and if a new idea necessitates a completely new mindset, or requires a sharp paradigm shift, it is often rejected out of hand. This is a natural and quite sensible way to approach the acceptance of new ideas, as to be receptive to any new idea that comes along runs the risk of destabilizing an entire thinking process. But it presents a problem for anyone with a new idea because to the rest of the world they are indistinguishable from cranks – which of course they might be.

This is the problem I had when I came to write this book. I thought I had some good ideas, but so do many people in lunatic asylums. How can you tell whether you are a loony? There is only one way – test the ideas out on sane and rational people who can judge them against their experiences in the world. But what if nobody listens to you?

The list serves are impossible places to make such tests because the barrage of protests from the more dogmatic subscribers distort or burn out any attempt at rational explanation. Then I remembered how I'd worked with ideas in the world of bricks and mortar. I'd used cafés and wine bars. I'd arrange to meet various groups of people for informal discussions where we'd bounce ideas off of each other, discuss theories, business ideas and plans. Providing the groups stayed small and intimate, great progress could be made without undue noise.

At the same time I'd picked up a book on communication strategies within large corporations. It pinpointed 'meetings' as being critically important nodes within a communication infrastructure. The book stated that long experience had shown that the optimum size of such nodal meetings should be between seven and nine people. With these thoughts in mind, I created a virtual café where I could arrange virtual meetings with a wide variety of people, splitting them up into small, efficient groupings. With these smaller groupings, the issue of noise was not such a great problem. More radical ideas could be discussed because they didn't have to conform to the common denominators of a large, mixed population. Differences could be discussed rationally and not clouded by different viewpoints all seeking a common ground.

The greatest advantage was in being able to separate out the different mind-sets. For example, the way in which a teacher views the world is quite different from that of, say, an entrepreneur; discussions quickly disintegrate into arguments if the backgrounds and outlooks on life are too disparate. Similarly, the way in which a specialist expert such as a programmer or a graphic designer interacts with the business environment is quite different from that of, say, a manager of a large project or a sales person. Being able to separate out these different mindsets by placing them at different tables, I was able to avoid semantic arguments and at the same time get a range of perspectives applied to the ideas.

Each grouping in its own way added new dimensions to the ideas. Also, ideas that were acceptable in one perspective but not in another could be identified and given alternative explanations in the book (which is why some ideas seem to be repeated in different forms and why everyone will have objections to some parts of the book).

To explain and describe the dynamics of this process in detail would probably take another book, but by way of example as to how this virtual café worked, here are a few of the hundreds of emails that resulted from this process while writing this book. (In fact, there were so many possible good examples I could have chosen from that I had to have some criteria for selection. So I decided to take this opportunity to add some balance to the book by using those that touched upon more contentious issues. In this way, I could perhaps compensate a little for some of the black and white treatment I've been forced to take, for the sake of brevity, in some of the more controversial areas.)

Culture clashes

I started the café with around 50 people. I used a random generator to decide who was at which table as I had no idea as to what would be the best way to decide the mixing. Some tables worked well with an immediate empathy developing within the groups. At others there were only cautious attempts at discussion. At one table there was a stony silence and at another things went disastrously wrong. This latter table I thought of as 'the table from hell'.

A problem, which nearly all the readers were puzzled by, was my unconventional approach to writing. It seemed inconceivable that I would begin to write a book where I had no idea as to what would turn out to be the conclusions. It took several chapters before most of them cottoned on to the idea that this was a dynamic process and they were part of the process of arriving at the conclusions. This was particularly a problem at my 'table from hell'. I discovered subsequently that the tone of a table's mood was usually set by the first one or two emails. A strongly negative first reaction put the whole table in a negative mood, with discussions rapidly descending into nit-picking; a positive first reaction usually resulted in an animated discussion, not only on the chapter in question, but on speculations on where the book was heading.

At the 'table from hell', the first two posters were both negative, one of whom was a university professor who objected to the whole approach of the first two chapters. He was challenged by a high school drop-out, who'd gone on to become an exceptionally talented, first-class hacker. A sample email follows, where the hacker (Ian Morrison, well known on the UK Director user's list as a sardonic baiter of any kind of pomposity) tears into the university lecturer's previous post a point at a time:

Brian wrote:
>*A lot of the analogies drawn from Peter's life to e-commerce are pretty hairy to me.*

Define hairy. I think it's a stupid word to use in this context.

>*The poker example Peter gave is familiar to most people with experience – it just illustrates the inter-dependence of things. This is where the concept breaks down – it assumes situations where we are all in competition, and there is a 'best' way or answer.*

Anyone who thinks we are not in competition is either naive or stupid. Everything we do in life is to clock up points. The only reason we exist is to carry forward our own DNA, and to destroy anything that interferes with that. With such dramatic orders, competition is what we thrive and rely upon.

>*In a poker game the group does not 'win', as the group has the same amount of money at the end.*

This suggests that the only reason for playing poker is for money. I'd differ to the point of personal insult.

>*The lesson of the Internet is not how we can use it, but that if we all work together everyone can win.*

People don't want to work together. People want to get rich without effort; I refer you back to Peter's son who just wanted to get the work done, and be gone. Collaborating with his father, despite the potential for learning (and insanity), was rejected because it's easier to learn for ourselves rather than trusting someone's pre-chewed knowledge.

>*The Internet is the first big example of how the profit motive can be bypassed. It is a wonderful thing in that regard.*

Wake up. The rose ink on your spectacles is going to run onto your bank statement if you're not careful. The Internet is the most disgusting example of commercially driven motives since commercial television. The net is used to not only bombard consumers with products, but also to stalk and categorize them. The day I can leave cookies enabled in my browser, and not shoot though a junkbuster proxy is the day I accept that the Internet is a wonderful thing for negating profit.

>*My personal view is that this misses the big picture. It's not about u_s_i_n_g the net, it's about being part of it. Something is happening all right, but it's not this. For example, could it be the Internet is the beginning of people realizing the limitations of doing things only for personal profit.*

Yes, mate. And we're all running Linux too, aren't we. Free the software, yadda yadda yadda.

>*These ideas are interesting, but not ground breaking. Suggest start again and think things through a little better.*

Wise words, if words were ever wise, from the wise man himself on practice as preach, and lack of therein.
Ian

I soon learned to split people up in a way that avoided such culture clashes.

Descending into chaos

Originally, Chapter 3 had contained a long mathematical description of chaos theory. It sparked off some extended theoretical discussions on one table, where I had a disagreement with somebody over the meaning of chaos. He wrote:

> If you really feel the need to put me straight on deterministic chaos, perhaps we should continue at a separate table? I fear that even an elementary discussion of such topics as phase trajectories, degrees of liberty, aperiodic oscillators, strange attractors, fractal dimensions, Hopf bifurcations, Fourier spectrums, Floquet matrices and so on is hardly appropriate at a table dedicated to the discussion of Chapter 3.
> James

I declined the offer. But, as many people had commented that a mathematical description of chaos theory was out of keeping with the established tone of the book, I asked everyone in the café for their opinions. It was voted out. I asked everyone then whether or not it should be included as an appendix. Jackie Kleinschmidt wrote:

> I think you could leave it out altogether, Peter, at least any attempt to explain chaos theory per se. You could make the same observations in ordinary lay terms just as well, and maybe even more clearly. From the whole chapter, what struck me was not anything you said about chaos theory specifically, but the observations you made about seemingly chaotic things and 'zen-ness'.
> Jackie

I did leave it out, deciding this description should go on my Web site rather in the book (***www.avatarnets.com/ewbook/chaos***).

Misplaced humour

Using black and white caricatures, mixed with tongue in cheek humour, didn't go down well with some readers, particularly the corporates. At one table a poster wrote:

> For example, the aborted 'green frog' lecture on evolutionary design was brilliantly told. The reader gains insight into the perspective of the author, who is transformed into a sympathetic, likable character during his ill-fated consulting gig. Further, it reveals volumes about the cultural rift between the author's mouth and the corporate ear.
>
> Although this failure to communicate is initially hilarious, it begins to hinder the author's credibility when he confronts the same misunderstanding with an academic. The academic is open to the author's radical ideas, and asks only that the author articulate these ideas. The author responds by launching into a critique that alienates all potential readers – corporate workers, software users, and academics.
>
> Paragraph after paragraph of sarcasm and other rhetoric follow. Most of it misses the mark, and insults the target audience of a book about e-commerce. By creating a stereotype of the corporate mind as obsessed with avoiding complexity and risk, he is only reiterating what the green frog story so clearly displayed: the author is taking an extremely limited view of the business world.
>
> A better strategy is to make fun of the worst of the worst, while also highlighting the best practices. This gives the reader a chance to side with the winners, and it gives the author a chance to avoid the impossible task of defending dozens of generalizations against waves of real business innovations, past and present.
>
> Even more importantly, this technique bolsters credibility by showing how the author's ideas helped create the Internet economy. He can take advantage of the brilliant people and courageous corporate minds that overcame the worst of the worst corporate inhibitors.
>
> Bruce

In fact, my intention had been to illustrate the different ways in which some corporations were missing out on e-commerce opportunities by letting Industrial Age attitudes handicap them. It was written in a way that I thought was a humorous, over the top caricature. Unfortunately, the humour didn't seem to get through to some people and I had to drastically tone it down (leaving it a bit bland in my opinion).

Object-oriented confusion

There seemed to be a very sharp division between the people who understood the concept of object-oriented thinking and those who didn't. In fact the concept is probably difficult to understand because of its very simplicity. Giles Askham made this point:

> ... the section on object-orientation. I find myself in the position of understanding object-oriented computer programming but reading a section explaining the concept to the lay person. It is therefore very difficult to try to read it with out bringing my own understanding to bear on the subject. It is difficult to know how fully anyone will grasp the concept from this section. I'm not even sure that a strong understanding is necessary; my hunch is, though, that it is very important in order to fully understand the book.
>
> When I started learning to program with Lingo I read many articles posted on different Web sites which attempted to explain the concepts involved in object-oriented programming (including some of your own, Peter). As I think you have already stated in the book, the fundamental principles are very simple; conceptualizing them, however, is not that simple, it takes a distillation of what you have read and what different pieces of code you have put into practice that finally leads to the eureka moment of full conceptual understanding.
> Giles

Perhaps it was an inability to fully appreciate the concept of object-oriented design strategies that led to the most contentious issue in the book: the appropriateness of managed teams in the environment of the Internet.

The main objections came from the people in the cafÈ who were in managerial roles, either in a conventional business structure or a con-tractor/subcontractor situation. They seemed to be under the impression that object-oriented design was an alternative to the way they worked rather than a complement to it.

It seemed inconceivable to them that you can appoint somebody to carry out a function without imposing some form of editorial or quality control over the work you ask them to do. Yet, this is exactly what object-oriented design is about.

The problem seems to be that the managers who object to this are trying to see object-oriented design in terms of their own managerial functions, but it doesn't apply to them at all: it applies to the people who employ them or hire their services.

The manager who objects to the idea of object-oriented design would probably be infuriated if their boss or client imposed a non-expert, critical judgement on their work or didn't have enough trust in them to accept at face value the work they carried out to the best of their skills and abilities.

Most managers and contractors have experienced the problem of the boss or client who criticizes their work at a level where they have little understanding of the criteria involved. In this situation, managers can see the logic of non-interference and thus object-oriented organization makes sense to a manager from this perspective.

The paradigm shift needed to appreciate object-oriented structures is to see it in this way. Bosses and clients must use object-oriented design thinking to avoid the temptation to interfere with the work of the people they have placed their trust in and managers must use their conventional managerial skills to justify that trust.

In the bricks and mortar world, and even to some extent in the information world, it is possible for bosses and managers, clients and contractors to employ object-oriented techniques in some situations and managerial techniques in other. But, in the highly complex environment of the Internet – which is heading increasingly towards specialization – mixing the two strategies is becoming less and less efficient.

The prime movers have too many problems to cope with to be able to find the time to learn enough detail in the variety of niche areas that they have to employ. They are forced to trust others that they have to rely on to do a job without quality control or supervision. The managers, for their part, have more than enough to cope with in just trying keep up with the ever-changing and expanding knowledge necessary to be proficient in their chosen managerial niche, to have time to consider the broader issues.

The key to understanding this paradigm shift is in realizing that object-oriented design and a managed team approach are not alternative choices as to the way to organize all spheres of activity. They are optimal methods to use in particular situations: the choice depending upon your level in the overall organization. At the system or strategy level you need to use object-oriented design, but, at the functional or technical level, you may need to function as a co-ordinated team.

Certainly a leader can be both a strategist and a manager (although unusual), but, the function of management has no role in object-oriented systems – only within the objects themselves (note, a managed team is considered to be an object in an object-oriented environment and object-oriented design is not concerned with what happens inside objects). An object-oriented system strategist, on the other hand, has no place in management, and it is not even a necessary requirement for them to be a leader.

If the reader has clicked upon the understanding of just this one single concept, the reading of the book would have been worthwhile.

Index